ECONOMICS, ENVIRONMENTAL POLICY, AND THE QUALITY OF LIFE

William J. Baumol
Princeton & New York Universities

Wallace E. Oates
Princeton University

with major contributions by
SUE ANNE BATEY BLACKMAN
Princeton University

Prentice-Hall, Inc., Englewood Cliffs, N.J. 07632

Library of Congress Cataloging in Publication Data

Baumol, William J
    Economics, environmental policy, and the quality of life.

    Includes bibliographical references and index.
    1. Environmental policy. 2. Economic policy.
I. Oates, Wallace E., joint author. II. Blackman, Sue Anne Batey, joint author. III. Title.
HC79.E5B374   301.31   78–i7933
ISBN 0-13-231365-0
ISBN 0-13-231357-X pbk.

The authors wish to acknowledge that their work contains material that was copyright ©
1963, 1970, 1971, 1972, 1973, 1974, 1975, 1976, and 1977 by The New York Times
Company. This material was reprinted by permission.

Printed in the United States of America

10 9 8 7 6 5 4

Prentice-Hall International, Inc., *London*
Prentice-Hall of Australia Pty. Limited, *Sydney*
Prentice-Hall of Canada, Ltd., *Toronto*
Prentice-Hall of India Private Limited, *New Delhi*
Prentice-Hall of Japan, Inc., *Tokyo*
Prentice-Hall of Southeast Asia Pte. Ltd., *Singapore*
Whitehall Books Limited, *Wellington, New Zealand*

Contents

Preface

Anyone who embarks upon an empirical study should be aware of two regularities which characterize such undertakings. First, the enterprise will almost certainly take longer than anticipated. Second, it will accumulate a long list of debts of gratitude which the author can easily acknowledge but cannot adequately repay. In neither of these respects is our study an exception. We expected the project to take a bit more than two years. In a fruitless attempt to avoid becoming yet another case of tardy completion, we adopted a three-year horizon as a fail-safe target. But the fates are not to be trifled with so easily; they sentenced us to a full five years of work for our presumptuousness in seeking to avoid their sway.

Over this period we were helped in many ways by many people. First, a role of critical importance was played by our sponsors at the National Science Foundation, whose generous support and seemingly unlimited patience helped us through our long task.

Second, we were dependent upon many associates for factual materials and for the work of catching errors and omissions in what we had written. There were others whose work went well beyond that; they undertook responsibility for particular pieces of analysis. For example, Jack Frisch carried out a careful study of trends in the prices of natural resources whose stocks may be threatened with depletion. His results were reported in the appendix to Chapter 6. Aristos Parris collected and analyzed for us data on meteorological conditions and their relation to concentrations of atmospheric pollutants, described in Chapter 20. Robert Plotnick surveyed and assembled the evidence on environmental problems and policies in socialist countries, which constitutes the subject of Chapter 5. Linda Martin explored the crucial practical problem of the metering of effluents. (See Chapter 20.) In addition, we are deeply indebted to others for their assistance with our study: Steve Cohen, Vernon Dixon, Victoria Elliott, Christine Greenhalgh, Judy Hawkes, Eva Lam, Sonia Maltezou, S. McLean, Wendy Mnookin, Nancy Morawetz, John D. Murray, L. D. Patterson, Steve Plaut, Julie Randall, John Scardino, Barry Schwartz, Johnathan Taylor, and Steve Williams. The fact that we can do no more than list their names indicates the inferiority of the coin with which we are able to repay their efforts.

Equally critical for our work was the careful and critical review of our manuscript by six readers of diverse expertise, who provided invaluable suggestions drawn from their extensive knowledge of the field. We can only say that without the comments of Gardner Brown, Richard Carpenter, A. Myrick Freeman, Marcia Gelpe, Edwin Mills, and Joseph Seneca, the book would have been less illuminating, far less accurate, less readable, and (perhaps worst of all) even longer than it is!

Finally, the two senior authors of this book insist upon the privilege of expressing their appreciation and admiration for the contribution of Sue Anne Batey Blackman. She assumed primary responsibility for two chapters; readers have singled out one of them, Chapter 19, for its originality and other virtues. In addition, her stamp is upon every other chapter of the book. It is no mere bow to nice custom when we say that we could not have done without her, and certainly we would not have wanted to!

1

Introduction:

ECONOMICS AND THE QUALITY OF LIFE

In the third of a century following World War II, we have witnessed the longest period of uninterrupted prosperity in the history of Western industrialized society. Although there were several recessions during this interval, they fade in comparison with the major economic collapses that plagued earlier periods. Yet the prevention of major depressions has proved to be less satisfying than most of us had anticipated. One no longer hears the exuberant assertions of the beginning of the postwar period that "50 million jobs" would solve all of society's problems. On the contrary, rising gross national product has not prevented a number of social and economic ills which, in their own way, are almost as debilitating as major depressions: the problems of minority groups, the degradation of the environment, the deterioration of the cities, and the rising costs of health care, education, and the arts.

Even if the growing abundance of the economy has not caused all these problems, it is obvious that neither has it succeeded in doing away with them. We have all too easily equated rising standards of living with "the good life"; only recently have we begun to have serious doubts about the association between the two.[1] A central theme of this book, however, is that society *can*

---

[1]The imperfect correlation between the level of national output and the quality of life is certainly not just a contemporary phenomenon. For example, it was no doubt the In-

have them both, but that this happy outcome will not happen by itself. On the contrary, the prognosis is that the economy, left to its present course, will produce more and more consumer goods, but will offer them to a society in which filth, noise, and other forms of pollution grow and in which public services continue to deteriorate. However, if society is willing to undertake the requisite corrective measures, we already have the basic knowledge and the resources to change this course of events.

This is not to say that a clean environment and the range of services essential to the good society will come free. It is, however, our contention that high levels of environmental quality and public services are consistent with relatively modest sacrifices of private consumption. They do not require halting all economic growth or dismantling our industrial system. Instead, what is needed is the design and enactment of a proper set of policies that will provide direct incentives to consumers, government agencies, and business to protect, rather than abuse, the environment. The outline of such a set of policies is the primary concern of this book. Our objective is to show how the application of the principles of economics can help to achieve *both* a continuation of abundance and improvement in the quality of life.

The analysis will show that the problems of environmental decay are embedded in our economic structure; they are not attributable simply to mismanagement, incompetence, or evil intentions—to villainous politicians, greedy businessmen, or inefficient bureaucrats. Rather, problems such as pollution and congestion are largely the result of what economists call "externalities" and are caused by a structural defect in the free enterprise system, which, incidentally, has its counterpart in the planned economies. This phenomenon is critical for the formulation of effective environmental policy, for only by understanding the sources of the problem can we design programs that can deal effectively with it and do so without imposing unnecessary burdens upon society.

Part 1 of this book deals with the factual and analytical materials necessary to the design of rational environmental policy. We begin with an examination of the actual trends in environmental quality. Here we find a mixed picture with some striking improvements alongside disturbing cases of continuing deterioration. In particular, we conclude that the risks, in certain areas, of environmental catastrophes of monumental magnitude imply that there are no grounds for complacency. We turn, in the remainder of Part 1, to the basic reasons for environmental abuse. By examining the structure of the pricing system, we can get at the source of the failure of the free enterprise, industrialized economies to provide adequate safeguards for the environment. Somewhat ironically, we also find that the planned socialist economies have experienced

---

dustrial Revolution and its contribution to output which transformed Glasgow from "one of the prettiest little towns in the British Isles" (as it was at the time of Adam Smith) into the large, slum-ridden city it became in the nineteenth century.

severe environmental degradation for reasons that are not altogether dissimilar to those of the Western experience.

Although the term "quality of life" eludes precise definition, we normally use it to refer to more than just the state of the natural environment. In addition to the cleanliness of our air and water and the condition of forest and field, the quality of life in our highly urbanized society depends critically on a wide range of amenities. Urban sprawl, decaying neighborhoods, and frustrating congestion become fully as important as the degradation of beautiful canyons or the extinction of animal species. Moreover, a broad collection of cultural activities (taking culture in its broadest sense) makes a significant contribution to the quality of life; education, health care, and the state of the arts all have profound effects upon our well-being. In Part 2 of the book, we extend the horizon of our analysis beyond the natural environment to consider the difficult problems of urban blight and various important services. We stress that our conclusions for public policy on these issues are, for a number of reasons, somewhat tentative, although we do believe that they provide some important insights into the kinds of measures that can, *and* those that probably cannot, produce real results. We conclude Part 2 with two chapters that explore the difficult issues posed, first, by the implications of pollution and its cleanup for the distribution of income between the wealthy and the poor and, second, by environmental problems in an international setting.

The primary thrust of the book is the design of policy to control pollution and other forms of damage to the natural environment; on this issue the principles of economics, supplemented by some lessons from the experience of recent policies, provide us with some very significant conclusions. This is the subject of Part 3: the design of effective environmental policy. Anticipating our conclusions, we find that there is no one policy measure that constitutes a panacea for all our environmental problems. We have at our disposal a wide range of policy instruments, and each, in proper conjunction with the others, has its role to play. What is clear is that past and present environmental policy has failed to make effective use of some of the available policy tools, for which we have paid a heavy price in wasted resources and reduced effectiveness of the programs that are in use. In particular, we shall contend that a major deficiency in recent policies has been their failure to enlist the pricing system for protection of the environment; by making pollution costly to both individuals and business firms, we can make it directly profitable to avoid activities that damage our air, rivers, and natural preserves.

Although it may seem a bit out of character for representatives of the so-called "dismal science," our message in this book is basically optimistic. The environmental problems with which we deal are serious and difficult, and we do not want to understate their complexity. But there do exist some basic principles for the design of public policy that promise to be effective for the regulation of environmental quality. This does not mean that remedial policies will be cheap and easy. Yet, we shall see that many of the problems associated with pollution can be dealt with by relatively painless measures that require surprisingly minor changes in our economic system. While some of them involve a substantial and growing commitment of resources, others are likely to prove comparatively inexpensive.

One may well ask, If these policies are so straightforward and so well understood, why haven't they been adopted already? The answer is not entirely clear, but some discussion of the issue is instructive because of its implications for the political feasibility of effective environmental policy. One of the most powerful forces for inaction is political inertia, fed by what has been called the tyranny of the small decision. The problems with which we are concerned have not sprung forth full grown; they have crept up on us little by little. Were we suddenly to find ourselves transformed overnight from communities with pure air and clear rivers into cities overwhelmed by stench, the public outcry might be far greater than it is. But each gradual increase in pollution can seem fairly innocuous. If we have survived yesterday's pollution levels, a little more doesn't hurt very much. The public seems to grow indignant only after shocking environmental crises, such as a sudden increase in deaths from respiratory diseases during particularly serious accumulations of pollutants. The small and virtually invisible change can sneak up on us unnoticed, until matters have grown very serious.

A second obstacle to effective policy has been the strong opposition from those interests that would find their activities circumscribed by environmental measures. Business reaction to the call for pollution abatement has certainly not been uniformly positive. Some firms have undertaken environmental research and investment programs, but even in those cases their response has been limited severely by responsibilities to stockholders and the fear of giving an advantage to competitors. There are many more examples of businesses that have demonstrated blatant unconcern with environmental problems: manufacturers of patently dangerous chemicals who have argued that the evidence against them was not yet conclusive(!); petroleum firms who have played down the risk of oil spills; and the parade of industrial lobbyists who have opposed virtually every environmental measure that threatened to be effective.

Fitting companions of this group are those legislators, journalists, and other leaders of opinion who in the name of practicality oppose every environmental proposal that departs from traditional practices. Speaking of such groups, Disraeli once remarked that "practicality" is the byword of those who propose to practice the blunders of their predecessors.

A fourth, and somewhat surprising, source of opposition comes from a group of dedicated environmentalists who reject as immoral and crass the use of economic incentives for environmental protection. This group appears to feel that environmental problems are too urgent and fundamental to reduce them to the level of dispassionate economic theory and that society should instead work for a greater moral commitment to a cleaner environment. Unfortunately, if greater moral commitment is the prerequisite for a better environment, it may wait indefinitely. As in the case of the Victorian gentleman who refused to remove his clothing to save a drowning person, morality may be preserved even though the cause is lost.

Part I

A PERSPECTIVE
ON ENVIRONMENTAL PROBLEMS

2

Trends in Environmental Quality

When we undertook this study several years ago, we had definite preconceptions about the general trends in environmental quality. Because of growth
in population and industrial activity, we were convinced that virtually all forms
of environmental damage were increasing and that, in the absence of powerful
countermeasures, they would continue to accelerate more or less steadily. A
preliminary study of available data seemed to support this view.[1] However, a
more careful and extensive re-examination of the evidence has led us to revise
this simplistic view of the course of environmental decay. We have found on
closer study that the trends in environmental quality run the gamut from steady
deterioration to spectacular improvement. This chapter presents our accumulated data on environmental trends; in Chapter 3 we shall attempt to evaluate
the implications of those trends.

---

[1] See William J. Baumol, "Environmental Protection, International Spillovers and Trade,"
The Wicksell Lectures for 1971 (Uppsala, Sweden: Almquist & Wiksells Boktryckeri Ab,
1971), pp. 15-16. These pages also represented the view at that time of Oates, who had
read and commented extensively on the manuscript during its preparation.

1. Collecting Evidence about the Environment[2]

Because widespread and systematic concern about environmental issues is relatively recent, it was not surprising that we found it difficult to obtain reliable evidence on environmental trends extending back more than a few years. Since the experience of a short period of time can often be deceiving and heavily colored by transient, irrelevant influences, we could not rely on easily accessible, short-term information.[3] The process of tracking down longer-term evidence took us beyond libraries to repositories of dusty records, to the Swedish Fisheries Bureau in Gothenberg, to the offices of St. Paul's Cathedral in London, and to the conservationists' offices in the Louvre. We want to emphasize that our survey in this chapter presents *all* the long-term data that we have been able to discover; systematic evidence over past centuries (or even decades) is, indeed, very scarce. However, what we have found is, in some instances, quite intriguing. Our searches often led to dead ends, but in other cases turned up evidence that revealed that broad statements reported in the popular press were often either misleadingly simplistic or completely untrue.[4] This has forced us to revise our earlier, naive view that environmental deterioration has been a universal, accelerating process whose source is modern industrialization and population growth.

A. Environmental Deterioration Caused by Natural Processes. Some environmental damage, whose source at first appears to be industrial pollution, is in fact primarily the result of natural forces. An instructive illustration is the

---

[2] In this chapter, we shall present numerous graphs and other figures to summarize the data that we have assembled. For anyone who wants to study the data more closely, we have either placed the actual numbers in an appendix or, where they are readily available, specified the source.

[3] For an illustration of the dangers in drawing conclusions about trends from data spanning even many decades, see Appendix A which examines water-flow figures for the Nile River that cover many centuries.

[4] A case in point, although not of major importance to this volume, is the matter of the progressive deterioration of works of art that are located out-of-doors. We had assumed from numerous studies in the press that there had been a marked acceleration in decay in recent years coincident with growing pollution. However, interviews with some of the world's leading authorities soon made our naiveté apparent. Where there is deterioration of these works of art, the causes are not completely understood and in some cases are clearly attributable in good part to natural phenomena. Even where visible deterioration has increased sharply in recent years, it is not safe to assume that the cause is recent. For example, a piece of stonework may have been decaying beneath its surface for centuries; when the weakened structure finally collapses, it can hardly be blamed on twentieth-century abuse. The experts did *surmise* that chemicals emitted into the atmosphere do increase the incidence of "stone sickness" which leads to the crumbling of buildings and sculptures, but repeatedly emphasized the absence of conclusive evidence confirming this plausible conjecture.

There are, of course, a few noteworthy exceptions—cases in which the evidence of accelerating deterioration is persuasive. For example, there are the casts of some portions of the Parthenon Frieze made by Lord Elgin in the early nineteenth century. A comparison

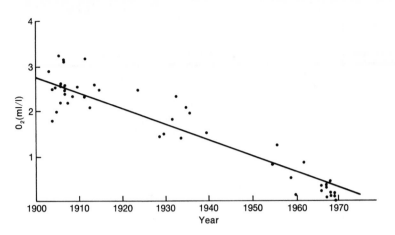

Figure 2-1 Oxygen Content of the Baltic Sea (in milliliters per liter), Station F 74 (depth of approximately 150 meters).

Source: Compiled from data from: (a) Counseil Permanent International Pour L'exploration de la Mer (ICES), *Bulletin des Résultats acquis Pendant Les Courses Periodiques,* Copenhagen (up to 1959); (b) *ICES Oceanographic Data Lists,* Copenhagen (1959-62); and (c) *Hydrographical Data,* Harsfiskelaboratorret, Göteborg (1963-69). For the actual figures from which this graph was drawn, see Appendix B, Table 2-B5.

quality of the deeper waters of the central Baltic Sea. The data in Figure 2-1 indicate that, in the central waters of the Baltic roughly midway between Stockholm and Helsinki, the oxygen content has been falling steadily from about 300 ml/l at the beginning of the century to virtually zero today. The data depicted in the diagram give the figures for only one of the sampling

---

of those casts with the originals in Athens confirms that, in the sixteen decades since Elgin was in Greece, the marbles have indeed suffered enormous visible deterioration relative to what they underwent in the more than twenty centuries before. Details that were sharp and clear in 1800 are virtually unrecognizable today (see the photographs in H. J. Plenderleith, *The Conservation of Antiquities and Works of Art,* 2nd ed. [London: Oxford Univeristy Press, 1971], plates 40A and B, p. 316). However, except for catastrophes such as the Florentine flood, there are few other documented examples of recent acceleration in deterioration.

Despite all that has been printed and said about the threat of modern industry to our artistic heritage, we were able to find very little *conclusive* evidence on the subject one way or another. Most of the authorities with whom we spoke were not even willing to conjecture that matters were getting worse. A notable case in point was St. Paul's Cathedral. London, at the end of the seventeenth century when St. Paul's was under construction, could hardly boast about the purity of its atmosphere. For example, a German tourist reported in 1710 that in order to see the vista from the tower of the cathedral, he had to get there very early in the morning "in order that we might have a prospect of the town from above before the air was full of coal smoke" (*London in 1710, From the Travels of Zacharias Conrad von Uffenbach,* trans. and ed. W. H. Quarrell and Margaret Mare [London: Faber and Faber, 1934], pp. 31-32). It is not surprising, therefore, that the new cathedral had to be cleaned within three decades after construction was started and before it was even finished. How, then, can one conclude with any degree of confidence that architectural stonework in London is being damaged more heavily today than it was three centuries ago?

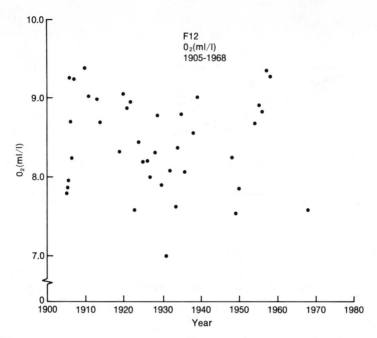

Figure 2-2   Oxygen Content (in milliliters per liter) at 100 Meters Depth at Station F 12 in the Bothnian Bay of the Baltic Sea between 1900 and 1968.

Source: Stig H. Fonselius, *Hydrography of the Baltic Deep Basins, III,* Fishery Board of Sweden Series Hydrography Report No. 23 (Lund, Sweden: Carl Bloms Boktryckeri, 1969): 46.

stations, but nearby stations show very similar trends. From such figures, some observers have concluded that the Baltic is becoming a "dead sea"; the inference has been that the pollution from its shores is destroying the Baltic.[5]

Yet it is by no means clear how closely the trends in oxygen content are related to pollution. For example, the northern part of the Bothnian Gulf of the Baltic, which is quite shallow, receives a considerable influx of pollutants from nearby paper plants[6] and is consequently one of the portions of the Baltic most heavily subjected to oxygen-demanding effluents. Yet the data on the oxygen content of this portion of the Baltic (see Figure 2-2) seem to exhibit no trend such as that displayed in the previous diagram. According to Stig H. Fonselius, the primary reason for the decrease in oxygen content in the central Baltic has been an increase in salinity.[7] Moreover, he attributes this rise in salinity to

[5] See, for example, Stig H. Fonselius, "Stagnant Sea," *Environment* 12 (July-August 1970): 2–3, 6, 28, 40.
[6] Ibid., p. 42.
[7] Stig H. Fonselius, *Hydrography of the Baltic Deep Basins, III,* Fishery Board of Sweden Series Hydrography Report No. 23 (Lund, Sweden: Carl Bloms Boktryckeri, 1969), p. 91. He lists, as the secondary reason for the increase, a rise in phosphorus concentrations which may well be related to the influx of sewage (pp. 90-91).

meteorological factors.[8] Specifically, "The main reason [s] . . . are changes in the atmospheric circulation which have been observed over a long period . . . [causing] a decrease in precipitation resulting in a corresponding decrease in runoff [that is, a diminution in the inflow from rivers feeding into the Baltic] ."[9] Examining the data on three rivers in the eastern Baltic region going back to the nineteenth century, he concludes, "There seems to be a general decreasing trend of the runoff in all three rivers from the beginning of the 20th century. If this is a true trend and it does continue there is not much hope for improved oxygen conditions in the Baltic deep water."[10]

Another rather curious illustration of environmental deterioration not attributable to recent human abuse is the case of "Cleopatra's Needle," the obelisk now standing in New York City's Central Park. Three sides of this monument are badly eroded, and the damage is often attributed to air pollution and continuous vibration from nearby traffic. We learned, however, that the obelisk, which originally stood at Heliopolis on the east bank of the Nile River, was tipped over by Persian invaders and remained on its side for some five and a half centuries until the Roman emperor, Augustus, had it moved and re-erected at Alexandria. From there it was brought to New York in 1880. According to E. M. Winkler, "The present east (undamaged) face probably faced downward during the monument's prostrate position between 500 B.C. and about 43 B.C." During that period there was "capillary migration from the ion-rich ground water on the flood plain silt of the Nile River."[11] That is, the stone absorbed Nile water and accumulated salt, which through normal capillary action was stored in the portions of the stone farthest away from the point of entry (that is, close to the other three sides). As a result "more than a few hundred pounds of granite flakings off the obelisk were cleaned up after a few years of exposure to the moisture-loaded atmosphere of New York City, which caused the hydration and expansion of the salts entrapped in the capillaries."[12] Much of the

---

[8] Ibid., p. 90.
[9] Ibid., p. 56.
[10] Ibid., p. 62. There is also some evidence suggesting that low-oxygen problems may have plagued the Baltic in the middle of the nineteenth century, well before the onset of extensive industrial activity. For the Vuoksi River in Finland, the uninterrupted data on runoff go back to 1847. While the Vuoksi does not itself flow into the Baltic, its runoff figures since 1900 follow a time pattern very similar to those for the two other rivers for which data are available only since 1900, a relationship that is hardly surprising since they are all presumably replenished from the same regional sources. This is significant, because it suggests that the behavior of the other rivers feeding into the Baltic could be expected to have paralleled that of the Vuoksi for the second half of the nineteenth century. Moreover, the figures suggest that, during the period 1847-1900, the runoff of the Vuoksi exhibited something of a rising trend. Indeed, in the 1850s the runoff was almost as low as it has been in recent times; this raises the likelihood that stagnation may have occurred in the Baltic in earlier periods too.
[11] E. M. Winkler, "Decay of Stone," *International Institute for Conservation, 1970 New York Conference on Conservation of Stone and Wooden Objects, I* (London: The International Institute for Conservation of Historic and Artistic Works, 1971): 6.
[12] Ibid.

remaining damage to the monument is probably attributable to "the strong abrasive action of drifting sand" while the monument stood in Heliopolis and Alexandria. Thus, Winkler concludes that "the disastrous disintegration of granites in city atmospheres, as exemplified by Cleopatra's Needle, is a myth. It is therefore hoped that the obelisk will be eliminated from textbooks of physical geology as 'a good example of weathering in cities.'"[13]

Not all damage to our environment can be traced to economic growth and industrialization.

B. Environmental Deterioration as an Historical Phenomenon. Another thing history makes very clear is that pollution is not a modern invention; technological developments have not always been an unmixed curse upon the environment. When the automobile began to replace the horse and rid the streets of odorous dungheaps, it was hailed as a major contributor to public health and sanitation. Certainly the modern city, whatever its state of cleanliness, is an improvement on the relatively tiny, but incredibly filthy, streets and waterways of medieval and Renaissance cities. It is reported that in about 1300 under Edward I, a Londoner was executed for burning sea coal in contravention of an Act designed to reduce smoke. During the reign of Edward I's grandson, some seventy years later, we find the following proclamation, one of many designed to protect the cleanliness of late medieval rivers and streets, all apparently equally unsuccessful (the reader will note especially the remarkable, if not wholly credible, assertion which we have italicized):

> Edward, by the grace of God etc., to our well-beloved, the Mayor, Sheriffs, and Aldermen, of our City of London, greeting. *Forasmuch as we are for certain informed that rushes, dung, refuse, and other filth and harmful things, from our City of London, and the suburbs thereof, have been for a long time past, and are daily, thrown into the water of Thames, so that the water aforesaid, and the hythes thereof, are so greatly obstructed, and the course of the said water so greatly narrowed, that great ships and vessels are not able, as of old they were wont, any longer to come up to the same city, but are impeded therein;* to the most grievous damage as well of ourselves as of the city aforesaid, and of all the nobles and others of our people to the same city resorting;—We, wishing to provide a fitting remedy in this behalf, do command you, on the fealty and allegiance in which unto us you are bound, strictly enjoining that, with all the speed that you may, you will cause orders to be given that such throwing of rushes, dung, refuse, and other filth and harmful things, into the bed of the river aforesaid, shall no longer be allowed, but that the same shall be removed and wholly taken away therefrom; to the amendment of the same bed of the river, and the enlarging of the watercourse aforesaid; so

---

[13] E. M. Winkler, "Weathering Rates as Exemplified by Cleopatra's Needle in New York City," *Journal of Geological Education* 13, No. 2 (1965): 50–52.

behaving yourselves in this behalf, that we shall have no reason for severely taking you to task in respect hereof. And this, as we do trust in you, and as you would avoid our heavy indignation, and the punishment which, as regards ourselves, you may incur, you are in no wise to omit. Witness myself, at Prestone, the 20th day of August, in the 46th year of our reign in England, and in France the 33rd."[14]

A description of the quality of the atmosphere in London in 1700 reminds us of its state two and a half centuries later:

the glorious Fabrick of St. Paul's now in building, so Stately and Beautiful as it is, will after an Age or Two, look old and discolour'd before 'tis finish'd, and may suffer perhaps as much damage by the Smoak, as the former Temple did by the Fire.[15]

The author goes on to point out:

By reason likewise of this Smoak it is, that the Air of the City, especially in the Winter time, is rendred very unwholsome: For in case there be no Wind, and especially in Frosty Weather, the City is cover'd with a thick *Brovillard* or Cloud, which the force of the Winter-Sun is not able to scatter; so that the Inhabitants thereby suffer under a dead benumming Cold, being in a manner totally depriv'd of the warmths and comforts of the Day . . . when yet to them who are but a Mile out of Town, the Air is sharp, clear, and healthy, and the Sun most comfortable and reviving.[16]

It is thus important to recognize that modern, industrialized society has no monopoly on pollution and environmental damage from either human sources or natural forces. Evidence of significant environmental damage does not necessarily mean that the damage is growing, and evidence that deterioration is growing may not mean that the source of the problem is human activity. We

---

[14] "Royal Proclamation against the Pollution of the Thames," *Memorials of London and London Life in the XIIIth, XIVth, and XVth Centuries, Being a Series of Extracts, Local, Social, and Political, from the Early Archives of the City of London, A.D. 1276-1419*, select., trans. and ed. Henry Thomas Riley (London: Longmans, Green and Co., 1868), pp. 367-68. A reviewer comments, "I assume that what seems incredible about the quote is that the refuse could block navigation. I think this was probably a legally necessary assertion even if not an objective truth. If my offhand memory of legal history serves me well, the King's power over the condition of the waterways stemmed from a navigational servitude in favor of the crown which gave the crown such powers over the waterways as were necessary to preserve the crown's right of navigation thereon" (letter from Professor Marcia Gelpe, University of Minnesota Law School, February 3, 1977).

[15] Timothy Nourse, *Campania Felix* (London, 1700), p. 352.

[16] Ibid. Perhaps the quotation should be taken with a grain of salt since Nourse was a violent critic of cities, but the evidence from other sources certainly suggests that his description was based on fact.

do not intend here to deny the seriousness of environmental decay, but rather to point out the complexities besetting an understanding and interpretation of levels and trends in environmental quality. With this in mind, we turn to the presentation of our accumulated data on these trends.

2. Cases of Mixed or Improving Environmental Trends

As we said at the beginning of the chapter, our examination of the available facts suggests that the trends in environmental damage are far less uniform than we had initially expected. This section presents some examples in which environmental quality is actually improving or in which a varied pattern of deterioration and/or improvement is apparent.

A. The Great Lakes. The deteriorating water quality of two of the most vulnerable of the Great Lakes (in terms of population and water volume), Lake

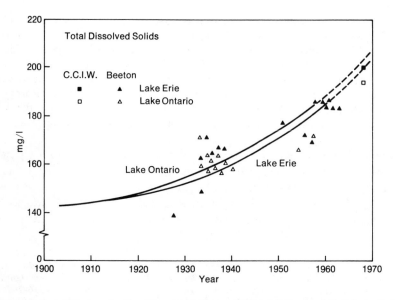

Figure 2-3   Changes in the Concentrations of Total Dissolved Solids in Lakes Erie and Ontario.

Source: Proceedings of the Conference on Changes in the Chemistry of Lakes Erie and Ontario, November 5–6, 1970, *Bulletin of the Buffalo Society of Natural Sciences* 25, No. 2 (1971).

Note: C.C.I.W. refers to Canada Centre for Inland Waters; Beeton refers to A. M. Beeton, "Eutrophication of the St. Lawrence Great Lakes," *Limnology and Oceanography* 19 (1965): 240–54; and Kramer refers to J. R. Kramer, "Theoretical Model for the Chemical Composition of Fresh Water with Application to the Great Lakes," in *Great Lakes Research Division* (Ann Arbor, Michigan: University of Michigan, 1964): 147–60.

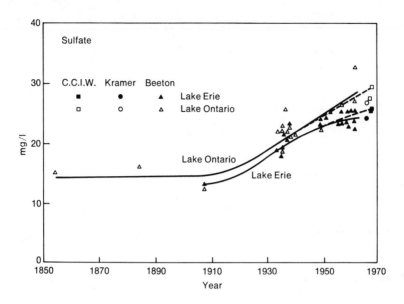

Figure 2-4   Changes in the Concentrations of Sulfate in Lakes Erie and Ontario.

Source: See Figure 2-3.

Erie and Lake Ontario, has received widespread attention. Figures 2-3, 2-4, and 2-5 show trends for these two lakes in the concentrations of three substances closely tied to industrial and municipal pollution: dissolved solids, sulfates, and calcium.[17] The figures show very clearly that, at least since early in the twentieth century, these concentrations have been increasing dramatically. Figures on concentrations of other substances in these lakes (chloride, sodium, and potassium, also associated with industrial wastes) tell much the same story (see Figure 2-6). But the water quality of Lakes Erie and Ontario differs sharply from that of the other Great Lakes. Although Lakes Michigan and Huron have suffered from an increase in dissolved solids (see Figure 2-7), this growth has been far slower than in Lakes Erie or Ontario. Moreover, Lake Michigan has suffered no growth in calcium content, and its concentrations of sodium and potassium leveled off soon after the turn of the century. Lake Superior's purity seems to have been increasing rather steadily or holding constant, at least in terms of the dissolved solids for which we have data. Figure 2-6 shows the great diversity in calcium, chloride, sodium, and potassium concentrations over time in the Great Lakes, with these chemicals apparently presenting an increasing problem only in Lakes Erie and Ontario. Sulfates, on the other hand, have increased in concentration in every one of the lakes except Lake Superior,

---

[17]We present in the next chapter a table of air and water pollutants that indicates their sources, characteristics, and effects on human health.

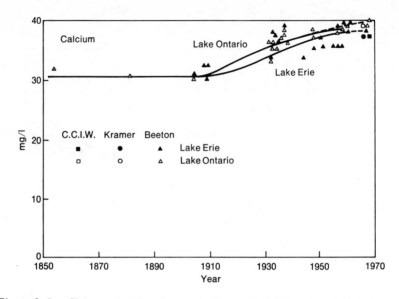

Figure 2-5   Changes in the Concentrations of Calcium in Lakes Erie and Ontario.

Source: See Figure 2-3.

the largest, deepest, and most isolated of the lakes.[18] A reporter could paint the most dismal picture of the state of the Great Lakes by singling out Lakes Erie and Ontario, while the investigator who chooses to study only Lake Superior could easily conclude that there is no cause for alarm.[19]

[18]The table below represents the latest figures on total dissolved solids, sulfates, calcium, chloride, and potassium available from the Great Lakes Basin Commission, Ann Arbor, Michigan, May 1977 (parts per million).

	Superior	Huron	Michigan	Erie	Ontario
Total Dissolved Solids	52	118	150	198	194
Sulfates	3.0	15	16	26	29
Calcium	13	25	32	37	40
Chloride	1.2	5.4	6	25	28
Potassium	0.5	0.8	1.0	1.0	1.0

[19]Environmental programs have apparently produced some recent improvements in the purity of some of the Great Lakes. See *New York Times,* May 23, 1974, p. 1, and June 9, 1974, Sect. 4, p. 2. The quality of Lake Superior, however, has been threatened by discharges of the Reserve Mining Company, which pours some 67,000 tons of taconite tailings into the lake every day Besides just dirtying the lake and its shores, it has been alleged by some experts that "the asbestos-like fibers emptied into the water—which is used in its

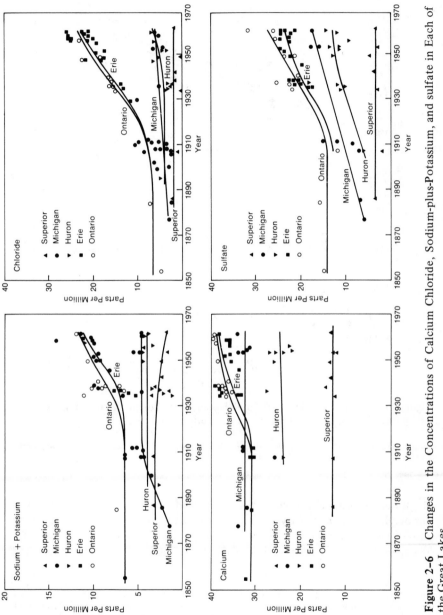

Figure 2-6 Changes in the Concentrations of Calcium Chloride, Sodium-plus-Potassium, and sulfate in Each of the Great Lakes.

Source: Beeton, "Eutrophication of the St. Lawrence Great Lakes," Fig. 3, p. 248.

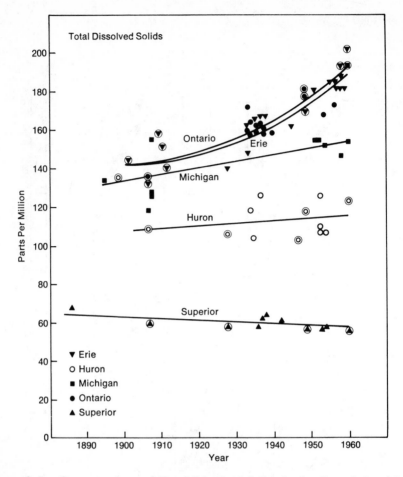

Figure 2-7 Concentrations of Total Dissolved Solids in the Great Lakes (circled points are averages of 12 or more determinations).

Source: A. M. Beeton, "Eutrophication of the St. Lawrence Great Lakes," *Limnology and Oceanography* 19 (1965), Fig. 1, p. 246.

B. Water Quality in the New York City Harbor. The quality of the waters surrounding New York City has a mixed history. Figure 2-8 shows the trend in dissolved oxygen concentrations in five waterways surrounding the city for the years 1910-70.[20] (Any biodegradable emissions such as human wastes, food

---

pure form as drinking water by Duluth and other communities—are a health hazard, since they have been known to cause diseases such as cancer among asbestos workers in other parts of the country, though sometimes not until 20 years after inhalation" (*New York Times,* June 9, 1974, Sect. 4, p. 2). Chapter 18 describes the long legal battles over this company's discharges into Lake Superior.

[20] To eliminate from the data the confusing and irrelevant year-to-year fluctuations that are

products, or waste paper are gradually transformed and assimilated by natural processes that use up oxygen. A waterway heavily polluted by biodegradable emissions will, therefore, tend to have a relatively low dissolved oxygen content.)[21] The decline indicated by the graph for the period prior to 1920 suggests that oxygen-using pollution in the city's waterways increased rapidly during the first years of the twentieth century. In about 1920, however, the process of deterioration suddenly halted. For the next three decades, the dissolved-oxygen level remained relatively stable, or even improved slightly. It has been suggested that the decrease in dissolved oxygen up to 1917 was the result, not of increased industrial activity in the area, but of rapid population growth. This population growth increased the amount of sewage dumped virtually untreated into the city's waterways. According to this view, it was the restriction of immigration from abroad that accounted for the stabilizing of water quality in New York's rivers. Unfortunately this explanation is only partly tenable at best, since the population of the city did continue to grow at least until 1930.[22]

In any event, by the early 1950s a major expansion in waste treatment facilities was begun, first in the East River and later in the Hudson. By the middle of the 1960s, dissolved oxygen concentrations had increased sharply in all five of the waterways described in the graph. Indeed, there was observable improvement throughout the Hudson River:

> almost all fishermen, marine biologists, environmentalists and government officials [are] agreeing that the river is cleaner now than it has been in recent years.
>
> By almost every measure available—amount of money spent, number of sewage treatment plants constructed, number of crabs returning, number and size of fish, visibility of sewage, number of people swimming—the 155-mile-long main stem of the Hudson River between New York City and Troy is improving.
>
> In the fishing season just ending, fishermen took in more and bigger blue-claw crabs, hauled in bigger weakfish, caught large numbers of "lafayettes" for the first time in 30 years. . . .[23]

---

heavily influenced by fortuitous meteorological conditions, the graphs represent five-year averages rather than the raw annual data from which the averages are derived. That is, the figure shown for 1912 actually represents an average of the data for 1910-14, the figure for 1913 is an average of the data for 1911-15, etc. For the raw data and the average data see Appendix B, Table 2-B2.

[21] We should emphasize that the level of dissolved oxygen is only one determinant of water quality; as we saw in the case of the Great Lakes, there are other important elements affecting the quality of a body of water. More on this will be said later.

[22] The population of the city as given by U.S. Census figures from 1900 to 1950 was: 1900, 3.4 million; 1910, 4.8 million; 1920, 5.6 million; 1930, 7.3 million; 1940, 7.5 million; 1950, 8.0 million (Ira Rosenwaike, *Population History of New York City* [Syracuse: Syracuse University Press, 1972], p. 133).

[23] *New York Times,* September 29, 1973, p. 1. However, the reader will note in Figure 2-8 that the most recent data for two of the rivers, the Hudson and the Lower East Rivers, indicate a reversal of this trend with dissolved-oxygen levels declining in the early 1970s.

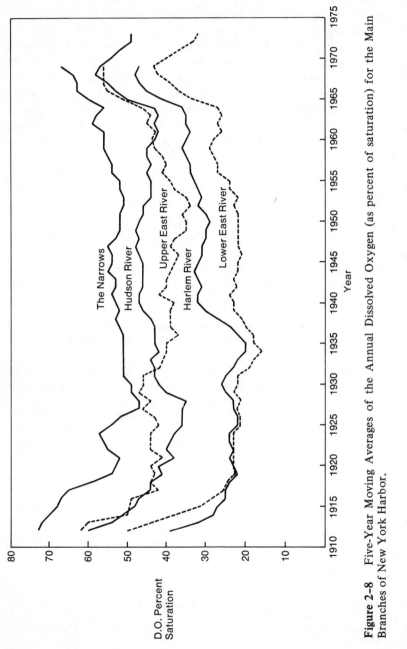

Figure 2-8 Five-Year Moving Averages of the Annual Dissolved Oxygen (as percent of saturation) for the Main Branches of New York Harbor.

Source: *New York Harbor Water Survey, 1970*, provided by City of New York, Environmental Protection Administration, Department of Water Resources, Bureau of Water Pollution Control. For actual figures, see Appendix B, Table 2-B2.

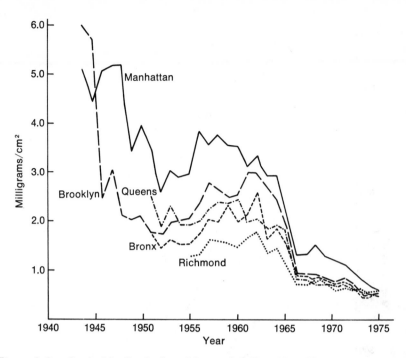

Figure 2-9 Settleable Particulate Matter for Five New York City Boroughs (milligrams per square centimeter).

Source: Department of Air Resources, 51 Astor Place, New York, N. Y. 10003.

C. U.S. Air Quality Trends. New York City's air quality has shown similar improvement in terms of certain pollutants. Figure 2-9 shows the trends in settleable particulate matter (soot) for all five boroughs of the city during the postwar period. The change is certainly startling. In Brooklyn the figure has fallen to about one-sixth of its 1945 level, and in Manhattan it has declined by more than two-thirds. Similarly, there has been a decline in the sulfur dioxide content of the atmosphere, not only in New York but in other major cities as well. The data depicted in Figure 2-10 show a dramatic improvement in New York and Chicago and more modest gains in the other cities such as Boston and St. Louis (although the latter two cities exhibited something of a reversal between 1971 and 1972). This sort of evidence suggests that environmental policy can be effective and can produce results that are both rapid and substantial.[24]

---

[24] Allen Kneese, in a letter to us, attributes much of the improvement in air quality, not to environmental policy, but to economic considerations which led to the substitution of oil and natural gas for coal "first in home heating (which was a terrible low level source of harmful and damaging substances) and later in industrial and electrical power generation.... This raises some interesting questions about what will happen when large scale reconversion to coal occurs." As we will discuss in a later chapter, the fuel crisis of the 1970s has brought great pressure for resumption of the use of fuels with higher sulfur

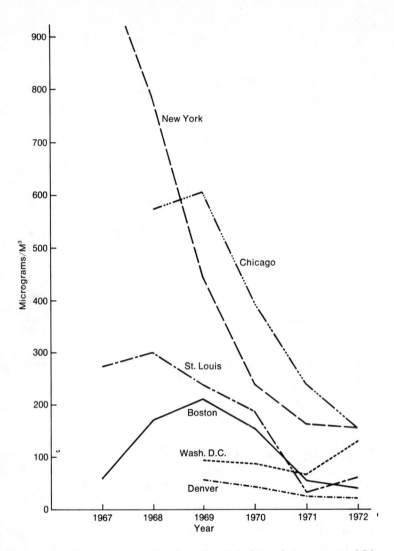

Figure 2-10 SO$_2$ Air Quality Data for Six U.S. Cities (micrograms of SO$_2$ per cubic meter).

Source: Derived from *Environmental Quality, The Fourth Annual Report of the Council on Environmental Quality* (Washington, D.C.: U.S. Government Printing Office, 1973), p. 273. They cite as their source: EPA data from the National Air Sampling Network.

Table 2-1 summarizes national emission trends for five major air pollutants for the period 1940-74. The figures indicate that between 1940 and 1970 emissions of these pollutants were steadily and significantly increasing. The Council on

content, and there is already some evidence of a concomitant deterioration of air quality in some U.S. cities.

TABLE 2-1

NATIONWIDE AIR POLLUTION EMISSIONS, 1940-74
(millions of tons)

Year	Sulfur Dioxide	Particulates	Carbon Monoxide	Hydrocarbons	Nitrogen Oxides
1940	22	27	85	19	7
1950	24	26	103	26	10
1960	23	25	128	32	14
1968	31	26	150	35	21
1969	34	27	154	35	22
1970	34.3	27.5	107.3	32.1	20.4
1971	33.5	25.2	104.9	31.4	20.8
1972	32.6	23.2	104.9	31.3	22.2
1973	33.2	21.0	100.9	31.3	23.0
1974	31.4	19.5	94.6	30.4	22.5

Sources: For the 1940-69 period, *Environmental Quality, The Third Annual Report of the Council on Environmental Quality* (Washington, D.C.: U.S. Government Printing Office, August 1972), Table 2, p. 6; for the 1970-74 period, *Environmental Quality, The Sixth Annual Report of the Council on Environmental Quality* (Washington, D.C.: U.S. Government Printing Office, December 1975), Table 32, p. 440.

Note: The CEQ cautions: "The techniques used to calculate these 1970-74 emissions differ from those used for 1940-1970. Consequently, although recent emissions appear lower, the pre-1970 estimates are not truly comparable with the post-1970 calculations" (*Sixth Annual Report*, p. 305).

Environmental Quality writes, "Since 1970, however, air pollution control programs appear to be stemming that growth. The estimated total nationwide emissions of particulates and carbon monoxide have been reduced significantly, and the other major regulated pollutants have remained near 1970 levels."[25] Table 2-1 shows "that between 1970 and 1974 particulate emission levels dropped by about 29%, sulfur dioxide declined 8%, carbon monoxide dropped 12%, and hydrocarbon emissions declined about 5%. On the other hand, nitrogen oxide emissions have increased an estimated 10% over the same period."[26]

D. London: Air and Water Quality Trends. Air quality in London displays striking parallels to the New York experience. London's long history of air pollution was largely the result of the heavy use of coal fires for both industrial and domestic heating. One of the consequences was the prevalence of filthy fogs, sometimes in garish colors produced by the chemical content of the air; such fogs became as much a symbol of London as Westminster Abbey and Big Ben. Only after the disaster of December 1952, during which in a two-week period abnormally high concentrations of sulfur dioxide and smoke resulted in

---

[25] *Environmental Quality, The Sixth Annual Report of the Council on Environmental Quality* (Washington, D.C.: U.S. Government Printing Office, December 1975), p. 305.
[26] Ibid., p. 305.

an estimated 4,000 excess deaths,[27] did Parliament adopt more stringent regulations for the protection of the atmosphere. The Clean Air Act of 1956 and
subsequent legislation established smoke-control zones in which strict codes
governed allowable smoke emissions.[28] The results have been impressive: pea-
soup fogs have disappeared, and the number of hours of sunshine in London
has climbed significantly. Figure 2-11 shows that there has been a 50 percent
increase in winter sunshine in Central London since 1950. More generally,
Table 2-2 indicates that emissions of smoke and, to a lesser extent, of sulfur
into the atmosphere throughout the United Kingdom have fallen fairly steadily
since the early 1960s.[29]

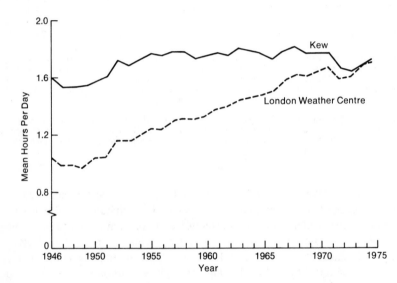

Figure 2-11   Trend in Hours of Winter Sunshine Recorded at London Weather
Centre and Kew Observatory.

Source: Cabinet Office, Central Statistical Office, Great George Street, London SW1P 3AQ,
Letter from R. W. Freeman, February 24, 1977. For data from which graph was drawn, see
Appendix B, Table 2–B3.

Note: Graph shows ten-year moving averages, December through February, plotted on last
        year of period.

---

[27] Lester B. Lave and Eugene P. Seskin, *Air Pollution and Human Health* (Baltimore: Published for Resources for the Future by The Johns Hopkins University Press, 1977), Chap. 9,
p. 188.
[28] Albert Parker, "Air Pollution Research and Control in Great Britain," *American Journal
Of Public Health* 47 (May 1957): 569.
[29] However, a reviewer points out that the decrease in smoke pollution may have resulted
in an increase in photochemical smog (the formation of which requires sunlight) and,
perhaps, even in the incidence of skin cancer.

TABLE 2-2

EMISSION OF SMOKE AND
SULFUR DIOXIDE (SO_2) IN
UNITED KINGDOM, 1955-75
(millions of tons)

Year	Smoke	SO_2
1955	2.35	5.05
1962	1.51	5.89
1968	0.89	5.74
1969	0.79	5.99
1970	0.72	6.12
1971	0.61	5.83
1972	0.50	5.63
1973	0.49	5.87
1974	0.46	5.43
1975[a]	0.39	5.11

Source: Cabinet Office, Central Statistical Office, Great George Street, London SW10 3AQ, letter from R. W. Freeman, February 24, 1977.

[a]Provisional

The English have also made considerable progress in the cleanup of some rivers and estuaries. We noted earlier the marked increase in recent years in the dissolved-oxygen content of New York City's rivers. Figure 2-12 depicts similar trends in levels of dissolved oxygen in the Thames near London. In contrast to the period of deterioration from the 1930s until 1954, when the dissolved oxygen content of the Thames just downstream from the City was close to zero, the curve for 1969 indicates a marked improvement. The Royal Commission on Environmental Pollution reported:

> The oxygen content of the Thames for some 10 miles above and 30 miles below London Bridge had been diminishing for decades, and the consequences were beginning to be very serious. In 1949 the Water Pollution Research Laboratory began an investigation into the causes of the deterioration. When these were diagnosed, the Port of London Authority launched a programme to improve the quality of the water. The success of this programme has been shown by the return of many kinds of fish. In 1957-58 a survey showed no fish between Richmond (15 miles above London Bridge) and Gravesend (25 miles below). By 1967-68 some 42 species were present and migratory forms were able once again to move through the polluted zone.[30]

---

[30]Royal Commission on Environmental Pollution, *First Report* (London: Her Majesty's Stationery Office, February 1971), p. 23.

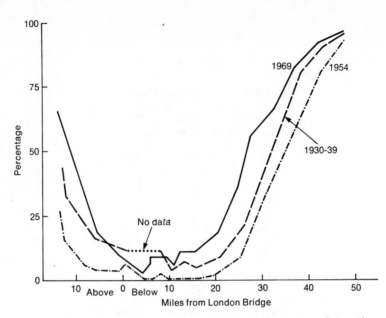

Figure 2-12   Analysis of Water of River Thames. Percentage Saturation with Dissolved Oxygen at High Water (average July–September).

Source: Royal Commission on Environmental Pollution, *First Report* (London: Her Majesty's Stationery Office, February 1971), p. 20.

These cases support the view that environmental policy can work. It does not follow, however, that the battle against pollution is essentially won or that improvement is universal and unambiguous. There are important and documented instances of progressive decline in environmental quality. In the next section, we will discuss some evidence of growing human abuse of the environment.

3. Cases of Deteriorating Environmental Quality

A. Another Look at Urban Air Quality. In the previous section we described the decreasing levels of atmospheric sulfur dioxide and particulate matter in New York and other cities as an example of improving air quality.[31] The trends in other measures of air quality are not so satisfying. Figure 2-13, for example,

---

[31] It now seems evident that, in fact, sulfur dioxide pollution is not as serious a threat to human health as are sulfate concentrations. Though SO_2 pollution in the cities has decreased markedly in the last decade (apparently largely because of the relocation to less populated areas of the main sources of urban SO_2, the municipal power plants), national ambient sulfate levels have remained fairly stable. This difference in the trends in sulfate and sulfur dioxide concentrations is apparently rather mysterious, since sulfates are a product of SO_2. We will say more about sulfates in the next chapter.

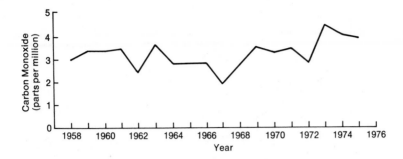

Figure 2-13 Carbon Monoxide Concentrations in New York City, 1958–75 (parts per million).

Source: Department of Air Resources, 51 Astor Place, New York, N.Y. 10003. Figures represent average annual measurements taken at Station Laboratory 121 (located at 121st Street) fifteen feet above street level. This station was chosen because it is the oldest in the city and its data are more complete. Most of the air pollutant measuring stations in New York City began operation after 1969. For figures from which graph was drawn see Appendix B, Table 2–B4.

shows that concentrations of carbon monoxide in New York City have, apart from short-term fluctuations, remained constant since 1958. This is also largely true for most European cities. Similarly, Figure 2-14, which depicts trends in the levels of suspended particulates in five major cities over a recent five-year period, shows that other cities have not done as well as New York in this respect. Indeed, the air in Denver has apparently been growing steadily more polluted in terms of particulate matter.[32]

B. Trends in Atmospheric Lead Pollution. A striking case of increasing environmental deterioration is the steady growth of lead concentrations in the earth's atmosphere. Analyses of ice layers in the Arctic and Antarctic regions have produced estimates of long-term trends in lead concentrations (and other pollutants). Figure 2-15 shows the findings of one of the most recent, and

---

[32] The evaluation of the overall pollution content of the atmosphere of a particular city or of a waterway is a complex matter, and data on any single pollutant or group of pollutants can easily be misleading. This point was made forcefully in a letter to us from Thomas McMullen of the Monitoring and Reporting Branch of the Environmental Protection Agency. Commenting on the data underlying Figure 2-9, he remarked, "This measurement can in no way be interpreted as an index of general air quality because the complex character of air pollution has been changing over recent decades. Dustfall levels have been diminishing as restrictions on use of soft coal, conversions of home heating systems to gas, and changes in industrial practices have reduced the quantity of larger particles emitted. However, concurrent growth in vehicular traffic, expansion of urbanization, and the burgeoning diversity of industrialization has increased the volume of other pollutant emissions and multiplied the variety of trace pollutants. I think it might be difficult to specify an index, implying reference to a base year or to some common denominator, applicable to the evolving nature of air pollution over the last several decades."

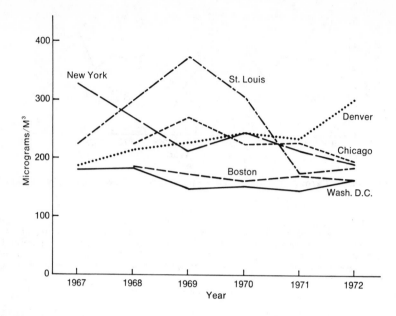

Figure 2-14 Total Suspended Particulates for Six Cities, 1967–72 (micrograms per cubic meter).

Source: *Environmental Quality, The Fourth Annual Report of the Council on Environmental Quality* (Washington, D.C.: U.S. Government Printing Office, Sept. 1973), p. 273.

apparently most systematic, of these studies.[33] The graph, which covers over twenty-five centuries, is certainly startling. It shows that, even in the remote regions of northern Greenland, there has been a persistent, accelerating rise in lead pollution; today lead concentrations at Camp Century, Greenland, are well over five hundred times "natural" levels.[34] The study's measurement of other "impurities" in the ice samples showed no discernible trends; that is, of the seven items whose concentrations were estimated as far back as 800 B.C., it was lead alone that exhibited any long-term growth pattern.[35]

The figures constitute grounds for genuine concern. Lead has been described as

> one of the most insidiously toxic of the heavy metals to which we are exposed, particularly in its ability to accumulate in the body and to damage the central nervous system including the brain. . . . It inhibits

---

[33] See M. Murozumi, T. J. Chow, and C. Patterson, "Chemical Concentrations of Pollutant Lead Aerosols, Terrestrial Dusts and Sea Salts in Greenland and Antarctic Snow Strata," *Geochimica et Cosmochimica Acta* 33, No. 10 (October 1969): 1247–94.

[34] Ibid., p. 1285.

[35] It should be noted that even the carefully gathered evidence of the Greenland study has been criticized on two grounds: first, similar results were not obtained in the Antarctic samples, and, second and perhaps more serious, the Greenland figures may reflect a very

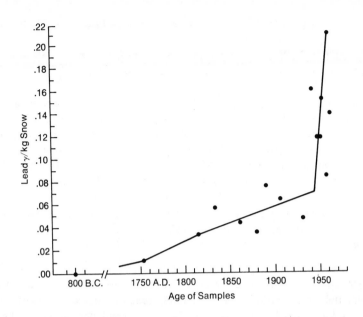

Figure 2-15 Industrial Lead Pollution at Camp Century, Greenland, Since 800 B.C., γ/kg (micrograms per kilogram).

Source: M. Murozumi, T. J. Chow, and C. Patterson, "Chemical Concentrations of Pollutant Lead Aerosols, Terrestrial Dusts and Sea Salts in Greenland and Antarctic Snow Strata," *Geochimica et Cosmochimica Acta* 33, No. 10 (October 1969): 1285.

enzyme systems necessary for the formation of haemoglobin . . . and has been said to interfere with practically any life-process one chooses to study. Children and young people appear specially liable to suffer more or less permanent brain damage, leading [among other things] . . . to mental

---

special source of lead contamination: "a major U.S. military base was established in Thule, Greenland, during World War II and a large camp was set up between 1959 and 1960 at Camp Century. This is only 80 [kilometers] from the Virgin Trench site where samples of snow, dated 1952-1965, were collected. The base was supplied by aircraft using leaded fuel . . . [thus] snow at the Trench site may well have been contaminated by these activities" (A. L. Mills, "Lead in the Environment," *Chemistry in Britain* 7 [April 1971]: 161). It may be relevant to note that Mr. Mills is chairman of the Institute of Petroleum's advisory committee on health. Both charges have evoked responses. The difference in the results for the Northern and Southern studies has been attributed to "barriers to north-south tropospheric mixing . . . which hinder the migration of aerosol pollutants from the northern hemisphere to the Antarctic" (Murozumi, Chow, and Patterson, "Chemical Concentrations," p. 1247). As for the second charge, an authoritative defender of the Greenland study has replied, "Firstly, the greatest amounts of lead were found to be deposited in the winter months when precipitation was heaviest and air traffic lightest. Secondly, the lead levels from sites between the Virgin Trench and the bases showed no elevation attributable to significant contamination from the bases. Thirdly, the Virgin Trench site was predominantly upwind from the bases. It is also worth noting that the major increase in ice-lead levels began about 20 years before the closer base was established" (D. Bryce-Smith, "Lead Pollution from Petrol," *Chemistry in Britain* 7 [July 1971]: 285).

retardation, irritability and bizarre behavior patterns. . . . More serious occupational exposure can lead to insanity and death. . . .[36]

Further evidence of long-term increases in lead concentrations is provided by a recent study in Peru comparing the lead content of six-century-old human bones with more modern samples. Lead concentrations in the modern bones were, on the average, over ten times as high as those in the earlier ones.[37] On the other hand, a Polish study showed ". . . that the levels of lead in modern Polish bones do not differ significantly from those found in bones from the 3rd century, although levels in the Middle Ages were often very high."[38] While there is strong evidence that the prevalence of this poison has increased markedly over the centuries, it is still impossible to reach completely unqualified conclusions.

C. The Accumulation of Solid Waste. We turn next to a source of indisputable environmental deterioration: the burgeoning *quantity* of solid wastes which society produces. Growth in population and in output per capita can be expected to increase the amount of solid waste. While time series for long-term trends in this area are not easy to obtain, the evidence available indicates that this has, indeed, been true. It is reported, for example, that in recent years the flow of solid wastes in New York City has been increasing 4 percent per year.[39] We have collected some data for Cincinnati that go back more than forty years. Figure 2-16 indicates that the amount of solid waste collected in Cincinnati has grown at an average rate of about 4.5 percent per year.[40] If records were obtained for other cities, they would no doubt show very similar results. There is no question that this trend poses ever-increasing problems for society. Already many cities are having trouble disposing of the mounting heaps of trash. Neighboring areas are reluctant to serve as the cities' dumps, and locations near cities that are suitable for landfill operations are getting scarce. Other methods of waste disposal are now recognized to create problems of their own. Burning garbage pollutes the air, while treatment of liquid wastes leaves a sludge which must be disposed of. Moreover, we are learning that dumping wastes into the

---

[36] D. Bryce-Smith, "Lead Pollution—A Growing Hazard to Public Health," *Chemistry in Britain* 7 (February 1971), p. 54. In a later note Bryce-Smith adds the significant point that "no other toxic chemical pollutant appears to have accumulated in man to average levels so close to the threshold for potential clinical poisoning" ("Lead Pollution from Petrol," p. 286). See also Table 3-2 in Chapter 3.

[37] See "Lead in Ancient and Modern Bones," *Scientist and Citizen* Vol. 10, No. 3 (April 1968), p. 89.

[38] Mills, "Lead Pollution," p. 161, citing a study by Z. Jaworoski.

[39] *New York Times,* March 27, 1970, p. 49.

[40] The figure of 4.5 percent was computed from data supplied by R. D. Behrman, Administrative Assistant, and A. H. Schuck, Acting Superintendent, Department of Public Works, Division of Waste Collection, City of Cincinnati, in letters of November 9, 1973, and February 17, 1977.

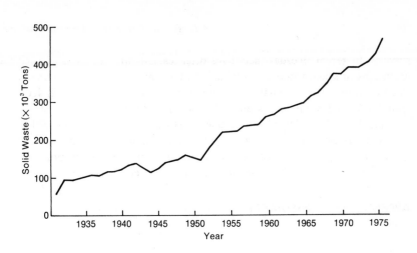

Figure 2-16   Total Tonnage of Solid Waste Received at City Disposal Sites, Cincinnati, Ohio, 1931-76.

Source: City of Cincinnati, Department of Public Works, Division of Waste Collection, Letters of November 9, 1973, and February 17, 1977, from R. D. Behrman, Administrative Assistant, and A. H. Schuck, Acting Superintendent. For data see Appendix B, Table 2-B1.

ocean nearby is not costless to society; sludge dumped into the sea can kill or contaminate marine life and pollute nearby waters and beaches. The changing composition of solid wastes also adds to the problem of disposal. For example, plastics (which are nondegradable and often have harmful combustion properties) make up an increasing percentage of solid wastes. All in all, the problem of solid waste disposal can hardly be viewed with equanimity; it surely represents a major environmental problem that is likely to grow worse.[41]

4. Conclusions

The trends in environmental deterioration are varied and uneven. While the evidence presented in this chapter may undermine some of the more rash and unqualified predictions of imminent ecological disaster, there is no justification for complacency and inaction. Unquestionably, various types of environmental damage directly associated with human activity have grown rapidly and without interruption for a very long period of time. Some of them, with little doubt, produce serious consequences. As we will see in the next chapter, certain forms of pollution, besides making existence uglier and far less pleasant, have almost certainly increased the frequency of illness and added significantly to death rates. Some forms of pollution may even pose serious hazards for human

---

[41] In Chapter 21 we will encounter another example in which environmental damage has been growing: the case of automotive emissions.

survival. In recent decades facts have often caught up with and surpassed the inventions of science fiction; we shall see that some of the more bizarre horrors threatened by environmental abuse cannot be ruled out with any high degree of confidence. But scare tactics are not necessary to make a case for strong environmental policy. The demonstrable ill effects of pollution on health and longevity, despite the untidy diversity of trends that accompany them, surely justify the adoption of effective countermeasures. In the next chapter we shall explore some of the likely consequences of environmental decay.

APPENDIX A: *A LESSON FROM VERY LONG TIME SERIES: THE CASE OF THE NILE*

This chapter has presented a number of time series for environmental data, some of considerable duration. Yet from a historical point of view they are relatively brief; few of them extend more than seventy-five years.

In one area, the study of climate, time-series data are available over extraordinarily long periods of time.[1] From the evidence of tree rings, glaciers, and other sources, experts have accumulated figures spanning hundreds of years. One of the most remarkable of these series provides the annual figures on the height of the Nile River. They seem not to have been assembled by scientists, but rather by tax authorities who based their tax levies on these data as an indicator of the agricultural prosperity of the Nile valley. Before presenting a graph that summarizes a substantial portion of the data (which extend more than seven centuries), let us consider briefly the data in Figure 2-A1, which gives, in five-year averages, the behavior of the annual low-water mark of the Nile River. The pronounced and steady downward trend over the period of more than thirty years should be clear enough. It may suggest the onset of a period of drought. Surely, the consistency of its decline presages unpleasant things for the succeeding years. An observer looking at this trend might well project dire consequences for the future of the river valley and its inhabitants.

Yet the companion Figure 2–A2, which gives the trend of the *high*-water levels over the same period, already provides grounds for doubt. There is still something of a downward trend, but it is not nearly so pronounced or persistent as the annual minima. Moreover, Figures 2-A3 and 2-A4 tell quite a different story; they repeat the data of 2-A1 and 2-A2 along with their sequels. The time paths can hardly be described as steady downward trends.

The full history, however, is revealed by our last graph, Figure 2-A5, which shows the variations in the height of the Nile from 641 through 1451. It is certainly not easy to discern any sharp trends in the data. The moral should be clear: it is dangerous to extrapolate from a consistent trend in a data series, even one persisting over decades.

---

[1] A good source on this subject is Emmanuel Le Roy Ladurie, *Histoire du Climat Depuis l'An Mil* (Paris: Flammarion, 1967).

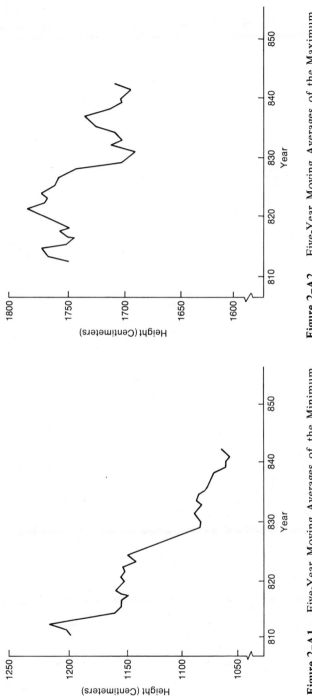

Figure 2–A1 Five-Year Moving Averages of the Minimum Height of the Nile River.

Figure 2–A2 Five-Year Moving Averages of the Maximum Height of the Nile River.

Source: S. A. Le Prince Omar Tousson, "Memoire sur l'Historie du Nil," Memoires Presents, A L'Institut D'Egypt et Publies Sous Les Auspices SA Majeste Fouad Ier, Roi D'Egypt, 10 (Le Caire: Imprimerie du l'Institut Francais d'Archeologie Orientale, 1925): 361–411. See Table 2–A1 for the data.

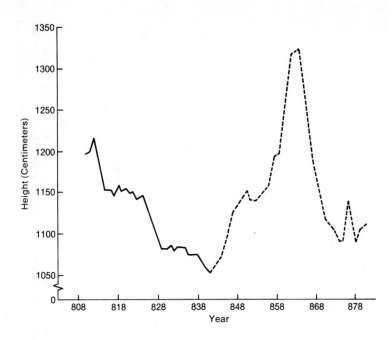

Figure 2-A3   Five-Year Moving Averages of the Minimum Height of the Nile River.

Source: See Figure 2-A1.

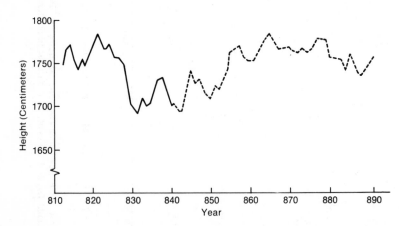

Figure 2-A4   Five-Year Moving Averages of the Maximum Height of the Nile River.

Source: See Figure 2-A1.

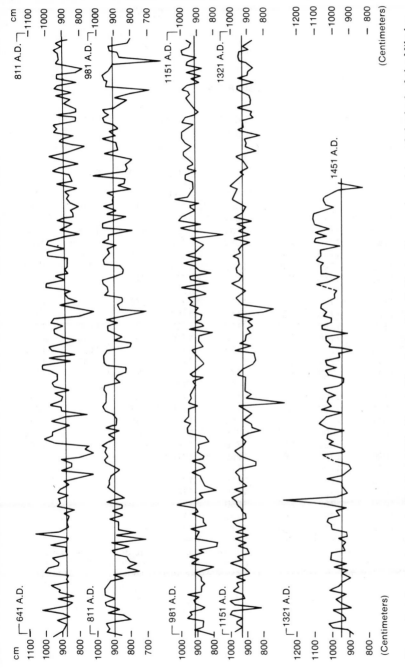

Figure 2–A5 Variations in Height of Nile Flood. The sloping line indicates the secular raising of the bed of the Nile by the deposition of silt. Height is in centimeters.

Source: C. E. P. Brooks, "Periodicities in the Nile Floods," *Memoirs of the Royal Meteorological Society* 2, No. 12 (January 1928): 10.

TABLE 2–A1

FIVE-YEAR MOVING AVERAGES OF THE HEIGHT OF THE NILE RIVER
(centimeters)

Year	Minimum	Maximum	Year	Minimum	Maximum	Year	Minimum	Maximum
811	1196		840	1062	1700	869	1149	1771
812	1202		841	1055	1701	870	1125	1766
813	1217	1746	842	1054	1696	871	1111	1765
814	1183	1767	843	1065	1692	872	1107	1769
815	1159	1773	844	1072	1718	873	1092	1766
816	1153	1749	845	1085	1741	874	1090	1765
817	1152	1742	846	1102	1724	875	1094	1772
818	1145	1756	847	1122	1733	876	1142	1781
819	1156	1746	848	1227	1728	877	1113	1781
820	1152	1762	849	1137	1712	878	1090	1783
821	1153	1775	850	1144	1709	879	1105	1758
822	1150	1782	851	1153	1725	880	1106	1757
823	1152	1769	852	1139	1720	881	1065	1757
824	1143	1767	853	1138	1731	882	1103	1757
825	1148	1771	854	1143	1753	883	1139	1747
826	1140	1758	855	1151	1764	884	1143	1763
827	1122	1756	856	1153	1769	885	1148	1752
828	1106	1756	857	1179	1767	886		1735
829	1091	1727	858	1194	1759	887		1733
830	1081	1702	859	1196	1755	888		1744
831	1081	1695	860	1224	1755	889		1752
832	1088	1687	861	1276	1764	890		1764
833	1080	1712	862	1295	1770			
834	1085	1700	863	1316	1778			
835	1085	1706	864	1319	1786			
836	1077	1722	865	1299	1787			
837	1076	1732	866	1250	1771			
838	1073	1735	867	1205	1768			
839	1073	1713	868	1176	1771			

Source: S. A. Le Prince Omar Toussoun, "Mémoire sur l'Histoire du Nil," *Mémoires Présentés A L'Institute D'Egypt et Publiés Sous Les Auspices SA Majesté Fouad Ier, Roi Egypt, 10,* (Le Caire: Imprimerie de l'Institute Français d'Archéologie Orientale, 1925): 361–411.

APPENDIX B

TABLE 2–B1

TOTAL TONNAGE OF SOLID WASTE RECEIVED
AT CITY DISPOSAL SITES, CINCINNATI, OHIO

Year	Combustible Waste	Year	Combustible Waste
1931	66,682.4	1954	215,959.9
1932	95,536.9	1955	218,108.8
1933	95,415.1	1956	218,753.1
1934	99,225.5	1957	230,714.8
1935	103,037.8	1958	231,169.5
1936	107,016.6	1959	235,622.2
1937	107,474.9	1960	253,871.8
1938	116,860.8	1961	259,743.7
1939	118,314.4	1962	271,585.0
1940	121,022.5	1963	278,582.6
1941	130,897.7	1964	281,376.0
1942	138,114.5	1965	287,922.1
1943	124,507.4	1966	307,333.8
1944	116,483.4	1967	315,054.2
1945	120,625.1	1968	335,732.5
1946	138,072.4	1969	360,388.0
1947	142,786.9	1970	360,843.1
1948	147,390.6	1971	379,080.0
1949	158,023.6	1972	379,066.0
1950	150,803.5	1973	384,576.0
1951	144,543.8	1974	404,097.7
1952	171,628.4	1975	415,432.5
1953	195,201.9	1976	469,086.8

Source: City of Cincinnati, Department of Public Works, Division of Waste Collection, Letters of November 9, 1973, and February 17, 1977, from R. D. Behrman, Administrative Assistant and A. H. Schuck, Acting Superintendent.

Note: Corresponds to Figure 2–16 in text.

TABLE 2–B2

FIVE-YEAR MOVING AVERAGES OF THE ANNUAL DISSOLVED OXYGEN
FOR THE MAIN BRANCHES OF NEW YORK HARBOR,
HUDSON RIVER AND LOWER EAST RIVER (Percent of saturation)

Year	Hudson River	Lower East River	Year	Hudson River	Lower East River	Year	Hudson River	Lower East River
1912	60%	50	1933	44%	18	1954	44%	24
1913	54	44	1934	42	16	1955	44	24
1914	51	38	1935	43	18	1956	45	27
1915	48	32	1936	43	18	1957	44	27
1916	47	28	1937	43	20	1958	45	28
1917	44	25	1938	44	21	1959	45	29
1918	44	24	1939	46	23	1960	43	28
1919	41	22	1940	47	23	1961	42	26
1920	42	23	1941	47	24	1962	43	27
1921	38	23	1942	46	22	1963	42	26
1922	40	23	1943	46	23	1964	43	37
1923	39	23	1944	46	22	1965	50	33
1924	38	23	1945	46	22	1966	53	37
1925	36	22	1946	47	21	1967	55	39
1926	36	22	1947	48	22	1968	58	42
1927	36	22	1948	47	22	1969	57	43
1928	35	21	1949	48	22	1970	55	40
1929	40	23	1950	47	22	1971	52	37
1930	42	22	1951	46	22	1972	49	33
1931	43	22	1952	46	23	1973	49	32
1932	43	19	1953	44	22			

Source: *New York Harbor Water Quality Survey, 1970,* provided by City of New York, Environmental Protection Administration, Department of Water Resources, Bureau of Water Pollution Control.

Note: Corresponds to Figure 2–8 in text.

TABLE 2-B3

HOURS OF WINTER SUNSHINE (DECEMBER TO FEBRUARY)
AT LONDON WEATHER CENTRE AND KEW OBSERVATORY

Year	Mean Hours Per Day		Year	Mean Hours Per Day		Year	Mean Hours Per Day	
	Kew	London		Kew	London		Kew	London
1939	1.64	1.19	1952	1.73	1.18	1965	1.77	1.55
1940	1.58	1.15	1953	1.71	1.18	1966	1.75	1.57
1941	1.56	1.11	1954	1.75	1.20	1967	1.80	1.64
1942	1.55	1.06	1955	1.78	1.25	1968	1.83	1.69
1943	1.57	1.05	1956	1.77	1.24	1969	1.79	1.69
1944	1.54	1.04	1957	1.78	1.30	1970	1.80	1.70
1945	1.56	1.04	1958	1.78	1.31	1971	1.79	1.73
1946	1.58	1.05	1959	1.74	1.32	1972	1.70	1.64
1947	1.53	1.00	1960	1.76	1.35	1973	1.67	1.62
1948	1.53	1.00	1961	1.78	1.41	1974	1.72	1.69
1949	1.54	0.98	1962	1.76	1.43	1975	1.77	1.72
1950	1.59	1.05	1963	1.80	1.51			
1951	1.62	1.06	1964	1.79	1.53			

Source: Cabinet Office, Central Statistical Office, Great George Street, London SW1P 3AQ, England, letter from R. W. Freeman, February 24, 1977.

Note: Corresponds to Figure 2-11 in text.

TABLE 2-B4

CARBON MONOXIDE CONCENTRATIONS IN NEW YORK CITY,
1958-75 (parts per million)

Year	Carbon Monoxide	Year	Carbon Monoxide	Year	Carbon Monoxide
1958	3	1964	3	1970	3.2
1959	3.4	1965	3	1971	3.4
1960	3.5	1966	3	1972	2.7
1961	3.5	1967	2	1973	4.5
1962	2.5	1968	3	1974	4.1
1963	3.7	1969	3.5	1975	4.0

Source: See Figure 2-13.

Note: Corresponds to Figure 2-13 in text.

TABLE 2-B5

OXYGEN CONTENT OF THE BALTIC SEA AT STATION F(INLAND)
74 (17) (in ml/l)

Date	Depth	Oxygen	% of Saturation	Date	Depth	Oxygen	% of Saturation
May 30, 1903	162	286	33.4	Jul 10, 1932	173	232	27.3
Aug 6, 1903	159	178	20.8	Jul 13, 1933	161	138	16.1
Nov 28, 1903	141	250		Jul 13, 1934	155	207	24.4
May 23, 1904	150	254	29.7	Jul 16, 1935	147.5	192	22.9
Nov 7, 1904	155	198	23.2	Jul 8, 1939	157	150	18.0
Aug 17, 1905	146	324	38.2	Jul 23, 1954	185	82	10
May 24, 1905	150	218		Jul 26, 1955	155	123	14.7
	155	259	30.3	Jul 19, 1958	143	52	6.2
Nov 11, 1905	140	257		Jul 20, 1959	155	13	1.5
May 6, 1906	150	313		Jul 21, 1961	150	85	10.3
	167	311	36.3	Jul 14, 1965	150	33	
Aug 8, 1906	150	255			170	21	2.5
	175	239		May 20, 1966	150	37	
Nov 12, 1906	140	249			165	36	4.3
Aug 15, 1907	143	218		Nov 19, 1966	140	8	0.9
Aug 17, 1908	150	232	27.2	Nov 6, 1967	150	41	
Jul 11, 1909	175	252	29.5	Dec 10, 1967	150	12	
May 28, 1911	155	316	36.7		160	18	
Oct 6, 1911	150	233	27.3	Feb 14, 1968	150	14	
May 20, 1913	172	257	30.2		170	10	
May 20, 1914	167	245	28.8	Apr 18, 1969	150	0	
Jun 8, 1923	146	246	29.1		175	0	
Jul 18, 1928	160	142	16.9	Jul 18, 1969	150	0	
Jul 13, 1929	159	145	17.3		175	0	
Jul 13, 1931	135	180					

Source: See Figure 2-1.

3

The Risks of a Deteriorating Environment*

In Chapter 2 we examined trends in environmental quality; in this chapter we shall investigate some of the implications of those trends. The evidence shows incontrovertibly that the real cost of pollution is high. At the very least, water pollution damages aquatic life and interferes with commercial fishing; air pollution imposes cleaning costs on the community; and both forms of pollution cause aesthetic damage that is extremely difficult to quantify. But more important than these economic and aesthetic costs are the effects of pollution on human health and the danger that pollution may reach critical levels with catastrophic results for large numbers of people.

To illustrate the kinds of health hazards encountered in a polluted environment, the next sections examine two classes of pollutants: (a) the major air pollutants, which have been a prime concern of policy makers in the last decade,

---

*This chapter contains a great deal of technical scientific material about which the authors can claim no expertise. We have had to rely in most instances on reports and studies from various parts of the scientific community. Physicists or chemists may, therefore, have real quibbles with our presentation or interpretation of some of the specifics. However, we have felt it essential to try to present, as best we could, a systematic description of the most serious threats to humanity associated with environmental abuse. In particular, the central thesis of the chapter rests on the broad character of the evidence, rather than on any single matter.

and (b) a variety of chemical pollutants that are often grouped under the heaa-
ing "toxic substances." We cannot attempt in our limited space to describe all
the hazards of every sort of pollutant; scientists have only just begun to investigate some of these hazards, and will no doubt discover as yet unrecognized
links between pollution and health. But a look at the effects of these two
groups of pollutants should make clear the dangers involved.

1. Pollution and Human Health

Tables 3-1 and 3-2 provide information about various pollutants; they
describe their sources, principal characteristics, and what is known about their
health effects. We have not attempted a complete list, but have sought instead
to describe those pollutants mentioned most frequently in newspapers and
magazines and those discussed in this book.

Our central concern is the extent of the hazard associated with each pollutant. As the tables indicate, this varies greatly: some pollutants turn out to be
less hazardous than is generally supposed; or at least the evidence about their
health effects is too incomplete to permit any confident evaluation of their cost
to mankind. Others, however, are demonstrably dangerous: they are definitely
related to increased illness and mortality. At least a few are fatal in concentrations that may be encountered in the environment; either they are directly
poisonous or they induce cancers or other fatal illnesses. In some cases, the
effects are likely to manifest themselves only many years after exposure. The
emission of these pollutants can amount to the planting of a time bomb whose
destructive effects will be felt only in the distant future.

Before examining the effects of the pollutants in more detail, we should
discuss briefly the nature of the evidence. In general, there are few systematic
and comprehensive data relating pollution to human health except for mortality.
In many cases, the available data are spotty and unsystematic. Many are derived
from comparisons of the health of persons living in relatively polluted and un-
polluted environments. These studies often do not control for other differences
such as occupation (farm vs. factory), age, personal habits (smoker vs. non-
smoker), and so on; the results are consequently less trustworthy than we would
like. However, the consistency of many of the findings lends some added confidence to the conclusions.

To evaluate the effects of toxic substances, in particular, researchers frequently rely on experiments using animals whose physiological reactions are
similar to those of humans. The conclusions of these experiments are necessarily
somewhat tentative with regard to their implications for human health. Critics,
particularly groups opposed to strong environmental programs, often dispute the
interpretations of such findings and label them inconclusive (even though such

TABLE 3-1

MAJOR AIR POLLUTANTS

THE PRINCIPAL CHARACTERISTICS, SOURCES, AND HEALTH EFFECTS OF
PARTICULATE MATTER, SULFUR DIOXIDE, HYDROCARBONS, NITROGEN OXIDES,
CARBON MONOXIDE, PHOTOCHEMICAL SMOG, SULFATES, AND LEAD

1. *Particulate Matter*

 a. Main Characteristics: Any solid or liquid particles dispersed in atmosphere, such as dust, pollen, ash, soot, metals, and various chemicals; particles often classified according to size, as settleable particles (larger than 50 microns), aerosols (smaller than 50 microns), and fine particulates (smaller than 3 microns).

 b. Principal Sources: Natural events such as forest fires, wind erosion, volcanic eruptions; stationary combustion, especially of solid fuels (e.g., power plants that burn coal), construction activities, industrial processes, atmospheric chemical reactions.

 c. Principal Health Effects: Directly toxic effects or aggravation of the effects of gaseous pollutants; aggravation of asthma or other respiratory or cardiorespiratory symptoms; increased cough and chest discomfort; increased mortality.

2. *Sulfur Dioxide (SO_2)*

 a. Main Characteristics: Colorless gas with pungent odor; oxidizes to form sulfur trioxide (SO_3) which forms sulfuric acid with water.

 b. Principal Sources: Combustion of sulfur-containing fossil fuels, smelting of sulfur-bearing metal ores, industrial processes, natural events such as volcanic eruptions.

 c. Principal Health Effects: Classed as mild respiratory irritant; most SO_2 inhaled is absorbed in upper respiratory tract and never reaches lungs; penetrates when clings to particulate matter; aggravates respiratory diseases including asthma, chronic bronchitis, emphysema; can result in reduced lung function, irritation of eyes, possible increased mortality.

3. *Hydrocarbons (HC)*

 a. Main Characteristics: Organic compounds in gaseous or particulate form, e.g., methane, ethylene, acetylene; component in formation of photochemical smog.

 b. Principal Sources: Incomplete combustion of fuels and other carbon-containing substances, such as in motor vehicle exhausts; processing and distribution and use of petroleum compounds such as gasoline and organic solvents; natural events such as forest fires and plant metabolism; atmospheric reactions.

 c. Principal Health Effects: Acute exposure causes eye, nose, and thoat irritation; chronic exposure suspected of causing cancer; some groups of combustion hydrocarbons especially implicated in induction of cancer in laboratory animals.

TABLE 3-1 (Continued)

4. *Nitrogen Oxides (NO$_x$)*

   a. Main Characteristics: Brownish-red gas with pungent odor.
   b. Principal Sources: Primarily from internal combustion engine; also high temperature stationary combustion (power plants) and atmospheric reactions; may occur around explosives plants.
   c. Principal Health Effects: Major role as component in creation of photochemical smog; also has distinct effects apart from those associated with smog; has been shown to be toxic to experimental animals; some studies indicate NO$_2$ produces disease in animals that have human counterparts (emphysema, other lung disease); in study of school children in high NO$_2$ area (near TNT plant) found that children contracted significantly more respiratory disease than children in control area; has been shown to aggravate respiratory and cardiovascular illnesses and chronic nephritis.

5. *Carbon Monoxide (CO)*

   a. Main Characteristics: Colorless, odorless gas with strong affinity for hemoglobin in blood; usually aware of presence of CO only after early poisoning symptoms appear (such as nausea, headache, dizziness, difficulty in breathing).
   b. Principal Sources: Incomplete combustion of fuels and other carbonaceous materials, industrial processes, cigarette smoking, forest fires, decomposition of organic matter; natural processes produce ten times as much CO as automobile and industrial processes combined, but problem is high concentrations in urban environments.
   c. Principal Health Effects: Absorbed by lungs; reduces oxygen-carrying capacity of blood; creates reduced tolerance for exercise, impairment of mental function, affects fetal development, aggravates cardiovascular disease; several studies show at prolonged low-level exposure results in diminution of visual perception, manual dexterity, ability to learn and perform intellectual tasks; other studies have produced no such adverse effects at low levels of exposure.

6. *Photochemical Oxidants (Smog)*

   a. Main Characteristics: Oxidizing type of pollutant found in many urban areas; results from chemical combination of reactive hydrocarbon vapors with nitrogen oxides in presence of sunlight; the resulting production of photochemical oxidants consists of a number of toxic compounds: ozone, peroxyacetyl nitrates (PAN), aldehydes, other chemical compounds.
   b. Principal Sources: Hydrocarbons mostly from motor vehicle exhausts and nitrogen oxides from motor vehicle exhausts and stationary combustion sources; photochemical smog a problem not only in southern California (notorious for smog levels) but also in desert cities of southwest and eastern cities which now may be receiving more sunlight because of reduction in smoke layer. Meteorological conditions necessary for formation of oxidants: stationary high accompanied by adequate sunshine with low early morning wind speeds.
   c. Principal Health Effects: Aggravation of respiratory and cardiovascular diseases, irritation to eyes, respiratory tract, impairment of cardiopulmonary function; some concern about possible mutagenic effects of

TABLE 3-1 (Continued)

ozone; in Los Angeles one study showed no association between "alert days" when oxidant levels were high and mortality increase; poorer athletic performance has been related to high oxidant levels; possibility of developing tolerance to oxidant pollution such as has been shown for experimental animals may account for the relatively few changes associated with chronic exposure.

7. *Sulfates*

    a. Main Characteristics: Aerosol formed by sulfur oxides; in moist environment appears as sulfuric acid (H_2SO_4) mist or rain.

    b. Principal Sources: Atmospheric reactions of SO_2; secondary chemical reactions in atmosphere from other sulfur compounds. Recent indications that automobiles with catalytic converters (designed to decrease hydrocarbon and carbon monoxide emissions) may emit more sulfates than autos without converters.

    c. Principal Health Effects: Aggravation of respiratory diseases, including asthma, chronic bronchitis; reduced lung function; irritation of eyes and respiratory tract; increased mortality.

8. *Lead (Pb)*

    a. Main Characteristics: Heavy, soft, malleable gray metallic chemical element; often occurs (as environmental contaminant) as lead oxide aerosol or dust.

    b. Principal Sources: Leading sources of human exposure: ingestion by young children with pica (abnormal craving for nonfoods) who eat leaded paint and dirt, occupational exposure in industries such as smelting and battery-making, airborne lead from nonferrous metal smelters, auto exhausts along highways; agricultural use of leaded arsenates; lead salts in some pottery glazes released when in contact with slightly acidic liquid, or heated; in "moonshine" whiskey because often made in apparatus with lead-welded copper tubing or in old automobile radiators.

    c. Principal Health Effects: Enters primarily through respiratory tract and wall of digestive system; more than 40 percent of lead inhaled is absorbed into bloodstream; accumulates in body organs; symptoms of lead poisoning not very specific; early signs are impairment of mental function, behavior problems, and anemia; higher levels cause vomiting, cramps, serious impairment of kidneys, nervous system, possible brain damage; study on rats and mice fed lead for life in concentrations comparable to levels in U.S. tissues showed early mortality, shortened lifespan, increased susceptibility to infection, visible aging and loss of weight, hardening of the arteries and heart attacks (see Schroeder); another study concluded: "Studies on the fetal mouse show that lead levels at about the currently accepted safe blood levels cause developmental deficiencies in certain individuals. . . . Extrapolation of these effects in the mouse to lower doses and other populations suggests that individuals are being destructively altered at currently acceptable environmental-lead-induced body lead burdens. It seems clear that this destructive process could be halted by the immediate elimination of lead from gasoline and continued public health measures to identify and remove lead-containing materials from the environment . . ." (see Berry, Osgood, and St. John, p. 529).

TABLE 3-1 (Continued)

Sources: George L. Waldbott, *Health Effects of Environmental Pollutants* (St. Louis: C. V. Mosby Company, 1973); World Health Organization, *Health Hazards of the Human Environment* (Geneva: World Health Organization, 1972); M. A. Q. Khan and John P. Bederka, Jr., eds., *Survival in Toxic Environments* (New York: Academic Press, Inc., 1974); *Environmental Quality, The Sixth Annual Report of the Council on Environmental Quality* (Washington, D.C.: U.S. Government Printing Office, 1975); James W. Berry, David W. Osgood, and Philip A. St. John, *Chemical Villains, A Biology of Pollution* (St. Louis: C.V. Mosby Company, 1974); Henry A. Schroeder, M.D., *The Poisons Around Us, Toxic Metals in Food, Air, and Water* (Bloomington, Ind.: Indiana University Press, 1974); *Photochemical Oxidant Air Pollution*, Report of the Air Management Sector Group (Paris: Organization for Economic Cooperation and Development, 1975); *Air Quality and Automobile Emission Control*, Vol. 4 (Washington, D.C.: U.S. Government Printing Office 1974); and *Environmental Quality, The Seventh Annual Report of the Council on Environmental Quality* (Washington, D.C.: U.S. Government Printing Office, September 1976).

TABLE 3-2

SELECTED TOXIC SUBSTANCES IN THE ENVIRONMENT

1. *Arsenic (As)*

    a. Main Characteristics: Volatile, highly toxic chemical element; cumulative protoplasmic poison; properties of both metal and nonmetal; occurs naturally in coal and oil; usually found as the sulfide, compounded with oxygen as arsenides, arsenates, and arsenites.

    b. Principal Sources: Main use in past was in pesticides and herbicides; now has very limited agricultural use (with advent of organic chemical pesticides); some nonagricultural uses (weed-killing along roadways, tennis courts); used in paint, glass, ceramics industries; in wood preservatives; large quantities produced from smelting of lead, copper, zinc, gold ores; cotton gins; burning of coal.

    c. Principal Health Effects: Severity of toxic reaction depends on concentration and type of compound; most compounds extremely toxic although the element itself relatively nontoxic; acute poisoning results in gastrointestinal inflammation, nausea, vomiting, diarrhea, feeble, irregular heartbeat, coma, sometimes death; carcinogenic in acute occupational exposure (nasal cancer); some studies have shown teratogenic effects in experimental animals; chronic exposure leads to muscle weakness, loss of appetite, vomiting, gastrointestinal pains, constipation, inflammation of nasal and oral mucous membranes; coughing, skin lesions, graying of skin; exposure is associated with bronchitis, other respiratory disease, dermatitis, skin cancer. Epidemiological studies of occupationally exposed persons have reported liver, skin, lung, and lymphatic cancers and adverse effects on thyroid gland.

2. *Asbestos*

    a. Main Characteristics: Class of natural fibrous silicates; two important forms—chrysotile (most important as environmental contaminant) and amphiboles (amosite and crocidolite); very widely used in environment.

    b. Principal Sources: Exposure from numerous sources including road building, construction, mining of asbestos, thermal insulation, as-

TABLE 3-2 (Continued)

bestos plants, transportation of asbestos, cement, floor tiles, attrition
of brake linings, fireproofing, demolition of old buildings where
asbestos was used as spray insulation, asbestos pipes, asbestos filters,
effluent from mining operations, plants; occupationally exposed
workers are themselves a source of contamination; found in a number
of drinking water supplies.

  c. Principal Health Effects: Occupational exposure to airborne asbestos
fibers has caused asbestosis (characterized by fibrosis of lungs and
shortness of breath), lung cancer, pleural and peritoneal mesothelioma;
studies have shown connection between asbestos and gastrointestinal
cancer in workers; water-borne asbestos effects not as clear or fully
documented; some studies suggest that mesothelioma may be hazard
for general public because it can be caused by a very small number
of fibers; most effects from occupational exposure but neighborhood
cases indicate risk to general population.

3. *Barium (Ba)*

  a. Main Characteristics: Soft, silvery metallic element; occurs in lead and
zinc ore deposits.

  b. Principal Sources: Used in industrial processes; as alloy with lead,
calcium; added to diesel fuel to suppress black smoke emissions; non-
poisonous insoluble barium sulfate used in gastrointestinal x-raying.

  c. Principal Health Effects: Prolonged occupational inhalation of
barium dusts can lead to benign dust disease, baritosis; some acid
soluble barium salts very toxic; poisoning symptoms include hypertension of muscles, violent peristalsis, arterial hypertension, convulsions, cardiac disturbances, kidney damage.

4. *Beryllium (Be)*

  a. Main Characteristics: One of most toxic nonradioactive elements
known; light stiff metal with high melting point; increasing use in
modern technology.

  b. Principal Sources: Commonly used as component in alloys, particularly
copper; major use in past was in fluorescent lighting industry; discon-
tinued in 1949 but brought to public attention occupational disease
of beryllium workers, berylliosis; beryllium contamination of the
environment largely confined to industrial plants that refine it or that
use it in alloying or machining.

  c. Principal Health Effects: Gains access to body primarily through
lungs; acute poisoning from short-term exposure to high dose characterized by inflammation of entire respiratory system, bronchitis,
chemical pneumonitis, edema of lungs, coughing, shortness of breath,
weakness, weight loss, anemia; chronic form of poisoning more insidious (may take up to thirty years to develop); early symptoms are
similar to acute form; disease progresses to degeneration of most body
functions and death; individuals living as far as three quarters of a
mile from beryllium factory have contracted beryllium poisoning.

5. *Cadmium (Cd)*

  a. Main Characteristics: Soft, silver-white heavy metallic element, related
to zinc and mercury; no cadmium ore as such; cadmium occurs as

TABLE 3-2 (Continued)

sulfide or carbonate in zinc, copper, lead ores; one of most harmful of metal toxins with very widespread effects.

b. Principal Sources: Half of all cadmium consumed in U.S. used by electroplating industry; used in nickel-cadmium battery industry in manufacture of negative terminal plates; as a stabilizer in plastics, pigment in plastics, paint; manufacture of metal alloys, photographic supplies, glass, rubber curing; contaminant from mining and smelting of lead, copper, zinc; constantly present wherever zinc is present (e.g., galvanized pipes); released as fine mist or dust during burning of cadmium-containing products. Food contamination an important source of exposure (especially fish).

c. Principal Health Effects: Most common route into body through inhalation from industrial processes; some through ingestion; appears to be inverse relationship between cadmium absorption and zinc intake (a required body mineral); with low zinc intake (deficiency) body tends to absorb higher quantities of cadmium; symptoms of cadmium poisoning—occupational exposure produces general tiredness, nervousness, dryness of mouth, impaired sense of smell, shortness of breath, sore throat, chest cramps, pain in small of back, poor appetite; most characteristic symptoms of long-term cadmium exposure, pulmonary emphysema, cirrhosis of liver, cloudy urine; cadmium accumulates in body organs; suspected nervous system impairment, adverse cardiovascular effects; suspected correlation between cadmium and hypertension (high blood pressure); one study compared atmospheric cadmium content in several cities with death rates due to hypertension; suggested causal relationship between cadmium and hypertension (see Schroeder); later studies showed no such correlation but presence of zinc (also related to hypertension disorders) may have been complicating factor; some experimental evidence of carcinogenicity in laboratory animals; implicated in human prostate cancer; exposure to large doses of cadmium characterized by degeneration of bones; one study concluded "Cadmium has probably more lethal possibilities than any of the other metals." (Berry, Osgood, and St. John, p. 86.)

6. *Chlorine (Cl)*

a. Main Characteristics: Dense greenish-yellow gas with irritating odor; strong oxidizing agent.

b. Principal Sources: Preparation, processing, liquefaction of chlorine; chemical, pulp, paper processes.

c. Principal Health Effects: Pulmonary edema, pneumonitis, bronchitis.

7. *Chromium (Cr)*

a. Main Characteristics: Hard metallic element highly resistant to corrosion; occurs in environment (as a contaminant) as aerosol or dust.

b. Principal Sources: Used in electroplating industry; in manufacture of stainless steel, in tanning and photographic industries; combustion of coal and refuse.

c. Principal Health Effects: Carcinogenic (has caused cancer of the respiratory system in chromate-producing industry workers and experimental animals); direct contact produces dermatitis, skin ulcers.

TABLE 3-2 (Continued)

8. *Fluoride*

   a. Main Characteristics: Hydrogen fluoride is a highly reactive gas; compound of fluorine (corrosive, poisonous gaseous chemical element) and one or more elements.

   b. Principal Sources: Production of phosphate fertilizer, aluminum metal, brick, tile, steel, glass; combustion of coal; ocean dumping of waste fluoride can cause air pollution when vaporization occurs; small amounts of fluoride used in some municipal water supplies to promote dental health; found naturally in some water.

   c. Principal Health Effects: Accumulates in young organism more readily than in adult; has been reported that in areas with fluoride pollution from industry, increased erythrocite (red blood cell) level, fluoride in teeth, urine, nails, hair of children; small doses apparently beneficial to dental health; high dose toxic over long period of time; can cause depression of collagen formation (fibrous protein in connective tissue, bone, and cartilage), bone resorption, and increase in bone crystal; one study found that occupationally exposed mothers bore infants with duodenal deformities; studies have linked high fluoride content in drinking water to increase in mongoloid births.

9. *Mercury (Hg)*

   a. Main Characteristics: Heavy, silver-white metallic chemical element; toxic properties have long been known; pure metallic form nontoxic, certain mercury compounds, especially methyl mercury, extremely lethal.

   b. Principal Sources: Occurs naturally from erosion and weathering; pollution results from mining, refining of mercury, combustion of fuels and refuse, widespread use of mercury pesticides; used to treat seed as fungicide, mildewcide in paints and textiles, in paper and pulp industry to prevent slime formation, improve storage properties; in chlorine-alkali industry as electrode; used in lamps, batteries, switches; water pollution can occur from waste water of industries that use mercury compounds and from agricultural runoff where mercuric pesticides used; greatest risk to general population: consumption of contaminated fish.

   c. Principal Health Effects: Mercury inhalation poisoning occupational hazard in some industries (felt hat industry, e.g.); toxic effects of acute methyl mercury poisoning well documented; symptoms mostly neurological—lack of muscular coordination, tremors, constriction of visual field, difficulty in swallowing; can progress to deafness, blindness, paralysis, kidney failure, death. Whether the large amount of inorganic mercury that remains in sediments in inland and coastal waters downstream from industrial polluters (even though industries have generally halted or drastically reduced the amount of mercury discharged) is being changed by natural processes into the lethal methylated form to any significant extent is a subject of controversy. "There has been a great deal of confusion both in the scientific literature and in the popular press concerning the extent of mercury contamination of natural origin in freshwater and saltwater fish. The formation of methyl mercury from inorganic mercury is a reaction catalyzed by microorganisms, and therefore, by definition, the formation and accumulation of methyl mercury in fish is a natural

TABLE 3-2 (Continued)

process. Microorganisms undoubtedly had the capacity to synthesize methyl mercury long before the evolution of fish . . . certain species of fish naturally contain significant concentrations of methyl mercury in their flesh. . . . Furthermore, some inland lakes that have a naturally high organic content in sediments and a naturally high inorganic mercury content in the lake bed provide conditions for the synthesis of methyl mercury and its accumulation in the fish. Clearly, however, natural methyl mercury contamination of fish is a localized problem; industrial pollution in advanced societies has vastly magnified the problem, making it more widespread. It must be emphasized that the contribution to the mercury problem by industry is to relocate inorganic mercury into areas where rapid synthesis of methyl mercury is assured." (Wood, p. 36)

10. *Nickel (Ni)*

    a. Main Characteristics: Hard, gray-white metallic chemical element; ferromagnetic and highly resistant to oxidation; occurs most commonly in oil and coal deposits and with iron and copper ores.
    b. Principal Sources: Used in manufacture of stainless steel, other heat-resistant steel; production of nickel alloys, alloy steel manufacture, anodes in electroplating industry; nickel-aluminum compounds used as catalysts in hydrogenation, dehydrogenation of organic compounds, bleaching, drying of oils, water purification, catalytic combustion of organic compounds in exhaust of combustion engines; several nickel compounds used as fuel additives; found in asbestos, coal, crude oil; principal source of atmospheric nickel burning of coal and petroleum products (also municipal incineration); food contamination during processing, especially baking powder, cider, breakfast cereals.
    c. Principal Health Effects: Metal relatively harmless; direct contact may cause some dermatitis; atmospheric nickel compounds enter respiratory tract and absorbed through skin; nickel salts, especially gaseous nickel carbonyl, very toxic; nickel carbonyl found to produce cancer of lungs and nose in humans and experimental animals; acute exposure to nickel carbonyl produces chest pain, dizziness, vomiting; chronic occupational exposure—diseases may take up to twenty years to develop.

11. *Pesticides* (the man-made chemical compounds)

    a. Main Characteristics: Vary with specific pesticide (see below). In general, very widely used; in 1973 over 45,000 registered pesticides.
    b. Principal Sources: Become pollutants when transferred outside area of deliberate use for agricultural or public health reasons, during accidental release, uncontrolled disposal from manufacturing plants, agricultural users; general population exposed through various large and small agricultural operations, forestry work, urban sanitation, food storage, home, garden, lawn use.
    c. Principal Health Effects: Vary with specific pesticide (see below).

    Chlorinated Hydrocarbons

    a. Main Characteristics: Include DDT (DDE, DDD), benzene hexachloride, heptachlor, lindane, dieldrin, aldrin, isodrin, endrin, chlor-

TABLE 3-2 (Continued)

dane, toxophene; DDT most widely used of chlorinated hydrocarbons; first gave spectacular results in crop increases and eradication of disease associated with insects (malaria); chlorinated hydrocarbons, because of wide use (although now being replaced by other pesticides) and persistence in environment (do not break down into nontoxic substances) are very prevalent in environment; half-life of toxic residues up to twenty years; characterized by very high vapor pressure (easily evaporate from soil and enter air). Nearly all uses of DDT, aldrin, dieldrin, heptachlor, and chlordane have been banned in U.S.

b. Principal Effects: DDT most widely studied of the pesticides; early symptoms of poisoning: headache, dizziness, loss of appetite (i.e., ill-defined illness similar to other chronic poisoning); some evidence that persons with disturbed liver function adversely affected by exposure to DDT; major documented effects of DDT: stimulation of nervous system characterized by hyperactivity, muscle tremors; stimulation of enzyme synthesis (can decrease level of certain hormones such as estrogen); carcinogenicity (DDT has increased rate of tumor formation in mice, rats, trout; aldrin, dieldrin, heptachlor carcinogenic in mice); genetic changes in experimental animals; cases of human poisoning by chlorinated hydrocarbons rarely documented— diagnosis of damage from long-term exposure usually made in retrospect; some deaths attributed to acute exposure (e.g, after large municipal spraying programs, heavy and repeated household use); other important effects: reproductive failure in fish, fish kills, decimation of aquatic food population, curtailment of bird breeding (interference with eggshell formation which causes eggshell breakage); birds of prey apparently especially vulnerable; decreases in their populations speculated to be result of use of DDT and other chlorinated hydrocarbons. Berry, Osgood, and St. John conclude "The fact that several of the chlorinated hydrocarbons are nerve poisons, upset normal functioning of enzyme systems, exhibit hormonelike activity, inhibit photosynthesis by plants, and are carcinogenic in test animals makes the extreme health hazard potential of this class of pesticides obvious" (p. 149).

Organophosphates

a. Main Characteristics: Second generation phosphorus-containing synthetic pesticides; in United States have largely replaced chlorinated hydrocarbons; include atrazine, simazine, parathion, malathion, azodrin, diazinon, TEPP, phosdrin, methyl parathion, disulfoton, Guthion, ronnel, systox; often more toxic (particularly parathion, TEPP) but not as persistent as chlorinated hydrocarbons; thought to produce no long term effects in the environment; very poisonous to harmful and beneficial insects alike; serve (like DDT) to reduce diversification of species.

b. Principal Effects: Heavy occupational exposure can cause nausea, headache, vomiting, abdominal cramps; several deaths reported each year from such acute occupational exposure; produces convulsions and muscle twitching in experimental animals; some very toxic to insects but nontoxic to humans (malathion); parathion most important organophosphate in terms of toxicity to man; has caused serious illness and death as result of spillage during transport or storage; chronic exposure can cause illness in agricultural workers often misdiagnosed as food poisoning, heat stroke, or gastroenteritis; exposure

TABLE 3-2 (Continued)

to DDVP (used in pest strips) thought to lower cholinesterase level (enzyme important to functioning of nervous system), adversely affect liver; some indications experimentally that exposure may lead to birth defects and cancer.

Carbamates

a. Main Characteristics: More recent development; include insecticides, Baygon, carbaryl; fungicides, nabam, zineb, ferbam; slug and snail-killer, zectran; nonpersistent in environment; major effects limited to area of application; considered less toxic than chlorinated hydro-carbons or organophosphates.

Herbicides (defoliants)

a. Main Characteristics: Used to destroy noxious weeds and shrubs along highways, median strips between lanes of highways, along railroads, for lawn and garden use; include chlorophenoxy acids, 2,4-D and 2,4,5-T; urea derivatives, fenuron and diuron; triazines; acylanilides.
b. Principal Effects: 2,4-D and 2,4,5-T generally of low toxicity to animals; exposure may cause some irritation and discomfort; indirect effects more important—destroy food supply for some animals; also destroying water-fouling weeds leads to rapid decomposition; uses up oxygen in water and makes less habitable for fish, other animals; in experimental animals have produced teratogenic and carcinogenic effects.

Fungicides

a. Main Characteristics: Two widely used fungicides are captan and folpet (phthalimides). Have been shown to be carcinogenic, terato-genic, and mutagenic to experimental animals; some concern about use because of chemical similarity to thalidomide (a known teratogen); studies on these effects are inconclusive.

12. *Nitrosamines*

a. Main Characteristics: Any of a series of organic compounds derived from amines (derivative of ammonia) and containing the divalent $= N \cdot NO$ radical. Occur throughout environment in foods, drugs, tobacco, drinking water, air.
b. Principal Sources: Direct discharges from manufacturing processes; also formed during the reaction of natural amines such as amino acids in food with nitrogen compounds emitted from automobiles, power plants, and used in commercial fertilizers. Also can be formed in human stomach from the nitrate and nitrite salts commonly used in meat and poultry products to inhibit botulism and enhance color.
c. Principal Health Effects: Laboratory tests have shown the substance to be carcinogenic and mutagenic.

13. *Polychlorinated Biphenyls* (PCBs)

a. Main Characteristics: Widely used nonflammable dielectric (does not conduct electric current but can contain an electric field) chlorinated

TABLE 3-2 (Continued)

hydrocarbon industrial compound (chemical cousin of DDT); very prevalent in environment.

b. Principal Sources: Used in electrical equipment, transformers, capacitators, fluorescent lamp ballasts, heat exchangers, hydraulic and heat transfer fluids, coating for electric wires, lumber, metal, concrete; added to numerous products such as paint, printing ink, carbonless reproducing paper; used in adhesives, sealants, solvents; added to varnish, floor tile; used in investment casting processes; enter water through effluent from plants that use it, through the leaching of lubricants in dumps and landfills; most released as water pollution in highly industrialized areas; do not readily break down in environment; most important source of potential harm to general public through food chain; high concentrations of PCBs have been found in fish and other wild animals; accidental industrial release into waterways and accidental release into food ingredients and animal feed during manufacturing process also potential hazard.

c. Principal Health Effects: Correlated to lethal effects in game birds; reduced reproductive capacity in fish-eating mammals, mink and seals; reduced resistance to viral infections in experimental animals; one study indicates that PCBs may be carcinogenic; accidental ingestion of high concentrations of PCBs has caused a disorder called "Yusho Disease" characterized by severe skin disorders, eye discharge, loss of hair, numbness in extremities, headaches, abdominal pain, vomiting, deformed nails, joints, and bones, poorly developed teeth; the after-effects of the disease can include permanent disturbances of central nervous system, especially in young children who display symptoms at birth, changes in heart and blood vessels, deformities in fingers, toes, wrists, ankles, vertebrae accompanied by pain. Laboratory studies on primates have produced hair loss, skin lesions, liver changes, reproductive losses. Carcinogenic in rodents. Occupationally exposed persons have experienced nausea, dizziness, eye irritation, nasal irritation, asthmatic bronchitis, dermatitis, fungus, acne.

14. *Vinyl Chloride (VC)*

a. Main Characteristics: Plasticizers used in the production of polyvinyl chloride, the most commonly used clear plastic; imparts flexibility, workability; not chemically bonded to matrix of PVC so can easily escape into air and water where becomes pollutant.

b. Principal Sources: Routes of entry into environment are air, water, and solid waste (air most important); occupational exposure in plants that manufacture or use VC (two major sources of VC emissions: polyvinyl chloride plants and ethylene dichloride-vinyl chloride plants); potential sources of exposure to general population due to use (as opposed to manufacture of) VC are aerosol containers, plastics used to wrap or package food, drinking water; used widely in industry, home, and medical science; in wall coverings, upholstery (account for "new car" smell), appliances, pesticide sprays, industrial oils, cosmetics, perfumes.

c. Principal Health Effects: In experimental animals at relatively low doses affect calcium metabolism, increase incidence of abortion, produce fetal abnormalities; VC has been shown to cause or contribute to the development of angiosarcoma (liver cancer), other

TABLE 3-2 (Continued)

cancers, and noncancerous disorders in persons with occupational exposure and in experimental animals exposed to VC; studies have also
suggested that increased rates of birth defects occur in communities
where PVC manufacturing plants are located.

15. *Sulfides and mercaptans*

    a. Main Characteristics: Gaseous sulfur compounds with unpleasant odor.
    b. Principal Sources: Processing of petroleum, coking of coal, paper pulp-
ing processes, inadequately treated sewage, solid waste.
    c. Principal Health Effects: Discomfort, nausea, headache, loss of ap-
petite, allergic reactions.

16. *Radioactive substances (Cobalt-60, Strontium-90, etc.)*

    a. Main Characteristics: Gaseous, liquid, or solid substances that give off
ionizing radiation.
    b. Principal Sources: Natural sources (rocks, soils, cosmic rays); nuclear
weapons testing; nuclear power generation; uranium mining, refining,
machining processes.
    c. Principal Health Effects: Leukemia, bone cancer, genetic damage.

17. *Polybrominated Biphenyls (PBBs)*

    a. Main Characteristics: Highly toxic flame retardant; persistent and
bioaccumulative.
    b. Principal Sources: Have been used commercially as flame retardant
additives in synthetic fibers and molded thermoplastic products (in-
corporated into the plastic housings of many commercial products,
e.g., typewriters, calculators, microfilm readers, radio and TV parts,
thermostats, shavers, hand tools); released into environment during
manufacturing processes; has contaminated cattle feed; subsequent
ingestion of cattle and milk products caused poisoning.
    c. Principal Health Effects: No long-term toxicity data available; short-
term laboratory studies show interference with reproductive and liver
functions, promote nervous disorders, teratogenic; experimental data
show PBBs more toxic than PCBs.

18. *Kepone*

    a. Main characteristics: Persistent, extremely poisonous chlorinated
organic compound, similar to another toxic compound, Mirex; both
used as pesticides, fire retardants, and plasticizers. Long life in
environment. Bioaccumulative.
    b. Principal Sources: Released during manufacture (careless discharge
of waste water and dispersion into atmosphere around plants). Seafood contamination also threat to humans—potential danger of spread
of Kepone in seafood far from original polluted area through tidal
movements and current movements and dispersal by migratory fish.
    c. Principal Health Effects: Has produced serious illness among workers
in Kepone-manufacturing plants and may through aerial dispersion and
dissemination in food cause long-term health effects and cancer in the
general population; occupational exposure has produced trembling,

TABLE 3-2 (Continued)

neurological disorders, skin changes, hyperexcitability, hyperactivity, muscle spasms, testular atrophy, low sperm count, estrogenic effects, sterility, breast enlargement, liver lesions, and cancer. In rats, exposure has produced adverse reproductive effects. Complete toxicity information for humans incomplete since first recorded human exposure very recent.

Sources: James W. Berry, David W. Osgood, and Philip A. St. John, *Chemical Villains, A Biology of Pollution* (St. Louis: C. V. Mosby Company, 1974); George L. Waldbott, M.D., *Health Effects of Environmental Pollutants* (St. Louis: C. V. Mosby Company, 1973); World Health Organization, *Health Hazards of the Human Environment* (Geneva: World Health Organization, 1972); M. A. Q. Khan and John P. Bederka, Jr., eds., *Survival in Toxic Environments* (New York: Academic Press, Inc., 1974); Henry A. Schroeder, M.D., *The Poisons around Us: Toxic Metals in Food, Air, and Water* (Bloomington, Ind.: Indiana University Press, 1974); *Environmental Quality, The Sixth Annual Report of the Council on Environmental Quality* (Washington, D.C.: U.S. Government Printing Office, 1975); T. H. Maugh, "Polychlorinated Biphenyls: Still Prevalent but Less of a Problem" *Science* 173 (1972): 338; M. G. Mustafa, P. A. Peterson, R. J. Munn, C. E. Cross, "Effects of Cadmium Ion on Metabolism of Lung Cells" in *Proceedings of the Second International Clean Air Congress,* ed. H. M. Englund and W. T. Beery (New York: Academic Press, Inc., 1971); P. Kotin and H. L. Falk, "The Role and Action of Environmental Agents in the Pathogenesis of Lung Cancer; Part I, Air Pollutants" *Cancer* 12 (1959): 147; Environmental Protection Agency [FRL 454-1] [40 CFR Part 61] *National Emission Standards for Hazardous Air Pollutants,* Proposed Standard for Vinyl Chloride; *Summary Characterization of Selected Chemicals of Near-Term Interest,* Office of Toxic Substances (U.S. Environmental Protection Agency, Washington, D.C., April 1976); *Environmental Quality, The Seventh Annual Report of the Council on Environmental Quality* (Washington, D.C.: U.S. Government Printing Office, 1976); John M. Wood, "A Progress Report on Mercury," *Environment* 14, No. 1 (January–February, 1972), pp. 33–39.

evidence has often formed the basis for major medical innovations). Other studies involve observation of individuals occupationally exposed to heavy concentrations of toxic substances. Even when the results of such studies are quite conclusive, however, their implications for the general population are far from clear, since usually only a tiny proportion of the population will ever be subject to such heavy exposure. It is conceivable that a substance will have highly toxic effects in sizeable doses, but will be relatively harmless if its concentration falls below some unknown threshold. As we shall see in later chapters, the existence of such thresholds is frequently assumed in the formulation of regulatory standards, though there often seems to be little evidence of their existence in fact.

In drawing together the various studies of the health effects of pollution, we must single out one source which constitutes the single most systematic, exhaustive, and sophisticated review of air pollution and health. Lester Lave and Eugene Seskin of Carnegie-Mellon University have examined with great care virtually every available piece of evidence on the effects of air pollutants in their recently published volume, *Air Pollution and Human Health.* Having reviewed, evaluated, and compared all the available studies, they have analyzed the statistics used in these studies as well as data obtained elsewhere. Consequently, we attach much weight to their findings. As we shall see, they conclude that the dangers attributed to a number of pollutants have been exaggerated. But they find that some pollutants do constitute a most serious threat to human health.

In summarizing the evidence of the relationship between pollution and health, we find it convenient to deal with three major categories of emissions: air pollutants from stationary sources, automotive emissions, and toxic substances (whether emitted into air and/or water).

A. Air Pollutants from Stationary Sources. Stationary sources generate three major air pollutants: particulates, nitrogen oxides, and sulfur dioxide. These sources, which include power-generating stations, industrial plants, construction projects, and solid-waste disposal units, are the origin of most of the sulfur dioxide, a large portion of the particulates, and nearly half of the nitrogen oxide pollution in the atmosphere.[1]

Sulfur dioxide has long been the target of environmental legislation, but recent studies indicate that the real danger to human health (as well as to building stone) is posed by the sulfates, which are the product of atmospheric chemical reactions of various sulfur compounds, including sulfur dioxide. As mentioned in the previous chapter, sulfur dioxide levels have declined in recent years, particularly in the cities. Unfortunately, for reasons that are not well understood, sulfate levels have not declined correspondingly.[2] Indeed, they have remained remarkably stable (see Figures 3-1 and 3-2). This is extremely disturbing, since the evidence suggests that sulfates are the most damaging of the

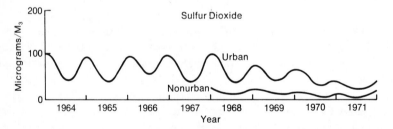

Figure 3-1   U.S. Sulfur Dioxide Level, 1957-71, National Air Sampling Network (NASN).

Source: *Environmental Quality, The Sixth Annual Report of the Council on Environmental Quality* (Washington, D.C.: U.S. Government Printing Office), p. 333.

---

[1]*Environmental Quality, The Sixth Annual Report of the Council on Environmental Quality* (Washington, D.C.: U.S. Government Printing Office, 1975), p. 307.
[2]The Council on Environmental Quality in its Seventh Annual Report writes, "Atmospheric sulfates, especially sulfuric acid aerosol, are derived from SO_2 emissions, being formed through several chemical reactions in the atmosphere. . . . It is possible to have high sulfate levels and low SO_2 . . . because sulfates may be windborne from considerable distances. Sulfur dioxide emissions from rural sources, such as ore smelters or powerplants, may be converted to sulfate and transported to areas where SO_2 emissions and atmospheric levels are low" (*Environmental Quality, The Seventh Annual Report of the Council on Environmental Quality* [Washington, D.C.: U.S. Government Printing Office 1976], p. 217).

common air pollutants. Numerous studies have revealed a wide range of adverse effects on human health: increased daily mortality, aggravation of heart and lung disease in the elderly, accentuation of asthma, increased incidence of acute respiratory disease in children, and increased incidence of chronic bronchitis. Suspended particulate matter, especially particles made up of toxic chemicals and the tiny respirable particles which can penetrate the lungs, is also a major hazard to health. Lave and Seskin conclude that "the measures of air pollution (sulfates and suspended particulates) were significant factors in explaining variations in the total death rate across areas of the United States. . . . For total cancers and for cancer of the digestive system in particular, there was a close association with air pollution (particularly sulfates) in 1960, although the 1961 replication did not indicate the same level of importance. Deaths from cardiovascular diseases and their subcategories also showed a close association with sulfate pollution in 1960; in this case, the 1961 results tended to strengthen the relationship."[3]

On the other hand, nitrogen oxide, the third of the principal air pollutants from stationary sources, seems to be a less universal threat than sulfur emissions and particulates. There appears to be little conclusive evidence of damage to adults from this source. Some evidence indicates a relationship between nitrogen oxide concentrations and infant mortality; one study of school-age children living near an explosives plant, where concentrations are usually high, determined that these children contracted repiratory diseases more frequently than those in a control group. These studies suggest some reason to treat nitrogen oxide emissions with care, but the evidence is by no means so compelling as for sulfur compounds and particulates.[4]

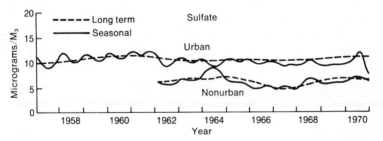

Figure 3-2   U.S. Sulfate Level, 1957–71, National Air Sampling Network (NASN).

---

[3] Lester B. Lave and Eugene P. Seskin, *Air Pollution and Human Health* (Baltimore: Published for Resources for the Future by The Johns Hopkins University Press, 1977), Chap. 11, pp. 238–39.
[4] For a careful review of the literature on the health effects of nitrogen oxide, see *Air Quality and Automobile Emission Control,* A Report by the Coordinating Committee on Air Quality Studies, National Academy of Sciences & National Academy of Engineering Prepared for the Committee on Public Works, U.S. Senate, Pursuant to S. Res. 135, Vol. 4, "The Costs and Benefits of Automobile Emission Control," Sept. 1974, Serial No. 93-24, U.S. Government Printing Office, Washington, D.C., 1974.

B. Pollution from Automobiles and Other Mobile Sources. Automobiles, trucks, aircraft, and other vehicles run by internal-combustion engines are responsible for most of the man-made carbon monoxide in the atmosphere, about half of the hydrocarbons, half of the nitrogen oxides, and, in areas where there are no industries that produce or use lead, about 90 percent of airborne lead pollution. The mobile sources also bear primary responsibility for photochemical oxidation (smog).

The effects of carbon monoxide have been studied widely. At high levels of concentration, this pollutant is quite hazardous: it produces, among other effects, impairment of mental function, reduced coordination, increased reaction time, and strain on the heart. However, at the lower levels of concentration found even in areas with heavy automobile traffic, the evidence is spotty and conflicting; some studies report effects similar to those just mentioned, while other studies have not detected them. It has proved difficult, for example, to separate the health effects of cigarette smoking from those of carbon monoxide at low concentration levels.

Hydrocarbons have been studied to a much lesser extent. Some studies have found them to be carcinogenic (cancer-inducing) in experimental animals. Others report that acute exposure causes eye, nose, and throat irritation. However, the evidence on hydrocarbon effects seems inconclusive.

In the presence of sunlight, hydrocarbons together with nitrogen oxides are transformed into smog. Besides being extremely unpleasant and ugly, smog can accentuate pulmonary disease and impair physical performance (e.g., athletic performance). However, these effects appear to be reversible; normal functioning apparently is restored after some period in a cleaner atmosphere.

The case of lead is rather different. As we mentioned in Chapter 2, there is no question that atmospheric lead pollution is a most serious, and potentially lethal, threat. Exposure can cause anemia, severe intestinal cramps, impairment of the nervous system and kidneys, and brain damage. The only issue under dispute is whether current ambient lead concentrations are sufficient to cause significant health problems. The evidence on this is conflicting; independent research studies have generally found that current concentrations are dangerously high, while studies financed by the lead industry usually report no observable ill effects. The complete elimination of lead from gasoline, for example, continues to be the subject of controversy and resistance by the petroleum industry.

The evidence concerning adverse health effects from airborne pollutants emitted by mobile sources (other than lead) appears less conclusive and persuasive than that for stationary sources. Lave and Seskin write, "we have based our justification of [stationary-source air pollution] abatement programs on the benefits to human health alone. Our most conservative estimate of the effect of a 58 percent reduction in particulates and an 88 percent reduction in sulfur oxides (reductions corresponding to proposed control levels) would lead to a 7.0 percent decrease in total mortality (and presumably at least an equal decrease in total morbidity). This would amount to a national annual benefit of $16.1 billion in 1979 (1973 dollars). We have confidence that substantial abatement of air pollution from the major stationary-source categories of solid waste disposal, stationary fuel combustion, and industrial processes is warranted."[5] However, they "find that the association between emissions from mobile sources and mortality is less strong than the association between air pollution from stationary sources and mortality. This conclusion holds even for areas such as Los Angeles, where high levels of automobile-related air pollution have existed for two decades."[6]

C. Toxic Substances. The great variety and exotic character of many of the toxic chemical substances discharged by industrial and other processes make it impossible to provide any overall characterization of their health effects. Some of these materials are the products of recent technology, and the study of their health effects is still very incomplete. Moreover, the long delay by the U.S. Congress in enacting regulation to control the use of toxic substances has impeded systematic study of their health effects by government agencies.[7]

Table 3-2 listed a variety of toxic substances that are released into the environment in many different ways.[8] The substances range from such natural elements as arsenic, cadmium, and mercury to man-made industrial chemicals, such as polychlorinated biphenyls and vinyl chlorides, which have no natural counterparts. Some of these substances (such as cadmium and vinyl chlorides) are very toxic in high concentrations; workers exposed occupationally or persons accidentally exposed to high doses suffer very serious effects (for example, occupational exposure to vinyl chloride has been linked to the incidence of a rare liver cancer). However, their effects at lower concentrations are less well understood. Other substances (asbestos is one) are harmful even at very low levels of exposure. In a few instances where toxic effects have been demonstrated, substances such as the chlorinated hydrocarbon pesticides (for example, DDT, aldrin, and dieldrin) and the arsenic-containing pesticides have been banned and replaced by newer chemicals. In the United States, organophosphate pesticides (such as malathion and parathion) are largely replacing chlorinated hydrocarbon pesticides; the organophosphates have little in the way of side effects on humans if used properly (though they do cause a number of deaths

---

[5] Lave and Seskin, *Air Pollution,* Chap. 11, p. 244.
[6] Ibid., p. 244.
[7] A federal Toxic Substances Control Act became law in the fall of 1976.
[8] The sources for this material appear at the end of the Table.

every year as a result of mishandling). Although they are generally extremely toxic to insects, the long-run environmental effects of these pesticides (which harm beneficial as well as destructive insect life) may not be known for some time.

There has been much alarm about the concentrations of polychlorinated biphenyls (PCBs) in many U.S. waterways. The disastrous consequences of exposure to high concentrations of PCBs are well documented. In particular, the accidental ingestion of large quantities of PCBs in Japan (and several other countries) caused a serious disorder known as Yusho Disease. The symptoms of this disease range from severe skin eruptions, pigment changes, and general malaise to permanent disturbances of the nervous system, cardiovascular problems, and deformity. However, the primary concern for the health of the general population is not this sort of accidental ingestion of huge quantities of PCBs (such accidents are very rare and have never occurred in the U.S.). Rather the low but persistent concentrations of PCBs in virtually every major body of water in the U.S. are of greater significance for the average citizen. Little is know about the low-level toxicity of PCBs. The few studies carried out so far have been done with experimental animals and have produced such effects as reduced reproductive capacity, lessened resistance to infection, and possible carcinogenicity.

Another suspect and widely used industrial chemical is vinyl chloride. Best known for its use in the production of plastics, this chemical has been linked to cancer in occupationally exposed workers. However, its low-level effects are more conjectural. In experimental animals, low doses have increased the incidence of abortion, produced fetal abnormalities, and affected calcium metabolism.

The wide dispersion of low concentrations of many toxic substances (such as PCBs and vinyl chloride) is the most important concern for the typical person who will never come into contact with occupationally high levels. Many of these substances have only very recently been recognized as hazardous, and consequently little is known about them—how they are broken down and transported in the environment and what their effects are. The continued manufacture and proliferation of such substances without proper testing and control poses unknown dangers to the public and should, in our judgment, be a prime concern of environmental policy makers.

Remarking on the state of the environment, one of the most prominent environmental economists, Allen Kneese, commented to us that

> as contrasted with earlier periods we are indeed discharging a larger mass of materials to the environment. But they are generally at locations more remote from populations, in space and elevation, and, with the exception of solid waste, less visible. What we are doing may be quite insidious in its effects, however. CO_2, fluorocarbons, chlorinated hydrocarbons, heavy metals, radioactivity, plant nutrient materials and numerous others one could mention all have little immediate visible effect but may be quite

insidious in their longer-term effects. These effects will usually be difficult
or impossible to reverse . . . in some ways the newer [pollutants] while
taking much longer [than the better known pollutants] to make their
effects felt have much more ominous implications.[9]

Kneese's remarks have plenty of support in recent reports. A few illustrations:

Hercules Inc. of Glen Falls, which makes color pigments . . . admits dumping substantial amounts of cyanide, arsenic, cadmium, mercury and lead
into the Hudson. . . . None of this . . . is in violation of any law.[10]

"The Delaware River water near Trenton contains one of the highest levels
of chloroform [a suspected carcinogen] found in all the nation's major
waterways, a federal government report revealed yesterday. The first large-
scale monitoring of American industrialized waterways found New Jersey
rivers and channels among the most polluted in the country. New Jersey
water samples contained a wide variety of chemicals considered poisonous
and suspected of helping cause cancer and birth defects, according to the
national survey for the U.S. Environmental Protection Agency."[11]

[Even] the most technically sophisticated [municipal water] treatment
plants . . . let poisonous heavy metals, such as cadmium and mercury,
slip into the water, where they can be absorbed by fish to endanger
consumers.[12]

The volume of PCB's that [the General Electric Company] has been
allowing to wash into the [Hudson] River has affected fish in far greater
measure than the United States Food and Drug Administration has up to
now regarded as tolerable for human health . . . The Hudson may be worse
than any other body of water in the country in this respect, but it is far
from being the only grave example. [PCB-contaminated] carp taken from
the Mississippi have been buried by order of the Food and Drug Administration. Excessive amounts of [PCB's] have also been found in fish in the
Ohio River, in oysters in a Florida bay, in the Great Lakes, the Housa-
tonic, and many other American waters . . . [and] are suspected of having
contaminated the drinking water of several communities in Illinois, California, and Massachusetts.[13]

[9]Letter from Professor Allen V. Kneese, December 30, 1975.
[10]Richard Severo, "Decision Is Awaited On Move By State To Bar Dumping PCB's in the
Hudson," *New York Times,* January 3, 1976, p. 25.
[11]John O. Membrino, "Poison Level High in Delaware River," *The Trentonian,* Nov. 23,
1977, p. 1.
[12]L. Langway and J. Edgerton, "Oceans and Sound are Dirtier Still," *New York Times,*
Sunday, March 24, 1974, Sect. 4, p. 6.
[13]"Action on PCB's," editorial, *New York Times,* December 22, 1975, p. 28.

Recently some scientists have suggested that as much as half of the Great
Lakes pollution may come from the sky—particles of phosphorus, heavy
metals, pesticides and toxic industrial compounds that get into the air and
then come down in rain, snow or just as dust. . . . [The Great Lakes Water
Quality Board of the International Joint Commission, a U.S.-Canadian
body that is the principal watchdog agency on quality of Great Lakes'
water, reported in 1976 that:] The chief concern for Lake Ontario . . . is
the bio-accumulation of toxic contaminants such as polychlorinated
biphenyls . . . and Mirex in fish and wildlife. Mercury contamination of
fish is a problem in the western basin of Lake Erie. In Lakes Huron and
Michigan, PCB's in fish are a major concern. In Lake Superior, items of
concern include accumulation of PCB's and mercury in fish and high concentrations of asbestiform fibers in the water. Lake Ontario in 1975 revealed almost a total reproductive failure of some herring gull colonies. . . .
The adult gulls were found to contain 15 organochlorine compounds and
14 polynuclear aromatic hydrocarbon compounds (e.g., PCB's and DDT
and its metabolites) in their tissues. The concentrations of Mirex ap-
proached concentrations of DDT.[14]

2. Environmental Abuses and Planetary Catastrophes

The evidence provided in the previous section confirms the dangers of
environmental abuse to human health and longevity. But some scientists have
suggested that environmental damage can take even more frightening and riskier
forms. One example is the contention that certain human activities may have
major climatological consequences.[15] The proposed diversion of water from the
Arctic region to replenish the vanishing Caspian and Aral Seas in the Soviet
Union has been said to pose such dangers as the melting of the polar icecaps.[16]
Air pollution, too, is suspected as a source of profound effects upon the global
climate. Some have argued that air pollution is likely to increase the heat reten-
tion of the earth's lower atmosphere, while others have contended that it may
decrease the ability of heat from the sun to get through to the surface of the
earth.

The growing concentration of carbon dioxide (CO_2) in the atmosphere is
the object of particular concern and has been widely studied. CO_2, which is
emitted during the combustion of fossil fuels, has a long life in the atmosphere:

---

[14]Gladwin Hill, "Efforts to Clean Up Great Lakes Gain, But New Problems Emerge," *New York Times,* July 25, 1976, p. 20.
[15]See, for example, William R. Friskin, *The Atmospheric Environment* (Baltimore, Md.: Published for Resources for the Future by The Johns Hopkins University Press, 1973), Chapter 2.
[16]Marshall Goldman, *The Spoils of Progress: Environmental Pollution in the Soviet Union* (Cambridge, Mass.: M.I.T. Press, 1972), pp. 262-63. An opposing view is that the same project would cause the Arctic ice cap to spread!

approximately half of all CO_2 ever generated by industry is still airborne. William D. Nordhaus writes, "it appears that carbon dioxide will be the first industrial emission to affect climate on a global scale, with a "significant' effect appearing sometime in the next twenty years. . . ."[17] He goes on to conclude, "The significant point is that there are predicted to be very large increases in [global] temperature in the coming decades, taking the climate outside of any temperature pattern observed in the last 100,000 years."[18] William Friskin observes, "we are left with some uncertainty on the short term (say, the next 50 years) as to whether carbon dioxide and the greenhouse effect will raise the [earth's] temperature significantly, or whether increased atmospheric turbidity due to man-made (or caused) aerosols will lower it significantly. There is a possibility that, since the doubling times are presently different, first the former and then the latter will occur. . . . On the longer term (say, more than 100 years) we have the more serious problem of beginning to warm the climate directly with our own energy conversion."[19] He concludes, "it is clear that if the industrial revolution continues at the present rate, it is only a question of time until man's activities begin to change the earth's climate."[20]

While, as economists, we are in no position to evaluate these views, they certainly do underscore the fact that humans do not really know what they are doing as they tinker with their surroundings. The same can be said of the stratospheric consequences of the introduction of supersonic transport jets (SSTs) and the widespread dispersion of chlorofluoromethanes (fluorocarbons). These activities have been linked with a decrease in the ozone in the stratosphere. Ozone in the stratosphere absorbs virtually all of the sun's harmful ultraviolet radiation; this prevents the radiation from reaching the earth's surface, where it would have adverse effects on people, animals, and plants and could upset the heat balance of the globe with major climatological consequences.

SSTs, which fly at stratospheric heights, have been found to emit nitrogen oxides (NO_x), resulting in a net decrease in ozone. A National Academy of Sciences report found that the NO_x emissions from a large fleet of several hundred SSTs and subsonic high altitude planes projected for 1990 would reduce stratospheric ozone by significant amounts in the absence of adequate emission controls.[21]

Of even greater concern is the widespread dispersion of chlorofluoromethanes (CFMs), which are used as propellants in aerosol spray cans, working

---

[17]William D. Nordhaus, "Economic Growth and Climate: The Carbon Dioxide Problem," presented at American Economic Association Annual Meeting, Altantic City, New Jersey, September 1976, p. 3.

[18]Ibid., p. 4.

[19]Friskin, *Atmospheric Environment*, p. 64.

[20]Ibid., p. 66.

[21]Climatic Impact Committee, *Environmental Impact of Stratospheric Flight: Biological and Climatic Effects of Aircraft Emissions in the Stratosphere* (Washington, D.C.: National Academy of Sciences, 1975), Table 4, p. 29.

fluids in air conditioners and refrigerators, and agents for producing certain solid plastic foams. It has been established that the accumulation of CFMs in the stratosphere leads to a reduction in the amount of ozone. The exact extent of this reduction is not known, but a National Academy of Sciences committee reported, "Continued CFM release at 1973 levels could by the year 2000 produce about half of the direct climatic effect caused by CO_2 increase over the same period, although the magnitude of both effects on climate is less certain. Thus, the CFM effect may well deserve serious concern. . . . In our present state of knowledge it would be imprudent to accept increasing CFM use and release, either in the U.S. or worldwide."[22]

Any appreciable reductions in stratospheric ozone, which would increase ultraviolet radiation, might result in increased incidence of malignant melanoma (a serious form of skin cancer which is frequently fatal), increased incidence of basal- and squamous-cell carcinomas (less serious skin cancers, rarely fatal, but usually expensive and sometimes disfiguring), and unknown effects on plants and animals.

Surely the possibility of ozone depletion, like the climatological consequences of air pollution, is a matter far too serious for human survival for us casually to ignore it. Even if the evidence on these matters is incomplete, the threat they pose at the very least justifies serious study of the hypotheses; in some cases even provisional prohibition of the suspected activities may be appropriate, until we accumulate evidence that clears the charges against them. There is a fundamental principle of rational conduct that applies in all such cases, a principle that is all too likely to be overlooked in the formulation of policy. It asserts that the severity of the policy that should be undertaken in defense against some peril depends on both the likelihood of the threat *and the character of the damage that it threatens*. This means that it often makes sense to protect oneself against a dangerous event whose occurrence is highly unlikely if its consequences can be catastrophic. A rational insurance program makes provision for financial support during serious illness or a disastrous fire that destroys one's home. Statistically, either of these is unlikely for any particular individual, but the consequences in the event that it does occur are so appalling that the cost of insuring against it is thoroughly justified. In the same way, it makes good sense for the human race to take steps to protect itself from types of environmental damage that the casual observer may consider uncomfortably close to science fiction.

3. The Special Problems of Nuclear Energy

In any event, recent decades have shown that science fiction is sometimes more prophetic than fictitious. While we are not completely certain about the

---

[22]*Halocarbons: Environmental Effects of Chlorofluoromethane Release,* Committee on Impacts of Stratospheric Change (Washington, D.C.: National Academy of Sciences, 1976), p. 3.

effects of supersonic flight or the climatological consequences of air pollution, there is at least one human activity that brings with it some truly awesome and more predictable perils: the production of energy by nuclear fission.

The fuel crisis in 1974-75 and again in 1976-77 gave new impetus to the proliferation of nuclear facilities for the generation of electricity (although trends in their construction and operation costs and public opposition to nuclear power plants have slowed their construction below the rates that had been anticipated). It is widely recognized that nuclear power generation does pose dangers. However, the magnitude of the peril is not generally known. We offer a rather lengthy excerpt from a piece entitled *The Faustian Bargain,* because it describes the issue very clearly and because it represents a carefully reasoned discussion of the matter by an economist, Allen Kneese, who is widely recognized for his knowledge of environmental issues and the levelheadedness of his judgment.

If so unforgiving a technology as large-scale nuclear fission energy production is adopted, it will impose a burden of continuous monitoring and sophisticated management of a dangerous material, essentially forever. The penalty of not bearing this burden may be unparalleled disaster. This irreversible burden would be imposed even if nuclear fission were to be used only for a few decades, a mere instant in the pertinent time scales. . . .

The recent failure of a small physical test of emergency core cooling equipment for the present generation of light-water reactors was an alarming event. This is in part because the failure casts doubt upon whether the system would function in the unlikely, but not impossible, event it would be called upon in an actual energy reactor. But it also illustrates the great difficulty of forecasting behavior of components in this complex technology where pertinent experimentation is always difficult and may sometimes be impossible. . . .

No doubt there are some additional surprises ahead when other parts of the fuel cycle become more active, particularly in transportation of spent fuel elements and in fuel reprocessing facilities. As yet, there has been essentially no commercial experience in recycling the plutonium produced in nuclear reactors. . . . Plutonium is one of the deadliest substances known to man. The inhalation of a millionth of a gram—the size of a grain of pollen—appears to be sufficient to cause lung cancer.

Although it is well known in the nuclear community, perhaps the general public is unaware of the magnitude of the disaster which would occur in the event of a severe accident at a nuclear facility. I am told that if an accident occurred at one of today's nuclear plants, resulting in the release of only five percent of only the more volatile fission products, the number of casualties could total between 1,000 and 10,000. The estimated range apparently could shift up or down by a factor of ten or so, depending on assumptions of population density and meteorological conditions.

With breeder reactors, the accidental release of plutonium may be of greater consequence than the release of the more volatile fission products.

Plutonium is one of the most potent respiratory carcinogens in existence. In addition to a great variety of other radioactive substances, breeders will contain one, or more, tons of plutonium. While the fraction that could be released following a credible accident is extremely uncertain, it is clear that the release of only a small percentage of this inventory would be equivalent to the release of *all* the volatile fission products in one of today's nuclear plants. Once lost to the environment, the plutonium not ingested by people in the first few hours following an accident would be around to take its toll for generations to come—for tens of thousands of years. When one factors in the possibility of sabotage and warfare, where power plants are prime targets not just in the United States but also in less developed countries now striving to establish a nuclear industry, then there is almost no limit to the size of the catastrophe one can envisage.

It is argued that the probabilities of such disastrous events are so low that these events fall into the negligible risk category. Perhaps so, but do we really know this? Recent unexpected events raise doubts. How, for example, does one calculate the actions of a fanatical terrorist?

The use of plutonium as an article of commerce and the presence of large quantities of plutonium in the nuclear fuel cycles also worries a number of informed persons in another connection. Plutonium is readily used in the production of nuclear weapons, and governments, possibly even private parties, not now having access to such weapons might value it highly for this purpose. Although an illicit market has not yet been established, its value has been estimated to be comparable to that of heroin (around $5,000 per pound). A certain number of people may be tempted to take great risks to obtain it. . . .

. . . part of the Faustian bargain is that to use fission technology safely, society must exercise great vigilance and the highest levels of quality control, continuously and *indefinitely*. As the fission energy economy grows, many plants will be built and operated in countries with comparatively low levels of technological competence and a greater propensity to take risks. A much larger amount of transportation of hazardous materials will probably occur, and safety will become the province of the sea captain as well as the scientist. Moreover, even in countries with higher levels of technological competence, continued success can lead to reduced vigilance. We should recall that we managed to incinerate three astronauts in a very straightforward accident in an extremely high technology operation where the utmost precautions were allegedly being taken.

Deeper moral questions also surround the storage of high-level radioactive wastes. Estimates of how long these waste materials must be isolated from the biosphere apparently contain major elements of uncertainty, but current ones seem to agree on "at least two hundred thousand years."

Favorable consideration has been given to the storage of these wastes in salt formations, and a site for experimental storage was selected at Lyons, Kansas. This particular site proved to be defective. Oil companies had drilled the area full of holes, and there had also been solution mining in the area which left behind an unknown residue of water. But comments of the Kansas Geological Survey raised far deeper and more general questions about the behavior of the pertinent formations under stress and the operations of geological forces on them. The ability of solid earth geophysics to predict for the time scales required proves very limited. . . .

Because the site selected proved defective, and possibly in anticipation of political problems, primary emphasis is now being placed upon the design of surface storage facilities intended to last a hundred years or so, while the search for a permanent site continues. These surface storage sites would require continuous monitoring and management of a most sophisticated kind. A complete cooling system breakdown would soon prove disastrous and even greater tragedies can be imagined.

Just to get an idea of the scale of disaster that could take place, consider the following scenario. Political factors force the federal government to rely on a single above-ground storage site for all high-level radioactive waste accumulated through the year 2000. Some of the more obvious possibilities would be existing storage sites like Hanford or Savannah, which would seem to be likely military targets. A tactical nuclear weapon hits the site and vaporizes a large fraction of the contents of this storage area. The weapon could come from one of the principal nuclear powers, a lesser developed country with one or more nuclear power plants, or it might be crudely fabricated by a terrorist organization from black-market plutonium. I am told that the radiation fallout from such an event could exceed that from all past nuclear testing by a factor of 500 or so, with radiation doses exceeding the annual dose from natural background radiation by an order of magnitude. . . .

Sometimes, analogies are used to suggest that the burden placed upon future generations by the "immortal" wastes is really nothing so very unusual. The Pyramids are cited as an instance where a very long-term commitment was made to the future and the dikes of Holland as one where continuous monitoring and maintenance are required indefinitely. . . .

None of these historical examples tell us much about the time scales pertinent here. One speaks of two hundred thousand years. Only a little more than one-hundredth of that time span has passed since the Parthenon was built. We know of no government whose life was more than an instant by comparison with the half-life of plutonium.[23]

4. Conclusions

The view that emerged from our study of environmental trends in Chapter 2 was far more disparate and heterogeneous than we had expected. But while the facts do not support the view that there is imminent ecological disaster in every

---

[23] Allen V. Kneese, "The Faustian Bargain," *Resources*, No. 44 (Washington, D.C.: Resources for the Future, Inc., Sept. 1973), pp. 1–4. See also, T. B. Cochran, *The Liquid Metal Fast Breeder Reactor, an Environmental and Economic Critique* (Washington, D.C.: Resources for the Future, Inc., 1974).

human activity or that all economic growth necessarily increases environmental deterioration, they provide no comfort to the proponent of business as usual. We have seen that at least some environmental problems are growing and are likely to continue to do so, that some are certain to exact serious costs in human health, and that some impose on humanity frightful risks that we cannot even begin to quantify.

It is important to recognize that, despite their uncertainty, the seriousness of these perils may be sufficient to justify long-term commitment of substantial quantities of resources to their control. Good sense dictates that we insure ourselves against ecological disasters, particularly against those that are effectively irreversible. Uncertainty about such environmental dangers does not call for us to delay action; on the contrary, the very riskiness inherent in certain types of damaging activities may suggest their curtailment.

From review of facts, we must now turn to analysis. The next chapter describes the economist's explanation of the failure of the free market economy to prevent abuses of the environment. The analysis is somewhat abstract and theoretical, but it is essential for an understanding of the nature of the problem and of some of the means that can be used to deal with it effectively.

4

The Mechanism of Environmental Damage
in a Free Enterprise Economy*

In the last two chapters we have surveyed the damage that human activity has done to the environment. This chapter shows that there are features in our economic system that act as systematic inducements to environmental abuse. Without an understanding of the nature of these inducements, the design of environmental programs is likely to go awry. That is why it is necessary to examine the relation between environmental damage and the incentive structure of the economy.

In its production of consumer goods—shirts, dishwashers, and pinball machines—the performance of our economy has been remarkable. Never before and nowhere else has an economy spewed forth so many consumer products so efficiently. As Marx and Engels put it, "The Bourgeoisie, during its rule of scarce one hundred years, has created more massive and more colossal productive forces than have all previous generations together."[1] This contrasts sharply with our economy's very mixed performance in providing some of the other amenities usually considered part of the good society. The free enterprise system has

---

*This chapter summarizes materials that are familiar to economists who will no doubt prefer to skip over it.
[1] Karl Marx and Friedrich Engels, *Manifesto of the Communist Party*, Sect. I.

obviously not done so well as a supplier of pure air and water or quiet surroundings.

Both sides of the matter—the economy's outstanding efficiency in producing consumer goods and its mediocre performance in providing social benefits—have long been studied by economists. In 1776 Adam Smith's *Wealth of Nations* explained why a free enterprise system is so responsive to consumers' demands in the marketplace. In 1920 another British economist, A. C. Pigou, showed why the performance of a profit system in supplying social amenities is apt to be less satisfactory.[2] It is important to understand the logic of both of these analyses, because it indicates how we can repair the operation of a free market economy to provide the proper incentives for the protection of the environment.

We must note first that economists generally do not set themselves up as arbiters of any "correct" quantity of resources to devote to environmental programs. They do not argue that people *should* want to devote fewer resources to, say, turning out motorcycles and television sets and that people *ought to* use these resources instead to clean up the air and water. Economists emphasize that they have not been granted any privileged knowledge about the ideal allocation of resources. The analyses we describe in this chapter rest on no such presumption. Pigou's logic shows clearly that, because of features inherent in its structure, a free enterprise economy will respond inadequately *to the wishes of the general public* in its supply of social amenities. In an affluent society, the public's wish for dayglow Frisbees or goosedown parkas will be the business world's command. But if the public wants purer air just as strongly, the response of business will be virtually nil.

1. The Competitive Price System as an Invisible Hand

In a free enterprise system the more efficiently a business firm satisfies the demands of consumers, the more it profits. If its products do not meet the specifications of the public or if it does not produce its commodity as inexpensively as possible, competitors will take its business away. These competitive pressures are a remarkably powerful inducement for the efficient provision of consumer goods and services. Every firm must constantly be on the lookout, not only for a better mousetrap, but also for ways to produce it less expensively. Note that producers serve the consumer not out of a sense of morality or commitment to public service, but out of their own self-interest, and sometimes even as a matter of economic survival.

Prices play a fundamental role in this process. They guide three critical functions of the economy: they match the output of goods and services to

---

[2] A. C. Pigou, *The Economics of Welfare* (London: Macmillan, 1920).

consumer desires; they apportion the limited supply of commodities; and they prevent waste. We need not linger over the first of these functions since it will not play a critical role in our discussion; moreover, the mechanism involved is fairly obvious. The basic point is that if consumer tastes change, switching, for example, from high-cholesterol lamb to lower-cholesterol veal, the price of lamb will fall and that of veal will rise. Farmers will consequently be forced to shift their investment from one product to the other to obey the wishes of consumers.

More important for our purposes is the role of prices in doling out and conserving scarce items. When a commodity becomes scarce, its market price will inevitably rise. This immediately implies something which may strike the noneconomist as paradoxical, if not downright perverse: the public can sometimes benefit from a rise in prices!

How can it ever be possible for consumers to benefit from price rises? We hope to convince the reader that in fact this can be true in *many* cases. The logic of the idea is clearly brought out by an example provided by Mountiford Longfield, a nineteenth-century professor of economics at Trinity College, Dublin.[3] Longfield wrote:

> . . . suppose the crop of the ordinary food used in any country, as potatos in Ireland, was to fall short in some year one-sixth of the usual consumption. If this scarcity did not indicate and in some measure correct itself by an increase of price, the whole stock of provisions destined for the supply of the year would be exhausted in ten months, and for the remaining two months a scene of misery and famine beyond description would ensue. But this in fact does not take place, for prices do rise and cause an immediate diminution in the ordinary daily consumption, so that the existing stores hold out until the season for an arrival of a new supply. Undoubtedly some distress is endured during this interval, from the want felt by many of the poor of a proper quantity of food; but this distress is necessarily incident to a diminished supply, and would be incalculably increased instead of being diminished, if human legislation should attempt to regulate the prices. . . . But when prices reach a certain height, an opinion frequently arises among the sufferers that it is not caused by a scarcity. . . . They suppose that there are provisions enough, but that the distress is caused by the insatiable rapacity of the possessors . . . [and] they have generally succeeded in obtaining laws against engrossing, amassing, or forestalling provisions, and thus they remove the imaginary, and aggravate the real cause of their distress . . . and it enables the ¿ɔɔer people to dispense with that harsh but necessary abstinence which alone can prevent the provisions from being entirely consumed long before a new supply can be obtained.[4]

---

[3]It is noteworthy that the lecture from which the quotation is taken was given some ten years before the great potato famine which brought indescribable suffering to the Irish population, and a great wave of Irish emigration to the United States.

[4]Mountiford Longfield, *Lectures on Political Economy* (Dublin, 1834), pp. 53–56.

The critical role of the price mechanism in relation to goods in limited supply is that it sends those supplies *where* they are needed most and makes them available *when* they are needed most. If grain is abundant in one area and scarce in another, the price differential that will arise will induce a flow of grain from the place of comparative abundance to the area of shortage. If there is a fair amount of grain in the warehouses from last year's crop but the crop about to be harvested is poor, the "futures price" (the price for delivery in later months) will rise relative to the current price. Grain will consequently be held back from current consumption and saved until later when the need for it will be greater. In this way the market mechanism husbands the available supplies of goods and gets them to the persons to whom they matter most, when and where they are needed most.

There have been times when society was unwilling to accept the social consequences of the unimpeded operation of the price mechanism. Price controls during war (and other) times, ceilings on interest rates, and rent controls in some cities are all recent examples of restraints on the price system. Historically, each limitation on price has been accompanied by a shortage of the good in question. In these cases, distribution of the limited supply has sometimes degenerated into chaos, with goods going predominantly to individuals with "the right connections." In other cases, chaos has been prevented by the imposition of direct rationing as a substitute for the price system. Often black markets come into being and commodities are sold at high illegal prices. In this latter case, prices are effectively restored as the apportioning mechanism (but in a way that is more costly and less efficient than if the pricing system had been left to its own in the first place).

The apportionment produced by the price system has much to be said for it. Consider the extreme opposite case: fixed rationing that takes no account of varying consumer preferences. Everyone is assigned a half pound of cheese and a half dozen eggs whether or not he or she happens to love the former and detest the latter. The apportionment that is achieved by the price system, in contrast, gets more of the available eggs to those who prefer eggs and more of the cheese to cheese lovers. Customers spend their money on the commodities they like. The pricing system thus tends to allocate goods and services according to individual tastes and incomes. On the other hand, apportionment by price always weighs most heavily upon the poor. When goods are scarce, rising prices hit hardest at the poor who are most vulnerable to the pressures for reduced consumption. This is the most effective rallying point of those who advocate alternative means to deal with shortages.

An important function of the price mechanism for our study is its ability to discourage wasteful use of resources in the production process. Business firms devote a great deal of effort and research to reduce the quantity of expensive resources used in making their products. In fact, input prices can have a profound effect on their usage. In economies where wages are low, there is little investment in labor-saving equipment, while in high-wage societies there is a constant search for new machines to replace human labor. There are remarkable examples of great care and expense laid out to prevent waste in precious metal industries. In platinum-using industries, the clothing of workers is cleaned every day in order to reclaim the bits of this precious metal which have lodged in the cloth. We emphasize that a competitive, free enterprise system virtually necessitates such cost-minimizing efforts. For without them the firm will be unable to match the prices of competitors.

In summary, inherent in the price system are extremely important incentives that guide resources to the production of those goods and services that consumers want to buy, incentives that encourage efficient methods of production. As we shall see next, there are good reasons to expect that this mechanism will not work nearly so well when it comes to the provision of the social amenities.

2. The Shortcomings of the Price System in Supplying Social Amenities

There are many services that the general public desires, but for which it is very difficult to charge an appropriate price. An extreme case includes goods and services, called *pure public goods,* which if supplied to any one consumer are automatically provided to many others. A classic example is pesticide spraying to destroy malaria-bearing mosquitoes in a particular area. There is no way a mosquito-free neighborhood can be provided to some residents of the area without making it available, simultaneously, to everyone else who lives there. But if a profit-making business is to sell its product, it must be able to *exclude* nonpurchasers from the consumption of that product. In the case of malaria elimination, a pesticide spray company cannot charge individual residents since all the nonpayers in the region will also benefit from the spraying. For the same reason, no private business firm will undertake the supply of national defense, public health measures, the elimination of crime in a city, or any of the other services which can be considered public goods. There is simply (under existing institutions) no way to market such a good or service.

A less extreme version of this problem crops up in a much broader category of economic activities. These are activities that affect not only the welfare of the supplier and the purchaser of a product, but also (unintentionally) yield incidental benefits or cause incidental injuries to some third party or parties not directly involved in the exchange. These unintended side effects are called *externalities* or *spillovers;* that is, these activities spill over upon persons outside the immediate transaction. An example of an external *benefit* is the case where a business decides to bury high tension electric lines in order to avoid the high maintenance costs of overhead wires. Other people in the area benefit not only because an eyesore has been removed, but also because there is some reduction in personal danger during storms.

In our discussion we are interested primarily in the *detrimental* externalities or spillovers that constitute the source of many of our most serious environmental problems. Air pollution is a prime example. A factory that pours smoke into the atmosphere does not do so as an end in itself, but as an incidental side effect of the process of production. The smoke that increases laundry costs in the neighborhood, that reduces the pleasure of living there, and that may constitute a health hazard is a spillover effect; it is omitted entirely from the firm's calculations of its receipts and costs. The fact that the business that causes a detrimental externality pays no part of its cost helps to explain why the market mechanism does such an imperfect job of protecting the environment. One can think of the cleanliness of the air, the purity of the water, and the attractiveness of a neighborhood as public resources that can be used up by production processes. Just as the manufacture of some product may require x ounces of steel or y kilowatt hours of electricity, it may use up z units of pure air through its discharges of smoke. There is, however, an important difference in the way in which the firm treats these inputs. The company has to pay for the steel and electricity it uses. But under most current arrangements, the use of the atmosphere is usually free of charge to the firm, and is not considered in its cost calculations.

We may, then, describe the externalities with which we are concerned to be products of an institutional arrangement under which a number of society's resources are given away free. Landlords who let their properties deteriorate "use up" the quality of the neighborhood, difficult though measurement of that quality may be, just as surely as a steel maker uses up society's coal resources. Fresh air, clean water, and attractiveness of the neighborhood are all available for the taking, and that is precisely where the difficulty lies, for a zero price is an invitation to the user to waste the resources for which he pays nothing.

The problem of externalities can be viewed as one involving the absence of well-defined *property rights.* No one owns our clean air or water and, as a result, there is no price placed upon it. Though it is abundantly clear that we do not have unlimited quantities of clean air and water, we have failed to use the price system to apportion these scarce resources properly. This suggests one obvious instrument that policy makers can use to deal with externalities. By *requiring* the generators of externalities to bear the cost—by making the polluters pay—society can discourage the flow of undesirable spillovers. This is an approach to the matter favored by many economists. We will see that there is reason to expect this approach to be effective in many cases. But it may be able to do more than that. It may bring to the provision of social amenities all of the responsiveness to consumer demands, and all of the pressures for efficiency in the use of resources that the price mechanism enforces in the production of ordinary consumer goods. If a system of charges upon the generators of externalities can come anywhere near to matching this claim, it will indeed have much to be said in its favor. This will be a key issue in our analysis of the choice of policy instruments in Part 2 of this book.

3. Externalities and the Frustration of the Public Desires

Externalities are of crucial importance to our analysis because they limit the effectiveness of the market mechanism in satisfying consumer desires. For example, consider a steel mill or an electric generating station that emits smoke which increases laundry and cleaning costs for miles around; suppose, moreover, that the accumulation of laundry bills far exceeds the cost of smoke-elimination devices. Since the steel mill does not pay the laundry bills itself, there is no financial pressure to induce it to limit its outputs of smoke, even though (comparing the laundry costs with the cost of the smoke-control equipment), it obviously would benefit society to have such devices installed. Moreover, because part of the cost of the steel production is borne not by the steel manufacturer but by those who pay the resulting laundry bills, the production and sale of steel-using products will be stimulated (by the financial saving to producers of steel). Steel output will be expanded, not because of a growth in consumer demand, but by the implicit subsidy that occurs when others pay part of the real cost.

In sum, where such spillovers occur, the private enterprise system will respond imperfectly to the desires of the public. The output of products yielding undesirable spillovers will typically be undesirably large; it will exceed what would be produced if the firms were forced to pay for the damage they inflict as a byproduct of their activities. Where there are significant externalities then, the price system does not act as an efficient servant of the public's preferences.

4. The Pervasiveness of Externalities

While there is widespread agreement that externalities can impair the functioning of the market system, it is sometimes implied that these spillover effects are rather rare and represent relatively minor shortcomings in the workings of the price mechanism. This is simply not so. Externalities pervade virtually every sector of our economy; they are an unavoidable element of the productive process; and their consequences tend to grow disproportionately with increasing population and expansion of the economy's activities.[5]

---

[5] This section draws on the illuminating discussion in A. Kneese, R. Ayres, and R. d'Arge, *Economics and the Environment: A Materials Balance Approach* (Washington, D.C.: Resources for the Future, Inc., 1970).

It is not hard to compile a substantial list of important externalities: familiar examples include industrial emissions of noxious wastes into many lakes and rivers and discharges of air pollutants into the atmosphere. As we have seen, the deleterious effects of these externalities, particularly in heavily industrialized and populated areas, are a matter of record. However, some of the most pervasive externalities are generated, not by industrial operations, but by individual activities. The automobile is a notorious producer of detrimental spillovers. Automobile exhausts increase laundry expenses, make it more difficult to breathe, and even shorten lives. The heavy cloud of pollutants that hangs over crowded roadways, the widespread traffic delays, and the heavy accident rates in such areas again suggest that externalities created by the activities of consumers are not exceptional phenomena.

Every manufacturing or consumption process inevitably creates wastes. These wastes take many forms: junked automobile bodies, household garbage, chemical residuals, slag from mining, and heat discharges into rivers from electric generating plants. The laws of conservation of energy and mass provide the ultimate evidence of the unavoidable connection between production and externalities, for they show that wastes simply *cannot* be made to vanish. The relationships of physics tell us that, after a society completes its initial use of a piece of steel, the only way in which it can prevent the steel from adding to the accumulation of wastes in one form or another is to put it to some other use (recycling). Any input must become a waste product the moment the economy finds no further use for it. There may be technical processes which transform the waste product into more convenient physical forms, but there can be no process that eliminates that waste![6]

In saying this, it must be emphasized that society can influence the form taken by these wastes so as to reduce the consequent damage. It can also influence the quantity of waste that is recycled rather than dumped into the environment. Here pricing can also play a major role. If generators of waste do not pay the full social cost of its removal, they will be encouuraged to be more wasteful. If taxes impose a price disadvantage upon recycling, this activity will be discouraged.

Wherever the cost of removal of waste does not reflect its full social costs (and that is generally the case), detrimental spillovers will occur. An example is municipal garbage-removal services where charges to the individual household frequently do not reflect the cost of the collection operation. Even where there is a charge, it normally corresponds only to the labor and investment costs of the disposal process, not the damage imposed by the smoke and disease that may emanate from the dump. As a result, households have little incentive to

---

[6] This "closed" character of our economic system is described dramatically in Kenneth Boulding's famous essay, "The Economics of the Coming Spaceship Earth," in Henry Jarrett, ed., *Environmental Quality in a Growing Economy* (Baltimore: The Johns Hopkins University Press, 1966), pp. 3–14.

reduce the amounts of trash and garbage they generate or to cooperate with programs to recycle. *Our central point is that externalities are not exceptional phenomena; they are everywhere about us, embedded in the workings of our economy.*

5. Concluding Comments

This chapter has outlined the economist's analysis of some fundamental economic difficulties that degrade the quality of life. It has shown why, where externalities are absent, the price mechanism does an amazingly effective job of directing the economy in terms of producing goods which consumers demand and producing them with great efficiency. We have seen that even high and rising prices serve as a bitter but salutary medicine that can help to keep otherwise serious shortages under control. But in economic activities that produce significant externalities, the market cannot be relied upon to respond effectively to the wishes of the public. The analysis shows that most of our environmental problems stem from what may be described as a limitation of the pricing system. We stress that this is not a manifestation of conspiracy or malfeasance by any particular group; rather, the problem of externalities is inherent in the organization of the economy itself, which permits individuals, firms, *and* government agencies to use up and damage society's resources, but escape the resulting social costs. This suggests that a pricing policy that requires polluters to pay for this damage is one way to deal with the problem. The analysis also suggests that externalities are widespread and important, and that in the absence of effective policies, the social damages resulting from externalities may well grow increasingly serious as population and industrial activity expand.

While externalities or spillovers weaken the power of the market mechanism to serve consumers effectively, it does not follow that environmental problems will arise only in free enterprise economies. On the contrary, there is strong evidence that planned economies have similar problems, perhaps slightly different in character, but surely comparably serious. However, the reasons for their occurrence are, naturally, somewhat different from the causes in a free market economy. The next chapter describes some of the environmental troubles of the Soviet Union and other planned economies and discusses some of their sources.

5

Pollution Problems
in the Planned Economies*

We will find in this chapter that the Soviet Union and the other centrally planned economies have experienced virtually every type of environmental degradation that has plagued the free enterprise countries. But our purpose is not invidious comparison. Rather, we can hope to learn from the experience of the Soviets and other planners what common influences underlie our common problems, and what special difficulties they may have encountered that we might do well to avoid.

Contrary to what some socialist theorists have suggested, a central lesson of the Soviet experience is that governmental ownership and central planning do not automatically do away with the abuse of a society's natural resources and its quality of life. State enterprises, just like private firms, may find it easiest to pour their liquid wastes into the nearest waterway and to emit their fumes into the atmosphere. This reminder is important for us because we are apt to forget that, even in a free market economy, governmental activities

---

*This chapter is derived entirely from secondary sources. It will be obvious enough that the authors can claim no special expertise on the subject. Indeed, it might not have been possible for us to write this chapter without the availability of the fine work of Marshall Goldman, who has surveyed environmental problems in the USSR more thoroughly than anyone in the U.S. His book, *The Spoils of Progress* (Cambridge, Mass.: M.I.T. Press, 1972), is nontechnical and makes fascinating reading.

produce quite a significant share of environmental damage. In the defense establishment, military aircraft contribute substantial amounts of noise and exhaust fumes; the disposal of obsolete military weapons, including radioactive materials and nerve gases, also constitutes a serious danger. Civilian governmental activities, as well, generate their share of pollution: municipal sewage plants pour great quantities of raw or partially treated wastes into waterways. Massive government projects, like the ill-fated Tocks Island Dam and the Cross-Florida Barge Canal, can also create environmental dangers. Indeed, the official status of government agencies can make them even more resistant than private organizations to efforts designed to circumscribe their environmentally damaging activities.

Another lesson from recent Soviet history (as well as our own) is that common ownership of a resource often leads to its abuse. As we will discuss in succeeding chapters, a natural resource that is owned by everyone (and hence by no one in particular) can become a cheap dumping ground for wastes, an inexpensive source of raw materials, and an attractive location for destructive activities; people are free to help themselves without compensating the remaining members of the community for what they lose from such wanton utilization.[1] Lake Erie in the United States and Lake Baikal in the Soviet Union are both spectacular victims of these dangerous sources of malfunction in economic arrangements; decisions have been made on the assumption that these valuable resources are free for the taking, though in both cases their misuse has proved highly costly to society.

Finally, our study brings out a third common problem: the grandiose construction complex.[2] This is the view that *any* construction that alters the environment in favor of "progress" is a good thing; that virtually any pristine piece of nature—a canyon, a lake, or a mountain—can be improved upon by human intervention; and that every massive alteration (even marginally justifiable by a shaky benefit-cost calculation) represents a net gain to society and a monument to mankind's creative powers. The Soviet Union's long romance with massive hydroelectric installations (its recurrent theme at international expositions) has exacted its toll, not only in aesthetic damage, but in economic losses as well: the destruction of valuable fish resources and the sacrifice of

---

[1] *Unrestricted* common property is the key problem here rather than "public" property in the Marxian sense of state ownership.

[2] It has been referred to as the "Corps of Engineers mentality" (or alternatively the "edifice complex"), but the former appellation may be unfair. There seems to be evidence that the U.S. Corps of Engineers has recently begun to respond to increasing public interest in the environment and to take an active role in the area. For an illustrative report on the Corps of Engineer's role in helping to protect the Florida Keys, see "Builders and Ecologists Clash Over the Future of Key Largo," *New York Times,* February 23, 1975, p. 41. One of our reviewers, however, makes the comment that our new verdict for the Corps is somewhat premature: "They are still pyramid builders . . . the Soviet Union has no monopoly on monument construction. Our Bureau of Reclamation and Corps of Engineers remain builders and drainers of the first order" (Professor Joseph Seneca, Rutgers University).

agricultural and vacation areas are two examples. As we will illustrate in this chapter, in the Soviet Union, where the governmental role in the economy is so pervasive, some of the monumental achievements literally dwarf any such environmental "improvements" that U.S. agencies have managed to produce.[3]

1. Differences in Soviet and U.S. Problems[4]

All of this is not meant to imply that environmental problems in the United States and the Soviet Union are essentially the same. On the contrary, there are systematic differences, and these are precisely the sort one might expect. In the Soviet Union consumption per capita is considerably less than it is in the United States, partially because per-capita output is still considerably smaller, but also because the Soviet Union has devoted a relatively large proportion of its output to producers' goods: the construction of plant and equipment. As a result, there are fewer automobiles in the Soviet Union than in the United States or Western Europe. One might consequently expect that exhaust emissions and related pollution would be far less in the Soviet Union. On the other hand, brakes on Soviet government activities (such as those to which we are accustomed in the United States—pressure from the public, the Congress, the Bureau of the Budget, Department of the Interior, and the Environmental Protection Agency) virtually do not exist. Moreover, a larger share of GNP flows through the public sector in the Soviet economy. Consequently, we might well expect potentially destructive projects in the Soviet Union to be grander in scale and more pervasive than they are in the West.[5]

The evidence supports our hypothesis on automotive pollution. Table 5-1 reports data for five major automotive air pollutants. We see that for only one of these pollutants are Soviet emissions more than half of those in the United States, and in three cases they are less than a quarter of the U.S. level. These differences become even more impressive when one recognizes the far larger

---

[3] The paucity of information available on most centrally planned economies makes it necessary to focus the discussion on the experience of the USSR. We offer only some fragmentary material on environmental programs in China and the countries of Eastern Europe. For a sanguine view of the prospects for environmental policy in China, see K. William Kapp, " 'Recycling' in Contemporary China," *Kyklos* 27 (1974), Fasc. 2, pp. 286–303. See also Leo A. Orleans, "China's Environomics: Backing Into Ecological Leadership," in *China: A Reassessment of the Economy, A Compendium of Papers Submitted to the Joint Economic Committee,* U.S. Congress (Washington, D.C.: U.S. Government Printing Office, July 10, 1975), pp. 116–44.

[4] This section draws heavily on R. J. McIntyre and J. R. Thornton, "Environmental Divergence: Air Pollution in the U.S.S.R.," *Journal of Environmental Economics and Management* 1 (August 1974): 109–20.

[5] One reader notes, however, that ecologists and other scientific groups in the USSR have a certain amount of status, and this should count for something. Also, there do exist exceptions to the supremacy-of-output rule; e.g., in the USSR a profitable species like the polar bear is carefully protected (not so in the U.S.).

TABLE 5-1

POLLUTANTS EMITTED IN THE U.S. AND THE USSR IN THE LATE 1960s
(millions of tons)

	Particulates	SO_2	CO	HC	NO_x
U.S.	28	33	100	32	21
USSR	17	16	19	7	1
USSR as % of U.S.	61%	48%	19%	22%	5%

Source: V. Mote, "The Geography of Air Pollution in the U.S.S.R." (Ph.D. dissertation, University of Washington, 1971), p. 231, as cited in R. J. McIntyre and J. R. Thornton, "Environmental Divergence: Air Pollution in the U.S.S.R.," *Journal of Environmental Economics and Management* 1:119.

geographic area and population of the Soviet Union, which means that *relative* average concentrations of these pollutants (and relative per capita emissions) in the Soviet Union are likely to be even lower than the figures in the table suggest.[6]

In sum, even though the general environmental problems in the two countries have many instructive similarities, it is certainly incorrect to imply that there simply are no significant differences.[7] We turn now to a broader discussion of environmental problems in the Soviet Union.

2. Pollution Problems in the Soviet Union: A Sampling

In parts of the Soviet Union, damage to the environment has reached dramatic levels. Soviet industry and agriculture discharge millions of tons of acids, petroleum wastes, metals, and salts into waterways, after treating only a very small proportion of these effluents. Forests have been cut in areas in which

---

[6] McIntyre and Thornton make the point that, while it is true that the *mix* of output (and hence effluents) differs significantly between the USSR and the U.S., it is also true that the receptor patterns are much different as well. That is, Soviets tend to live where they work, while commuting over significant distances is common in the U.S. Damages from pollution in the Soviet Union might thus belie the seemingly lower pollutant emission totals, because the pollutants and people are physically in contact to a greater degree. Here, higher incomes permit us to escape by dichotomizing our lives, at least with respect to physical location.

[7] One ironic difference is the much greater willingness in the Soviet Union to use pricing methods to assure effectiveness of a program of reuse of containers as a recycling device. For example, it is reported that "Recycling is a habit born of necessity in the Soviet Union; the Russians simply do not throw away bottles, boxes, bags and papers as westerners do. . . . Bottles are redeemed by stores as a matter of routine—yogurt, for example, sells for 30 kopecks, of which 10 kopecks is the deposit on the bottle. In Moscow, some of the collec-

reforestation is difficult, with the soil left free to wash into streams.[8] In 1970 a Russian conservation official estimated the costs of water pollution at over six billion rubles annually;[9] others estimate the yearly toll of erosion at over 3.6 million rubles.[10]

There have been spectacular catastrophes: the Iset and Volga Rivers have actually caught fire, and the continuingly heavy concentration of combustibles they carry threatens a recurrence (reminiscent of 1969 when the Cuyahoga River in Cleveland caught fire). Millions of fish perished, at least in one instance, in a sudden discharge from a chemical plant in Volgograd,[11] and many once fertile fishing grounds have been rendered devoid of all life.

Economic development also threatens the inland seas of Russia. The coast of the Black Sea is being destroyed by a combination of unorganized building, insufficient shore protection, antilandslide installations, and the removal of sand and pebbles for use in building.[12] Lake Baikal, the earth's deepest lake which contains hundreds of unique species of water life, is contaminated by wood and pulp mills that have yet to comply with 1969 pollution control orders.[13] In the next section, we shall discuss the unusual problems of the Aral and Caspian Seas.

The most notorious sources of environmental damage in the U.S. have their counterparts in Russia too. The recently completed Alaskan pipeline is more than matched by a Soviet pipeline which runs from Siberia to the western refining centers. This line has already ruptured with damages extending to the Caspian Sea and wide land areas.[14] Pesticides are used heavily in the USSR, and reports of consequent deaths of large animals and birds are common. In 1970, the use of herbicides increased 2.5 times over the 1965 level, and this too is reported to have killed wildlife.[15]

Air pollution problems have apparently also been growing. The adoption of a few simple control measures in the 1950s improved matters temporarily,

tion depots . . . offer special coupons for people who bring in 20 kilos of waste paper. With these coupons they are qualified to buy rare and desirable [popular] books. . . . People pick up such substantial amounts of change from bottle refunds that there is even a Soviet joke about it. 'I am earning 150 rubles a month; my wife makes 120 rubles and we pick up another 120 rubles from empty bottles and still we do not seem to have enough money to make ends meet'," (*New York Times,* January 26, 1975, Business and Finance Section, p. 61). This should be compared with the rocky road travelled by proposals for compulsory container deposits in the U.S., which is discussed in Chapter 18.

[8] David E. Powell, "The Social Costs of Modernization: Ecological Problems in the USSR," *World Politics* (July 1971), pp. 618–34.

[9] *New York Times,* April 9, 1970, p. 12. One ruble is approximately $1.11 at the *official* exchange rate.

[10] Goldman, *Spoils of Progress,* p. 170.

[11] Powell, "Social Costs of Modernization," p. 622.

[12] *Izvestia,* January 28, 1969, p. 2 as in *Current Digest of the Soviet Press,* Vol. 21, No. 4, February 12, 1969, p. 28.

[13] *New York Times,* April 2, 1972, p. 5.

[14] *New York Times,* March 22, 1971, p. 9.

[15] Philip R. Pryde, "Soviet Pesticides," *Environment,* November 1971, pp. 16–24.

but industrial growth has since undone their effects. Two specialists from the Forestry Laboratory of Gosplan (the central planning agency) have observed

> The growth of industrial establishments and large enterprises of factories and mills, as well as the development in the last few decades of automotive transport in Moscow, as in many other large cities in the USSR, caused the discharge into the air of millions of tons of gas, smoke, dust, and other pollutants. Accumulated smoke forming a dense, dirty smog can often be seen over large industrial cities. Quite frequently this dense, dirty fog hangs over the city at a height of 500 meters, and even the ultra-violet rays have difficulty penetrating it even in the heat of summer. In most cases, these rays do not reach the earth's surface.[16]

Because of emissions from chimneys, there are 40 percent fewer clear daylight hours in Leningrad than in Pavlovsk, a town only twenty miles away. As in the United States, there is evidence that polluted air has killed forests which are located downwind from smokestacks and has damaged the health of residents. Metallurgical plants, after severely polluting the air in their vicinity, have been forced to build long tunnels to provide the pure air needed for their own manufacturing processes! Rejection rates as high as 96 to 98 percent have been reported in electronic shops contaminated by impure air.[17]

While less is known about other economies of the Soviet type, they also suffer from pollution. Smoke from soft coal emitted by home heating systems hangs over the cities of Eastern Europe. "Pollution levels comparable to New Jersey" are to be found in the industrial districts of Poland, Hungary, and Czechoslovakia. A Hungarian trade union newspaper estimates the cost of air pollution at $700 million a year, largely a result of reduced harvests in areas near chemical plants. The Balkan states, long underdeveloped, now contend with air and water pollution emitted by their new factories.[18]

3. The Case of the Caspian and Aral Seas

The Caspian and Aral Seas have undergone perhaps the most spectacular of the environmental changes introduced by human intervention in the Soviet Union. These two bodies of water are located in an extremely arid region where evaporation rates are high and rain is scarce. They depend heavily on the supply

---

[16]M.Y. Nuttonson, ed., *The Susceptibility or Resistance to Gas and Smoke of Various Arboreal Species Grown Under Diverse Environmental Conditions in a Number of Industrial Regions of the Soviet Union. AICE Survey of USSR Air Pollution Literature,* Vol. 3 (Silver Spring, Maryland: American Institute of Crop Ecology, 1970), pp. 13–14, as cited in Goldman, *Spoils of Progress,* p. 124–25.
[17]Goldman, *Spoils of Progress,* p. 140.
[18]*New York Times,* January 3, 1970, p. 2.

of water from the rivers that feed them. During Stalin's regime, the Soviets undertook enormous hydroelectric and irrigation projects; much of this activity focused on the Volga River, a prime source of water for the Caspian. Thirteen large dams and numerous canals and reservoirs were built along that river. Simultaneously, newly constructed dams and related projects altered the courses of many other rivers affecting these seas.[19] The diversion of all this water from the Caspian and the Aral has had serious consequences. In 1929 the level of the Caspian Sea, and in 1960 that of the Aral Sea, began to fall rapidly. The rate of fall of the Caspian has increased almost tenfold. The Aral, whose average depth is a bit over 16 meters, is expected to fall more than 4 meters between 1960 and 1980, and its area is projected to decline from some 65,000 square kilometers in 1960 to about 20,000 square kilometers in 1980. By the year 2000 all that may remain of the sea is a salt marsh.[20]

The social costs of all this activity have taken many forms. A great deal of valuable land was lost by flooding and salination resulting from the dam construction. The loss of water from these seas has reduced their ability to dilute pollutants. As a result of this and the disruption of breeding grounds, valuable fish, notably the sturgeon (and its caviar), have grown more scarce, though they have been replaced at least in part by less valuable species. In addition, fishing villages and steamship ports, formerly on the shore of the seas, now find themselves as much as thirty miles inland. Even the climate in the area has apparently been affected: winters have become longer and summers shorter. After the disappearance of the Aral, it has been suggested that the area may suffer from dust and salt storms and eventually become uninhabitable.[21] We should note, incidentally, that some of these problems do not fall on the Soviet Union alone. Iran, too, lies on the Caspian Sea, and the quality of its waters and its sturgeon and caviar supplies have presumably suffered.

Because the consequences of the shrivelling of these seas are so disturbing, there has been considerable interest in measures to protect and revive the Caspian and Aral (though some geographers have argued that it is not worth what it would cost to save them). Unfortunately, several of the proposed cures are more frightening than the disease. One project, major portions of which have already been completed, involves transporting water from Siberia across thousands of kilometers. This project actually calls for reversal of the flow of rivers with the aid of chains of pumping stations to make the water go in the uphill southern direction over the equivalent of the area's "continental divide." It may involve the construction of a canal nearly 2000 miles in length.

Naturally such a grandiose project has produced new fears: more water loss through evaporation, more loss of land by flooding and salination, and disruption of the underground water table for hundreds of miles. Local climatic

[19]Goldman, *Spoils of Progress*, pp. 221-23.
[20]Ibid., pp. 216-17.
[21]Ibid., pp. 225-38.

conditions may be altered, and the cut-off of river flows into the Arctic Ocean may unleash tremendous and unpredictable forces that, it has been argued, may change the climate of the Northern Hemisphere, perhaps rendering it subtropical. Fear has even been expressed that the spinning of the earth might be affected.[22] Surely, these engineering projects are, in themselves and in their potential consequences, grand in scale!

4. Soviet Institutions and Environmental Quality

To try to understand the sources of environmental deterioration in the Soviet Union (as in our earlier discussion of the pricing system in capitalist nations), we must examine the objectives and incentives operating in the economy. The Soviet experience suggests that the priorities and economic incentives adopted by Soviet planners have not been successful in promoting conservation and protection of the environment. Much of the difficulty has as its source the heavy emphasis upon increased production, almost regardless of its social costs.

In the early 1920s, Lenin and his followers found themselves in control of a giant underdeveloped nation seriously weakened by World War I and civil strife. To build a successful Soviet state amid the surrounding and hostile capitalist countries, they felt it necessary to give high priority to rapid industrialization and to the acceleration of economic growth. This goal has remained the major focus of Soviet economic policy in the half century that has passed since the revolution.

To carry out this policy Soviet officials have typically relied upon a system of production quotas, which specify *only output volumes*. We cannot stress this too strongly. *The set of economic incentives confronting plant managers primarily promotes output levels; plant managers have little motivation to do much about pollution and other social costs.* Note here the interesting parallel to the structure of incentives in a free market economy. In the latter, the basic economic incentive is to maximize profits; in the Soviet Union, the incentive is to maximize outputs. In either case the individual producer has little reason to take into account the costs he imposes on others through polluting activities.

Managerial salaries in the Soviet Union have been tied to fulfillment or overachievement of target outputs, and have been practically independent of any external damage incurred in the process, at least until the reforms of 1966. Managers now can be fined when convicted of polluting activities but, as in the United States, fines are often negligible in magnitude. "The manager would rather pay a fine of 500 rubles if it means he can earn a premium of 5000-10,000 rubles for overfulfilling his plan."[23] Quite often the fine is paid out of

---

[22] Ibid., Chap. 8.
[23] *Sotsialisticheskaia industriia*, August 15, 1790, p. 2, as cited in Goldman, *Spoils of Progress*, p. 67.

the funds of his enterprise (which frequently include special provisions for such expenses!), and he then suffers no personal loss at all. In such an atmosphere, it should not surprise us that the country's resources, especially "free goods" such as air and water, have been used wastefully, without regard for the ecological consequences.

With all the emphasis on production, there is little incentive to invest in pollution-control devices. Money spent on such equipment typically contributes nothing to output and may even impede production activities. Moreover, if enterprises strive to maximize production per ruble of invested capital, nonproductive installations can only reduce performance.[24] When asked why a new filter was not installed in his plant, the manager of a paper factory replied,

> "It's expensive. . . . The Ministry of Timber, Paper and Woodworking is trying to invest as few funds as possible in the construction of paper and timber enterprises in order to make possible the attainment of good indices per ruble of capital investment. This index is being achieved by the refusal to build purification installations."[25]

There are countless cases in which funds have been allocated for effluent control but not spent, even though the devices were required by law.

Accordingly, the low levels of pollution-control technology in the Soviet Union are easy to understand. Most purification devices suffer from inefficient and often untested designs, poor workmanship, capacities too low for the jobs assigned them, and inadequate maintenance. This simply has not been an objective of high priority. Soviet programs have not encouraged students to specialize in pollution-control technology and have introduced only limited and poorly coordinated instruction. Salaries of persons responsible for the abatement of pollution are below those in other factory departments, bonus opportunities are fewer, and there is general hostility from production managers and local officials.[26]

While both the United States and the Soviet Union have treated air and water as essentially free goods, the Soviet Union has extended this treatment to other natural resources. Communist ideology holds that all resources belong to the state, and it has been argued that they should be provided freely to any authorized user. For many years state mining and oil enterprises paid nothing at all for the use of the land and its resources. Although such use is no longer free, the price paid is still so low that these enterprises find it more profitable to move their operations from one mine or oil field to the next as they exhaust the richest and most accessible deposits, rather than continue a less efficient

---

[24] Powell, "Social Costs of Modernization," p. 625.
[25] *Current Digest of the Soviet Press,* March 24, 1965, p. 25, as cited in Goldman, *Spoils of Progress,* p. 188.
[26] See Powell, "Social Costs of Modernization," pp. 623–24.

extractive process at an old site. As a result, recovery rates have been very low compared to those in other countries, and large quantities of salvageable materials are often discarded. A few Soviet economists have gone so far as to advocate measures similar to effluent charges under which each plant would pay (at least approximately) the social costs of its activities, and would thereby be provided with a strong incentive to reduce the damage it imposes on the community resources.[27] However, so far, any such program has foundered on the view that in a socialist society resources must belong to everyone and so must be free to anyone who wishes to use them, at least for "legitimate" purposes. Thus

> Almost no calculation [is] made, for example, of the losses we would suffer if the industry discharged every year so much poisonous wastes into the air, or dumped so much water polluted with harmful substances, the effect it will have on the health and longevity of the people, how much it will decrease the available amounts of drinking water, irrigation water, etc.[28]

5. Pollution-Control Measures in the Soviet Union

Many of the corrective policies that have been proposed or undertaken in the Soviet Union are very similar to the measures that have been suggested for a market economy. Soviet agencies have issued appeals to conscience; they have sought to persuade managers to curb the emissions of their plants voluntarily. As in other societies, this approach seems to have achieved few tangible results. A variant on the voluntaristic approach has been the attempt to convince firms to extract valuable byproducts from wastes they formerly discarded with a resulting increase in output and reduction in levels of effluents.

In addition to the use of exhortation, the Soviets have enacted a comprehensive set of laws and regulations for the protection of the environment, some dating back to Lenin's time. These regulations set water and air quality standards, require approved purification devices before factories are permitted to begin operations, and prohibit various damaging practices (such as the removal of pebbles from the Black Sea shore or the cutting of timber in certain locales). However, the effectiveness of these laws has been undercut by lax enforcement and very low penalties for violations. The number of polluters actually prosecuted is small, and the courts are lenient with them. Even though

---

[27]It is worth noting that a number of the East European countries do use an effluent charge system (this is true, for example, of Hungary, East Germany, and Czechoslovakia), whereas most of the capitalist countries don't. In principle, the policy in effect proclaims that the polluter should bear the costs of his actions but in practice the charges are quite low relative to secondary treatment costs.

[28]*Pravda Ukrainy,* August 29, 1967, as cited in Powell, "Social Costs of Modernization," p. 625.

prosecutions have increased slightly, they usually are brought against individual violators, while government agencies are granted virtual immunity. Yet public institutions—factories, farms, municipalities—are responsible for the bulk of Russia's environmental problems. The penalties provided by the law include fines, jail sentences for managers responsible for the prevention of pollution, and the complete shutdown of polluting enterprises. Forced closings have rarely been attempted. As one critic complained, "If . . . an enterprise does not fulfill its production plan, its executives have to make a strict accounting to the party organization, the trust and the ministry. But when this same enterprise pollutes the air and releases dirty water into a river, . . . it is hardly likely that anyone will demand an accounting from the guilty parties."[29]

6. Some Fragmentary Information from Mainland China

Reliable and systematic evidence on the maintenance of environmental quality in Communist China is scarce, but there is some and it presents a rather mixed picture. At the United Nations Conference on Human Environment in Stockholm in 1972, the Chinese declared that "we hold that the major social root cause of environmental pollution is capitalism . . . seeking high profits, not concerned with the life or death of people, and discharging poisons at will."[30]

However, reports from China suggest that they too have experienced some dramatic episodes of environmental damage. Like the Soviets earlier in the century, the Chinese found themselves in a state of retarded economic development in a relatively hostile world atmosphere. Their response was to place heavy stress on rapid economic growth which, as in the Soviet Union, has had some adverse side effects on the environment. One observer reports that:

> It would be easy to assume that in a country where only 15 percent of the population live in urban areas and where vehicular traffic is insignificant, air pollution would not be a serious problem. In fact, it isn't for most people—but those who live in the large industrial centers have had to breathe air that is as bad as is likely to be found anywhere in the world. The normal pollution of industry is greatly intensified by the widespread use of coal for both power and heat, and China's northern cities in particular are notorious for the constant heavy pall of pollution, which becomes incredibly heavy in the winter.[31]

He goes on to note that ". . . Chinese managers of factories, who are also judged by their ability to show 'profit', were reluctant to spend limited capital in ways that would not reflect higher productivity."[32]

---

[29]*Pravda Ukrainy*, September 10, 1967, as found in Powell, "Social Costs of Modernization," p. 626.
[30]Taken from Orleans, "China's Environomics," pp. 118-19.
[31]Ibid., p. 132.
[32]Ibid., pp. 132-33.

On the other hand, there have been a number of impressive reports involving not only certain instances of reduced air and water pollution, but also of substantial progress in health and sanitation. Particularly in the 1970s, the Chinese have launched new efforts aimed at protection of the environment, some of which involve extensive recycling of wastes. But as late as 1973, a visitor, following a meeting at the Institute of Hygiene in Peking which stressed environmental matters, found himself a few days later at China's largest iron and steel works where "the smoke was so heavy that visibility was limited to no more than a couple hundred yards. I attempted to inquire about the air pollution and what was being done about it. No one seemed to know what I was talking about, and of course, no one had heard of the Institute of Hygiene nor of any prescribed standards."[33]

7. A Concluding Comment

It is clear that central planning does not necessarily provide a better guarantee against environmental abuse than does the invisible hand of the free market system. Each requires special institutional arrangements for the control of externalities and the protection of society's irreplaceable resources. As we have seen, both economic systems have suffered in this area from rather similar shortcomings in their organizations: *in neither do polluters bear the costs that their actions impose upon the community.* In both cases there has been heavy reliance upon direct controls that are severe in appearance but which are often, in fact, all but toothless. In both systems public agencies dream up and carry out, against all opposition, projects of gigantic proportions that may leave indelible scars upon the surface of our planet.

The Soviets may be more vulnerable to damage from some of these sources, while we are more likely to suffer from others. We have, indeed, seen evidence that we have experienced greater damage associated with heavy consumption, particularly of energy and especially from the consumption of fuel in our widespread use of automobiles. On the other hand, the Soviets are apparently more prone than we to the ravages of gigantic engineering projects whose environmental consequences are inadequately taken into account.

But that, perhaps, is not the most important moral. The fact is that from the point of view of quality of life, all countries are struggling with severe environmental problems. We must, therefore, be prepared to look to one another for fruitful ideas and effective programs, and we must not be deterred by the labels of measures as "bourgeois" or "socialistic."

---

[33] Ibid., p. 134.

6

Are We Running Out of Resources?

Certain recent studies have raised the spectre of complete exhaustion of some of the world's critical resources.[1] They tell us that, in the absence of drastic countermeasures, within a matter of decades mankind is likely to run out of petroleum, natural gas, and other vital fuels; to deplete virtually all the sources of various minerals such as mercury, copper, and silver; and to have cultivated essentially all remaining and still usable land. In brief, the world economy will be brought to the brink of catastrophe by the exhaustion of essential resources.

In this process the captains of industry are usually named as the villains. The contention is that their callous treatment of resources has resulted in the destruction of our forests and the ravaging of the land by strip mines. There is more than a little truth to these charges. But, although industry's record on resource conservation has not always been exemplary, we will contend (somewhat paradoxically) that the problem is not primarily the result of the untrammeled functioning of the market system. On the contrary, it is due to a failure to extend its role sufficiently. Industry, individuals, *and* governments

---

[1] See, for example, the report of the Club of Rome: Donella H. Meadows et al., *The Limits to Growth* (New York: Universe Books, 1972), which we will examine explicitly in Chapter 9.

have felt free to despoil resources, largely because they were *not* subject to the harsh discipline of the market mechanism and its heavy penalties for waste. As we saw in Chapter 4, the price mechanism will ordinarily prevent the sudden exhaustion of any important input, for as its scarcity increases, its price will rise and this will reduce its use accordingly. In this way, the price system can prevent an orgy of unabated waste that results in the disappearance of one resource after another.

In this and the following three chapters, we shall explore the issue of resource exhaustion. We begin with a survey of the facts concerning available stocks of key resources and then consider just how the pricing system allocates resources over time. We can then take a close look at the logic underlying some of the more frightening predictions of economic collapse from depletion of the world's resources.

1. Estimates of Scarcity of Various Resources

Each year the U.S. Bureau of Mines publishes estimates both of the U.S. and world demand for mineral resources and of the quantities of *identified* supplies of these resources. In Table 6-1, we present some recent estimates. Of particular interest is the last column in the table: it shows the ratio of identified stocks of resources to their expected demand over the whole period from 1974 to 2000. This provides a measure of the adequacy of known supplies of resources relative to their anticipated demands, a kind of "reserve-demand" index. A perusal of this column of figures indicates that this ratio varies considerably among different resources: for iron ore, for instance, identified supplies are almost 10 times the total demand for the last quarter of this century. In contrast, for two resources, fluorine and uranium, the ratio is less than one, which would seem, on first reflection, to indicate that we will exhaust the supplies of these two items prior to the turn of the century.

Even though they suffer from various sorts of inaccuracy, these figures for proven reserves are, unfortunately, all too often taken at face value and have served as the bases for some dire and rather naive predictions. But reserves are not "proven" by happenstance. Mineral exploration is expensive and is undertaken only when it is justified by prices, anticipated demands, and the levels of stocks currently known. As a result, active exploration typically takes place only as previously discovered reserves are used up; frequently, new reserves are found as fast, or even faster, than previously proven reserves run out. R. W. Wright has recently compared the reserve-demand indices for minerals for the years 1950, 1960, and 1969.[2] Although he obtained his basic data from three

---

[2] R. W. Wright, "Ferrous and Non-Ferrous Metal Resources," *Centennial Volume, American Institute of Mining, Metallurgical and Petroleum Engineers* (Dallas: Storm, 1971), p. 18.

TABLE 6-1

COMPARISON OF WORLD CUMULATIVE PRIMARY MINERAL DEMAND FORECASTS, 1974–2000, WITH WORLD MINERAL RESOURCES, 1974

Commodity	Units	Primary Mineral Demand 1974–2000			Identified Mineral Resources			Ratio of Identified Resources to Cumulative Demand[a]		
		United States	Rest of World	World	United States	Rest of World	World	United States	Rest of World	World
Aluminum (Bauxite only)[b]	million s.t.	316	646	962	50	6,260	6,310	0.2	9.7	6.6
Antimony	thousand s.t.	864	1,917	2,781	130	5,450	5,580	0.2	2.8	2.0
Arsenic	thousand s.t.	675	696	1,371	3,800	9,400	13,200	5.6	*	9.6
Barium	million s.t.	36	83	119	230	770	1,000	6.4	9.3	8.4
Beryllium	thousand s.t.	15	8	23	80	1,138	1,218	5.3	*	*
Bismuth	million lb	87	183	270	36	257	293	0.4	1.4	1.1
Cadmium	thousand s.t.	238	506	744	1,780	19,030	20,810	7.5	*	*
Chromium	million s.t.	21	80	101	2	1,155	1,157	0.1	*	*
Cobalt	million lb	793	1,774	2,567	1,684	7,756	9,440	2.1	4.4	3.7
Columbium	million lb	367	1,018	1,385	320	31,970	32,290	0.9	*	*
Copper[b]	million s.t.	78	275	353	410	1,640	2,050	5.3	6.0	5.8
Fluorine	million s.t.	38	96	134	15	60	75	0.4	0.6	0.6
Germanium	thousand lb	1,600	4,020	5,620	1,500	7,000	8,500	0.9	1.7	1.5
Gold	million t.oz	224	832	1,056	240	1,660	1,900	1.1	2.0	1.8
Indium	million t.oz	30	35	65	20	89	109	0.7	2.5	1.7
Iron ore	billion s.t.	3	19	22	18	197	215	6.0	*	9.8
Lead	million s.t.	31	105	136	119	211	330	3.8	2.0	2.4
Lithium	thousand s.t.	217	213	430	927	1,178	2,105	4.3	5.5	4.9
Manganese	million s.t.	46	362	408	74	3,526	3,600	1.6	9.7	8.8
Mercury	thousand fl	1,300	5,300	6,600	900	16,610	17,510	0.7	3.1	2.7
Molybdenum	billion lb	3	6	9	35	28	63	*	4.7	7.0
Nickel	million s.t.	7	22	29	15	108	123	2.1	4.9	4.2
Palladium[b]	million t.oz	26	55	81	80	475	555	3.1	8.6	6.9
Platinum[b]	million t.oz	27	70	97	120	725	845	4.4	*	8.7

TABLE 6-1 (Continued)

Commodity	Units	Primary Mineral Demand 1974–2000			Identified Mineral Resources			Ratio of Identified Resources to Cumulative Demand[a]		
		United States	Rest of World	World	United States	Rest of World	World	United States	Rest of World	World
Rhodium[b]	million t.oz	2	4	6	10	50	60	5.0	*	*
Selenium	million lb	59	63	122	347	1,038	1,385	5.9	*	*
Silver	million t.oz	4,500	9,000	13,500	5,700	16,930	22,630	1.3	1.9	1.7
Strontium	thousand s.t.	700	1,050	1,750	1,700	A	A	2.4	*	*
Tantalum	million lb	81	54	135	3	573	576	–	*	4.3
Tellurium	million lb	11	5	16	82	245	327	7.5	*	*
Tin	thousand l.t.	1,400	6,100	7,500	85	20,300	20,385	0.1	3.3	2.7
Tungsten	million lb	780	2,490	3,270	958	10,400	11,358	1.2	4.2	3.5
Zinc	million s.t.	57	182	239	130	1,530	1,660	2.3	8.4	6.9
Asbestos	million s.t.	26	162	188	20	255	275	0.8	1.6	1.5
Graphite	million s.t.	3	17	20	10	300	310	3.3	*	*
Phosphate rock	million s.t.	1,319	5,449	6,808	7,000	76,900	83,900	5.3	*	*
Potash	million s.t.	228	839	1,067	400	A	A	1.8	*	*
Natural gas	trillion c.f.	522	1,160	1,682	439[c]	NA	NA	0.8	NA	NA
Petroleum[d]	billion bbl	198	520	718	74[e]	NA	NA	0.4	NA	NA
Uranium	thousand s.t.	1,065	1,773	2,838	356	1,508	1,864	0.3	0.9	0.7

Source: United States Department of the Interior, *Mineral Facts and Problems*, 1975 ed., Bureau of Mines Bulletin 667 (Washington, D.C.: U.S. Government Printing Office, 1975), p. 33.

Note: Identified resources are specific bodies of mineral-bearing material whose location, quality, and quantity are known from geologic evidence supported by engineering measurements with respect to the demonstrated category, and include reserves and subeconomic resources. NA = not available. A = adequate. *Ratio of 10 or more.

[a]Excludes minerals where U.S. and rest of world ratios are more than 10.
[b]Includes hypothetical and speculative resources.
[c]Measured and inferred reserves.
[d]United States includes natural gas liquids.
[e]Measured, indicated, and inferred reserves.

different sources (and does not discuss their comparability), his findings, summarized in Table 6-2, are nevertheless highly suggestive. Wright concludes that for the noncommunist states "reserves are increasing in relation to consumption in the case of lead, iron, and oil, but decreasing in the case of zinc and nickel. The figures for copper, tin, and bauxite are inconclusive; and one can probably eliminate nickel on the grounds that the number of years of life in 1969 was still very considerable, leaving zinc as giving apparent cause for anxiety."[3]

P. T. Flawn, who has aso calculated reserve-demand indices for some thirty-two minerals, notes how little the indices have varied over time; he explains that "new discoveries have more or less kept pace with withdrawals from the reserve bank account and maintained a steady production/proved reserves ratio . . . [probably because] companies do not believe it good practice to invest large sums of money in development before it is necessary."[4] He follows up his estimates with a documented analysis of expected demand, discoveries, and substitutions both for the world and for the United States. Flawn suggests that there is a real danger of silver and mercury shortages in the foreseeable future, that copper may become scarce in the United States, that a shortage in gold is approaching, and that uranium may quickly become scarce if exploration continues to lag. Of course, these conclusions, too, are rather suspect. The proven reserves of a particular resource may have failed to grow, not because its supply is about to "run out," but because market conditions did not make sufficient exploration worthwhile.

TABLE 6-2

RESERVE-DEMAND INDICES FOR NON-COMMUNIST STATES
OF SEVERAL CRITICAL METALS, 1950-69
(million metric tons)

	1950	1960	1969
Copper	63	49	59
Lead	18	16	26
Zinc	26	26	22
Tin[a]	25	25	25
Bauxite	–	252	279
Nickel[a]	140	195	135
Iron[a]	527	686	>1000?
Oil	25	39	32

Source: Roy W. Wright, "Ferrous and Non-Ferrous Metal Resources," *Centennial Volume, American Institute of Mining, Metallurgical and Petroleum Engineers* (Dallas: Storm, 1971), p. 18.

[a]Possible as well as probable reserves.

---

[3]Ibid., p. 18.
[4]P. T. Flawn, *Mineral Resources* (Chicago: Rand McNally, 1966), p. 273.

2. Rising Extraction Costs vs. Absolute Exhaustion

The central issue is not one of *total* exhaustion of our resources; it is, rather, a matter of increasing costs of extraction. The basic principle is that, if demand outstrips new discoveries of ore concentrations, mining normally moves on to more expensive sources (that is, to lower-grade ores or deposits with greater difficulty of extraction).[5]

Proven reserves refer to the known stock of the item that is economically exploitable *under current technology and under current or expected economic conditions.* These reserves vary with price because, as prices rise, it may pay to include in the feasible reserve ores of relatively low grade, high impurity, great depth, or poor location which are more expensive to extract. This relationship between price and the quantity supplied is known in economics as the *supply curve.* The single figure that is sometimes given as the estimated level of reserves refers, in effect, to one point on this supply curve (usually that point corresponding to the current price of the resource).

In some instances, a study may report the general shape of the supply curve for a particular resource. This is, in fact, a much more informative way of describing available reserves, for it indicates the additional quantities of a resource that can be extracted at progressively higher cost. As one example, Table 6-3 reports estimated mercury reserves in relation to market price for

TABLE 6-3

MERCURY RESERVES OF UNITED STATES AT SELECTED PRICE LEVELS

Mercury Price per Flask	Potential Total Production (flasks)
$100	46,000
200	140,000
300	379,000
500	827,000
1,000	1,287,000
1,500	1,465,000

Source: U.S. Bureau of Mines, *Mercury Potential of the United States,* Information Circular 8252 (Washington, D.C.: U.S. Government Printing Office, 1965), p. 22.

---

[5] Recently one writer has, however, questioned the conventional assumption that as high-grade resources are exhausted, abundant quantities of lower-grade stocks of the same resources can be found. Apparently, many geologists now believe that the lower-grade stocks are often scarcer than the high-grade reserves. See D. A. Brobst, "New Systems Approach to the Analysis of Natural Resource Scarcity" (Paper presented at a forum of Resources for the Future, Washington, D.C., October 18-19, 1976).

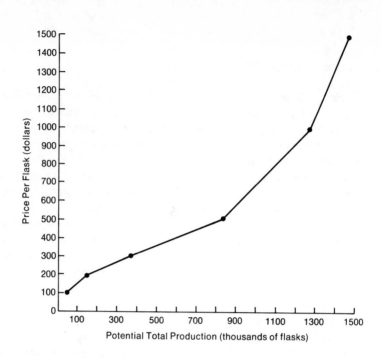

Figure 6-1 Mercury Supply Curve.

Source: See Table 6-3.

the United States. In Figure 6-1 we depict this information in the form of a supply curve. The curve shows the relationship between the price of mercury and the quantity of available reserves; it indicates the larger amounts that will be available at higher prices.[6] Note how responsive mercury reserves are to increases in price. For example, doubling in price from $100 to $200 per flask is estimated to triple reserves. Ultimately the curve begins to level off; this implies that, after some point, increasing price begins to lose its power to call forth substantially larger supplies.

As a last resort, we can always turn to ordinary rock or even sea water as a source for needed resources. This is not so absurd as it may sound. Table 6-4 indicates the concentrations of certain important minerals in crystal rock and in the world's oceans. With a sufficient input of energy, we could indeed "mine the seas."[7] All this, however, is to underscore the basic point: the prob-

---

[6]This supply curve differs from the normal supply curve in that it is a stock-price relationship rather than a flow-price relationship; it relates price to the quantity of available reserves at a point in time, rather than to the quantity supplied per unit of time. We might call it a "stock supply curve."

[7]See Harrison Brown, James Bonner, and John Wier, *The Next Hundred Years* (New York: The Viking Press, 1957).

TABLE 6-4

ABUNDANCES OF IMPORTANT MINERALS IN ROCK AND SEA WATER

Element	Symbol	Abundance in Crustal Rocks (parts per million)	Abundance in Sea Water (mg/l)
Aluminum	Al	81,300	0.01
Antimony	Sb	0.2	0.0005
Chromium	Cr	200	0.00005
Copper	Cu	45	0.003
Gold	Au	0.005	0.000004
Iron	Fe	50,000	0.01
Lead	Pb	15	0.00003
Magnesium	Mg	20,900	1350
Manganese	Mn	1,000	0.002
Mercury	Hg	0.5	0.00003
Molybdenum	Mo	1	0.01
Nickel	Ni	80	0.002
Phosphorous	P	1,180	0.07
Platinum	Pt	0.005	–
Silver	Ag	0.1	0.0003
Sulphur	S	520	885
Tin	Sn	3	0.003
Tungsten	W	1	0.0001
Uranium	U	2	0.003
Vanadium	V	110	0.002
Zinc	Zn	65	0.01

Sources: For crustal rocks, B. Mason, *Principles of Geochemistry* (New York: Wiley, 1958), p. 44; for seawater, E. D. Goldberg, "The Oceans as a Chemical System," in M. N. Hill, *The Sea* (New York: Wiley, 1963), 2: 4-5.

lem of resource exhaustion is, in truth, one of the rising cost of obtaining additional quantities of resources, not one of imminent absolute exhaustion.

3. Rising Cost as a Test of Increasing Scarcity

Our discussion of the supply curve suggests another way to test whether there is, in fact, an increasing scarcity of minerals. We can examine the trend over time in the cost or the price of each resource to see whether it has been rising significantly. Although prices can be influenced by the policies of a cartel or by other quasi-monopolistic arrangements as well as by regulatory intervention, the trends may still be highly suggestive. Certainly it is hard to believe that any resource whose price falls consistently without regulatory interference is really growing very scarce relative to prospective demand.

Following this logic, Barnett and Morse assembled the unit costs of extraction of thirteen minerals for the period 1870 to 1957.[8] They found that costs in fact declined rapidly for all the minerals except lead and zinc, for which the decline was quite small. Rejecting several other explanations, they concluded that the bulk of the cost savings were attributable to technological advances in resource extraction.

The data used by Barnett and Morse end in 1957, and so we have reexamined price trends for fifteen minerals including oil and natural gas, using data extending from 1900 through 1975, a total of more than seven decades.[9] Table A in the Appendix shows for each year from 1900 to 1975 the ratio of the price index for each mineral to the wholesale price index.[10] That is, it gives the price of each resource measured in dollars of constant purchasing power. As we might expect, the series are somewhat erratic: mineral prices have fluctuated roughly in the same pattern as wholesale prices but with somewhat greater amplitude. To smooth out the irregularities in the price figures we calculated nine-year averages of the prices; these appear for selected years in Figures 6-2, 6-3, and 6-4. (Note that the years 1900-1903 and 1972-75 are "lost" in the process of calculating the moving averages.)

The most striking fact that emerges is that, over the period considered (which encompasses nearly three-quarters of a century), the prices of seven of the fifteen resources investigated actually fell *after correction for changes in the value of the dollar.* These items include lead, copper, aluminum, mercury, magnesium, liquid natural gas, and natural gas, (though the price of the last of these was subject to extensive regulatory intervention). None of the price rises can really be considered very substantial; in constant dollars most of them rose at a rate of less than 1 percent per year. We should note that the price decreases tend to be concentrated toward the beginning of the period, while increases begin to preponderate toward its end. This may suggest increasing scarcity in recent years (particularly since 1960), but is hardly evidence of imminent exhaustion.[11]

----

[8] These were petroleum and natural gas, bituminous and anthracite coal, iron ore, copper, lead and zinc, fluorspar, sand and gravel, stone, phosphate rock and sulfur. H. J. Barnett and Chandler Morse, *Scarcity and Growth* (Baltimore: Published for Resources for the Future by The Johns Hopkins University Press, 1963), Part 3, Chaps. 8 and 9.

[9] We used those minerals for which price data are readily available: crude oil, anthracite and bituminous coal, natural gas, liquid natural gas, iron ore, copper, lead, zinc, tin, aluminum, platinum, magnesium, mercury, and antimony. The tests were designed and carried out by Jack Frisch.

[10] The price data for energy sources and wholesale prices through 1955 are taken from S. H. Schurr et al., *Energy in the American Economy, 1850-1975* (Baltimore: Published for Resources for the Future by The Johns Hopkins University Press, 1960) and U.S. Bureau of Mines, *Minerals Yearbook* (Washington, D.C.: U.S. Government Printing Office), various issues. Mineral prices for the entire period and the wholesale price index since 1955 are taken from American Metal Market, *Metal Statistics* (New York: Fairchild), various issues.

[11] Although the trends of costs or prices of natural resources are surely suggestive as to their relative scarcity over time, they are far from conclusive evidence. Several authors have recently pointed out certain shortcomings in these cost-price trends as a measure for indicating national resource scarcity. As one example, current technological improvements

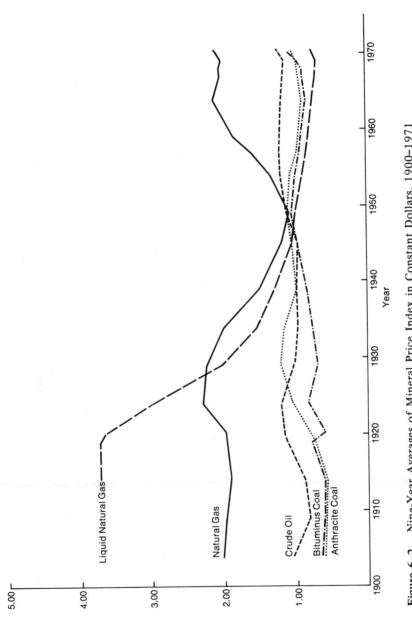

Figure 6-2 Nine-Year Averages of Mineral Price Index in Constant Dollars, 1900–1971 (using wholesale price index to correct for purchasing power of the dollar).

Source: Table 6–A1, Appendix.

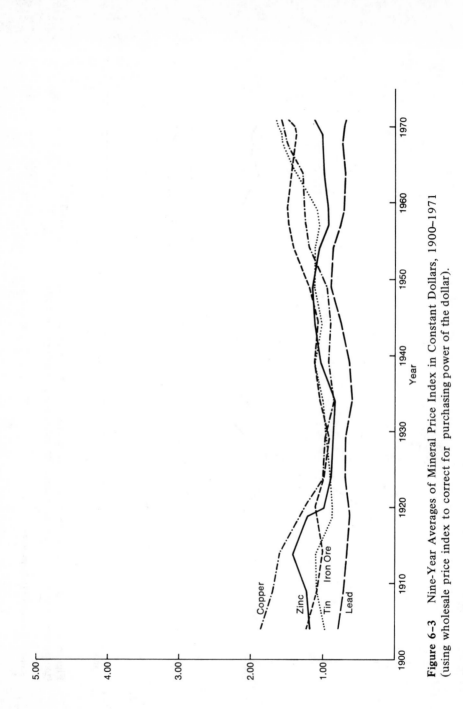

Figure 6-3 Nine-Year Averages of Mineral Price Index in Constant Dollars, 1900–1971 (using wholesale price index to correct for purchasing power of the dollar).

Source: Table 6–A1, Appendix.

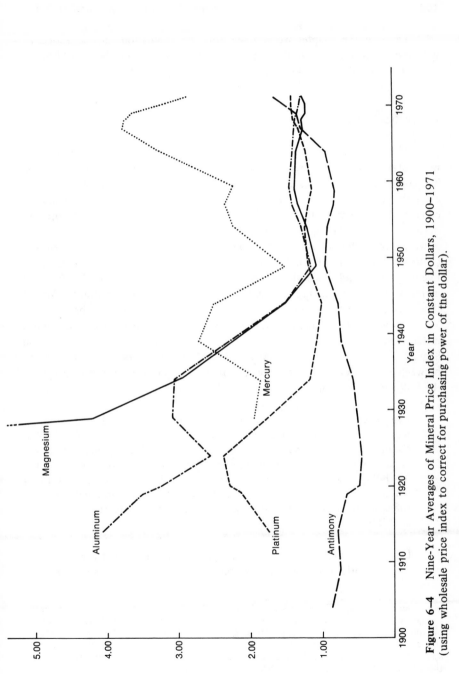

Figure 6-4 Nine-Year Averages of Mineral Price Index in Constant Dollars, 1900–1971 (using wholesale price index to correct for purchasing power of the dollar).

Source: Table 6–A1, Appendix.

Later in the chapter we will see how this evaluation can be reconciled with the great rash of scarcities experienced in certain periods in the 1970s: the shortages of gasoline, heating fuel, natural gas, newsprint, and even toilet tissue.

4. The Growing Demand for Resources

The industrial revolution brought with it growing demand for power and raw materials such as the world had never seen. The fantastic rate of expansion has continued throughout the twentieth century. It has been estimated, for example, that, in the first two decades of the twentieth century, mankind consumed more energy than it had used in total over all the previous centuries of its existence. During the following two decades, we again employed more power than in the totality of the past (including the part of the twentieth century that preceded it). Moreover, a similar statement has held for each twenty-year period since then. We see in Figures 6-5 and 6-6 the dramatic increases in recent energy consumption. Moreover, simple extrapolation of these trends suggests how enormous future demands for energy may be.

Obviously, the utilization of these resources in different parts of the world is far from uniform. It is heaviest in the Western industrialized societies and heaviest by far in the United States. The difference in consumption patterns between the United States and the rest of the world is brought out strikingly in the following quotation:

> Even if world population growth stopped in 1972, world iron production would have to be increased about sixfold, copper production almost sixfold, and lead production about eightfold to bring global per capita consumption to the present United States level . . . to raise all of the 3.8 billion people of the world of 1972 to the American standard of living would require the extraction . . . of some 250 times as much tin, 200 times as much lead, 100 times as much copper, 75 times as much zinc, and 75 times as much iron.[12]

Dramatic figures on heavy resource utilization and rapidly growing demand in the world as a whole have inspired a chorus of forecasts of imminent

---

in extraction techniques may more than offset the fact that available deposits are becoming less accessible and/or are deteriorating in quality. Thus unit costs could fall over this period, but this says nothing about future costs of extraction which, conceivably, could suddenly rise quite dramatically. For a careful examination of price measures as an indicator of scarcity, see Gardner Brown, Jr. and Barry Field, "The Adequacy of Measures for Signaling the Scarcity of Natural Resources" (Unpublished manuscript, presented at American Economic Association Annual Meeting, Atlantic City, N.J., September 1976).

[12] See Paul R. Ehrlich and Anne H. Ehrlich, *Population, Resources, Environment* (San Francisco: Freeman, 1972), pp. 72-73.

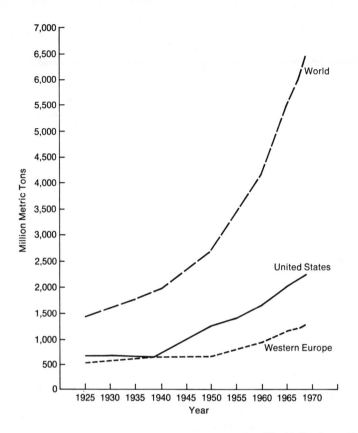

Figure 6-5 Energy Consumption by Selected Major World Regions, Selected Years, 1925–68 (all figures based on coal equivalents).

Source: Graph derived from figures in Joel Darmstadter, with Perry D. Teitelbaum and Jaroslave G. Polach, *Energy in the World Economy, A Statistical Review of Trends in Output, Trade and Consumption Since 1925* (Baltimore: Published for Resources for the Future by The Johns Hopkins University Press, 1971), p. 10. For actual figures from which graph was drawn see Table 6-A2, Appendix.

doom. We will examine some of these prophecies more systematically in Chapter 9, but let us note here that, fortunately, these apocalyptic visions suffer from at least one critical oversight: their implicit assumption that trends in demand are immutable and beyond the reach of normal economic influences. In particular, these forecasts typically assume that demand is completely unresponsive to price changes.

Yet such an assumption flies in the face of virtually all economic experience. There is generally a wide range of uses for most resources along with considerable scope for the substitution of alternative inputs. Petroleum is used to make plastics, to heat homes, to carry out industrial processes, to transport

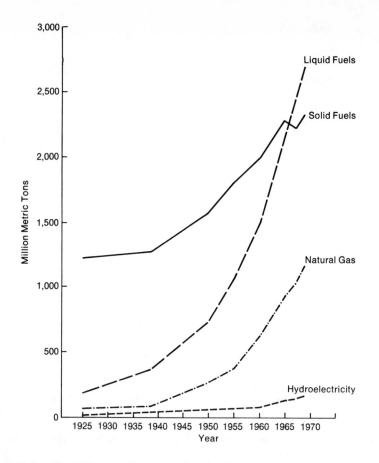

Figure 6-6 World Energy Consumption, by Source, Selected Years, 1925–68 (all figures based on coal equivalents).

Source: Darmstadter et al., *Energy in the World Economy,* p. 13. See Appendix Table 6-A3 for figures.

goods, to drive people to work, or for weekend pleasure trips. As its price goes up, portions of industry can and do switch readily to substitutable fuels. We soon find that plants are built closer to their sources of inputs or their markets to economize on transportation, that families insulate their homes more effectively, that people purchase smaller cars that use less gasoline, and, at the same time, that they cut down on less essential trips.

Indeed, during the fuel crisis of 1973-74 that is precisely what happened. The market for large vehicles all but collapsed, while demands for small cars simply could not be satisfied. More generally, there seem to have been "surprising reductions in quantities demanded. Crude oil supplies available in the United States from both domestic production and imports declined from their peak [over a three-month period] by 9.6%. However, crude oil stocks in the United States increased 1.2% over the same time period."[13]

The point is that, as a resource grows scarcer, its price normally tends to increase as a result of the forces of supply and demand. That, in and of itself, serves to keep demands in check. This is true whether an item is commonly regarded as a "necessity" or a "luxury"; a commodity which is totally unresponsive to changes in its price has yet to be found. Moreover, as we shall discuss in the next chapter, the higher price provides an incentive to recover and recycle used resources.

Even so, one must not assume away the prospective problems implied by the growing consumption of resources. Higher prices can help check the expansion in resource use through reduced consumption and increased recycling and, at the same time, can induce more search and production to expand supply, but neither reduced demand nor expanded exploration can make our finite resources limitless. In addition, a growing world population with rising incomes will work in the direction of increasing demand for the resources.

There surely are valid grounds for concern over the waste and abuse of resources that occur in our economy. It is therefore of some importance to examine the sources of the problem and to consider the means available to deal with it. To this we turn in the next chapter.

---

[13]Walter J. Mead, "Discussion of 'Dynamic Demand Analysis of Selected Energy Resources' by H. S. Houthakker, P. K. Verleger, and D. P. Sheehan" (Paper prepared for a Joint Session of the American Economic Association and the American Agricultural Economic Association, New York City, December 29, 1973), p. 3.

APPENDIX

TABLE 6-A1

RATIO OF MINERAL PRICE INDEX TO WHOLESALE PRICE INDEX
(base: 1947 = 1.00)

Year	Oil	Anthracite Coal	Bituminous Coal	Natural Gas	Liquid Natural Gas	Iron Ore	Copper	Lead	Zinc	Tin	Aluminum	Platinum	Magnesium	Mercury	Antimony
1900	1.63	.54	.66	3.12		1.35	2.07	.79	1.05	1.02					.85
	1.34	.62	.68	2.55		1.10	2.12	.80	1.00	.93					.83
	1.05	.64	.68	2.39		1.44	1.44	.70	1.12	.87					.75
	1.21	.71	.74	2.37		1.27	1.61	.72	1.27	.90					.58
	1.11	.65	.66	2.36		.95	1.55	.73	1.17	.90					.58
	.79	.62	.63	2.05		1.13	1.86	.79	1.34	1.00					.85
	.91	.61	.64	1.84		1.30	2.24	.93	1.37	1.23					1.64
	.85	.60	.62	1.93		1.47	2.27	.83	1.28	1.12					1.16
	.88	.62	.63	2.04		1.08	1.50	.68	1.02	.89		.89			.60
	.80	.56	.57	1.83		1.02	1.38	.64	1.10	.84		.88			.54
1910	.67	.55	.57	1.86		.94	1.30	.64	1.08	.93	3.45	1.14			.52
	.72	.61	.61	2.13	3.10	.92	1.36	.69	1.23	1.25	3.32	1.63			.51
	.82	.63	.59	2.04	3.89	.91	1.67	.66	1.39	1.28	3.45	1.62			.49
	1.05	.63	.60	2.05	4.09	.94	1.57	.64	1.12	1.21	3.58	1.58			.47
	.91	.62	.61	2.21	2.99	.84	1.39	.57	1.05	1.00	2.89	1.62			.55
	.71	.61	.58	2.17	3.18	.87	1.77	.68	2.80	1.06	5.20	1.66	50.77		1.88
	.99	.56	.55	1.76	4.51	1.01	2.29	.81	2.16	.97	7.52	2.39	34.08		1.31
	1.02	.50	.69	1.43	4.38	1.45	1.73	.75	1.04	1.00	4.62	2.14	12.13		.78
	1.16	.53	.70	1.53	3.80	1.12	1.31	.58	.85	1.26	2.63	1.98	9.75		.42
	1.11	.61	.64	1.46	3.69	.92	.98	.42	.72	.90	2.46	2.03	9.32		.26
1920	1.53	.65	.87	1.51	3.39	1.21	.81	.53	.71	.62	2.10	1.76	7.33		.24
	1.36	1.05	1.06	2.56	3.93	1.05	.93	.47	.71	.58	2.30	1.89	9.41		.22
	1.28	1.06	1.11	2.84	4.17	1.10	.99	.60	.85	.64	2.05	2.48	11.69		.25
	1.02	1.11	.95	2.46	2.64	1.15	1.04	.73	.94	.81	2.68	2.84	8.78		.34
	1.12	1.14	.80	2.34	2.51	.95	.95	.83	.92	.97	2.92	2.97	7.91	1.27	.49

TABLE 6-A1 (Continued)

Year	Oil	Anthracite Coal	Bituminous Coal	Natural Gas	Natural Gas Liquid	Iron Ore	Copper	Lead	Zinc	Tin	Aluminum	Platinum	Magnesium	Mercury	Antimony
	1.25	1.05	.70	2.24	2.89	.88	.97	.88	1.04	1.06	2.78	2.82	5.87	1.43	.75
	1.45	1.15	.73	2.35	2.80	.90	.99	.85	1.04	1.24	2.86	2.69	5.65	1.63	.71
	1.05	1.13	.74	2.28	2.11	.86	.97	.72	.93	1.28	2.82	2.02	5.04	2.20	.57
	.93	1.11	.69	2.27	2.23	.81	1.07	.66	.89	.99	2.62	1.93	4.02	2.27	.47
	1.03	1.13	.67	2.13	2.09	.86	1.35	.73	.97	.90	2.66	1.64	4.15	2.28	.42
1930	1.06	1.22	.70	2.18	1.88	.90	1.08	.65	.77	.70	2.92	1.21	3.93	2.40	.39
	.69	1.40	.75	2.37	1.34	.96	.82	.59	.74	.64	3.38	1.11	3.29	2.23	.41
	1.03	1.41	.72	2.44	1.38	.98	.64	.50	.68	.65	3.81	1.29	3.16	1.59	.38
	.78	1.30	.73	2.33	1.61	1.05	.78	.59	.90	1.13	3.75	1.14	3.00	1.60	.44
	1.03	1.17	.83	1.98	1.46	1.06	.81	.52	.81	1.33	3.05	1.15	2.64	1.75	.53
	.93	1.04	.79	1.79	1.50	1.02	.78	.51	.79	1.20	2.72	.99	2.65	1.60	.76
	1.04	1.06	.78	1.68	1.63	1.05	.84	.59	.88	1.09	2.69	1.25	2.62	1.79	.67
	1.05	.91	.80	1.46	1.52	1.16	1.10	.70	1.07	1.20	2.46	1.42	2.45	1.89	.79
	1.10	1.02	.88	1.54	1.42	1.21	.91	.61	.86	1.02	2.70	1.08	2.70	1.73	.70
	1.02	.97	.85	1.57	1.52	1.20	1.01	.66	.96	1.24	2.75	1.12	2.47	2.45	.71
1940	1.00	1.04	.87	1.42	1.03	1.25	1.03	.67	1.15	1.21	2.52	1.14	2.43	4.04	.79
	1.00	1.00	.89	1.39	1.12	1.17	.96	.67	1.21	1.09	2.00	.99	1.94	3.78	.71
	.93	.93	.86	1.28	.99	1.04	.85	.66	1.18	1.00	1.50	.87	1.64	3.55	.70
	.89	1.01	.93	1.25	1.09	1.00	.81	.64	1.13	.96	1.44	.83	1.44	3.37	.68
	.89	1.10	1.00	1.21	1.16	.99	.80	.63	1.21	.95	1.43	.83	1.43	2.04	.68
	.89	1.14	1.03	1.14	1.06	1.01	.79	.62	1.10	.93	1.40	.81	1.40	2.28	.66
	.90	1.16	1.01	1.08	.86	.98	.81	.68	1.02	.86	1.23	1.18	1.23	1.44	.63
	1.00	1.00	1.00	1.00	1.00	1.00	1.00	1.00	1.00	1.00	1.00	1.00	1.00	1.00	1.00
	1.24	1.05	1.11	1.00	1.29	1.15	.97	1.14	1.19	1.18	.97	1.34	.92	.89	1.01
	1.28	1.13	1.14	1.02	1.12	1.31	.91	1.02	1.14	1.24	1.11	1.20	.97	.90	1.13
1950	1.22	1.15	1.09	1.01	.97	1.29	.96	.85	1.24	1.15	1.11	1.20	.98	.83	.82
	1.10	1.11	.99	1.02	.93	1.29	.97	1.00	1.43	1.38	1.08	1.27	1.00	2.12	1.11
	1.13	1.12	1.02	1.12	.93	1.36	1.00	.97	1.34	1.38	1.13	1.35	1.03	2.02	1.14
	1.22	1.17	1.04	1.34	.99	1.39	1.20	.80	.92	1.08	1.23	1.33	1.13	2.02	.94

TABLE 6-A1 (Continued)

Year	Oil	Anthracite Coal	Bituminous Coal	Natural Gas	Natural Gas Liquid	Iron Ore	Copper	Lead	Zinc	Tin	Aluminum	Platinum	Magnesium	Mercury	Antimony
	1.26	1.03	.95	1.47	.91	1.40	1.23	.84	.89	1.03	1.26	1.25	1.17	2.75	.80
	1.25	.95	.94	1.51	.85	1.43	1.54	.90	1.01	1.06	1.36	1.23	1.29	3.03	.84
	1.21	.96	.98	1.52	.91	1.47	1.66	.92	1.07	1.10	1.45	1.44	1.41	2.62	.88
	1.31	1.02	1.00	1.54	.85	1.50	1.16	.82	.89	1.01	1.49	1.23	1.41	2.42	.86
	1.26	.99	.94	1.60	.85	1.53	1.00	.67	.79	.99	1.43	.89	1.39	2.21	.77
	1.21	.93	.93	1.74	.85	1.53	1.18	.67	.88	1.06	1.43	1.00	1.38	2.19	.76
1960	1.20	.87	.91	1.88	.87	1.52	1.22	.66	.98	1.05	1.57	1.11	1.38	2.02	.75
	1.21	.90	.89	2.04	.78	1.53	1.15	.60	.89	1.18	1.47	1.12	1.39	1.90	.82
	1.21	.89	.87	2.89	.78	1.52	1.18	.53	.89	1.19	1.38	1.11	1.38	1.84	.84
	1.21	.94	.85	2.13	.72	1.46	1.18	.61	.92	1.21	1.31	1.08	1.39	1.83	.84
	1.21	.97	.86	2.07	.72	1.45	1.23	.75	1.03	1.63	1.37	1.18	1.38	3.01	1.02
	1.17	.90	.84	2.06	.73	1.43	1.32	.86	1.08	1.81	1.39	1.28	1.36	5.39	1.08
	1.14	.83	.84	2.01	.77	1.38	1.32	.79	1.04	1.61	1.34	1.26	1.31	4.04	1.05
	1.16	.83	.85	2.04	.79	1.38	1.37	.73	1.00	1.51	1.37	1.39	1.31	4.47	1.05
	1.14	.86	.84	2.04	.68	1.34	1.53	.67	.95	1.42	1.36	1.45	1.28	4.79	1.02
	1.15	.96	.86	2.00	.61	1.31	1.71	.73	.99	1.52	1.39	1.48	1.23	4.37	1.24
1970	1.14	1.04	1.04	1.98	.65	1.38	1.92	.74	1.00	1.55	1.42	1.52	1.19	3.45	2.97
	1.18	1.10	1.14	2.04	.68	1.47	1.63	.64	1.03	1.50	1.39	1.37	1.18	2.43	1.43
	1.13	1.07	1.19	2.00	.66	1.47	1.53	.67	1.04	1.46	1.21	1.35	1.15	1.74	1.13
	1.15	1.05	1.17	2.05	.75	1.29	1.57	.63	1.08	1.66	1.02	1.43	1.02	1.47	1.16
	1.68	1.46	1.82	2.43	1.08	1.72	1.54	.75	1.56	2.43	1.16	1.47	1.35	1.66	2.59
1975	NA	NA	NA	NA	NA	2.11	NA	.64	1.54	1.91	1.24	1.23	1.69	.87	2.30

Sources: For fuels: Until 1955, Sam H. Schurr and Bruce C. Netschert, *Energy in the American Economy, 1850-1975* (Baltimore: Published for Resources for the Future by The Johns Hopkins University Press, 1960), pp. 545-47. From 1956 to 1975, average prices of energy minerals from U.S. Bureau of Mines, *Minerals Yearbook* (Washington, D.C.: U.S. Government Printing Office, various issues). Wholesale price index derived from American Metal Market, *Metal Statistics* (New York: Fairchild, various issues).

For minerals: Mineral price index and wholesale price index constructed from American Metal Market, *Metal Statistics*, various issues.

Note: NA = not available as yet.

TABLE 6-A2

ENERGY CONSUMPTION BY SELECTED MAJOR WORLD REGIONS,
SELECTED YEARS, 1925-68
(million metric tons coal equivalent)

Year	United States	Western Europe	World
1925	717.7	517.0	1,484.5
1938	669.4	619.2	1,790.1
1950	1,201.0	583.9	2,610.9
1955	1,370.3	748.2	3,358.2
1960	1,550.1	849.5	4,196.1
1965	1,881.6	1,117.2	5,474.6
1967	2,055.0	1,168.0	5,888.0
1968	2,173.0	1,242.0	6,306.0

Source: Joel Darmstadter, with Perry D. Teitelbaum and Jaroslave G. Polach, *Energy in the World Economy, A Statistical Review of Trends in Output, Trade and Consumption Since 1925* (Baltimore: Published for Resources for the Future by The Johns Hopkins University Press, 1971), p. 10.

Note: Corresponds to Figure 6-5 in text.

TABLE 6-A3

WORLD ENERGY CONSUMPTION, BY SOURCE,
SELECTED YEARS, 1925-68
(million metric tons coal equivalent)

Year	Solid Fuels	Liquid Fuels	Natural Gas	Hydroelectricity
1925	1,230.0	196.7	47.9	9.8
1938	1,291.8	375.8	99.7	22.8
1950	1,593.2	722.2	252.1	43.4
1955	1,816.6	1,092.7	389.6	59.2
1960	1,998.5	1,499.0	612.6	86.0
1965	2,290.8	2,159.1	912.1	112.6
1967	2,209.0	2,489.0	1,064.0	126.0
1968	2,315.0	2,702.0	1,157.0	132.0

Source: Darmstadter et al., *Energy in the World Economy*, p. 13.

Note: Corresponds to Figure 6-6 in text.

7

Conservation of Resources
and the Price System

1. The Role of Common Property Provisions[1]

Many, if not most, of the resources suffering abuse from industrial activity are properties that belong wholly or in part to the entire community. Waterways and the atmosphere are obvious examples. Beautiful mountains and valleys are not so clearly common properties; like other pieces of land, they are often bought and sold. But even though they belong legally to particular individuals, their beauty is, in an important sense, part of the legacy of the entire community.

While few things excite such general indignation as the misuse of resources that "belong to everyone," no resources are more difficult to protect from abuse. The trouble is that resources that belong to everyone *in general* belong to no one in particular, and become natural prey of the unscrupulous and the irresponsible.

An illustration shows the temptations inherent in common-property

---

[1] On this subject, see biologist Garrett Hardin's widely read essay, "The Tragedy of the Commons," *Science* 162 (December 13, 1968): 1243-48. A more detailed treatment is available in J. H. Dales, *Pollution, Property, and Prices* (Toronto: University of Toronto Press, 1968).

institutions. If a community of 5,000 people owns a property, say, a lake, in common, and one of those 5,000, the owner of a sawmill on the lake, creates $100,000 worth of water-pollution damage to the lake, he or she suffers only $20 or 1/5,000 of that damage; the rest of the cost of the damage is spread among the other members of the community.[2] Furthermore, even if the sawmill owner were to be moved by conscience to refrain from polluting the lake, competition may allow no choice in the matter. So long as some unprincipled business rival is prepared to take advantage of the opportunity to save on abatement costs by letting (most of) the damage to the common property be borne by others, our original sawmill owner cannot afford to bear the entire cost alone. Competition can force the hand of even the best-intentioned decision maker.

The issue is described well in a book that appeared early in the nineteenth century:

> Supposing that the earth yielded spontaneously all that is now produced by cultivation; still without the institution of property it could not be enjoyed; the fruit would be gathered before it was ripe, animals killed before they came to maturity; for who would protect what was not his own; or who would economize when all the stores of nature were open to him? . . .
>
> In this country, for instance, where the only common property consists in hedge-nuts and blackberries, how seldom are they allowed to ripen. . . .[3]

2. Current Pricing and Future Supplies of Resources

Just what does private ownership do to protect resources for the use of future generations? Obviously firms and individuals are more careful with their own property than with property that is not theirs exclusively. Yet it would seem that the owners of a forest might serve their interests equally well either by maintaining the forest for their heirs or by leaving a barren waste after they die and avoiding the expense of reforestation.

The machinery that penalizes such destruction is the market value of the property itself. We know the earnings of stockholders are composed of two parts: dividends and capital gains. Stockholders who do well on dividends but whose securities meanwhile fall in market value have little reason to con-

---

[2] One can think of this $100,000 either as the loss to the community in terms of reduced fishing, recreation, and available clean water, or alternatively as the cost of cleaning up the pollution to restore the purity of the lake (where we assume the cost of the cleaning to be apportioned equally among the members of the community).

[3] Mrs. J. H. Marcet, *Conversations in Political Economy*, 3rd ed. (London, 1819), pp. 60–61. The book, written by a friend of David Ricardo, was one of the first textbooks in economics. It is all in the form of a discussion between a Mrs. B and her young friend, Caroline, who invariably succumbs quickly to her mentor's economic arguments.

gratulate themselves on the profitability of their investment. The same logic applies to any property: a factory, a piece of farm land, a mine, or a forest. An owner's interests are never well served by a decision to increase the flow of current income if that causes a disproportionate fall in its market value.

How the future affects the *current* market value of a property is most easily indicated by illustration. Consider two hypothetical forests. The first is cut down over a period of ten years to yield $1 million in lumber, but the land is left an unusable mass of stumps. The second forest is cut down over the same period, but is simultaneously cleared and replanted so that at the end of the decade it is restored to its original condition. The first forest will then be virtually worthless at the end of the period, while (assuming no change in lumber or land prices over the time interval) the latter will have retained its original value. The careless destruction of the forest will deprive future consumers of some forest products, but in a market that functions effectively owners will themselves be harmed *because the market value of their property will fall by an amount equal to the present value of those future products.* If they care for their *own* interests, property owners will effectively look out for those of the future as well.[4]

If the future yield of reforestation is greater than its cost, it will be worthwhile from the point of view of the community. But then it will also be profitable to the owners of the forest. Note that, even if the yield comes after the death of the owners, reforestation is still in the owners' interest: the decrease in the *current* market value of their property will be greater than the amount of money they save by failure to replant, since potential purchasers will value the lost future output in the same way the owners would, had they survived.

The upshot of our discussion is that the market system contains powerful forces that can compel the most selfish decision makers to consider the interests of the future. If they fail to do so, they will be penalized correspondingly. To all this, however, there are two important provisos:

1. This analysis holds only for resources that are accorded the full protection of the price system; we have already seen, for example, that it does not work for common property resources.
2. The analysis requires for its working a market mechanism that functions well, without the interference of monopoly elements, *inappropriate* government intervention, or other externalities.

Later in the chapter we will see that in practice these requirements are not always met, and that this can cause problems sufficiently serious in certain

---

[4]This does not mean that replanting is always in the private or the social interest. It may make sense to clear some woods to make room for housing, for example. Neither is it always appropriate to make sacrifices for the future; in a poor community it may be irrational to take workers away from food production to speed up the construction of a factory that will benefit the population only many years later.

instances, to warrant explicit corrective measures. But these reservations do not invalidate the basic point: it is not the institution of private property that underlies our society's resource-depletion problems. On the contrary, much of the trouble lies in our failure to extend the range of property ownership sufficiently.

3. The Economics of Resource Depletion

We have thus seen that the pricing system allocates scarce resources among the different time periods and rations their use among competing alternatives at each point in time. Serious depletion in the supplies of a particular mineral will cause its price to rise, thereby discouraging its use, inducing the substitution of other inputs, and, at the same time, stimulating exploratory activity to seek out additional deposits of the now more valuable resource.[5] Moreover, the high prospective price will discourage immediate consumption and thereby strike a balance between current and future utilization of the remaining mineral stock. For this reason, forecasts of the disappearance of this or that resource probably will not be borne out by future developments unless we help the process along. We will, of course, have to adapt our patterns of consumption and production as particular raw materials begin to grow scarce, but the price system works to make the changeover a relatively gradual one. The price mechanisms will induce consumers and producers to introduce substitutes by making the scarce resource ever more expensive.

There is a real danger that threatens this course of events. The rising prices of "essential" resources that we have just described will probably elicit from consumers demands for price controls. But controls that effectively prevent prices from reflecting the increasing scarcity of a resource will leave it essentially unprotected. Consumption will continue unabated or even grow. In this scenario, we may well use up vital resources, but we will have no one but ourselves to blame.

We emphasize that this is no far-fetched and remote possibility. There are already demands for price controls on certain scarce resources. Despite all the clamor about the international fuel crisis and the prospect of continuing energy shortages, politicians feel compelled to push for pricing policies that will keep these resources "within everyone's reach." There *are* valid arguments against fully unrestricted price movements (for example, on the ground that they are inequitable between rich and poor). But certainly one cannot have it both ways: we cannot undermine the pricing process, but do nothing to ration scarce resources by some other means.

---

[5] Note, in this regard, the striking acceleration in the search for oil deposits since the increase in oil prices in recent years. It is hardly accidental that the discovery of rich deposits in the North Sea, Mexico, and elsewhere followed so quickly on the price rises.

4. A Recent Experience with a Scarce Resource: The 1973-74 U.S. Fuel Crisis

The fuel crisis of the winter of 1973-74 is a classic example of the effects of tampering with the price system without any attempt to institute an effective alternative scheme for rationing. Long before the advent of the crisis, there were repeated warnings that the growth of demand for fuel in the United States was rapidly outstripping those domestic supplies *that were relatively inexpensive to extract.* However, a number of public policies served to keep the domestic prices of oil and some of its substitutes at artificially low levels. First, domestic production and the depletion of domestic reserves have been favored by a variety of government subsidies for petroleum production, most notably the depletion allowance (which reduced the effective tax rates for the petroleum industry relative to those applicable to business generally), and the favorable treatment of certain drilling costs. At the same time, the Federal Power Commission had regulated the price of natural gas (a byproduct of oil production) and kept it well below the price of substitute fuels; this tended to discourage production of this energy source.

Over the postwar period, after correcting for changes in the purchasing power of the dollar, the prices of these fuels actually fell; in the case of natural gas, the real price fell *substantially.* All of this has encouraged profligate use of fuel, discouraged exploration for natural gas, and depleted the domestic reserves of inexpensive petroleum. Americans were encouraged to buy large gas-guzzling automobiles, and were offered little incentive for insulation of their homes to reduce fuel consumption. In brief, the low prices of energy to producers and consumers in the United States had generated a highly energy-intensive economy. At the same time, the imposition of environmental controls restricting the use of "dirty" fuels such as high-sulfur coal served to reduce usable supplies. A day of reckoning was virtually bound to come, and the Arab oil boycott seems only to have moved the date a bit earlier.

Now, while the oil boycott was perhaps not predictable, these other influences could have been foreseen and, in fact, were predicted well in advance of the crisis. Despite this, apparently nothing was done to arrange for a gradual rise in the prices of petroleum products, nor was there any plan for an effective rationing program.[6]

The result was a solution that seems to have combined the worst possible features of every conceivable policy. Prices were held back and then were

---

[6] Apparently, the lesson of this experience has still not been learned by some. According to the *New York Times* (March 15, 1975, p. 28) a group of 102 Congressmen has been advocating a 5 to 8 percent reduction in gasoline supplies accompanied by neither rationing nor increased taxes (higher gasoline prices) because "shrinkage of gasoline supplies by 8 percent would cause no filling station lines."

allowed to rise sharply and rapidly, permitting no orderly adjustments in production, purchase, and location decisions. But while prices were permitted to
rise, they were not allowed to rise far enough to eliminate the gap between
supply and demand. Thus consumers had neither inexpensive fuels nor the
supplies they wanted at the prevailing prices. On the east coast, there was virtual
anarchy in the distribution of fuel supplies: most gasoline stations had inadequate gas supplies; wherever there was gas, cars were lined up in long queues
(each car using up substantial quantities of gas in the process); often by the
time only half the line had been served, supplies had run out. The switch in
demand from large to small automobiles was so abrupt it left producers and
dealers stuck with unsalable inventories of large cars and equipment for the
manufacture of these larger vehicles. Moreover, there were many instances of
"price gouging" by gas-station operators, outright stealing of gasoline for resale
on the black market, and the dangerous storage of hoarded supplies of gasoline
in private garages. Truckers and gasoline-station operators went on "wildcat"
strikes, and some independent gas stations went out of business altogether.
The policy makers ended up (to paraphrase the late Francis Ysidro Edgeworth)
producing the chaos congenial to their mentality, and their reaction to that
chaos was to consider price rollbacks and the imposition of special taxes upon
the oil companies, both of which were virtually certain to intensify the shortages.

In the short run, then, it seems clear that national policy could have
chosen either a set of controlled prices together with an effective rationing
system, or a set of uncontrolled prices to allocate the available supplies. The
former might have been preferred for the protection it offered less-affluent
purchasers of fuels; the latter because it can help to stimulate supplies by offering higher prices to producers, and because it avoids the bureaucratic machinery
needed to administer a rationing process.

In the long run, however, we probably don't have a choice. No free society
seems prepared to tolerate a permanent system of rationing; we will, in all likelihood, eventually return the control of fuel prices to the forces of supply and
demand. What does this augur for the future? Will it lead to astronomical fuel
prices? Does it mean a major break in our way of life, with fuel consumption in
particular and living standards in general falling below any range in our experience?

This sort of forecast is always hazardous. However, there have been some
studies of the responsiveness of both demand and supply to price changes, which
take account of costs of supplies from alternative sources and of substitute fuels
and which explore the prospects for new technological developments. The
results of these studies do not support the most pessimistic of the prognostica-
tions. The studies generally agree that some further rise in fuel prices is to be
expected, but at least some of the estimates suggest, for example, that the
market-clearing price of gasoline in the absence of additional taxes may rise

some ten or twenty cents per gallon (*in 1974 prices*) from their 1973-74 levels.[7] A price of, say, seventy cents (or even one dollar) per gallon certainly cannot be regarded with pleasure, but neither can it be seen as the end of civilization as we know it. Drivers in western European countries and Japan have been paying much higher prices for some time, and their way of life has nevertheless been approaching that in the United States with remarkable rapidity.

At these higher prices we will perhaps end up using fuels more carefully: less air conditioning, better insulated houses, smaller cars, more public transportation, and fewer power-using gadgets. But overall we can expect to continue to grow more prosperous, as have Japan and Europe with higher fuel prices. Nor is a significant retreat in environmental goals called for by that sort of forecast.

As oil prices rise, it will become profitable to extract oil from shale, to liquefy coal, and to obtain fuels from other sources whose "proven" reserves suffice for prospective demands hundreds of years into the future.[8] Meanwhile, there is every reason to suppose that we or our descendants will perfect new techniques to extract energy from other sources (such as solar and geothermal energy) where available quantities are virtually unlimited and whose environmental damage promises to be minimal.

5. Limitations of the Price Mechanism

We must be careful not to overstate the virtues of the price mechanism. No one who has studied its workings carefully will deny that it is extremely powerful, but many students of the subject have raised serious questions about its effectiveness in allocating resources between the present and the future. They have suggested that is has built-in biases toward inadequate provision for tomorrow.

Economists generally accept the outlines of our earlier argument that misuse of resources hurts today's proprietor and not just the community of the future. However, they suggest that, at least under some circumstances,

---

[7] See, for example, Walter J. Mead, who calculates that the equilibrium price is fifty-nine cents per gallon; "Discussion of 'Dynamic Demand Analysis of Selected Energy Resources' by H. S. Houthakker, P. K. Verleger, and D. P. Sheehan" (Paper prepared for a Joint Session of the American Economic Association and the American Agricultural Economic Association, New York City, December 29, 1973). Note that this price calculation is expressed in 1973 dollars, and will naturally have to be adjusted upward as the process of general inflation continues. Obviously, such estimates of the free market price of gasoline in the future are highly speculative, and it is certainly conceivable that prices will rise well above the figure suggested, particularly if some of the taxes that have been proposed are enacted into law.

[8] See, for example, W. D. Nordhaus, "The Allocation of Energy Resources," in A. M. Okun and G. L. Perry, eds., *Brookings Papers on Economic Activity,* No. 3 (Washington, D.C.: The Brookings Institution, 1973), pp. 529-70.

waste is likely to hurt today's property owner less than it harms future generations; they argue that, while the market mechanism protects resources to some
extent, it may not do so adequately.

There are four sources of disparity between the private and social costs of
resource conservation:

a. differences in risk
b. certain externalities inherent in provision for the future
c. imperfect knowledge
d. inappropriate types of governmental interference

Let us examine each of these briefly.

A. Risk to the Individual and the Community. Investments in the future are
more likely to benefit the community than the investors themselves. One reason
for this is the danger to individual investors that they may run into financial
difficulties, so that, as a result, their property will fall into the hands of others.
The owner of a forest or a mine who becomes insolvent loses his or her property,
but it is not lost to the community. Such an investment may well prove worth
its cost from the community's point of view, and yet not from the viewpoint
of the original investor who has lost the property. Thus, individuals may be
unwilling to undertake risky investments for fear of bankruptcy, even though
such investments would be beneficial to the community as a whole. A related
reason is the insurance principle. This asserts that, with a sufficiently large
number of independent cases, aggregate risk decreases and, for all practical purposes, virtually disappears. No one can say how long a particular healthy individual will survive, but an insurance company predicts with a high degree of
confidence the *proportion* of its many thousands of policy holders who will
survive any given number of years. Similarly individuals who invest in the conservation of their property have relatively few if any offsetting risks from other
investments to insure them against failure. But to society, where many investments are constantly underway, another such investment may be like writing
another policy to an insurance company.

On both grounds then (the risk of bankruptcy and the insurance principle), private ownership may not provide for our posterity as extensively as
society may wish.

B. Externality Aspects of Provision for the Future. All members of the community may take pleasure in the knowledge that the future is well provided
for. But this (unsalable) benefit to others does not enter the profit and loss
accounts of the proprietor who must foot the bills for particular conservation
activities.

There is a related phenomenon referred to as "option demand." Imagine a beautiful site owned by a proprietor who charges admission to campers and other visitors that use it and employs at least part of these funds for the upkeep of the area. Certain individuals may have no particular desire to visit the place for the present; yet they would like to keep the option open in case they should change their minds or in case their children should some day want to make a visit. Thus, once again, proprietors who conserve their resources provide a benefit to others (that is, to future visitors) that is not reflected in their own profits. They will be correspondingly unwilling to expend as much for the future as would best serve the public interest.

C. Imperfect Knowledge. In the reforestation case we suggested that the market will penalize owners who fail to replant by a corresponding reduction in the price of their property. But what if potential purchasers do not know about the decrease in the land's prospective yield? Of course, poor information may lead to either too little or too much investment for the future.

D. Inappropriate Government Interference. We have already discussed the danger of price controls inadvisedly imposed on scarce resources. Other government activities can also contribute to the destruction of the community's resources, among them projects to dam rivers that flood canyons and undermine a region's ecology and the indiscriminate construction of roads and airports. Such acts do not distort the workings of the price system; rather, they circumvent it. Here, too, the result may be either excessive or inadequate amounts of investment.[9]

6. On Equity and Reliance on Pricing for Conservation

In their advocacy of the price mechanism as an instrument to conserve resources, economists have undoubtedly given inadequate attention to the implications of these policies for distributive equity. Rising prices of scarce resources weigh most heavily upon those who have the least to spend. The wealthy may reduce their consumption of scarce goods as their prices rise, but they do not have to do so if price alone rations their use. The poor may have little choice in the matter.

Sometimes, then, policy makers may have good grounds for considering alternative measures, notably the direct rationing of scarce items. Particularly for short periods during which an emergency allows no time for the design and production of substitutes, rationing may be more acceptable than a sharp and painful price increase.

---

[9]Of course, an ideal cost-benefit analysis which took account of *all* the consequences for society would prevent such governmental acts. But, unfortunately, not all government decisions are made on such an ideal calculus.

In saying this, we must, however, reemphasize that rationing itself incurs serious social costs,[10] and that experience indicates that it rarely works for more than very short periods. One must always remember that a decision to avoid both rationing *and* freedom of price movements is tantamount to a decision for chaos: artificial shortages, a breakdown of distribution arrangements, long queues, and the formation of black markets.

It is also important to recognize that much can be done to ameliorate the distributive effects of price rises produced by dwindling supplies. Indeed some such measures will have to be undertaken if the pricing approach to resource conservation is to achieve political acceptability. There are, in fact, some obvious and direct redistributive provisions that can accompany rising prices. Or one can at least reduce the effects upon the poor by helping to provide them with attractive substitutes for increasingly costly items. For example, improved public transportation can in some cities help to offset the consequences of rising gasoline prices upon lower income groups.[11]

A bit of ingenuity can sometimes alleviate some of the more distressing consequences of increased prices of necessities. One example is the suggestion (embodied in the Administration's energy proposals in 1977) that a tax per gallon be imposed on gasoline use, with every car owner receiving a fixed annual rebate equal to the *average* tax payment by all Americans. In this way no person need be deprived of purchasing power, and those who reduce the use of fuel more than the average would receive a net increase in their disposable income.

Whatever the approach we adopt, we simply cannot ignore the equity issue. Rising prices *do* produce inequities, and we must be prepared to deal with them both as a matter of justice and as a practical matter of political feasibility. Later in the book we will return to a careful examination of the relationships between environmental policy and income distribution. But for noneconomists, in particular, the issue arises to haunt each and every chapter, particularly where we advocate the use of pricing as the appropriate instrument of environmental policy.

7. Concluding Comments

In our imperfect world there is no reason to expect the price system to work perfectly in preserving sufficient quantities of resources for tomorrow. As the preceding discussion indicated, there may be built-in biases that lead to

---

[10] Recall that these costs include not only the administrative costs of operating the rationing program, but also the failure to generate the increase in supplies that will be forthcoming in response to a higher price.

[11] Unfortunately, this will be effective only in some areas. In sprawling cities such as Los Angeles and Phoenix, public vehicles with fixed routes may be able to contribute little to help meet the overall demand for transportation.

some extent to a systematic underprovision for the future by private enterprise.

But whether the price system allocates too much or too little to the
future is probably not the most critical issue. The fact is that it does a great
deal to prevent the wanton destruction of resources.[12] The view that the free
enterprise system is the source of our resource-depletion problems is, in an
important sense, highly misleading. We are not arguing here that the workings
of the economic system are beyond criticism and uniformly beneficent. But so
far as the issue of resource depletion is concerned, the pricing mechanism can
do much to prevent excessive current consumption.

----

[12] A noteworthy exception occurs where resource destruction is the result of an externality—that is, the result of the activities of groups who have no financial stake in the particular
resource. As we saw in Chapter 4, industrial activity that depletes the atmosphere or the
resources of the sea cannot be controlled adequately by the price system because those who
cause the damage do not suffer corresponding financial penalties.

8

The Tyranny of Compounding

It may seem strange, in a book on environmental issues, to devote a chapter to the arithmetic of compounding, but problems of compound growth are, in fact, a central theme in much of the environmental literature. Several recent forecasts of the collapse of modern civilization as we know it are all based on some relatively simple extrapolations of compound growth.[1] It is, therefore, extremely important to explore the nature of geometric expansion (that is, compounding growth), both to see how this can help us understand change over time and, equally important, to be forewarned against simplistic extrapolations of current growth rates that yield mechanical predictions of future disaster.

Growth is itself a recurrent theme in the discussions of quality of life: growth in output, growth in population, growth in pollution, growth in the costs of some of "the better things in life." In savings accounts in commercial banks, the principal and the accumulated interest are compounded; that is, they *both* earn interest. In estimating future levels of population and pollution, it is a common practice simply to calculate recent growth rates and extrapolate

---

[1]We will examine some of these forecasts in the following chapter.

them ahead with the arithmetic of compounding. For example, in demographic forecasts, such calculations assume that any addition to the population will, in turn, produce offspring (who will also produce offspring, and so on).

1. The Explosive Character of Compounding Growth

In this chapter we first explain the workings of the compounding process, for many of the calculations of forecasters are based upon this simple arithmetic. In particular, it is of foremost importance to recognize the fundamental sky-rocketing nature of even modestly compounding rates of growth: *compounding growth always and unavoidably becomes explosive in the long run.* After an initial period of mild increase, the interest on the accumulated interest invariably begins to predominate and the process takes off. Where an assumption of con-tinued compounded growth is justified, the arithmetic of compounding can help to warn us of any exacerbated problems that explosive growth will bring. However, where a premise of compounding growth is not implied by the facts, it follows that predictions based on this assumption will be very far off the mark; they may cause panic when in fact there is little or no cause for hysteria.

The evidence suggests that many of the magnitudes relevant for the quality of life are compounding at a percentage rate which may at first seem rather moderate. For example, world population is increasing at approximately 2 percent per year compounded. And measured in dollars of constant purchasing power, the cost of education per student has been growing about 4 percent per year over the postwar period. In an era when double-digit inflation rates no longer shock us, these magnitudes are not likely to be startling. But if their effects are calculated over any substantial period, they are not so negligible. Since in this book we are concerned primarily with rather long-term problems, we must examine with some care the longer-period effects of compounding.[2]

---

[2]Even those who are used to working with compounding processes sometimes do not grasp how explosive they are. An incident involving the authors of this book may help to make the point. A few years ago we were studying some matters centering about the reigns of Elizabeth I and James I. Fortunately, there exists a time series of English price statistics, about as reasonably founded and constructed as one can hope for, going back before 1300. Figure 8-1 is a graph of these fascinating data. In particular, notice that the period of the late Tudors and early Stuarts (1510, one year after the accession of Henry VIII, to 1650), was one of rapid inflation; in fact, it was one of the most serious inflations in English history with prices rising eightfold during the 140-year period.

The point in this story is that, while awaiting the results of a computer calculation to determine the average annual rate of increase in prices during that period (using all the figures and not just the data for the first and last years), we and several colleagues guessed at the answer. All of us came out far too high. It turned out that *a price rise a bit below 1.5 percent per year was sufficient to produce the great Tudor inflation.* We were, of course, misled by recent experience. In a world where a 4 percent annual rate of inflation is taken to constitute stability and 2 percent seems virtually unattainable, we could, perhaps, not have been expected to think of one of the most notorious inflations in English history in terms of 1.5 percent per year.

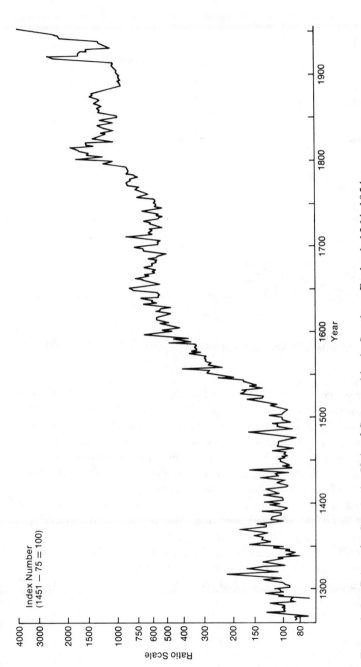

Figure 8–1 Price of a Composite Unit of Consumables in Southern England, 1264–1954.

Source: Ernest H. Phelps-Brown and Sheila V. Hopkins, "Seven Centuries of the Prices of Consumables, Compared with Builders' Wage-Rates." *Economica* N.S. 23 (November 1956): 296–314.

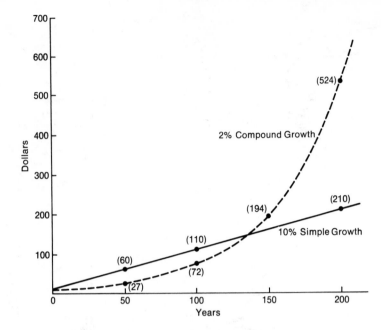

Figure 8-2   Effects of Simple and Compounded Interest Rates Compared.

A simple graph helps to illustrate the explosive nature of a steady compounding process. Consider a pair of ten dollar investments: one accumulates *simple* interest at an annual rate of 10 percent, while the other *compounds* at a steady 2 percent. Figure 8-2 shows how the two principals accumulate over a period of about 200 years. The broken line shows the characteristic path of compounding growth. In our graph it rises moderately for the first hundred years or so.[3] After that it really begins to shoot upwards until, toward the right-hand end of the graph, it rises almost vertically. In this way compounded growth will invariably catch up with and surpass the steady expansion (as illustrated by the straight line in the diagram) that is characteristic of uncompounded growth, no matter how small the growth rate of the former or how large the growth rate of the latter. The issue is only how long a period is required for the one to overtake the other, and that is a matter of the magnitudes of the growth rates.

---

[3]The long period of modest expansion is attributable to the 2 percent figure we selected for our illustrative growth rate; at, say, 7 percent only thirty years would have been required to achieve the same expansion.

2. Doubling Periods with Various Compounding Rates

It is actually quite easy to estimate the longer-term consequences of various rates of compounding with the aid of a simple table. Such a table indicates for each specified rate of interest the length of time required for it to produce a doubling of the initial magnitude. Table 8-1 gives these figures for rates of growth from 1 to 10 percent.

The table tells us, for example, that at a 2 percent rate of growth the world's population will double every 35 years. That means that in 140 (4 × 35) years it will have doubled four times; that is, it will have risen to sixteen (2 × 2 × 2 × 2) times its initial level. More generally, Table 8-2 shows how one can calculate, approximately, the magnitude of a variable such as population, whose initial magnitude we designate as *p,* after the passage of *x* number of doubling periods. What it shows is that as time varies "arithmetically," the variable undergoing a constant percentage growth will expand "geometrically"; that is, as time proceeds through the sequence of periods 1, 2, 3, 4, etc., the size of the growing variable increases in the doubling sequence 2, 4, 8, 16, etc.

TABLE 8-1

DOUBLING PERIODS FOR VARIOUS COMPOUNDING RATES

Annual Growth Rate (percent)	Number of Years for Doubling (approx.)
1	70
2	35
3	24
4	18
5	14
6	12
7	10
8	9
9	8
10	7

Note: There is a simple device that permits one to remember this useful table (or rather to calculate it). Just note that any entry in column 1 multiplied by the corresponding entry in column 2 equals either 70 or 72. Thus, to find the doubling period for an *x* percent rate of growth, simply divide *x* into either 70 or 72 (whichever it goes into evenly), provided *x* is an integer between one and ten, inclusive.

Finally, Table 8-3 spells out, in terms of actual numbers of years, the implications of Table 8-2 for several specific growth rates. Table 8-3 indicates, for example (last entry in last row), that for a variable to grow to thirty-two times its initial magnitude it will require (last column) 350 years if its growth rate is 1 percent, 175 years if its growth rate is 2 percent, only 90 years if its rate of expansion is 4 percent, and just five decades if it is increasing at a rate of 7 percent.

Looked at the other way, we see that after (approximately) 70 years, any item growing at an annual rate of 1 percent will have doubled in size, any variable increasing at a 2 percent rate will have quadrupled, any item growing at 6 percent will have increased sixteenfold, while anything growing at 7 percent per year will have risen to 128 times its initial value! (This last figure not shown in the table.)

The utter simplicity of the calculations must be emphasized. They involve no more than the arithmetic of the doubling sequence 2, 4, 8, 16, 32, etc. We underscore all this because compounding plays so important a role for some of the basic issues discussed in this book; it is thus very convenient that readers be able to check for themselves where things are heading as a result of

TABLE 8-2

MAGNITUDES AFTER INDICATED NUMBERS OF DOUBLING PERIODS

Number of years	0	x	$2x$	$3x$	$4x$	$5x$	$6x$
Magnitude of variable	p	$2p$	$4p$	$8p$	$16p$	$32p$	$64p$

Note: Here x represents the doubling period corresponding to the relevant growth rate as given in the second column in Table 8-1, and p represents the principal (i.e., the original amount that is growing).

TABLE 8-3

MAGNITUDES AFTER INDICATED TIME LAPSE
FOR SEVERAL GROWTH RATES

Growth Rate (percent)	Number of Years					
1	0	70	140	210	280	350
2	0	35	70	105	140	175
4	0	18	36	54	72	90
7	0	10	20	30	40	50
Magnitude Attained	p	$2p$	$4p$	$8p$	$16p$	$32p$

any current trends that actually continue on a path of steady compounding growth.

An illustration will bring out the power of compounding very clearly. As has already been noted, the earth's population has been rising at an annual rate of about 2 percent per year. Professor Ansley Coale of the Office of Population Research at Princeton University has carried out calculations like those of Table 8-3 to determine what continuation of this growth rate implies for longer periods of time. His arithmetic shows that:

1. If population were to grow at today's rates for another 600-700 years, every square foot of the surface of the earth would contain a human being.
2. If it were to expand at the same rate for 1200 years, the combined weight of the human population would exceed that of the earth itself.
3. If that growth rate were to go on for 6000 years (a very short period in terms of biological history), the collection of bodies crosspiled on the surface of the globe would constitute a sphere whose diameter was growing with the speed of light![4]

The preceding calculations, as Professor Coale will readily agree, clearly cannot be taken seriously as forecasts of the future. Population density will never reach one person per square foot, let alone the level suggested by the two other absurdities that emerge from the arithmetic. Yet such calculations do have very serious and significant implications for the future. They show that current growth rates unavoidably lead to impossible consequences. This means that, long before such a stage has been reached, we will certainly have altered today's growth rates. The issue is not *whether* any fixed growth rate will ultimately be terminated, but *how* the change will be achieved. If human habits of procreation do not change by themselves and no policy measures are undertaken to bring about the change in a relatively painless manner, the environment will carry out the job for us. For, then, the unhappy eventualities that we associate with Malthusian doctrine must surely come to pass. Long before we reach a density of one person per square foot, famine, disease, and perhaps other plagues will decimate the population.[5]

Long-term extrapolations from constant percentage growth rates, then, usually *do* indicate a policy choice that is open to the decision maker. The choice is not that between achievement and prevention of the results deduced from the calculation, for our finite earth cannot support the astronomical

---

[4] Ansley J. Coale, "Man and His Environment," *Science* 170 (October 9, 1970): 132-36.
[5] There is evidence that excessive density in animal populations can produce fatal psychological and physiological reactions. Animals in crowded conditions are found to have enlarged kidneys, livers, and adrenals, all symptoms associated with extreme stress. In such colonies increases in homosexuality, sadism, and infant and female mortality have been observed, both under experimental and natural conditions. See Edward T. Hall, *The Hidden Dimension* (New York: Doubleday, 1966), Chaps. 2 and 3.

magnitudes that such an extrapolation must ultimately yield. The decision before us is the choice among the means available to bring the process to an end; considering the very unpleasant consequences that can, in the long run, result from a policy of muddling through, the importance of a careful process of program selection should be obvious.

However, as Lord Keynes reminded us, "In the long run we are all dead"; short periods are vitally important, especially for environmental policy making. There is evidence that, in some areas, the accumulation of *certain types* of pollutants is growing at rates as high as 5 percent per year.[6] Over a short period, such rates of growth can often continue more or less constant, though their compounded consequences (as we have seen) can sometimes be startling (and startlingly unpleasant). A 5 percent annual increase in pollution levels means that, *if that compounded rate continues,* in less than thirty years the pollution concentrations will have increased to four times their level today. Similarly, we find that in the postwar period, *after correction for the effects of inflation,* the cost of education per student has been rising more than 4 percent per year. The budgetary implications for our municipalities thirty-five years in the future are quite dramatic.

There is always another possibility: a compounding rate of growth may in fact peter out by itself, or current trends may even reverse themselves. In short, forecasts of the future that rely on the assumption of steady compound growth should be based only on strong factual or analytic evidence. We will see presently some problems which may arise if this precaution is ignored.

Finally, we should point out that there is nothing inherently evil about compounding growth. It all depends on what it is that grows exponentially. As one illustration, economists concerned with economic development have found that in recent history modern industrialized countries have exhibited more or less continuing expansions in output per capita as a result of "technological change." In a study of economic growth in the United States, Edward Denison estimates that over the period 1929-69 we have experienced *on the average* a compounding rate of growth of about 1½ percent per annum that is attributable solely to increased outputs per unit of input; that is, we have in an average year gotten 1½ percent more goods and services from the same labor and capital input than in the preceding year.[7] This sort of compound growth, unlike other cases we have examined in this chapter, clearly works to the advantage of mankind and the environment, and may go far in postponing the depletion of resources that has been held up as an imminent threat.[8]

---

[6] For example, this is reportedly true of the lead content of the atmosphere in San Diego (*New York Times,* August 8, 1970, p. 35).

[7] Edward F. Denison, *Accounting for United States Economic Growth 1929-1969* (Washington, D.C.: The Brookings Institution, 1974), Table 9-4, p. 127.

[8] A reviewer points out that we should not expect anything to grow at a constant compound rate forever. Technology is no different in this respect.

9

On Limits to Growth

For some observers, the prospect of the exhaustion of resources is an integral part of a larger prophecy for the future of the planet which foresees continued economic growth inevitably leading to a collapse of civilization as we know it. Unless drastic steps to limit growth are taken very soon, the new prophets of doom foresee a "sudden and uncontrollable decline in both population and industrial capacity."[1] As Jay Forrester, a professor of engineering at the Massachusetts Institute of Technology, puts it, "We may now be living in a 'golden age' when, in spite of a widely acknowledged feeling of malaise, the quality of life is, on the average, higher than ever before in our history and higher now than the future offers."[2]

In somewhat varying garb, this dire prediction has been offered by a number of biologists and scientists from other fields including, for example, Barry Commoner and Paul and Anne Ehrlich.[3] The forecast has even assumed a quanti-

---

[1] Donella H. Meadows, Dennis L. Meadows, Jørgen Randers, and William W. Behrens III, *The Limits to Growth: A Report for The Club of Rome's Project on the Predicament of Mankind* (A Potomac Associates book published by Universe Books, New York, 1972. Graphics by Potomac Associates), p. 23.
[2] *World Dynamics* (Cambridge, Mass.: Wright-Allen Press, 1971), p. 12.
[3] Barry Commoner, *The Closing Circle* (New York: Alfred A. Knopf, 1972); Paul and Anne Ehrlich, *Population, Resources, Environment* (San Francisco: Freeman, 1970).

131

tative form. Two recent studies use elaborate computerized models of the world, which trace out paths of future history characterized by a violent collapse of the world system.[4]

These frightening forecasts, which emanate from the work of a variety of scientists and systems analysts, certainly deserve the closest scrutiny. In fact, the response has been an outpouring of articles, reviews, and conferences numbering in the hundreds, all attempting to evaluate the validity and implications of the findings of these modern prophets of doom. Those who have found the analyses persuasive have called for strong and immediate measures to arrest population growth and the continuing process of industrialization; their prescription calls for a transition, more or less rapid, to a world of "zero economic growth" (ZEG).

This chapter explores the argument and claims of the no-growth proponents in order to assess the plausibility of the analysis and to draw out its implications for the formulation of effective environmental policy.

1. The Argument for Zero Economic Growth

As we noted in the introduction, the indictment against continued economic growth has come from a variety of sources. The more intuitive discussions are typified by the work of biologist Barry Commoner, a perceptive and informed student of environmental problems. He bases his opposition to growth on a wide variety of serious ecological developments: the deterioration of Lake Erie, the unpleasant and unhealthy blankets of smog over the Los Angeles basin, and the contamination of water and food supplies from growing accumulations of nitrates in the soil. Commoner writes, "My own judgment, based on the evidence now at hand, is that the present course of environmental degradation, at least in industrialized countries, represents a challenge to essential ecological systems that is so serious that, if continued, it will destroy the capability of the environment to support a reasonably civilized human society."[5] To avert this disaster, Commoner reasons that "there must be some limit to the growth of total capital, and the productive system *must* eventually reach a 'no-growth' condition. . . ."[6] This we might describe somewhat loosely as the empiricist's case for the limitation of economic growth.

At the other end of the spectrum are the mathematical models which attempt, by a process that is essentially deductive, to embody the basic characteristics of the ecological system in a set of equations. Such work was initiated

---

[4] See Forrester, *World Dynamics*, and Meadows et al., *The Limits to Growth*. Not all of the "futurologists" can be characterized by such an extreme pessimism. Some seem to be quite optimistic. See, for example, Herman Kahn, *The Next 200 Years, A Scenario for America and the World* (New York: Morrow, 1976).
[5] Commoner, *Closing Circle*, pp. 217–18.
[6] Ibid., p. 274.

by Professor Jay Forrester and followed up by an international team under the direction of Professor Dennis Meadows; the work of Meadows and his associates was supported by an influential group of thirty people from ten countries, who although of diverse backgrounds and interests, were united by a deep concern with "the present and future predicament of man." In April 1968 the group assembled in Rome and formed the Club of Rome which undertook "to foster understanding of the varied but interdependent components—economic, political, natural, and social—that make up the global system in which we all live; to bring that new understanding to the attention of policy-makers and the public worldwide. . . ."[7]

To make a long story short, the Club of Rome underwrote an ambitious effort to build a mathematical model of the world system. This culminated in the publication in 1972 of *The Limits to Growth,* which reports the findings of the Meadows team. The highly publicized projections (or, more accurately, simulations) of the Club of Rome model, which indicate that continued growth leads inevitably to a catastrophic collapse of the world ecological and economic systems, have met with quite varied receptions ranging from the highest praise to one review which characterized the whole study as "Garbage in and garbage out."

The most striking characteristic of this entire literature, whether it be the verbal arguments of Barry Commoner or the complex mathematical model of the Club of Rome, is a single premise that constitutes its basic foundation: *we live in a finite world of limited space, resources, and capacity to absorb pollution, and continued growth must inevitably, at some point, reach one or more of these limits.* This, incidentally, is not a new argument. In 1798, Thomas R. Malthus published his influential *Essay on Population* in which he contended that, without checks on population growth, the expansion of the population would outrun the supply of food with misery, pestilence, and famine the inevitable consequence. Malthus postulated a geometrical (compounding) rate of growth of population which, if left uncontrolled, would overwhelm the productive capacity of the limited supply of land. For this reason, it has seemed quite appropriate to refer to members of the No-Growth Society as the neo-Malthusians.

The basic logic of the neo-Malthusian argument, as built into the Club of Rome's models, is quite straightforward. As Commoner puts it, "It is a fundamental fact of nature, then, that the base of human existence represented by the ecosphere and mineral resources is limited in its size and rate of activity."[8] Add to this the assumption that increasing output implies the depletion of limited resources and a rise in levels of pollution, and the conclusion of inevitable collapse is assured. According to the Club of Rome model this collapse will not take

---

[7]Meadows et al., *Limits to Growth,* p. 9.
[8]Commoner, *Closing Circle,* p. 120.

very long—perhaps only a few more decades. We saw in the preceding chapter the dramatic arithmetic of compound growth, where one becomes two, two becomes four, four becomes eight. . . . It doesn't take long for the numbers to become truly staggering; cancerous expansion of this kind can allow its victim only very little time. The policy implications of this line of reasoning are equally clear: to circumvent disaster, we must stop short of the limits imposed by nature on our activities. In short, we must, as a condition for the survival of civilization, move to a no-growth world.

2. Predictions from the Club of Rome Model

Before we illustrate the results of the report, we may note that they were derived by a process that specialists in the area call computer simulation. Literally this means that one assumes some mathematical relationship to be true and uses the computer to determine what sort of future it implies. But the result obviously cannot be taken literally as a forecast. Indeed, the very process of choosing the equations in effect assumes away the forecasting problem, because the projected outcomes are implicit in the assumed relationships. The frequent assumption in the Club of Rome model that population and other variables will continue to grow at compounded rates may or may not turn out to have some basis in fact, but we cannot *know* that this will be so without considerably more knowledge of the facts than anyone has accumulated to date. Thus one must not be misled by the mathematical character of a simulation analysis into believing that its forecasts are blessed (or cursed) by inevitability.

It may prove helpful here to look at some of the results generated by the "World Model" of the Club of Rome.[9] The research team postulated a system of several interrelated equations to describe basic behavioral and technological relationships. In particular, the Club of Rome model includes equations in which population growth increases with food output, and in which the rates of resource depletion and pollution levels rise with the level of industrial output. Along with these equations, the research team then fed in some numbers for the size of the initial stock of resources and population. The rest of the job was simply a matter of letting the computer trace out the implied path of the future of the world system.

We reproduce in Figure 9-1 a sample computer run of the Club of Rome model (one they called their "standard run"). The horizontal axis represents time measured in years, from 1900 at the left to the year 2100 on the right. As

---

[9]In a more recent report the Club of Rome has revised its position and adopted a view of future prospects that is more moderate. We nevertheless concern ourselves here with the earlier report because our purpose is more to illustrate the dangers in the approach they had adopted than to criticize the Club or its positions. For the later study, see Donella H. Meadows et al., *The Limits to Growth,* 2nd ed. (New York: New American Library, 1974).

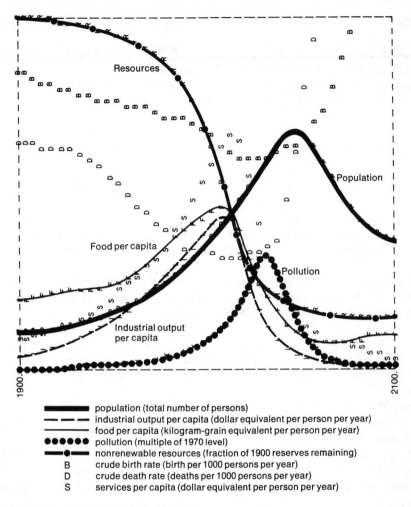

▬▬▬▬	population (total number of persons)
— — —	industrial output per capita (dollar equivalent per person per year)
————	food per capita (kilogram-grain equivalent per person per year)
●●●●●●	pollution (multiple of 1970 level)
▬●▬●▬	nonrenewable resources (fraction of 1900 reserves remaining)
B	crude birth rate (birth per 1000 persons per year)
D	crude death rate (deaths per 1000 persons per year)
S	services per capita (dollar equivalent per person per year)

Figure 9-1   World Model Standard Run.

Source: Donella H. Meadows, Dennis L. Meadows, Jørgen Randers, and William W. Behrens III, *The Limits to Growth: A Report for The Club of Rome's Project on the Predicament of Mankind* (New York: A Potomac Associates book published by Universe Books, 1972. Graphics by Potomac Associates), p. 23.

we move from left to right, we are thus, in effect, moving through time and can see what is happening to world population, output, resources, and so on. Over the early part of the period, population and industrial output per capita continue to grow (presumably reflecting the first sixty to seventy years of the twentieth century). However, note the catastrophic collapse that occurs a little over half-way through the period: first industrial output and food per capita plunge precipitously followed by later and rapid declines in the absolute size of the population. In fact, by the year 2100, the standard of living (as measured by food and industrial output per capita) has sunk to levels below those that prevailed at the beginning of the simulation period in 1900. The collapse of the world economy is complete. The authors describe the process:

> The behavior mode of the system . . . is clearly that of overshoot and collapse. In this run the collapse occurs because of nonrenewable resource depletion. The industrial capital stock grows to a level that requires an enormous input of resources. In the very process of that growth it depletes a large fraction of the resource reserves available. . . . Finally investment cannot keep up with the depreciation, and the industrial base collapses, taking with it the services and agricultural systems, which have become dependent on industrial inputs. . . . Population finally decreases when the death rate is driven upward by lack of food and health services.[10]

So, the disintegration of the world economy as shown in Figure 9-1 is simply the result of running out of resources. However, it is worth noting the conclusion that Meadows and his associates draw from this:

> *We can thus say with some confidence that, under the assumption of no major change in the present system, population and industrial growth will certainly stop within the next century, at the latest.*[11]

A chilling prognostication!

In other simulation runs in which the demands on resources are eased, the research team finds other causes of world collapse: pollution levels in excess of the environment's assimilative capacity, population in excess of that supportable by potential food production, and so on. Sooner or later, the expansionary paths traced out by the computer hurtle downward as some limit in the World Model is exceeded.

3. A Critique of ZEG

The basic logic of the neo-Malthusian position appears, on the face of it, extremely compelling—indeed, almost irrefutable. If there are such limits (which would seem to be guaranteed since the planet is certainly finite), then it appears that we must curtail growth in order to stay within "bounds." However, a closer look at the meaning of economic growth and the nature of production processes suggests that the argument is not so obvious. Moreover, it is critically important to set this matter straight, for the social implications of ZEG, as we will see later, are truly momentous.

---

[10]Meadows et al., *Limits to Growth* (1972), p. 125.
[11]Ibid., p. 126.

Let us consider first the issue of economic growth (the expansion over time in the output of goods and services), and return later to the matter of an increasing population. We recall from an earlier chapter the fact that (aside from fuels) most resources, while limited, are not really consumed in the sense that they vanish forever. As Kenneth Boulding reminds us with his image of "Spaceship Earth," the iron and tin we dig out of the ground and use to make various products are still with us, even if in a somewhat altered form.[12]

Moreover, a large fraction of these resources can, in principle, be recovered and reused; we may have to melt down metal containers to recover the tin or aluminum, but such things as certain types of glass containers can be reused after very little more than cleansing. One of the main reasons why recycling activities are not more widespread is that, at the moment, there exist ample supplies of most minerals; it is still cheaper to dig the ore from the earth than to recover used metals from discarded products. However, we can be sure that, as certain resources become scarcer and their prices rise accordingly, recycling will become increasingly profitable. One interesting example of this is the gradual disappearance of the once-familiar heaps of junked automobiles and abandoned vehicles on the streets; the value of the metals they contain and the techniques for their recovery have now reached a point where it is economically viable to recycle the materials. We will have more to say about recycling in a later chapter, but here we simply note that, with the exception of fuels, most resources are potentially reusable.

It is nevertheless true that, although reusable, the stocks of these resources are not infinite. The same aluminum presumably cannot be used in two containers at the same time. Thus, the fixity of resources would consequently appear to establish limits on levels of economic activity. Chapter 6 examined the known reserves of the world's primary mineral reserves and found these reserves, in most cases, to be quite substantial. However, with compound rates of growth of output, the neo-Malthusians warn us that we will eventually exhaust even these abundant reserves.

There are two extremely important and basic rejoinders. First, much of the thrust of economic growth comes from what economists call "improvements in technology." And by this they mean something quite specific: *increased output per unit of input.* A fundamental element of economic growth is that we learn to get more from less: transistors replace tubes, and refrigerators eliminate the need for daily deliveries of ice. Economists interested in the process of economic growth have actually tried to estimate what percentage of the increase in output is attributable to improved technology. In the preceding chapter we cited Edward Denison's calculations indicating that, over the period 1929-69 in the United States, the increase in output per unit of input was on average roughly

---

[12] "The Economics of the Coming Spaceship Earth," in Henry Jarrett, ed., *Environmental Quality in a Growing Economy* (Baltimore: The Johns Hopkins University Press, 1966).

1½ percent per annum while national output grew at an average (compound) annual rate of a little over 3 percent.[13] However, even this figure understates the magnitude of the increase in efficiency of resource use. Denison estimates that about one-third of the remaining 1½ percentage points of average annual growth was the result of increased education and skill of the labor force. This suggests that only about one-third of the growth in national output had its source in increased use of *physical* inputs. So even if we were ultimately to become subject to tight resource constraints, we could still expect some continuing increases in output because of more effective use of the same fixed stock of resources.

Second, and equally important, is the substantial range of substitutability among inputs that characterizes most production processes. As a resource becomes relatively scarce, the market signals this to users in the form of a higher price; this in turn provides the incentive for switching to other resources or finding other ways to economize on its use. The petroleum shortage, as we noted earlier, generated a marked shift in demand from larger to smaller automobiles.[14]

We thus find that continuing technological improvements and the scope

---

[13]Edward F. Denison, *Accounting for United States Economic Growth 1929-1969* (Washington, D.C.: The Brookings Institution, 1974), p. 127.

[14]The surprising scope for flexibility in production was illustrated dramatically during World War II in the course of the Allied bombing of Germany. Bombing strategists were quick to focus on what they saw as a critical point of vulnerability in the German war effort: the manufacture of antifriction (ball) bearings. Two facts were considered of central importance. First, nearly all the major instruments of German war capacity made extensive use of antifriction bearings, and the production of the balls for the bearings was a job of the highest precision, requiring in some instances tolerances of only a millionth of an inch. The second notable feature of the German antifriction bearing industry was its geographical concentration which made the factories vulnerable to bombing.

The result was a high priority on the bearings factories as targets for heavy bombing, and beginning in the summer of 1943 the Allied air forces conducted a series of forty bombing missions aimed at the bearings plants. The damage inflicted, although far from total, was severe, with bearing output falling to less than half of its earlier levels. This appeared particularly devastating in view of German plans for a great expansion in armaments production in 1944.

What is remarkable about this episode is that, in addition to drawing on reserves of bearings and concentrating effort on restoration of the plants, the Germans found another way to meet this crisis. They simply redesigned their vehicles of war to reduce their use of antifriction bearings. Within four months the redesign was completed and embodied in actual construction so that, for example, German aircraft (the Junkers and Messerschmidt fighters), some of which had previously required as many as 1,000 antifriction bearings, now used only one or two hundred and in some cases less than fifty. In the end, the Germans made good on their boast, *"Es ist kein Geraet zurueck geblieben weil Waelzlager fehlten"* (no equipment has been held up because of a shortage of bearings). (For a comprehensive summary of this episode, see *The United States Strategic Bombing Survey: The German Anti-Friction Bearings Industry* [Washington, D.C.: U.S. Government Printing Office, January 1947].)

Similarly, on this side of the Atlantic, when our sources of natural rubber in the Pacific were cut off by the Japanese, we found a way to produce synthetic rubber. The point is that production processes are rarely of a character so rigid that there is no room for substitution of one input for another.

for input substitution in production processes seriously undercut the no-growth argument. This was made clear recently in a careful study of the Forrester model by Professor William O. Nordhaus of Yale University.[15] The Forrester world model (and also the Club of Rome models) do not contain in their structure any allowance for continuing technological improvement or for substitution in production. In fact, Forrester assumes a fixed stock of exhaustible, nonreproducible resources which is continually eaten away by ongoing production activities in such a way that each added unit of output implies the irretrievable loss of a fixed amount of resources. Nordhaus refers to this as Forrester's "iron law of resource use." However, we have seen that this sort of assumption simply does not describe the way the economic system functions: most resources are not irretrievably lost; scarce resources can typically be replaced by substitutes; and some increased output emerges from improved technology without any increase in inputs.

To try to render the model somewhat more realistic, Nordhaus replaced the Forrester production equations with others allowing for some substitution among inputs in the processes of production. Nordhaus' revised version of the Forrester model predicts a future strikingly different from the Club of Rome's vision of cataclysmic collapse. Instead, it forecasts continuing (compounding) expansion in *per-capita* consumption over the next century, even with continued growth in the world's population. This is evident from Figure 9-2, which depicts the results of the Nordhaus computer runs. The "reference path" in Figure 9-2 is Forrester's simulation, while the four curves indicating continuing growth in consumption *per capita* each embody a different assumption concerning population growth, but allow for input substitution.

We hasten to add that the Nordhaus adaptations of the world models do not mean that everything is automatically going to be fine, and that we need not concern ourselves with resource conservation. The moral of the exercise is really that one can easily be misled by grandiose mathematical models of the future of the world. Long-run economic forecasts (e.g., those widely attributed to Malthus and Marx) have not often fared very well, and dressing them up in a set of equations does not necessarily make them any more valid.

4. Economic Expansion and the Growth of Population

We turn now to the issue of population growth. Here, the sheer space limitations of the earth indicate that continuing population growth must eventually lead to crowding and congestion on a scale that would be unpleasant and, perhaps, destructive.[16] There is probably some "optimal" population size (or

---

[15] "World Dynamics: Measurement Without Data," *Economic Journal* 83 (December 1973): 1156–83.
[16] One reviewer comments: "The *level* of population is only part of the issue. Its geographic distribution also has important environmental implications. Thus, consider the much greater

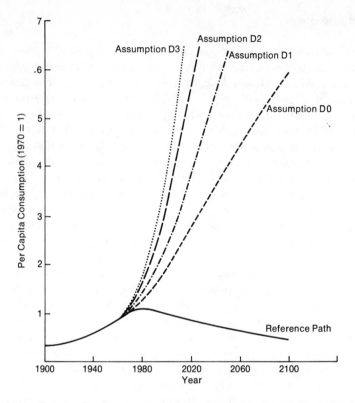

Figure 9-2 Results for Simple Model with Substitution and Alternative Population Paths.

Source: William O. Nordhaus, "World Dynamics: Measurement Without Data," *Economic Journal* 83 (December 1973): 1182.

perhaps range of sizes) for the world in the sense that inhabitants of the planet would be somewhat worse off if the population were either substantially larger or smaller than this figure. It's hard to know just what this magic number is, but we can be quite sure that an ever-increasing population must ultimately become excessively large.

While this much may be clear, it is another matter simply to extrapolate current rates of population growth into the future and predict catastrophe from overcrowding. There is still considerable uncertainty concerning patterns of fertility and birth rates. What we do know suggests that growing affluence itself usually dampens the rate of new births. More accurately, studies suggest that a "demographic transition" takes place during the process of economic growth so that the rate of population growth first rises and then falls with the level of

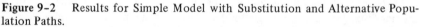

resource demands of an additional infant born in the United States, as compared to one born in a less-developed country."

economic development. In fact, the evidence indicates that the countries which have the most serious birth-rate problems are the less-developed lands, for whom growing population constitutes an obstacle to economic growth. The recent precipitous decline in U.S. birth rates lends further support to this view; as has been widely publicized, it appears that the United States has reached a fertility level at, or slightly below, the replacement rate (as have a number of western European countries). Although future patterns of fertility are highly uncertain, it is quite possible that we are on the way to a stable population as a result of purely voluntary behavior patterns. At any rate, the evidence does suggest that a halt in the growth of world output is likely, if anything, to retard the lower birth rates associated with the higher incomes, education, and access to birth-control measures that continuing economic development permits.

5. On the Desirability of Economic Growth

It's important to underline precisely what we have argued in the preceding section. We have tried to suggest that *continued economic growth is possible;* it does not inevitably lead to a catastrophe of worldwide dimensions, as the neo-Malthusians contend. This is not to say, however, that ZEG is undesirable.

Some observers, like Professor Ezra Mishan of the London School of Economics and Political Science, have argued that the social and cultural costs of continued economic growth are excessively high.[17] Mishan argues that the "cult of efficiency" and "unchecked commercialism" that characterize the developed economies have taken a tremendous human toll in terms of displaced craftsmen, international conflicts among "growth-obsessed governments," and a general degradation of the quality of human life.

> Generations have passed, and, like the woods and hedges that sheltered it, the rich local life centered on township, parish and village, has been up-rooted and blown away by the winds of change. Today no refuge remains from the desperate universal clamour for more efficiency, more excitement, and more novelty that goads us furiously onward, competing, accumulating, innovating—and inevitably destroying. Every step forward in technological progress, and particularly in the things most eagerly antic-ipated—swifter travel, depersonalized services, all the pushbutton comforts and round-the-clock synthetic entertainment that are promised us—effec-tively transfers our dependence upon other human beings to dependence upon machines and, therefore, unavoidably constricts yet further the direct flow of understanding and sympathy between people. Thus in the

---

[17]See, for example, Mishan's *Technology and Growth: The Price We Pay* (New York: Praeger, 1969).

unending pursuit of progress men are driven even farther apart and come
to depend instead, for all their services and experiences, directly upon the
creations of technology.[18]

While this argument represents a serious indictment of modern industrial
societies, it is essential to note how it differs from the neo-Malthusian arguments.
The Club of Rome and its partisans say that continued economic growth is
impossible; Mishan, in contrast, tells us that it is *undesirable*. The key distinction
here is that the Mishan position implies a choice: we *can* follow a course of
continued growth if we choose, but we can also select a style of civilization
which places emphasis on different sorts of values. This issue is admittedly an
extremely complex one that involves a great many noneconomic value judgments about what constitutes the "good life." On this, let us simply offer a few
brief observations. First, it is frankly very difficult to envision a transition to a
no-growth economy without an elaborate system of central planning and controls. An extended set of ceilings and associated regulations would be necessary
to restrain the output of each industry and to coordinate the mix of different
outputs in the economy. This in itself implies the creation of a large bureaucracy
and sets of controls that we would regard as themselves the likely source of
many difficulties including, perhaps, a potential threat to our political liberties.[19]
Second, even if we were to reach a state of ZEG without too many dislocations, this choice is likely to involve certain other "costs." One of the likely
casualties of ZEG is the amelioration of poverty. Much of the world continues to
exist at a subsistence standard of living, and a halt in growth in the near future
would in all likelihood condemn future generations to a similar fate. As Robert
Solow points out, "The rich Western nations have never been able to agree on
the principle of allocating as much as one percent of their GNP to aid undeveloped countries. They are unlikely to be willing to share their wealth on any
substantial scale with the poor countries. Even if they were, there are so many
more poor people in the world that an equally shared income would be quite
low. The *only* prospect of a decent life for Asia, Africa, and Latin America is
more total output."[20] Thus, there is indeed a tradeoff between progress toward
a more equitable income distribution and that toward a quieter, cleaner world of
zero growth. Even in the United States itself, continued growth promises the
most feasible and painless method of raising incomes at the low end of the
spectrum; an electorate will probably be far less willing to transfer part of its

---

[18] Ibid., pp. 154–55.
[19] An alternative possibility is a major reorientation of values: an abandonment of material-
istic motivations. In some societies, material drives are indeed far weaker than in ours. But
it should be noted that it is by no means clear how to induce such a change in values. It is
naive to suppose that such measures as cessation of advertising or even a political revolution
will automatically bring it about. In any event, even if we know how to manipulate the
values of the general public, to whom would we be prepared to entrust this awesome power?
[20] "Is the End of the World at Hand?" *Challenge* 16 (March-April 1973): 41.

current income to poorer families than to allow a part of the *increment* in national income to go to less affluent households. One can also make a plausible case that ZEG would intensify international conflict in the resulting scramble for a fixed basket of world output.

Finally, we stress that programs of environmental protection will themselves be costly. The achievement of desired standards of air and water quality and other amenities will require large commitments of resources. The public sector will have to channel large sums into the public treasury to finance the treatment of wastes, environmental clean-up programs, and the provision of additional services to enhance the quality of life. In addition, the adoption of recycling techniques and other methods of production involving less pollution implies increased costs in the private sector, which consumers will have to bear in the form of higher prices for many goods and services. The use, for example, of cleaner, but more expensive, sources of energy means increased costs and prices. The Council on Environmental Quality estimates that the attainment of the nation's legislated targets for environmental quality will require pollution-control expenditures over the decade 1975-84 of $486 billion (in 1975 dollars).[21] In brief, our efforts to upgrade the environment will themselves require substantial resources which growth can help to make available.

6. Some Concluding Remarks

Let us emphasize, in concluding our discussion of the issue of economic growth, that we share with Barry Commoner and others a deep concern over the degradation of the environment. The smog that envelops many of our cities, the pollution of our waterways, and the excessive levels of congestion and noise that plague many of our metropolitan areas represent a real deterioration in the quality of life, and, if unchecked, pose a serious threat to the future of mankind. We also share with them a distrust of growth for growth's sake.

On all this, we are in full agreement with the proponents of zero economic growth. Where we tend to part company, however, is over the most realistic *and* effective cure for the disease. We saw in earlier chapters that the mechanism of environmental decay is not so much a matter of economic development and industrialization as it is our failure to build into the economic system proper safeguards against excessive levels of the activities that pollute the environment. We have, in effect, taken society's increasingly scarce supplies of clean air and water and given them away without charge.

In our view, the appropriate response to environmental problems is not to bring a complete halt to the expansion of the economy, but rather to build into

---

[21] *Environmental Quality, The Seventh Annual Report of the Council on Environmental Quality* (Washington, D.C.: U.S. Government Printing Office, September 1976), p. 167.

it a powerful set of incentives to reduce those activities that degrade the environment. With such incentives as a basic part of our economic structure, we do not foresee the inevitable catastrophe envisioned by the neo-Malthusians. Continued growth and the associated increases in standards of living are consistent with improvement in environmental quality, *if* we adopt the measures needed to induce individual producers and consumers to economize on their use of environmental resources. And that is the objective of this book: to outline the kinds of policies that will provide the desired protection of the environment and of the quality of life, without forcing the economy into absolute stagnation.

Part II

CRITICAL POLICY ISSUES
FOR THE QUALITY OF LIFE

10

The Provision of Urban Services

This book deals primarily with the natural environment: the purity of the air, the cleanliness of our waterways, and the maintenance of society's nature preserves. But it is important to point out as emphatically as possible that the quality of life depends on more than the preservation of our natural heritage alone. In a nation where the bulk of the population lives in cities and suburbs, the quality of life is eroded very directly by dirty streets, high crime rates, the deterioration of city schools, and ill-planned use of land.

This chapter and the next explore some of these issues. In a sense, they are a digression from our central topic of environmental policy in the more narrow sense. But we examine them here to stress that, from a broader conception of "the environment," we must deal with a wide range of urban problems that have a profound impact on the quality of life.

We introduce this examination of urban problems with a very specific issue: the rapidly rising costs of providing various local services. This is, of course, only one of the factors that has contributed to the deterioration of urban services, but we are convinced that it is of great importance. Moreover, it is a matter that is widely misunderstood and one for which systematic economic analysis can provide considerable illumination.

1. The Rising Cost of Urban Services: Some Figures and Perceptions

We can, perhaps, best introduce this issue by reproducing an "advertisement" that appeared recently in the *New York Times:*

WILL TAXES BE THE DEATH OF ATLANTA?

> Taxes go up. Services go down. And people move out. Not only in New York, Newark and Detroit. But even Atlanta, which some call the world's next great city.
> In the past four years, Atlanta tax collections soared by $17 million. . . .
> A homeowner gets socked with an 8% annual hike in his home valuation. Tax rates climbed too: 17% in 1975. Water and sewer fees almost doubled.
> Higher taxes and more revenues collected should mean improved services. Right?
> Wrong. Garbage collection went from twice weekly backyard to once-a-week curbside. Downtown gets dirtier, parks and classrooms more crowded.
> Any wonder 6,300 taxpayers leave Atlanta every year? . . .
> The real threat to Atlanta is not lack of money. It's poor management. Inefficiency. And lack of leadership at City Hall."[1]

Were this an isolated case, we could perhaps attribute it to some special circumstances in Atlanta. But we are all too well aware that the same story is repeated in nearly all the major cities in our nation and in many other countries. On closer examination, we find that a diverse set of urban services has in recent decades shared one very fundamental and disturbing characteristic: extraordinary rates of cost increases. Even before the unprecedented inflation rates of the early 1970s, we find, for example, that between the years 1947 and 1967 the cost of elementary education *per pupil* rose at a compounded rate in excess of 6½ percent per year.[2] Costs of hospital care increased even faster: over the period 1947 to 1963 cost per patient-day in U.S. hospitals rose at an annual compounded rate of 7.4 percent.[3] The pattern of cost increases for several other services—higher education, libraries, and the performing arts—exhibits similar magnitudes.

---

[1] Advertisement by American Federation of State, County and Municipal Employees Local 1644, in *New York Times,* May 1, 1977, Sect. 4, p. 17.

[2] D. F. Bradford, R. A. Malt, and W. E. Oates, "The Rising Cost of Local Public Services: Some Evidence and Reflections," *National Tax Journal,* June 1969, p. 190.

[3] Ibid., p. 195. In recent years, hospital costs have increased even faster. Martin Feldstein and Amy Taylor report that in the last decade, average cost per patient day rose at an annual rate of increase of 13.8 percent. See their "The Rapid Rise of Hospital Costs," Dicussion Paper No. 351, January 1977, Harvard Institute of Economic Research, Harvard University, Cambridge, Mass., p. 8.

Meanwhile, *in the remainder of the economy costs rose at less than 1½ percent per year over this period.*

Such rapidly increasing costs have in many cases led to significant decreases in the quality or the quantity of these services: streets have gotten dirtier; libraries have had to reduce the hours during which they are open; and hospitals have become increasingly overcrowded. Yet public spending on these services has hardly remained stationary. Between 1946 and 1969 expenditures of U.S. state and local governments, which are in considerable part devoted to such services, rose from $11 billion to $131 billion, *a more than tenfold increase in less than twenty-five years,* while GNP increased at less than half that rate.[4] Surely, budgetary increases of this magnitude should have permitted not only the maintenance of the quantity and quality of these services, but significant increases in both. Their failure to do so certainly requires explanation.

Observers have often attributed these problems to three basic causes: governmental inefficiency, growth in population, and inflation. But closer inspection shows they are not the real villains. In the United States, for example, many universities, hospitals, and theaters are privately run. Yet, the costs of these services are going up just as rapidly as those provided by government. Indeed, the cost of medicine has increased most quickly of all. Nor can the explanation be the growth in the size of the population. The postwar baby boom did increase the number of children to be educated. However, the educational figures cited earlier referred to cost *per pupil* (i.e., they were already adjusted to eliminate the effects of population growth). Finally, we cannot attribute the problem to inflation. If inflation were the explanation, in an economy where prices rose at 1½ percent per year we would also expect cost per pupil to rise at that rate—not at 6½ percent per year. Obviously, even after we take account of the effects of inflation, we still have some 5 of the 6½ percent growth in cost per pupil to be explained.

There is, of course, no single explanation for the rapidly rising costs of these services. Rural-urban-suburban migration patterns, a rising student population, the rather inflexible tax base in most cities, and a host of other problems have contributed to the financial plight of the urban public sector. Some of these problems may be peculiar to recent decades and may or may not persist in the future. However, we have argued elsewhere that there exists a chronic "cost disease" that infects not only governmental services, but also a wide variety of services provided by private industry and by private nonprofit institutions.[5] This cost disease threatens to price out of the market many of the

---

[4] Massive increases in state-local spending have continued in the 1970s. For fiscal year 1975 these expenditures were over $230 billion, which represents a rate of increase in state-local spending well in excess of that for the economy as a whole during the first half of the decade.

[5] For a formal treatment of the "cost-disease" problem, see W. Baumol and W. Oates, *The Theory of Environmental Policy* (Englewood Cliffs, N.J.: Prentice-Hall, Inc., 1975), Part 3.

services which we usually take for granted: elementary and higher education, medical services, the handicrafts, the live performance of music, drama, and dance, and libraries; in short, many of the things which we associate with a vital and appealing life.

We will contend that a substantial portion of the cost problems that beset these services is inherent in the nature of their technology. It is not a new problem; this cost disease has plagued the services for a long time and is likely to continue to do so for the foreseeable future. It appears, moreover, that there is no painless cure. We can predict with considerable confidence that the cost of these services will rise continually at a rate more rapid than costs for the economy as a whole. But there is nevertheless a bright side to the matter; as we will see, the very process that causes the problem generates the resources which can enable society to cope with it, *if its character is understood.*

2. Lagging Technological Progress in the Personal Services

To understand the source of the cost disease, we must consider the continual improvements in production methods that have increased over time the productive capability of labor—the goods and services an average worker can produce per hour. These increases in output per worker have occurred much more consistently in some productive activities than in others. In particular, there is a broad class of activities, which we will call (admittedly with some oversimplification) the *personal services,* that are relatively resistant to continuous productivity-increasing innovation.

Two closely related characteristics of the personal services inhibit steady increases in output per person. First, many of these services are inherently unstandardized so that their mass production is extremely difficult. Certain forms of medical care are a good example. Even when two patients have the same disease, the treatment appropriate for one may produce dangerously allergic reactions in the other. Standardization is equally difficult in such disparate services as special education, automotive and watch repair, and dance.

The second obstacle to rapid and continued productivity increases in the personal services is the frequently intimate connection between the *quantity* of labor and the quality of the end product. It is not easy, for example, to imagine how we can mechanize a teacher's reading and criticism of students' papers. An increase in instructor productivity (through an increase in the number of students per teacher) would in all likelihood have serious consequences for the quality of the "product." In the live performing arts, the obstacles to productivity increases are perhaps the most clear-cut of all. It takes 1½ hours of labor to execute a Schubert trio scored for a half-hour performance, and that is all there is to the matter. "Removing Judge Brack from the cast of Hedda Gabler would certainly reduce labor input to Ibsen's masterpiece, but it would also destroy the product. Nor could one increase the productivity of the cast by performing the play at twice the speed."[6]

We do not mean to say that any increases in productivity are impossible for these activities. Programmed teaching materials have no doubt raised the teacher's productivity to some extent; television and the jet airliner have permitted performers to reach many cities, either at once or in quick succession, and have thereby yielded spectacular increases in the productivity of actors and musicians; and more sophisticated communication and detection systems have facilitated the operations of police and firemen. But it is nevertheless much more difficult in the personal services to achieve regular and frequent increases in productivity than elsewhere in the economy. The techniques used today, for example, by a policeman in "pounding the beat," differ very little from those employed by his counterpart a century ago. In how many lines of manufacturing can the same be said?[7]

3. The Effects of Slow Productivity Growth: Rising Relative Costs

As productivity in the overall economy rises with the passage of time, the personal services find themselves at a growing cost disadvantage. In time, compounding can make this cost differential grow into a frightening magnitude. We can illustrate this by considering the history of two products: a personal service, say a haircut, and a manufactured good, say a fountain pen. Let us assume for simplicity that each is produced solely with labor and that in the initial year it takes one hour of labor to produce a haircut and one hour to produce a pen, so that the initial cost of a haircut and a pen is the same. If an hour of labor costs $1.00 in the first year, then the cost of each item will be $1.00. Let us suppose, however, that technical progress in the manufacture of pens generates increases in their output per hour of work at a rate of 3 percent annually, while the annual rate of increase in haircuts per labor-hour is only 1 percent.[8] Finally, we postu-

---

[6] Alan Peacock, "Welfare Economics and Public Subsidies to the Arts," *The Manchester School of Economic and Social Studies,* December 1969.

[7] It is sometimes objected that the preceding analysis misses improvements in the *quality* of many of the services. Productivity changes in some services, it is suggested, have taken the form of better output rather than increased quantity per unit of labor input. There seems little reason to doubt, for example, that an appendectomy today is a much better product than the corresponding operation in 1900. There is little question about the significance of such improvements for the welfare of the community. But it is important to recognize that they are largely irrelevant for the central point of our present discussion: the rising quantity of *money* required to procure the service. The fact is that neither a 1900 appendectomy nor a 1900 education is available today, no matter which of them the consumer prefers. It may be comforting to the harassed mayor of a city to be assured that the children of the constituency are getting a better education, but this does not help to raise the rapidly rising quantity of money needed to finance that education.

[8] These rates of increase in productivity are, incidentally, fairly realistic. A study of the barbering industry found that, over the period 1939 to 1963, output per worker had in-

late that wages in both industries rise at the same rate as productivity in the production of pens, namely at 3 percent per year (since, in practice, productivity gains in a firm or industry are usually matched by rising wage demands from labor unions).[9] Thus, for pens the rise in wages per hour is offset by the rise in output per hour, and the cost of a pen remains unchanged over time at $1.00. In contrast, productivity increases in the provision of haircuts cannot keep up with rising wages; as a result, the cost of a haircut increases steadily at 2 percent annually (the difference between the increases in wages and in output per hour). So, while the cost of a pen remains at $1.00, the cost of a haircut increases to $1.02 in the second year, to $1.22 by the tenth year, to $2.67 in the twentieth year, and finally, after the passage of a century, a haircut will cost over seven times as much as a pen.[10]

The evidence in fact shows that such differentials between the costs of many personal services and manufactured goods have persisted for over a century; in recent decades they have in several important instances been substantially larger than the differential in our preceding example. And this, we are convinced, has been a powerful force contributing to the growing financial distress of state and local governments throughout the United States and in other industrialized countries as well.

The case of education illustrates this process quite clearly. Consider, for example, a school with twenty-five pupils per teacher. If the teacher receives a pay increase of 5 percent per year (in line with pay increases elsewhere in the economy), it follows inexorably from the arithmetic that teacher salaries per pupil must also rise by 5 percent annually (assuming no rise in the pupil-teacher ratio). Since salaries make up the great bulk of the school budget, it is hardly surprising to find that cost per pupil in our public *and* private schools has risen far more rapidly than unit costs for the economy as a whole. This assumes real significance when we recognize that expenditures for education are by far the

---

creased at an average annual rate of 0.6 percent. In contrast, from 1947 to 1965, output per worker in manufacturing rose on average at 3.0 percent annually. See Victor Fuchs, *The Service Economy* (New York: Columbia University Press, 1968), pp. 51, 109.

[9]The labor markets for the personal services and in manufacturing are not isolated from one another. If wages of policemen, teachers, street cleaners, or barbers fall significantly behind those in manufacturing, in a prosperous economy labor will simply move out of the former occupations and look for jobs in the latter. Scarcity of labor supply will force wages in the personal services upward, close behind those in the remainder of the economy. The evidence suggests that over longer periods wages in the personal services keep up with those paid elsewhere much more closely than is sometimes believed.

[10]We should emphasize that, while our illustration has assumed (fairly realistically) that wages constantly rise, increasing money wages really are not the source of the problem. So long as wages in the two sectors of the economy maintain approximate parity, whether they rise or fall, the *relative* cost of the personal services must increase in the manner described. Suppose money wages were to remain absolutely fixed over time. In that case in our example, the dollar cost of a haircut would actually decrease 1 percent per year. But the cost of a pen would then fall 3 percent per year, so that the annual 2 percent differential rise in relative costs would remain.

largest item in state-local budgets. The fact that spending on education has in recent decades grown at a rate almost double that of GNP has been a source of tremendous pressure on local finances. Year after year, taxpayers in local school districts have been asked to approve budgets calling for large increases in expenditure accompanied by continuing rises in local property-tax rates. In some instances, they have simply refused to do so; such "taxpayers' revolts" have produced severe dislocations in schooling programs.

A projection of the future price implications of the cost disease may help to dramatize the general point. Assume that the cost of personal services continues to rise at about 4 percent per year faster than costs in the remainder of the economy. Using the techniques described in Chapter 8, we can readily calculate what they are likely to become at some stipulated future date, say thirty-five years from now. Table 10-1 presents such projected prices for several representative services. It should be noted that *these figures have been corrected to eliminate any effects of inflation;* they are expressed in real terms in dollars of 1978 purchasing power!

In summary, when one sector of an economy persistently lags behind the rest in terms of productivity growth, the products of that sector must invariably rise in cost relative to the cost levels in the rest of the economy, and that rise will be persistent and cumulative. The personal services, in short, are the victims of technological progress in other sectors of the economy, and their problems grow worse with the increased efficiency achieved elsewhere by innovation.

4. Rising Costs and the Supply of the Personal Services

With costs rising cumulatively over the foreseeable future, continued supply of the personal services will obviously run into a variety of difficulties. Already, we can see examples of at least four different developments. First, some services have virtually disappeared or at least their volume has fallen drastically. Handmade furniture is increasingly unusual; doctors' house calls are also largely gone. Second, although certain other services continue to be available, their quality has undergone progressive deterioration in an attempt to offset the pressure of rising costs. Dirtier streets, poorer postal service, subways with increasing accident rates, and larger classes and split sessions in some schools are a few examples. Third, certain other services will be transformed, in whole or in part, into unpaid amateur activities. Hand-thrown pottery, for instance, is now mostly produced as a hobby, and shaving is rarely done anymore by barbers. Finally, there are services, notably medicine and (at least until recently) education, for which the public has generally resisted any decrease in supply or quality. For this we have had to pay the price: expenditures have had to match cumulatively rising costs. Anyone who has recently purchased either of these services in the United States knows all too well how painful these rising costs can be.

TABLE 10-1

PROJECTED 2013 PRICES OF
SEVERAL SERVICES IN DOLLARS OF
1978 PURCHASING POWER

Annual tuition, room and board, private university	$25,000
Annual auto insurance fee	$ 2,500
Hospital cost per day	$ 600
Fee: Doctor's visit	$ 100
Top ticket price: Broadway musical	$ 75

5. Can Society Finance the Rising Costs of Personal Services?

It might seem that there is no real cure for the cost disease of the services, but if our analysis is correct, the disease, by its very nature, can provide for its own treatment. The analysis in essence shows that the rising *relative* cost of the personal services is part of the price of economic progress; it results from the cumulative increases in productivity in manufacturing (and agriculture), while productivity in the personal services remains unchanged or rises relatively slowly.

But the very process that generates the rising costs of the services automatically provides the wealth to permit society to continue to purchase them. If it wants to, the community could obtain ever-increasing quantities of personal services despite continuing increases in their prices. To do so, it needs only to shift *part* of the labor force from the manufacturing sector to the services. Taking an extreme example, suppose that output per worker in manufacturing rises at 3 percent per year, while in the services there is absolutely zero increase in productivity. If 1 or 2 percent of the manufacturing labor force were transferred annually to the production of services, then an ever-increasing supply of *both* manufactured goods and services would result. The output of services would rise, because more labor is continually being devoted to it and, at the same time, the decline in manufacturing workers would be more than offset by the continuing rise in output per worker. A process of this general type seems in fact to have characterized the historical experience of the advanced, industrialized countries. In the United States, for example, the share of total employment accounted for by the service industries has steadily risen, at the expense of the shares of agriculture and manufacturing. By the mid-1960s, the service sector of the economy absorbed over 50 percent of total employment, which led Victor Fuchs to describe the United States as the world's first "Service Economy."

A simple extrapolation of the sort we carried out earlier suggests the options before us and the magnitudes that may be at stake in the future. Assume, as before, that productivity in the remainder of the economy grows 4 percent faster than it does in the personal services. Then a calculation such as those described in Chapter 8 readily confirms the following:

1. If expenditures on the personal services are kept to today's amounts, with increases in dollar outlays limited to the rise in the overall price level, then the output of the personal services will actually fall by some 75 percent within thirty-five years!
2. Yet the output of personal services does not have to fall. For example, we can keep the outputs of the services to their current quantities and quality. This will require us to spend on them about four times the amount we lay out on them today (in dollars of current purchasing power). Yet rising productivity will nevertheless permit the per-capita output of manufactured goods to rise by 300 percent.
3. If, instead, society decides that the output of the personal services is to grow by the same percentage as the outputs of other products of the economy, then expenditure on the personal services must rise from about 25 percent of GNP today to more than 55 percent in thirty-five years! Yet in that case the nation's output of manufactured products will nevertheless still rise substantially, and permit more than a doubling of the per-capita supply of consumer goods and all other products.

The point is that society possesses the means to maintain, or even to increase, the output of personal services over time, should it desire to do so.

6. The Moral of the Cost-Disease Analysis

It is not our place as economists to argue that the public *should* want and *should* be willing to pay for fine medical care, an excellent educational system, clean streets, an abundance of library facilities, and a flourishing program in the arts. These are matters that the public will have to decide for itself. What is clear is that, if funds for such activities become increasingly scarce, there will be a profound effect upon the quality of life. Many of these services will either disappear or undergo serious deterioration in a variety of ways.

We reiterate that we have no special competence that gives us a special right to advocate the expenditures required for such services to prosper. Our only objective is to help prevent the progressive decay of these services because of a misapprehension that society can no longer afford them. A natural consequence of the virtually inevitable rise in their prices is a sort of money illusion that leads people to believe that they are being priced out of the reach of the community. But since their rising relative prices are merely a reflection of our growing productivity, that *is* merely an illusion, as our analysis has shown. After all, an economy that can more than double its per-capita output of manufactured goods and of personal services in thirty-five years is hardly threatened with either stagnation or inability to afford rising living standards.

7. An Outline of Part 2

In this chapter, we have examined one particular phenomenon—the rising cost of the personal services—which has, we believe, been a powerful force underlying the deterioration in the range and quality of a variety of urban services. In Chapter 11 we continue our exploration of urban problems with the focus shifting to patterns of land use and urban blight. Again we emphasize that the treatment of these problems of the urban "environment" is fundamental to the enhancement of the quality of life. To be candid, however, we must admit that our analysis of policy options to deal with these problems will be much more tentative in character than our policy proposals for the control of pollution. As we shall see in Part 3, economic analysis has some very direct and, we believe, compelling implications for the design of genuinely effective policies to protect the natural environment. We feel somewhat less confident about the appropriate means to treat our specifically urban ills, but we would feel somewhat remiss if we were to ignore a set of issues so fundamental to our concern with the quality of life.

The last chapters in Part 2 address two quite different issues that are crucial to the formulation of environmental policy. Chapter 12 treats the distributive problem: Who pays for and who benefits from environmental programs? Not only is this a basic matter of social justice, but it bears profoundly on the generation of widespread political support for environmental policies. Chapter 13 turns to still another issue in which the political element figures in a most fundamental way: the international aspects of environmental policy. Here there are two primary problems: the damage that one country inflicts on the environment of other nations, and the difficulty in coordinating national pollution control policies. Part 3 of this book will describe a set of programs for the protection of the environment that applies, in principle, in a global, as well as a national, setting. However, our concern in Chapter 13 is the political and economic pressures in the international arena that may make these policies difficult to carry out and the scope for effective unilateral action in the absence of international cooperation.

Part 2 of this book thus explores a rather diverse set of issues, but each is of critical importance for the quality of life. Moreover, they all pose serious problems for economic analysis, in part because the state of existing analysis is relatively unsatisfactory, but also because they are so profoundly related to political circumstances. For these reasons, we must acknowledge that the policy prescriptions in Part 2 rest on grounds much less firm than those underlying our conclusions in Part 3.

11

Land Use, Urban Blight,
and the Deterioration of City Life

In Part 1 we concentrated on environmental issues about which there is general agreement: we all want cleaner air and less polluted lakes and rivers. These objectives do involve hard choices; improvements in air and water quality come at a real cost in terms of the sacrifice of other goods and services. But at least we can argue that a cleaner environment is, in itself, a good thing.

However, we now turn to a topic of central importance to environmental quality (more broadly considered) that presents more serious difficulties, not only in designing effective policies, but even in the sense of defining society's objectives. Few areas of economic policy are likely to have a more profound effect on the future quality of life than decisions influencing patterns of land use. Yet there is much disagreement over what are "desirable" uses of land; in short, it is by no means clear what society wants to achieve. Nevertheless, the economist again has some important things to say about land-use policies, simply because an understanding of how market forces and public policies shape land-use decisions is essential to the formulation of effective programs to achieve society's objectives, whatever they are.

While there may be no overall consensus about the desirable form of the urban and rural landscape, one dimension of the problem has become a matter of general concern: the progressive deterioration of the cities. The exodus of the well-to-do and of jobs from the cities to suburban communities has, in many instances, left the cities as residual locations or "reservations" for lower-income families and for many of the social ills that beset our society. The amelioration of urban poverty, crime, and general deterioration has thus become an explicit target of public policy. On this matter there is less dispute about goals, although even here things are not absolutely clear. The main difficulty, however, in our view is the failure of policy makers to find ways to reverse the cycle of cumulative deterioration. Most past and existing urban-renewal programs seem, at best, to have had only modest and *transitory* effects on the problems of the cities; they have not succeeded in establishing a progressive and continuing revitalization of city life.

1. Alternative Prospects for the Future: The Choice of Land-Use Patterns

We can best illustrate the issues at stake in land-use policy by considering two extreme prospects for the end of this century. At one pole envision, a quarter century from now, a vast extension of suburban sprawl—enormous tracts of single-family houses each with its own lot. Los Angeles or Oklahoma City, now striking examples of suburban sprawl, would be the norm. The other possible extreme is a number of highly concentrated population centers—perhaps, futuristic linear cities clustered along fast, efficient public transportation corridors, surrounded by open countryside more or less "unspoiled" by industry or significant numbers of residences. These cities might offer a variety of neighborhoods ranging from high-rise apartment buildings surrounded by open space to more old-fashioned, small-scale buildings. The central organizing principle of this scenario would be economy in the use of land: clustering the population into small, high-density areas, while preserving unsullied, open space.

Many dedicated environmentalists are very likely to find the latter to be the more attractive option. However, the issue is by no means cut and dried. There is a very large, and perhaps growing, portion of the population to whom suburban living is an ideal. The Los Angeles model has an enormous attraction, and those whose goal is a piece of ground to call their own may be as entitled to their choice as those who treasure virgin forests and undrained wetlands.

Such differences, incidentally, may not simply represent haphazard variations in taste. It is at least plausible that they reflect differences in income class, in cultural background, and in social grouping. We will see in the next chapter that low-income groups make relatively little use of recreation areas such as national parks; for them it only seems natural that public expenditures on rather different items, perhaps hospitals and technical training programs, might have higher priority. It is therefore not surprising that lower-income groups are less enthusiastic than more affluent groups about nature preserves. Some socioeconomic groups also appear to have stronger preferences for individual homes on small lots (particularly those who have struggled out of poverty into the lower-middle income classes).

In sum, there is wide variation in taste among residential life styles, and society's choice among them is closely related to its income-distribution policies. The American dream of a quiet little home in the suburbs, and the Jane Jacobs vision of urban living are each shared by many. There simply is no consensus, and no one view of the matter which can be labelled "correct." Our land-use policies today will certainly leave their mark upon the life styles of succeeding generations. But neither we nor any self-appointed judges can claim to know the best course for society.

2. The Appropriate Goals of Urban Renewal

There is clearly much less dispute about the overall social goals involved in the second major topic of this chapter: urban deterioration. The decline of our cities, which has manifested itself both in physical deterioration and in the growth of a variety of social ills, is obviously as important for the quality of life as is the state of the natural environment. In both cases it is generally agreed that improvement is desirable in itself, subject only to considerations of expense and the availability of ways to achieve the desired improvements.

But even in the case of urban rehabilitation, once we go beyond the broadest generalities, the objectives again are not clear-cut. First, it is not certain that all cities should be revived. Some urban areas have long ceased to provide either the economic or cultural advantages usually characteristic of a large metropolis. Rather, they have become little more than shabby compact repositories for poor families who cannot afford any better location. Some thoughtful observers have recently begun to ask whether such places have any redeeming social value. If not, it may be better gradually to abandon such sites, rather than to try to patch up a community that in the long run is unlikely to prove economically sustainable. Particularly if in fact few people live in these cities by choice, while most share the dream of suburban living, it may be hard to make a good case for preservation of such cities. There is also some question about the best *type* of city. Tall buildings can house many people in a small area and help to preserve a great deal of open space. But they change the character of the neighborhood in a way that may sap the vitality of the community and destroy its variety. Improved roadways can help industry in the cities, but at the same time make the neighborhoods through which they cut unlivable.

Thus, the objectives of urban renewal are far from pat. Moreover, for reasons that we will examine presently, policy makers have been hard-pressed to come up with effective ways to implement *whatever* goals are decided upon.

3. On Means to Influence Land Use

Economic analysis *can,* however, contribute some insights into effective ways to achieve our land-use objectives, once they are chosen. To design an efficacious land-use program one must understand how individual choices, operating through the market and other institutions, determine the uses to which land is put. For example, if we do not understand the *mechanism* that leads to urban deterioration, we cannot hope to design a policy for rehabilitation that will really work.

We can readily list several major elements that have profoundly influenced land-use patterns in recent years: innovation and evolution in transportation, the postwar move to the suburbs, and a variety of public policies such as rent controls, real estate tax laws, and zoning regulations. These are, of course, all interrelated, as we will presently see. No doubt there are other important influences, many of them outside the economist's range of competence, but this partial list permits us to deal with a number of significant issues for land-use policy. We want to emphasize that anyone who is to have any reasonable hope of designing effective land-use policy must understand these powerful influences on land-use patterns. Any program that ignores or flies in the face of these forces is virtually doomed to failure.

4. Suburbanization and Transportation

The movement of middle- and upper-income families from the central cities is not just a matter of desire for more space. In part, it is a natural response to the rise in per-capita incomes since World War II at a pace and with a degree of persistence unparalleled in our history. As people get richer they want more amenities; spacious homes are among these amenities.[1]

At the same time the exodus from the cities was stimulated by changes in transportation facilities, both directly and indirectly. The direct effect is not quite as straightforward as it may seem. The automobile and the construction of superhighways appear to have made it easier to commute to the city. But, in fact, in many cases it is harder and more time-consuming for suburbanites to get into the cities today than it was in the interwar period, when suburban trains ran frequently and operated along a wider network. Today daily traffic jams in many cases have transformed automobile commuting into a penance that taxes the traveller's patience and pocketbook.

Changes in transportation have encouraged suburbanization in a way that is less widely recognized: they have facilitated the dispersal of industry as

---

[1] For a formal treatment of this process of suburbanization, see, for example, Edwin Mills, *Urban Economics* (Glenview, Ill.: Scott, Foresman, and Company, 1972).

160

much as that of individual residences. The network of highways has favored transportation of freight by truck instead of railroad. One of the main characteristics of truck traffic is that it is at its most efficient *outside* the central cities, where it can avoid traffic jams and crowded streets. Unlike the railroads it gains little advantage from a central depot in a large urban terminus. This change has coincided with innovations in factory and warehouse technology that also have helped to induce industry to leave the central city. Automated processes operate most easily in a single-story building; they often require plants that extend over very large areas and are likely to be prohibitively expensive in the center of a city. Thus, the growth in transportation by truck has made it easier for firms to relocate in a manner compatible with the requirements of the newer technology. And as industry moved out of the city, employees tended to be attracted to the suburbs along with it, partly because they wanted to go in any event, and partly to be nearer to work.[2]

This suggests that a land-use program that tries to recentralize industry will have no easy time of it. Industry has a heavy investment in its decentralized locations, and both its own technology and that of the transportation system that serves it make such a target extremely expensive. The recent rise in fuel costs and the attendant increase in transport costs may, perhaps, have done more to facilitate such a change than any set of land-use programs. By increasing the cost of shipment, rising fuel prices have offered a real bonus to centralization. Moreover, since railroads are more efficient users of fuel as measured per ton-mile of freight carried, the rise in fuel price in this way too is an impediment to further dispersal.[3]

5. Exodus from the Cities as a Cumulative Process

There is another aspect of the exodus from the cities that merits particular attention. The relocation to suburban areas of upper and middle socioeconomic groups and of industry is a process that feeds on itself. Policy makers must understand this process if they are to influence it. For a number of reasons, the more industry and higher-income groups leave the city, the more difficult or less attractive it becomes for those left behind to stay on there. That is, the exodus leads to further exodus. The most obvious contributor to this cumulative process is the central city's tax structure. As the city loses industries and individuals from socioeconomic groups most capable of paying taxes, those who remain must shoulder an ever-increasing tax burden (unless there is a concomitant cut in the provision of services). Every erosion in the tax base by the flight of tax-

---

[2]On all this, see Raymond Vernon, *The Changing Economic Function of the Central City* (New York: Committee for Economic Development, 1959).
[3]Pollution-control measures may have a similar effect, since railroads emit far smaller quantities of pollutant per ton-mile than do trucks.

payers is likely to require a rise in tax *rates* upon property values, and in other forms of taxation. But this, in turn, makes the city unattractive to the remaining taxpayers and may induce some of them to join the exodus. Each step in the process leads to the next: migration leads to higher tax rates; higher tax rates induce more migration; that then forces tax rates still higher, and so on in a chain of events that seems to end only with the complete deterioration of the city.[4]

Indeed, the role of taxes is merely one of the elements in this process. Urban blight itself can play a similar and equally significant role, for growing deterioration is also an important component of the cumulative process. The movement of higher-income groups out of the cities has not only reduced the tax base of the municipal government, but has also left the city to socioeconomic groups most in need of schooling, improved housing, and a variety of other servies. The result has been a deterioration in living conditions within the cities: poorer schools, neglected streets, increased crime rates, which have made the city even less desirable to those who can afford to move. This has led to further outmigration which, in its turn, produces a further reduction in the average wealth of those who remain, and so the process continues, apparently ad infinitum.

In such a process, each character individually is powerless to alter the course of events; one's best efforts to cope with the situation only make things worse. A person who migrates from the city might very well have preferred to stay and may be distressed by the blight enveloping the metropolis, but as an individual he or she is powerless to do anything about it. If a middle-class family decides to remain in the city, its own income has a negligible effect upon the overall economy of the city, but it subjects itself to poorer schools, the dangers of crime, and a variety of other social costs associated with urban deterioration. Business firms, too, are swept along in this process; they follow their employees to the suburbs where they contribute to the tax base and employment opportunities and thereby induce other firms and individuals to follow their example.[5]

We emphasize the cumulative character of these problems, because of its critical implications for the usual urban-renewal programs. Policy measures that may seem entirely appropriate are often no more than transitory palliatives. Federal grants for housing improvements, new school construction, or even direct

---

[4]For an empirical study of this cumulative flight to the suburbs, see D. Bradford and H. Kelejian, "An Econometric Model of the Flight to the Suburbs," *Journal of Political Economy* 81 (May-June 1973): 566–89.
[5]This brief discussion only highlights the most noteworthy of the cumulative processes that have helped to stimulate suburbanization. There are others. For example, urban residents will readily recognize the cumulative process underlying the deterioration of many local transportation systems. The typical scenario includes a decline in the number of riders that forces the authority to increase fares and reduce the quality of service, but that in turn produces a further fall in number of passengers, leading to still higher fares and yet poorer service, etc.

revenues (such as the federal revenue-sharing programs) may have the effect of briefly turning back the hands of the clock; they may in some respects restore an earlier state of affairs. But so long as these programs do not change the fundamental dynamics of the process—so long as they do not alter the sequence of deterioration and exodus—after a brief interval things will be back where they were.

These observations may help to explain why most recent policies designed to revive the cities have proved so disappointing and so transitory. It also suggests how much more radical any policies will have to be if they are to provide longer-term improvement. We will not go into the complex and technical issues relating to the control of cumulative processes. For our purposes it is enough to observe that the standard solutions to urban decay, which are so often undertaken as a matter of simple common sense, may be foredoomed to failure; they may serve only to waste enormous sums of money and produce disappointment and disenchantment with programs to "save the cities."

6. On Rent Controls[6]

Among the more popular policy measures to make life in the cities more attractive are rent controls. Their object is to prevent landlords from driving up the prices of available housing to a point where middle- and lower-income families can barely afford to live in them. But economists of a wide variety of political persuasions agree that there are, unfortunately, few measures less likely to achieve their purpose.

As far back as we have records, people have hoped that legislative fiat would do away with high prices. But this approach hardly ever achieves its purpose (at least over the longer run) and never fails to create problems for the future. Aside from the stimulation of ingenious means to evade such regulations, price controls invariably produce a decline in the supply and a deterioration in the quality of the very product with which the regulations are concerned.

In a period of rising prices, rent controls, in essence, become an attempt to force landlords to bear the cost of rising housing expenses. However, if they work, their effect is virtually to guarantee a halt to new construction, since no one will invest in an enterprise that has been rendered unprofitable by legislative action. Not only will new construction cease, but landlords will have little incentive to maintain and repair existing housing. In short, rent controls, if effective, will most certainly lead to a deterioration in a city's stock of housing. In some instances, it may actually lead to abandonment of dwelling units by the owner, a phenomenon that has been widespread in recent years in New York City. Abandonment does not amount simply to a reduction in housing stock; it typically

---

[6]For a useful collection of studies on rent controls in several countries, see F. A. Hayek et al., *Verdict on Rent Control* (London: Institute of Economic Affairs, 1972).

leaves behind a dilapidated eyesore, a potential source of fire to adjacent buildings, and a focal point for unsanitary conditions and petty criminal activities. One economist (whose views are generally considered to be to the left of center) has commented that bombing a city *probably* has more disastrous effects than rent controls, but that this judgment is by no means beyond dispute. Moreover, it is ironic that, in the long run, rent controls may well bring with them higher, rather than lower, rents to the community, as declining construction and increased abandonment reduce the supply of available housing, and as diminished maintenance outlays lower the quality of the remaining housing stock.

Yet the 1970s have witnessed a resurgence of rent-control legislation. Such programs were, in the 1960s, limited primarily to New York State (particularly New York City), but since that time they have spread to hundreds of communities including such major cities as Boston, Washington, Baltimore, and Miami Beach. A recent survey by the *New York Times* discovered that, in New Jersey alone, there are now about 110 communities with rent-levelling laws (including some of the older decaying center cities such as Newark, Paterson, and Jersey City).[7] The renewal of interest in such legislation stems largely from the rapid inflation in rents that took place in the late 1960s and early 1970s: the rent component of the consumer price index rose by 41 percent from 1967 to 1975. Irate tenants responded with demands for rent controls; local politicians heard these demands and responded with new laws. Yet closer analysis reveals that the overall consumer price index rose by 66 percent over this same period; thus, in nearly all metropolitan areas rents actually *fell* substantially relative to the general level of prices.

It has always been tempting to try to raise living standards by a mere legislative stroke. Unfortunately, like all acts of magic, such measures turn out to be illusions. Moreover, their consequences can be incredibly costly and destructive. Society may well have good grounds for giving priority to improvement in housing and to reductions in rents. But to achieve this goal, it must be prepared to pay the requisite cost.

7. On Property Taxes

Taxes always tend to induce changes in behavior, some of them desirable, some undesirable. A tax on industrial investment will inhibit the construction of plant and equipment and, more generally, may depress the level of economic activity, while a tax on emissions of pollutants will induce companies to decrease their discharges of these substances.

Like other taxes, property taxation generates a set of incentives. Moreover,

---

[7]Joseph P. Fried, "Spread of Rent Controls Spurs New Controversy," *New York Times*, March 7, 1976, pp. 1, 37.

property taxes on real estate are very substantial—far heavier than most people realize. Tax rates in cities frequently run to 8 or 9 percent of *total* property value. What this figure conceals is that *such a tax rate can amount to an 80 or 90 percent sales tax on housing services.* Since rents are roughly on the order of 10 percent of the value of a property, a tax of, say, 8.5 percent *on the property value* is the same as an 85 percent yearly tax *on the rental value* of that property. We may observe that, if an 85 percent sales tax were proposed for any other consumer good, it would undoubtedly be considered a crippling blow to the industry.[8]

Property taxes in rural and suburban areas typically are much lower than they are in the central cities. In New Jersey, a state which places a very heavy reliance on local property taxation, they have ranged typically from 2 to 5 percent of total value of property, while in the cities, as already indicated, they have run at 7 to 9 percent and sometimes even higher. Property tax rates in the center cities are often somewhere between two and three times as high as the average for the state. Obviously, this can affect land-use patterns very profoundly; such tax differentials introduce another serious impediment to the location of industry and of middle- and upper-class residents in the central cities. In this way too the tax system contributes to the spread of housing and industry.

There is at least one other way in which existing tax structures may contribute to deterioration of the inner city and to the exodus to the suburbs. It has often been suggested that most property taxes inadvertently favor those landlords who permit their properties to deteriorate; they act as a financial impediment to improvements. The problem is that the owner's tax bill is based on the assessed valuation of his or her property; more precisely, the property-tax bill is equal to the assessed value of the property multiplied by the local tax rate. Landlords who, for example, upgrade their buildings may find that they increase their tax bills, because the improvements can lead to a new and higher assessed valuation of their properties. Conversely, landlords who allow their properties to fall into a state of disrepair may find their tax bills reduced.[9]

Perhaps more important, even if the current regulations are not absolutely perverse, they certainly do not provide incentives for an improved housing stock.

---

[8]There is, incidentally, a lively debate at present among economists as to who actually pays the property tax. For a good summary of the differing points of view, see Henry Aaron, *Who Pays the Property Tax? A New View* (Washington, D.C.: The Brookings Institution, 1975).

[9]Recent research indicates that this particular problem is perhaps not as serious as has sometimes been suggested. For example, one careful study of this issue reports finding "no examples of reassessments occurring as a result of property improvements." Nevertheless, it is hard to believe that there is no relationship in the long run between the market value of a property and its assessment for tax purposes, and that is enough to provide at least some financial disincentive to expenditure for maintenance and improvement of property. On this see George O. Peterson et al., *Property Taxes, Housing, and the Cities* (Lexington, Mass.: D.C. Heath and Co., 1973), Chap. 4.

Without changing the *total* amount to be paid by landlords, it is possible to raise taxes on substandard properties and to offer a tax advantage to the landlord who improves his own property. Note that such a change, if designed to collect the same total amount of tax, is neither a windfall to property holders nor a penalty upon them. All that it modifies is the *structure* of the tax, in such a way that landlords must act in accord with the public interest in order to keep their payments down; it offers no bonus for destructive behavior.

8. Zoning Practices

One of the policy instruments used most widely for the control of land use is zoning: direct rules that set out a variety of practices that are prohibited by the community. Zoning laws may specify the maximum height of new buildings, set aside certain areas for structures of particular types, or require a minimum lot size for new family residences. Despite its popularity, zoning has given rise to considerable controversy, most notably about the inequities which it is said to have introduced.

On its face, zoning is a very attractive notion. It permits a locality to decide what sort of community it wishes to be. Residents can, for example, choose to keep their community relatively sparsely populated through a variety of zoning measures. Perhaps more important, the community can protect itself with appropriately designed ordinances from damage generated by unwanted migrants; for example, zoning regulations can prevent the entry of polluting factories. This gives the community some control over its own future development.

Moreover, the courts (at least until quite recently) have looked very favorably upon local zoning practices. So long as a local jurisdiction could make some sort of case that its zoning ordinances promoted the health and welfare of its residents, it encountered little effective opposition. Various court decisions (particularly the crucial Supreme Court ruling in 1926 in the case of *The Village of Euclid* vs. *Ambler Reality Co.*) permitted wide discretion for local zoning practices. By the end of the 1930s, virtually all large cities and hundreds of smaller towns had instituted zoning ordinances.

The problem with all this, as has become increasingly apparent with the continuing process of suburbanization, is that most zoning practices raise some very serious issues of equity. Close scrutiny of many ordinances reveals that they are essentially exclusionary devices to prevent the entry of those who are, for one reason or another, "undesirable." There are some instances of blatant racial discrimination in local zoning practices. In California in the 1880s, for example, when certain regulations to exclude Orientals were deemed unconstitutional, San Francisco and some other California communities simply zoned laundries out of the desirable parts of their jurisdictions and thereby confined many Orientals to certain districts.

Exclusionary zoning is not, however, solely (or even typically) the result of unreasoned prejudice. The entry of poorer households or households with many children can be very costly to other taxpayers. The poor may not be able to pay very much in taxes, and this leaves a larger share of the burden to others. Perhaps more serious, both the large family and the poor are likely to require heavy expenditures on municipal services (schooling, welfare, etc.) On both counts, the community that attracts to itself large numbers of these migrants is likely to find its previous residents subject to heavier tax burdens. It is not entirely surprising, therefore, that many communities are tempted into a program of "fiscal zoning" whose primary purpose is to keep away households that won't "pay their way."

The history of local practices to control land-use patterns is thus one in which local authorities have used a wide range of devices to exclude "undesirables" from their jurisdictions. A noted urban economist, Edwin Mills, has concluded that:

> . . . urban land use controls . . . have been used much more for exclusionary purposes than to control what economists normally think of as external diseconomies. The ostensible legal purposes of land use controls are to prevent such things as noise, air and water pollution, vibration and traffic hazards in residential neighborhoods. . . . But almost always, the desire by a politically influential group to exclude a racial, ethnic, occupational or income group from an area is part of the story. Often the exclusionary motivation is fuzzy, a desire to protect "neighborhood quality" or a familiar and customary residential composition, or merely a desire to prevent change. This conclusion is supported not only by the . . . history of land use controls but also by an examination of administrative practices. Studies to estimate carefully the damages that would be done by a particular proposed land use are rare in the administration of land use controls. Much more common are studies of the relationship between dwelling value, numbers of children, tax yields and school costs. Exclusion on racial grounds is of course illegal and is hence not an explicit consideration in land use control administration, but it cannot be doubted that it is frequently among the real reasons for the ways controls are used.[10]

As we noted, until recently such zoning ordinances have encountered no serious challenges. However, in 1975 the New Jersey Supreme Court promulgated a decision that is potentially revolutionary. In the Mt. Laurel case, the Court declared "fiscal zoning" to be illegal, because of its conflict with "regional housing needs."[11] The ruling stated that the Mt. Laurel ordinances had the

---

[10] Edwin S. Mills, "Economic Analysis of Urban Land Use Controls" (Unpublished manuscript, Princeton University, 1977), pp. 21-22.
[11] See Lester V. Chandler, "Exclusionary Zoning in New Jersey: The Mount Laurel Decision," in *Eighth Annual Report, Economic Policy Council,* State of New Jersey (Trenton, 1975), pp. 122-27.

intention and effect of excluding low-income households and that Mt. Laurel must devise a zoning plan that will enable a "fair share" of the region's poor to live in Mt. Laurel in more modest units that they can afford. The potential effects of this decision are obviously enormous; it could serve to open up the suburbs to poorer minority groups who have been effectively confined to the center cities. But while its potential consequences are great, implementation of the decision is extremely complicated and could easily stretch out over decades. We shall have to see what happens.[12]

Even zoning of property for commercial-industrial uses raises some tricky issues. Some observers, including the courts, have pointed out that jurisdictions with large commercial-industrial properties in their tax base can finance large outlays and ample public services and yet keep their tax rates low. This gives rise to substantial differences in per-capita expenditures by different municipalities on schools and other public services, differences that are often judged to be inequitable. These problems can be accentuated when commercial-industrial activities are located in one community, while the bulk of its employees inhabit another nearby jurisdiction, so that the tax advantage is reaped by the former municipality while the burden of supplying the required public services is borne by the other.

In consequence, some have proposed that the commercial-industrial tax base be "metropolitanized" (i.e., that uniform tax rates be imposed throughout a given metropolian area and that tax receipts then be shared on some agreed-upon formula by the various municipalities that make up the larger area). While there is some merit to this approach, there is another side to the story. Most communities already have some control over the entry of commercial-industrial property to their jurisdiction. Where they have chosen voluntarily to exclude or discourage it, their consequently reduced tax base is, in effect, the price they have chosen to pay in order to avoid the pollution, the congestion, and the other environmental damage that the industry is likely to bring with it. Communities that encourage the entry of industry are, in effect, undertaking to do society's dirtier work in return for the fiscal benefits. Typically, this is done by poorer communities (which, as we will see in Chapter 12, tend to have a lower demand for environmental amenities) as a means to help finance their public sector. Since it is the less-affluent communities that welcome commercial-industrial property, metropolitanization of the commercial-industrial tax base would, in effect, be a regressive measure, for it would restrict the freedom of lower-income communities to choose for themselves their preferred mix of industry and tax

[12]The New Jersey Supreme Court has already backed off to some extent on the applicability of the Mt. Laurel ruling. In a later decision, it found that communities that were already essentially fully developed in terms of single-family dwelling units were exempt from the need to provide additional housing for lower-income groups. In addition, the Court has given to the legislature the responsibility for determining guidelines for implementing the Mt. Laurel decision.

burden. It would impose upon them the preferences of the wealthier communities, even though the poor have neither the desire nor the ability to bear the financial burden.[13]

9. Other Fiscal Measures to Influence Land-Use Patterns

Up to this point, we have examined some of the major forces that have shaped existing land-use patterns. Our purpose has been to indicate some of the problems inherent in the formulation of land-use policies; in particular, we have seen that certain policies, while superficially attractive, can have some rather disturbing side effects.

Two important conclusions can be drawn from the analysis. The first is that land-use policies based on little more than intuition and "common sense" are likely to prove disappointing, wasteful, and sometimes actually destructive. Second, our discussion has indicated that there *are* means capable of influencing effectively the uses to which land is put. For better or ill, public policy does have important effects on land-use patterns. In this section, we will examine several additional policy instruments, which are perhaps a bit more innovative than those we have considered before. We do not intend to idealize these particular measures; our intent is rather to indicate that there exists a variety of extremely promising approaches that basically conservative policy makers have hardly begun to consider.

A. Density Charges: A Powerful Instrument for Land-Use Control. We will stress in Part 3 of this book the potential of fiscal incentives for the protection of the environment. Fees on emissions of pollutants into the air or water can provide strong incentives for firms and individuals to cut back on destructive waste emissions. It is likewise possible to use price incentives to help achieve our objectives for land use. One way of pursuing whatever land-use goals society decides upon is a reorientation of the tax structure that increases substantially the charges upon less desirable land uses and offers tax advantages to uses that promote the general welfare.

As an illustration, suppose that it is decided after extended debate and consideration that the ideal pattern of future land use will preserve unspoiled

---

[13]For an excellent study of this issue, see William Fischel, "Fiscal and Environmental Considerations in the Location of Firms in Suburban Communities," in E. S. Mills and W. E. Oates, eds., *Fiscal Zoning and Land Use Controls* (Lexington, Mass.: D. C. Heath and Co., 1975), Chap. 5. Another troublesome implication of metropolitanization is its consequences for the location of industry. If no community is permitted to benefit financially from its presence, who will be willing to welcome it and undertake the amenity and other costs of its proximity? Industry, after all, must operate somewhere. It seems appropriate that the community that agrees to accept it should receive some sort of financial compensation for its sacrifice.

locations and induce industry and homes to locate in already built-up areas. One simple way to do so is to impose on new construction a substantial tax (perhaps counterbalanced by other tax reductions) that varies with the residence and industrial density of the area. The tax formula might depend on the number of square feet of floor space already in existence, say, within one mile of a proposed building site. This would mean that those who build factories and homes in an area already densely filled with such structures would be charged virtually no such construction tax, since the square feet of floor space already in the vicinity would be very large. A structure built in a moderately dense area would, however, have to compensate the community by a substantial tax payment, and a factory or residence proposed for a nearly untouched area could find the tax prohibitive.

One of the advantages of such an arrangement is its automatic character. The formula is straightforward, and the vigilance of the tax collector is proverbial. There seems little doubt that such a piece of legislation, enacted for the country as a whole or by individual states, would drastically alter prospective land-use patterns by increasing density in already built-up jurisdictions while preserving those as yet undeveloped areas.

B. Land Value vs. Property Taxes as a Stimulus for Property Improvement. At the end of the nineteenth century an American economist, Henry George, made his reputation by proposing that there be only a single tax: a tax on the value of land to replace all other taxes.[14] While few economists would subscribe to the Henry George proposal in its entirety, a growing number have been attracted by a somewhat similar but more moderate proposal: that the tax paid by property holders in urban areas be based exclusively on the value of their land, regardless of the market value of the buildings erected on that land.

The purpose of such an arrangement is to make it profitable for owners to improve their property and to make it expensive for them to permit its deterioration. The point is that a landlord who left a slum building standing on a potentially valuable piece of land would not be protected by the worthlessness of the slum building from the heavy tax payments the land value justifies. To survive financially he or she would be forced to upgrade the building to bring its earnings more closely into line with the value of the land it occupies. On the other hand, the landlords with the best and most valuable buildings will find this tax advantage an encouragement to keep up their properties. There is some preliminary evidence from several areas where this approach has been tried experimentally, suggesting that it is capable of producing upgrading of neighborhoods.

The land tax must, however, be used with some caution because it does carry with it at least two potential dangers. First, if used in areas with substantial

---

[14] Henry George (1839–97) described his views most completely in his *Progress and Poverty* (1879). In 1886 he was nearly elected major of New York City.

quantities of vacant land it is likely to accelerate construction on that land, since under this arrangement an empty lot is taxed at its full potential value, with no dispensation to the landlord who permits it to lie fallow. It is therefore dangerous to use where one of society's goals is to *discourage* construction on unspoiled lands. Second, the land tax is likely to eliminate not only slums, but also some of the better-quality housing for lower-income groups. Since lower-income groups cannot be expected to pay heavy rents, the land tax could make it unprofitable to build low-income housing on valuable land.

Nevertheless, the shifting of the property tax liability off structures and onto land itself in our urban areas has much to commend it; it can provide a powerful fiscal incentive for a revitalization of the city's stock of structures.[15]

C. Deposits to Deal with Abandonment of Buildings. As we noted earlier, building abandonment has become increasingly prevalent. No one knows how many buildings are abandoned in urban areas every year, but it is becoming clear that it is a problem of substantial proportions.[16] Abandoned buildings become a site of crime, a threat to sanitation, a source of fire, and more generally a cause of deterioration of property values in the entire neighborhood. So far the cities haven't found an effective way to prevent landlords from causing this sort of damage to their neighbors or to require them to bear the cost of rehabilitation or removal of the vacant building. One of the main difficulties is that "slumlords" often hide behind a maze of legal entities that conceals their identity and effectively prevents their pursuit by the authorities after abandonment of the property. In some instances an owner may simply find someone on the street, who in return for a few dollars, will accept title to the building!

One way to prevent this may be a requirement that all owners of rental property post as a bond an amount of money sufficient to cover the cost of rehabilitation or removal of such a building, should it be abandoned. To minimize the burden upon property owners, the municipality that holds the deposited money could pay full market interest on the amount; the city government would treat these funds simply as part of its normal borrowing. The deposit would, of course, be refunded to the landlord on proof of sale to another bona fide owner and after the posting of a substitute bond by the new proprietor. The deposit would also be refunded if the landlord were to choose to take the building down, after taking appropriate steps to insure that the lot was kept in acceptable condition.

---

[15] On the issue of land taxation, see, for example, the collection of studies in Daniel Holland, ed., *The Assessment of Land Value* (Madison: The University of Wisconsin Press, 1970).

[16] One recent and careful study of the city of Pittsburgh found that "At year end 1973, for example, the City of Pittsburgh had obtained some 11,000 separate real estate parcels through treasury sales of tax delinquent parcels. Acquisitions over the preceding twenty-year period has proceeded at a rate of 200 to 500 properties each year, with the rate of property acquisition by the City increasing dramatically in recent years" (George Sternlieb and Robert W. Lake, "The Dynamics of Real Estate Delinquency," *National Tax Journal* 29 [September 1976]: 261).

D. Extended Homesteading. A number of cities have recently adopted programs under which abandoned properties are made available to lower-income families on the condition that these families undertake the rehabilitation of the buildings and agree to occupy them at least for some specified minimum period. The program seems to have proved moderately successful so far, though the evidence is still rather scanty.

However, we may note that the approach can be extended in a way that may transform it into a far more powerful instrument of both rehabilitation and job training. Unemployed residents of the inner city who volunteer for the program can be taught, partially on the job, the skills necessary for a professional job of rehabilitation of buildings abandoned or foreclosed for nonpayment of taxes. A fraction of the rehabilitated houses can then be turned over to those who have worked on them, with the remainder put up for sale to help in the financing of the entire enterprise.

The objective of the program would be to give the unemployed participants in the program a financial stake in the quality of their own residences and in the state of the neighborhood generally, and to permit them to acquire skills valuable to themselves and the community. By supplying such financial motivation, the upgrading of slum neighborhoods may indeed be facilitated; such programs could encourage a reversal of the ongoing process of progressive deterioration.

E. Equity in Public Housing. A somewhat related approach may be useful in preventing deterioration of public housing. One of the most persistent problems besetting slum rehabilitation programs has been the widespread dissatisfaction of residents with government housing projects. Many such projects have been treated badly by the residents, and as a result they have themselves turned into slum areas only a few years after their construction.

One approach to the problem that merits consideration is to turn the buildings into cooperatives or condominiums owned by the families that live in them. By arranging a gradual transfer of title to the tenants, with opportunity for resale after some specified period, the resident would be given a stake in the condition of the property. Social pressure and individual interest may then serve to reduce or prevent vandalism and elicit the effort required for effective maintenance. There is no guarantee that this will change matters overnight. However, without such a change there seems to be little prospect that public housing will be able to provide more than a very temporary improvement in slum conditions.

10. Conclusions

In this chapter we have discussed two interrelated problems of vital importance for the quality of life, and we have illustrated both the limitations and the strengths of what economics has to say about these issues. We have seen that economic analysis is at its weakest in dealing with the choice of social goals, a matter that ultimately must be decided by society at large, not by any group of analysts. The greatest contribution of economics is in the means to achieve the goals of society. Economics can explain why many of the current approaches to land use have failed and, more important, it can indicate a number of avenues that seem more promising. At the very least, it is clear that the future of both our cities and our countryside is in our hands; we do have the power to improve upon that future.

12

Who Pays and Who Benefits?

Bottlers, brewers and soft-drink manufacturers who would stand to lose business, along with labor unions worried about their members' jobs, had 30 lobbyists in the Capitol, urging legislators constantly to stop the bill. Legislators knew many of these lobbyists personally. But they had no way of being sure how many voters were out there. . . .[1]

It is probably no exaggeration to say that, in the world of political reality, the distribution of benefits and costs is *the* key issue in environmental policy. While economists are usually concerned about the economic *efficiency* of a proposed environmental program, most other observers are more interested in its *equity*. Most noneconomists, if confronted with a tax designed to reduce gasoline consumption, are concerned less about its effectiveness in curtailing gasoline sales than about its effects on the poor and on consumers who have no practical alternative to the automobile and therefore cannot reduce their gasoline consumption.

Though we are economists, with economists' biases, we accept without reservation the importance of the distributive issue in environmental policy. We believe it must be dealt with effectively, not only because attention to it is good political strategy, but because the subject *is* really crucial to the welfare of society. The fact that our discussion of distribution appears confined to only one chapter is not a consequence of our sense of the importance of the issue. It

---

[1]Lawrence Fellows, "The Life and Death of Connecticut's Bottle Bill," *New York Times,* June 12, 1977, Sect. E, p. 6.

174

reflects instead that studies of the distributive effects of environmental policies are still in their infancy. In this chapter, we shall report the findings of several excellent pieces of analysis. But much remains to be done before we can piece together a comprehensive picture of the distribution of the benefits and costs of environmental programs.

Moreover, the issue of distribution will not allow itself to be confined to a single chapter. It will unavoidably arise again at various points later in the book. And even where we do not mention them explicitly, distributive considerations must constantly haunt our analysis of policy determination for protection of the environment.

One of the central issues is the impact of these policies on different income groups. There is much evidence that the environmental movement draws most of its support from middle- and upper-income classes, and that lower-income groups are often either uninterested or openly hostile. There are several explanations. First, only those who are in comfortable economic circumstances can devote a significant proportion of their incomes to the "luxury" of environmental improvement and assign lower priority to increases in material goods. Poorer nations and poorer individuals must give higher priority to food, clothing, and housing. Second, the poor are far less able to protect themselves from any disruptive side effects of environmental measures. When polluting plants are shut down, both executives and blue-collar workers may be forced to hunt for new jobs. However, the latter typically have a smaller cushion of savings and less mobility so that their period of unemployment may be more painful and last longer. Third, it is sometimes alleged that the bulk of the benefits of environmental programs flow to the rich, while the burden of their costs falls disproportionately on the poor.

Whether or not all of these hypotheses are true is not entirely clear, but the widespread belief in the inherent inequities of environmental programs (regardless of the validity of the belief) is of vital importance for their political future. If these programs are to generate a wide base of public support, those who are less affluent must not believe that improvements in environmental quality come at their expense. Moreover, and of at least equal importance, considerations of equity argue that we must make certain that such programs are not exclusively "pro-rich."

The issue of the distributive aspects of environmental policy is an extremely complex one, subject to few simple generalizations. For example, we cannot judge the distributive consequences of a rise in fuel prices simply by comparing the direct consumption of gasoline and other fuels by the rich and the poor. Rising fuel prices affect other prices—those of steel, transportation, artificial fibers, and so on. Much of the impact on the distribution of income is likely to take this indirect avenue. As we shall see, evaluation of the ultimate impact of a particular tax measure is equally complex. Indeed, similar analytic problems beset all studies of the distribution side of our subject. Consequently, in this chapter we shall have to rely largely on suggestive evidence, conjectures, and more or less educated impressions as to who, in the end, enjoys the benefits and who bears the costs of these programs.

1. Benefits, Costs, and Their Distribution[2]

We must first characterize these benefits and costs. It is useful to separate the benefits into those that improve conditions in heavily populated areas and those that flow to more remote locations. In the first case, the environmental program will benefit people where they live and work, while in the second case, people will have to seek out the improved amenities. Environmental measures that reduce carbon monoxide levels in a city are an example of the first type of benefit, while the protection of a national park is an instance of the second. This distinction is important, because there is evidence that the poor tend to frequent national parks and other more distant protected areas far less than middle- and upper-income groups.

We can also divide the costs of environmental programs into two categories: transition costs and long-run (or continuing) costs. Transition costs include unemployment and the associated disruptions of retraining and relocating when businesses are forced to move or shut down altogether. Such losses are transitory; once the economy has readjusted itself to the requirements for a cleaner environment, there need be no additional dislocations of this sort. There will, however, be additional long-run costs. An automobile with pollution-control devices will continue to be more expensive to run, and an industry whose factories are not permitted to dump their wastes into nearby waterways will charge higher prices for its products. Environmental programs are likely to increase substantially *and* permanently the prices of fuels, transportation, and certain types of metals. The tax burdens resulting from the operation of treatment plants are not transitory either.

2. The Distribution of Benefits from Environmental Programs

The benefits from programs that improve the environment at an industrial or a residential center are likely to be shared by a broad range of income groups.

---

[2]For an excellent comprehensive survey of the literature on the distributive effects of environmental programs, see Paul R. Portney's "The Distribution of Pollution Control Costs: A Literature Review and Research Agenda," Prepared for the Panel on Sources and Control Techniques of the Environmental Research and Assessment Committee, National Academy of Sciences, February 1, 1976.

However, the pattern of sharing will vary from program to program and from one location to another. It is tempting to argue that the benefits from, say, the improvement of air quality in a metropolitan area will accrue equally to everyone, rich and poor. However, that is not generally true. From the outset, the rich usually occupy the areas that are generally more desirable. People with higher incomes are able to avoid areas closest to pollution sources—industries, highways, airports—while people who are less well-off are forced to settle for more polluted, but lower-rent, neighborhoods. Table 12-1 presents data for three major cities indicating the exposure of different income classes to several air pollutants. It shows clearly that air quality decreases systematically with the average family income of census tracts in Kansas City, St. Louis, and Washington, D.C.[3]

The wealthy are also better able to protect themselves from any discomforts in their neighborhoods. They are protected from crime by doormen and armed guards, from air pollution by air conditioners, from noise levels by insulating materials, and so on. By using their private means, the wealthy can make certain improvements in their personal environments.

In sum, the rich and poor do *not* suffer equally from environmental damage within a given city, and so they cannot be expected to share equally in its benefits. All this may suggest that, since their neighborhoods have the greatest room for improvement, the poor are in fact the prime beneficiaries of certain environmental programs. But for several reasons even this is far from clear.

First, environmental improvements may in fact be worth a great deal more to the rich than to the poor, particularly if the benefits are measured in money terms.[4] As already noted, the poor are likely to have other economic concerns that are far more pressing to them. They may, for example, assign less importance to the long-term consequences of the use of chemical insecticides in nearby farmlands, if the prohibition of these sprays increases food costs. Consequently, even if a given program improves the air for the poor somewhat more than it does for the wealthy, the latter may nevertheless place a higher valuation on the benefits.

---

[3] In a study of the New York region, Zupan also found that poorer families tend to reside in locations of comparatively low air quality. See Jeffrey M. Zupan, *The Distribution of Air Quality in the New York Region* (Washington, D.C.: Resources for the Future, Inc., 1973). The most recent and comprehensive study of the distribution of air quality in a large sample of U.S. cities provides further support for the proposition that, within cities, the poor tend to live in sections with the worst air quality. See Peter Asch and Joseph Seneca, "Some Evidence on the Distribution of Air Quality", *Land Economics,* forthcoming.

[4] One study that attempts to measure the damage costs of air pollution in terms of willingness to pay, in fact, finds that these costs are greater among the highest income groups. The implication is that, *measured in money terms,* the wealthy may well benefit more from programs to improve air quality than the poor. See L. P. Gianessi, H. M. Peskin, and E. Wolff, "The Distributional Implications of National Air Pollution Damage Estimates," to be published in F. T. Juster, ed., *Distribution of Economic Well-Being* (New York: National Bureau of Economic Research, forthcoming).

TABLE 12-1

AIR POLLUTION EXPOSURE INDEXES BY INCOME SIZE CLASS

Income Size Class (dollars)	Suspended Particulates (μgms/ml)	Sulfation (mg. SO_3/ 100 cm^2 per day)	Mean[a]
Kansas City			
0–2,999	76.7	0.22	1.16
3,000–4,999	72.4	0.20	1.09
5,000–6,999	66.5	0.18	0.98
7,000–9,999	63.5	0.17	0.93
10,000–14,999	60.1	0.15	0.86
15,000–24,999	57.6	0.14	0.80
25,000–over	58.1	0.12	0.76
St. Louis			
0–2,999	91.3	0.97	1.19
3,000–4,999	85.3	0.88	1.10
5,000–6,999	79.2	0.78	1.00
7,000–9,999	75.4	0.72	0.93
10,000–14,999	73.0	0.68	0.89
15,000–24,999	68.8	0.60	0.82
25,000–over	64.9	0.52	0.74
Washington, D.C.			
0–2,999	64.6	0.82	1.19
3,000–4,999	61.7	0.82	1.16
5,000–6,999	53.9	0.75	1.04
7,000–9,999	49.7	0.69	0.96
10,000–14,999	45.5	0.64	0.88
15,000–24,999	43.2	0.58	0.82
25,000–over	42.0	0.53	0.77

Source: A. Myrick Freeman III, "Distribution of Environmental Quality," in Allen V. Kneese and Blair T. Bower, eds., *Environmental Quality Analysis* (Baltimore: Published for Resources for the Future, Inc. by The Johns Hopkins University Press, 1972), p. 265.

[a]Unweighted index of both particulate and sulfation levels—a measure of "average air quality."

Second, improvements in the areas inhabited by the poor are likely to drive up rents. As we might expect, neighborhoods with high pollution levels tend to offer lower rents.[5] It has been suggested, for example, that the elimination of smog in Los Angeles and of crime in Harlem would bring with them an influx of wealthy individuals prepared to take over the housing now occupied

[5]See Ronald G. Ridker and John A. Henning, "The Determinants of Residential Property Values with Special Reference to Air Pollution," *Review of Economics and Statistics* 49

by the less affluent. Improvement of neighborhoods, such as the East Side and SoHo in New York and Islington in London, have already brought with them a stream of moneyed individuals seeking chic areas in which to live; the result has been moving costs and higher rental expenses for the poorer people who previously lived there.

The upshot of all this is somewhat unclear. Undoubtedly, some of the benefits of environmental programs go to every income class. Certainly, reduced illness and increased longevity are things no income group is likely to spurn. But the rich almost surely value aesthetic improvements more highly than the poor. There are, on the other hand, *some* environmental programs whose design appears clearly to be pro-poor. A measure that sets maximum levels on the pollution content in the atmosphere of a neighborhood seems likely to have a greater effect on the areas in which the poor live where, as we have seen, pollution is typically high; wealthy neighborhoods may have met the standards before the program was enacted, so that for them it may have absolutely no effect.[6] Another example of a program that can be presumed to be pro-poor is urban renewal, at least those measures designed primarily to get rid of slums and attract job opportunities to low-income neighborhoods. However, some argue that even these measures have imposed most of their real costs on the low-income groups.[7] Frequently the relocation costs have been borne almost entirely by slum residents, and in a tight housing market this has often led to higher rents. Reduction in the absolute and relative number of housing units of low quality have led to higher costs for consumers of such units and lower costs for middle- and upper-income classes. In addition, the disruption of neighborhoods has produced a loss of "social capital": neighborhood community centers, local businesses, and other gathering places. Thus, even these programs, though apparently intended to assist the poor, have not always proved entirely beneficial to the income class they were designed to serve. In sum, it is difficult to find examples of environmental measures whose advantages have flowed primarily and unambiguously to the low-income population.

(May 1967): 246–57. Using multiple-regression analysis, the authors studied median property values in 167 Census Tracts (1960) in the St. Louis Metropolitan Area. They found that, other things being equal, property values are significantly and inversely related to sulfation levels of the atmosphere. A number of later studies have confirmed this finding. Similarly, there is strong evidence that property values and rents tend to be lower in noisier neighborhoods.

[6] Asch and Seneca have found that, over the early 1970s, improvements in air quality have been more pronounced in sections of cities occupied by lower-income groups than in areas with higher-income residents. See their "Some Evidence on the Distribution of Air Quality."

[7] See Jerome Rothenberg, *Economic Evaluation of Urban Renewal, Conceptual Foundation of Benefit-Cost Analysis* (Washington, D.C.: The Brookings Institution, 1967). For contrary views, see James Q. Wilson, ed., *Urban Renewal: The Record and the Controversy* (Cambridge, Mass.: M.I.T. Press, 1966), especially Chaps. 11 and 12.

It is easy, however, to find examples of the opposite. Government investment in wilderness and recreation areas produces benefits, the bulk of which accrue to upper-income groups.[8] This is hardly surprising, since the use of many of these areas requires expensive equipment and heavy travel outlays. Yet calculations of distributive effects usually play only a small part in the evaluation of such conservation programs.[9]

3. The Distribution of Transition Costs of Environmental Programs

Having considered their benefits, we turn next to a more detailed discussion of the distribution of the *costs* of environmental programs; here we shall employ our earlier distinction between transition and continuing costs. The most striking feature of the transition costs is the very uneven pattern of their incidence. Some industries will be hit much harder than others. Fuels, metals, paper, chemicals, transportation, and a few other industries are virtually certain to bear the brunt of the effects, while others, like telecommunications and legal services, which are relatively clean, should be affected only very slightly.

The same is true of the geographic distribution of the effects. Transition costs will fall much more heavily on some communities than on others. If, for example, the automobile industry suffers a contraction as a result of environmental regulation, unemployment in Detroit can be expected to increase dis-

---

[8]See Charles J. Cicchetti, Joseph J. Seneca, and Paul Davidson, *The Demand and Supply of Outdoor Recreation* (Washington, D.C.: U.S. Department of the Interior, 1969). The authors use multiple-regression analysis to study the usage of outdoor recreation facilities. They found that, on the average, the higher an individual's income, the more likely he or she is to engage in swimming, water skiing, fishing, sailing, picnicking, sightseeing, and wildlife photography.

In another study, Jack L. Knetsch and Robert K. Davis used a questionnaire technique to ascertain what a sample of users were willing to pay for the services from a forest recreation area in Maine. Their findings indicated a substantially higher willingness-to-pay on the part of higher income users. See their "Comparisons of Methods for Recreation Evaluation," in Allen V. Kneese and Stephen C. Smith, eds., *Water Research* (Washington, D.C.: Resources for the Future, Inc., 1966), pp. 125–42.

[9]Typical of this is a very sophisticated cost-benefit analysis of a contemplated project for Hell's Canyon. The proposal was to employ that area for the generation of hydroelectric power, a project which would alter the area permanently and prevent its use for recreation. The primary object of the study was to investigate the value to be placed on a unique natural phenomenon threatened with irreversible change by a development project.

The authors conclude from their estimate of the flow of future benefits from the two alternative uses of the Canyon that the potential net benefits from preservation of the area are clearly greater than those of development. However, the authors say little about the distributive implications of the choice. Electricity seems to be consumed more heavily, as a proportion of income, by the poor while, as we have seen, recreation is utilized primarily by those in comfortable economic circumstances. However, in this particular case, it must be noted that the net gains from the preservation of the area seem to be so substantial that distributive considerations are unlikely to reverse the authors' conclusions. See John V. Krutilla, Charles J. Cicchetti, A. Myrick Freeman III, and Clifford S. Russell, "Observations

proportionately. Small towns whose primary sources of income and employment are a single, heavily polluting plant may be particularly vulnerable. There have been, in fact, several episodes of that sort. For example, in San Juan Bautista, California, stringent air pollution laws led to the shutdown of the Ideal Cement Company and the dismissal of its 130 workers. Mayor Leonard Caetano pointed out that, "Twenty per cent of our population depended on the plant directly for a living, and many others relied on that $2 million payroll circulating through town."[10]

These effects will not necessarily fall on one income group more heavily than another. Both high-salaried and low-salaried workers may find their jobs threatened. And while, as already indicated, the former may have greater financial reserves and geographic mobility, some elements in the situation do not work in their favor. Jobs for executives do not grow on trees. An unskilled worker who has frequently gone from job to job in the past may find it easier to get new employment (if the entire area has not become depressed) than a $50,000-a-year member of the management.

However, this is not how things are usually perceived. Fear of unemployment and loss of income seem to be felt more heavily among lower-income groups. When environmental interests halt or slow down the construction of a refinery or an airport, the protests about lost jobs usually come from blue-collar workers or the jobless. We shall see later that both opinion polls and election results confirm that there is an income-related difference in attitudes toward environmental legislation; one may well surmise that transition costs in the form of loss of jobs are a foremost consideration in the minds of those who are lukewarm or hostile to such measures.

We should emphasize that unemployment is indeed a cost that we can expect to be transitory. That is, any jobs lost as a result of the closing of polluting plants should not produce a permanent decrease in employment opportunities in the nation. The total demand for labor is determined by other government policies: its taxes, its overall expenditures, its monetary measures, and various localized policies. By keeping taxes sufficiently low, the government can stimulate demand for commodities and capital goods (factories, equipment, etc.) and, hence, the demand for labor, regardless of what is happening in any particular industry. Thus a worker who has lost a job in a polluting industry need only remain unemployed for as long a period as it takes to find a job in another industry. This is not meant to minimize the severity of the blow; even temporary unemployment can have serious financial and psychological effects on a family, particularly if it has little accumulated savings.

---

on the Economics of Irreplaceable Assets," Chap. 3 in Allen V. Kneese and Blair T. Bower, *Environmental Quality Analysis* (Baltimore: The Johns Hopkins University Press, 1972), pp. 69–112.

[10]*New York Times,* "Town Loses Its Lone Industry," September 8, 1973, pp. 39, 47.

However, there has been a tendency to exaggerate the unemployment caused by environmental measures. In particular, in several instances of plant closings that management attributed to the added costs of pollution control, it appears that the firms were already losing money and would have gone out of business anyway. Studies by the Environmental Protection Agency indicate that the major economic effect of environmental legislation has been to accelerate closings that would have occurred even in the absence of pollution-control requirements.[11] In short, owners have, to some extent, used environmental measures as a convenient excuse to shut down operations that were already unprofitable.

4. The Distribution of Continuing Environmental Costs

The real cost of environmental measures is, ultimately, the additional resources needed to run the economy in a less-polluting way. Smoke-suppression devices and recycling processes use up raw materials, fuel, and labor. The individual consumer will bear these costs in two forms: in higher taxes to pay for the operations of environmental agencies, and in increased prices when private industry passes on some (or all) of the increase in its costs. Whether industry is required to pay a pollution tax or is simply ordered to install pollution-control equipment, its costs will increase, and this puts an upward pressure on the prices of its products.

We note in another chapter that, from the point of view of effective environmental protection, these increased prices are desirable: they encourage shifts in purchases away from the products of polluting industries to goods and services whose production is less harmful to the environment. But these price increases may not always have desirable *distributive* effects. Suppose that a commodity whose output produces high levels of pollution is used largely by lower-income groups. In such instances, the costs of pollution abatement may fall disproportionately on the poor.

The issue, then, is "Who purchases the goods whose prices are increased?" If the items constitute a larger *share* of the purchases of upper-income groups than of purchases of less-affluent families, the price rises will be "progressive" in their effects; that is, *relative to their incomes,* the rich will pay more than the poor. If the items take up a larger portion of the budgets of the poor, then the price rises will be "regressive," and will effectively increase income inequality.

The task of determining the long-run distributive effects of environmental policy may then seem straightforward. The difficulty is that we do not know exactly where a given cost increase or a given rise in taxes will show up in the

---

[11] See *Environmental Quality, The Third Annual Report of the Council on Environmental Quality* (Washington, D.C.: U.S. Government Printing Office, August 1972), pp. 287–301.

form of price increases. Even if it is true, as some evidence seems to suggest, that gasoline purchases constitute a higher proportion of the outlays of the middle-income groups than those of the poor, that is not the only effect of more expensive gasoline. For example, food products that are transported by truck will certainly become more expensive, and this price increase is likely to weigh relatively more heavily on impoverished families.

The fact is that cost increases usually set in motion a complex chain of price increases, and no one knows precisely what the final price pattern will look like or who will bear what share of the burden. This is particularly the case where the product whose price has risen is an intermediate good rather than a final consumer good (that is, it serves as an input to other productive processes). The list of commodities whose production generates high pollution costs includes a lot of intermediate products: chemicals, fuels, and paper and pulp products. As their costs rise, this will obviously affect the prices of the consumer goods they are used to produce. But that is only the beginning of the story. As costs and prices rise, wages too are likely to be readjusted, and in a complex pattern. Wages in the industry whose operations are directly affected by an environmental program may be held back or even reduced by any resulting contraction in output. Simultaneously, wages in other industries may be pushed upward by the increased costs of the consumer goods those workers must purchase. This complicated pattern of wage changes in turn will influence the prices of both the goods the workers produce and those they consume. Even this only illustrates, and certainly does not exhaust, the complexities of the long-run price consequences of environmental policy.

In spite of these difficulties, there is one recent, comprehensive, and rather ingenious study of the distribution of the costs of U.S. federal environmental programs.[12] In this study, Nancy Dorfman and Arthur Snow have estimated the cost per family as a percentage of family income for income levels ranging from $2,000-4,000 per annum at the bottom to over $50,000 at the top.

The Dorfman-Snow procedure was to analyze separately the three major sources of long-run environmental costs: taxes to finance government expenditures on environmental programs, the costs of controlling auto emissions, and the distribution of price increases from higher abatement costs in private industry (other than the automobile sector.)[13] By combining the findings from

---

[12] Nancy S. Dorfman assisted by Arthur Snow, "Who Will Pay for Pollution Control?—The Distribution by Income of the Burden of the National Environmental Protection Program, 1972-1980," *National Tax Journal* 28 (March 1975): 101-15.

[13] An estimate of the distribution of these costs requires some assumptions about how they are to be financed. For the public-sector expenses, the authors assume that each level of government will increase taxes, rather than cutting other expenditures, and does so by increasing proportionately the rates on each of its major sources of tax revenues. The federal government, for example, is assumed to raise 74 percent of its required funds from the personal income tax and the remaining 26 percent from corporate income taxes (since this reflects the current shares of revenue from these two sources—aside from the payroll

these three parts of their study, Dorfman and Snow were able to generate, for different levels of family income, estimates of the total cost of pollution control as a percentage of income. Their estimates, which appear in Figure 12-1, indicate that the distribution of these costs is indeed quite regressive: they tend to fall significantly as a fraction of income as we move from lower to higher income families. It is also interesting that, as we move from 1972 to 1980, the distribution of costs appears to become increasingly regressive.

We should stress (as would Dorfman and Snow) that these findings must be considered highly tentative. They are based on a number of critical assumptions whose violation can significantly alter the results. Nevertheless, their study does provide some support for the prevailing supposition that the costs of environmental programs fall disproportionately on those at the lower end of the income scale.[14]

5. The "Perceived" Distribution of the Benefits and Costs of Environmental Protection

Obviously, the evidence is far from adequate. It is simply impossible, given the data that are available, to conclude firmly that all environmental programs are likely to be pro-rich or pro-poor. Yet one cannot reject the evidence that suggests they sometimes favor the rich, and perhaps do so more generally. Certainly there is a strong presumption that measures protecting natural wonders and wilderness areas are predominantly beneficial to the wealthy, and our tentative judgment is that, taken overall, a major effort to improve environmental quality is likely to favor the well-to-do.

What is perhaps most important for the enactment of environmental legislation is that this is the way the issue appears to be *perceived*. Three intriguing pieces of evidence show that there is a consistent pattern of dispropor-

tax). They then use existing estimates of the incidence of these taxes to apportion the tax burden among families at different income levels.

For the cost of auto emissions, Dorfman and Snow estimate the additional production and operating costs of new automobiles attributable to pollution-control devices and maintenance for each model year. Using depreciation schedules for the useful life of automobiles, they allocate the costs by family income class, using the data from a survey indicating the typical age of car and number of miles driven per year by families at different income levels. In the final part of their study they attempt to trace through the effects of pollution-abatement costs on the prices of final goods with the use of an input-output matrix. (An input-output matrix is a set of coefficients that indicates, for one additional unit of output of each commodity, how many extra units of *each* input is required. Using such a matrix, one can trace through the effects of a change in demand or costs for one or more goods on all the outputs and costs in the economy.) Their finding was that these indirect cost increases become so finely diffused among the many final goods and services in the economy that the incidence follows closely the pattern of total spending on consumption. With this result, they decided simply to distribute these costs among different income groups in proportion to total consumption expenditure (exclusive of rent).

[14]Not only does the distribution of benefits and costs of environmental programs vary

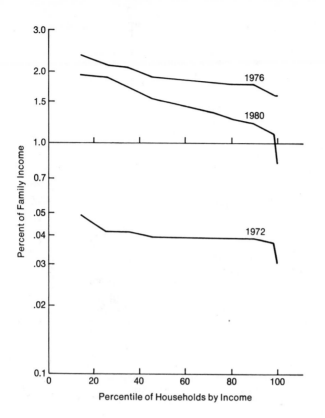

Figure 12-1 Distribution of Total Cost of Pollution Controls as Percent of Family Income 1972, 1976 and 1980.

Source: Nancy Dorfman assisted by Arthur Snow, "Who Will Pay for Pollution Control? The Distribution by Income of the Burden of the National Environment Protection Program, 1972–1980," *National Tax Journal* 28 (March 1975): 102.

tionately strong support for environmental programs among higher-income groups. In 1965 and 1970, the Opinion Research Corporation conducted a series of interviews in which they queried individuals on the seriousness of air and water pollution. They found that, the higher the income level of the respondent, the more likely was he or she to consider environmental problems to be "very serious." Figure 12-2 summarizes the ORC findings. It is noteworthy that by 1970 concern with these issues had grown substantially at all income levels, so that a higher proportion of the lowest income group (under $5,000) viewed environmental deterioration as "serious" than had been the case for the highest

among income groups, but one recent study suggests far more dramatic variations between people in different geographical locations in the United States. See L. P. Gianessi, H. M. Peskin, and E. Wolff, "The Distributional Effects of the Uniform Air Pollution Policy in the United States," Resources for the Future, Discussion Paper D-5 (March 1977).

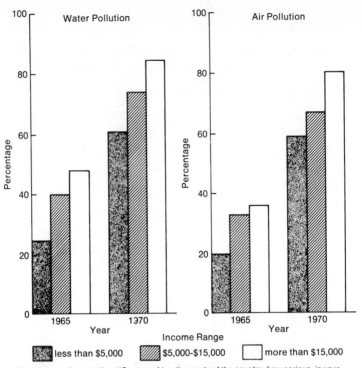

Figure 12-2 Environmental Concern by Income Level.

Source: *Environmental Quality, The Fourth Annual Report of the Council on Environmental Quality* (Washington, D.C.: U.S. Government Printing Office, September 1973), p. 82.

income group (over $15,000) in 1965! Yet for each year, the pattern was consistent: the wealthier the group, the more frequently its members considered pollution to pose a serious threat.

In a second series of surveys conducted by the Gallup Organization on behalf of the National Wildlife Federation, individuals were asked how great an increase in their family's expenses they would be willing to bear for the cleanup of the natural environment. Robert Dorfman has analyzed the results from these surveys and finds that "The main conclusion to be drawn is the unsurprising one that clean environment is a superior good and that at any stated price more people at higher income levels are willing to buy it than at lower incomes."[15]

---

[15]Robert Dorfman, "Incidence of the Benefits and Costs of Environmental Programs," *American Economic Review* 67 (February 1977): 336.

The third piece of evidence comes from the voting patterns of the electorate on environmental referenda. One particularly enlightening episode took place in a referendum in Santa Barbara County, California. Perry Shapiro, a professor of economics at the University of California at Santa Barbara, described the setting as follows:

> At issue was the development of a large ranch (El Capitan) fronting on the sea in the rural part of the county. The voters were to decide whether or not a private developer should be allowed a zoning variance to develop homesites in an established agricultural open space area. The project promised to generate an increase in local economic activity at the expense of environmental quality. The issue, as related in pre-election press reports, was one of environmental quality versus income, and there is good reason to believe this was the alternative between which voters chose in the polling booth.[16]

Professor Shapiro subjected the election returns to a careful statistical analysis and found a clear relationship between the level of family income in a voting district and the percentage of votes supporting the zoning variance. The higher the income level, the larger was the fraction of the votes against the development of El Capitan. Only in the low-income districts was there really substantial support for the variance.

We want to emphasize the importance of these findings. Although we may be somewhat uncertain about the actual distribution of the benefits and costs of environmental improvement, the *perceived* incidence of these programs seems clearly to be pro-rich. There does appear to be a real difference in the priority assigned to environmental quality between families of varying levels of income. This suggests the need to formulate and finance environmental programs in a way that makes them less onerous to lower-income families, both as a matter of social justice *and* as a means to generate the support necessary to institute effective environmental measures.

6. Conclusion: Integrating Distributive Provisions into Environmental Programs

Income redistribution is undoubtedly one of the most pressing economic issues of our time. Poverty and its associated social ills impose heavy burdens not only on the poor, but also on the remainder of society. Moreover, as the com-

---

[16]Perry Shapiro, "Voting and the Incidence of Public Policy: An Operational Model and an Example of an Environmental Referendum," Working Paper in Economics No. 8 (Santa Barbara, Calif.: University of California, May 1972), pp. 1-2. In several subsequent studies of voting patterns on other environmental issues, Professor Shapiro has obtained very similar results.

munity grows more productive and wealthy, it becomes increasingly difficult to justify the failure to undertake effective measures for the elimination of poverty, let alone programs that intensify the inequality in the distribution of wealth.

It would be easy to leave the matter here, adding a few pious platitudes, in the hope that someone, somehow, will do something to rectify inequalities that stem from environmental measures. But it seems to us that such general expressions of good wishes are not enough. There is real doubt about the justification of any measure that is designed to improve the quality of life, but whose burdens fall preponderantly on the poor. Moreover, as we have stressed, this perverse pattern of burdens may erode seriously the political support necessary for environmental programs.

The answer is, of course, not simply to abandon our environmental goals. As we saw in Chapter 3, there is strong evidence that pollution contributes significantly to illness and death; the poor, as well as the rich, can hardly be pleased with those prospects. In addition, as we reported earlier in our discussion of Figure 12-2, even the lowest income groups are growing more concerned about pollution problems. By 1970 some 60 percent of a sample of interviewees with family incomes under $5,000 per annum considered both air and water pollution problems to be either "somewhat" or "very" serious. In our view, the appropriate response is to try to incorporate explicit provisions into environmental programs to distribute their costs (and, if possible, their benefits) fairly. This does not mean that we should redirect environmental programs from their central purpose in order to turn them into vehicles for the redistribution of income. Such an attempt is likely to backfire and achieve neither goal.

We can best end the discussion with some concrete measures that illustrate how distributive provisions can be put into practice. The first and most obvious program to offset any unfortunate distributive consequence of environmental programs is the provision of adjustment assistance: unemployment compensation and retraining and relocation assistance, similar to that offered under programs of tariff reductions. These can go a long way toward offsetting the heavy transition burdens that are often the primary concern of those who fear the economic effects of environmental measures. Moreover, these are programs with which we already have some actual experience; they can be implemented.

A second provision that may help to reduce regressiveness in the distribution of costs is the assumption of a high proportion of the expense of environmental programs by the federal government. The federal tax structure is more progressive than that of most state and local governments; the additions to tax revenues required by environmental measures are more likely to be drawn predominantly from upper-income groups if they are collected by the federal government.[17]

---

[17] This is plausible but by no means certain. There are at least two grounds for doubt. First, given the various loopholes and tax shelters usually available to the very rich, the actual

A third approach utilizes a fiscal measure that we will explore in greater depth in a later chapter. For now, simply assume that the environmental authority issues a limited number of "pollution permits" that restricts the total emissions of pollutants to a level that is consistent with a prescribed and satisfactory standard of environmental quality. This might be accomplished by issuing a small number of "pollution certificates" to every family that could, for example, be required with gasoline purchases (like the rationing of food coupons during World War II). If these coupons are legally transferrable and salable, they will ultimately flow to those who can best afford them. However, the wealthy, who want to buy more of these coupons, must pay for the privilege and make the payment to those whose low income makes the sale of the certificates attractive. Society may thereby promote both its environmental and redistributive objectives: the output of pollutants will be limited by the number of authorizations issued, and funds will be diverted from those with greater ability to pay to those whose incomes are more limited.

Such a scheme may sound rather far-fetched (and perhaps it is). Nevertheless, there may be some circumstances for which it would be reasonably easy to implement and quite effective. The issuance of tickets, for example, for the use of various urban facilities (a limited number of parking spaces or access to certain roads during peak hours of use) might serve, on the one hand, to reduce congestion and delays and, on the other, to supplement the income of poorer families who would rather sell the tickets than make use of the facilities themselves. Perhaps the range of feasible applications of this approach is quite small. But it is not our intent to propose any single device capable of resolving all the distributive aspects of environmental programs. Rather, it is to suggest that, with a little imagination, we can devise measures that will alleviate some of the more perverse redistributive effects of programs to control pollution.[18] And here, as with many other important issues, one of the greatest dangers to effective policy lies in the propensity to equate imagination, ingenuity, and novelty with "impracticality."

---

progressivity of the federal tax structure is undoubtedly far more modest than it appears to be. Second, the relevant issue is the progressivity of the *new* taxes enacted by Congress to cover the costs of environmental programs. Even if current taxes are progressive, it does not follow that new ones will be.

[18] Another example is the recent Administration proposal that a tax per gallon of gasoline be accompanied by an annual fixed rebate to each family amounting to the (national) *average* tax payment on gasoline purchases. In that way, a family need lose no net income through the tax and can even save money by cutting back its use of gasoline (by driving smaller cars or by doing less driving than an average automobile owner). Since lower-income families typically consume less gasoline than more affluent households, the former should, on average, experience a net increase in their disposable income.

13

International Environmental Policy

The Atlantic was no longer blue but grey-green and opaque, covered with clots of oil ranging from pin-head size to the dimensions of the average sandwich. Plastic bottles floated among the waste. We might have been in a squalid city port.[1]

    International environmental problems and policy issues do not, in principle, require any alteration in our analysis. We can, for example, explain the problems of oil spills or the decimation of the whale population as examples of externalities in which the actions of one individual (or country) impose serious spillover costs upon others. However, if the international setting does not affect the validity of our analysis, it does complicate enormously the design of effective environmental policy.

    The special problems of international policy stem in part from the many independent jurisdictions whose decisions require coordination, and the common-property characteristics of a substantial portion of the world's resources. One country's decisions about pesticide use or fishing activities may have a profound effect upon the welfare of its neighbors. As we shall see, much of the deterioration of one nation's water or air may be the result of pollution whose sources are in other countries. In addition, a nation's environmental policy has implications for its position in the world economy; there is the fear, for example, that the costs of an aggressive domestic program of pollution con-

---

[1] Thor Heyerdahl, *The Ra Expedition*, trans. Patricia Crampton (London: Allen and Unwin, 1970), p. 208.

trol will result in higher export prices, loss of world markets, deterioration in the balance of payments, and an accompanying loss of jobs and income.

None of these problems would be more troublesome than they are for domestic environmental policy, if we could somehow arrange for the different governments to get together and agree on a common and effective program. The issues then would be essentially the same as those involved in the design of effective environmental measures for one country. But international cooperation has been hard to come by. There have been many international conferences on environmental problems, but at least up to now they have not gotten very far in establishing effective and enforceable systems for the protection of the global environment.

In the absence of needed international cooperation, the threat of the competitive disadvantage that unilateral pollution control may impose on a nation's export- and import-competing industries has often stifled attempts to introduce effective environmental programs; underdeveloped areas have shown particular reticence about instituting strong pollution measures for fear that their growth will be slowed. The result has been continuing abuse of international waters and air as individual countries subject their neighbors, as well as themselves, to the damage they impose on the environment.

1. Evidence of Transnational Environmental Damage

Cases of environmental damage across national boundaries are not rare. One particularly acute example is overfishing, sometimes to the point of the destruction of a species (which we will discuss in the next section). There is also a growing awareness of such international pollution problems as atmospheric lead contamination by private industry, the widespread dispersion of many pesticides, and the contamination of numerous international rivers.

Scientists know a great deal about the mechanism by which certain pesticides and other pollutants are distributed throughout the globe. Significant amounts are carried by rivers and ocean currents, but apparently most of this pollution is transported by the atmosphere. The speed with which air currents can move enormous quantities of pollutants over great distances is evidenced in dramatic fashion by the following selections from a report by Justin Frost:[2]

> Located on the Shetland Islands over 100 miles from the northern tip of Scotland, and more than 200 miles west of Bergen, Norway, Lerwick is farther removed from any agricultural activity than any of the other stations [used in a recent study of movement of pesticides]. Nevertheless, Lerwick registered comparable concentrations of dieldrin and the DDT

---

[2] "Earth, Air, Water," *Environment* 11 (July-August 1969): 14–33.

group, and had the highest concentrations of BHC of any of the seven stations. Moreover, the total concentrations of all pesticides was the highest recorded at any of the stations.[3]

> The . . . study not only indicates that pesticides are carried in the general atmospheric circulation throughout the year, but also gives direct evidence that very large quantities are involved. The seven stations sampled throughout the year appear to offer a reasonable sample of the magnitude of pesticide concentrations in the rain over the United Kingdom, the average concentration being 170 parts per trillion. On the basis of these figures, one can calculate that in the United Kingdom one inch of rainfall would deposit one ton of pesticides. Since the average annual rainfall in the United Kingdom is more than 40 inches, we can conclude that this area receives almost four times as much pesticides in rain as the Mississippi River dumps annually into the Gulf of Mexico.[4]

The study gives other illustrations indicating the remarkable capacity of air currents to transport pollutants:

> Near the end of 1958, for example, radioactivity at ground level due to debris from the testing of atomic weapons was almost entirely confined to the Northern Hemisphere, but within three months it had spread well into the Southern Hemisphere. Debris from French nuclear tests in September, 1968 at 21° S latitude (in the South Pacific) was detected in Arkansas at 34° N latitude about three weeks later.[5]

> One source of contamination of the atmosphere is pesticide-laden dust picked up directly from soils by storms. In January, 1965, five to six tons of dust per square mile were deposited in Cincinnati, Ohio, by a light rain at noon. The dust had been picked up in a large storm the day before in western Texas (where annual pesticide use is heavy) and correspondingly contained appreciable amounts of DDT, DDE, and chlordane, and trace amounts of heptachlor epoxide and dieldrin, totaling 1.3 ppm of chlorinated hydrocarbons. At the time the dust-fall occurred in Cincinnati the dust cloud resulting from the storm stretched for 1,500 miles in a 200-mile-wide band extending easterly from the southern tip of Texas 700 miles across the Gulf of Mexico to the Florida Panhandle where it curved northward 800 miles to Lake Erie.[6]

Residues of DDT have even been found in polar bears and other arctic animals.[7] Pollutants other than DDT also travel across national borders: Norway, for example, has been plagued by "black snow" which "was caused by combustion pollutants with a high content of sulphuric acid, which Scandinavian scientists

---

[3] Ibid., pp. 21, 23.
[4] Ibid., p. 23.
[5] Ibid.
[6] Ibid., pp. 23–24.
[7] George W. Irving, Jr., "Agricultural Pest Control and the Environment," *Science* 168 (June 19, 1970): 1423.

concluded had come from air over the Ruhr in West Germany."[8] Pollution shows little respect for national boundaries.

2. International Common Property

As we discussed in an earlier chapter, one of the major sources of environmental problems is the institution of common property: property which is owned by no one and which is therefore subject to abuse by everyone. A piece of land, which might yield abundant crops and whose soil might be carefully nurtured by a private proprietor, is all too likely to be poorly maintained and overused if it is held in common. It pays no individual to fertilize or do anything else to preserve and enhance the land's productivity, because the fruits of that labor will go largely to others.

Probably the most significant, economically, of the world's common properties are the oceans, seas, and other international waterways. As we may expect, these waterways have been the subject of a great variety of misuse. Two abuses, in particular, have become critical: the use of the seas and oceans as dumping grounds for noxious wastes, and the excessive utilization of its sealife.

There are some notorious examples of the use of international waters as garbage dumps: the disposal of radioactive wastes by European governments, of obsolete nerve gas by the United States, and of oil discharges from tankers at sea.[9] When Thor Heyerdahl crossed the Atlantic Ocean by raft, he reported "a continuous stretch of at least 1,400 miles of open Atlantic polluted by floating lumps of solidified, asphalt-like oil."[10]

The fish of the oceans are also common property. The resulting overfishing that has occurred is again predictable. A particularly dramatic and instructive example is the near-decimation of the prized blue whale.[11] The whale has long been hunted, not only for food and fuel, but also for the production of a wide variety of commodities ranging from shoe polish to cosmetics. However, in the

---

[8] John M. Lee, "Pollution Defies Europe's Borders," *New York Times,* January 11, 1970, p. 24. See also, Clyde H. Farnsworth, "Norse Seek Curb on Acid Rainfall," *New York Times,* November 27, 1970, p. 64.

[9] Incidentally, one noteworthy fact that emerges from these illustrations is the contribution of governmental activities to the world's pollution problems. It is all too easy to imagine that damage to the environment is the result of the irresponsible behavior of soulless corporations whose managements care for nothing but profits. However, government power-generation and sewage-disposal plants emit a large portion of the pollutants in our air and waterways, and military activities generate some of the most troublesome of the world's wastes.

[10] Terence Smith, "Treaty Is Urged to Forbid Flushing of Tankers at Sea," *New York Times,* November 3, 1970, p. 69.

[11] See George L. Small, *The Blue Whale* (New York: Columbia University Press, 1971); Faith McNulty, *The Great Whales* (Garden City, N.Y.: Doubleday, 1974); and Anthony

twentieth century, there have been striking developments in the technology of whaling; of particular significance has been the introduction of pelagic (open-sea) whaling, which involves large fleets of ships (including factory ships to process the kills of the catcher boats). With such fleets from many nations ranging the seas in pursuit of the whale, there remains virtually no sanctuary for these great mammals. The blue whale has been a favorite target of the fleets. These whales are very large (they can reach lengths of 80 feet or more) and are an excellent source of a variety of oils and flesh. Other whales tend to be somewhat leaner, and their oils are not always edible. The development of pelagic whaling led to dramatic increases in the kills of blue whales, particularly in the Antarctic. This has taken a heavy toll: before 1940, the world's oceans contained over 150,000 blue whales, but by 1976 estimates of the population were down to 6,000-13,000.[12] Moreover, fewer blue whales are living to maturity. In 1933 the average length of the blue whales taken in the Antarctic was 80.4 feet but by 1953, it had fallen to 77.5 feet; in 1963 it was down to 73.1 feet.[13] Since it requires about six years for a blue whale to become sexually mature and the female bears a calf on average only once each two years, the decimation of the adult population has critically reduced the number of the new young.

The fate of the blue whale is a disturbing illustration of the "common-property" problem. In contrast, a rancher who has exclusive ownership of a herd of cattle will carefully nurture the animals. It is in the owner's interest to see that they are cared for, grow to full size, and reproduce so as to maintain the herds in the future. But the blue whale is not so fortunate; it is owned by no one. In consequence, it is in the interest of each whaler to kill as many whales as he can before someone else can get to them.

3. The Prospects for Effective International Agreement

The key difference between international and national environmental

---

Netboy, "The Tragic History of the Blue Whale," *American Forests* 81 (January 1975): 42-44.
[12] D. G. Chapman, "Status of Antarctic Rorqual Stocks," Chap. 9 in William E. Shevill, ed., *The Whale Problem, A Status Report* (Cambridge, Mass.: Harvard University Press, 1974), p. 234; Netboy, "Tragic History of the Blue Whale," pp. 42-43; Statement of Christine Stevens, Society for Animal Protection Legislation, Hearings before the Subcommittee on Fisheries and Wildlife Conservation and the Environment of the Committee on Merchant Marine and Fisheries, House, 94th Congress, First Session, May 13, 1975, p. 36; Statement of Dr. Lee Talbot, Council on Environmental Quality, Hearings before the Subcommittee on Fisheries and Wildlife Conservation and the Environment, Ibid., p. 59; Victor B. Scheffer, "Exploring the Lives of Whales," *National Geographic* 150 (December 1976): 752-67. Twenty blue whales were caught in the 1965 season in the Antarctic. Since then blue whales have been on the International Whaling Commission's protected list and there are no figures of any legal kills since 1965 (although certain countries, such as Chile and South Africa, are still reported to be catching blue whales).
[13] Small, *Blue Whale*, p. 95.

problems is the greater difficulty of establishing an effective control mechanism. There simply is no international authority with enough power to regulate global environmental activities. In circumstances where one country's activities can create significant environmental problems for others, and particularly where a number of countries are jointly responsible for the deterioration of some feature of the environment (for example, in the case of the Baltic Sea, which receives pollutants from every one of the countries that border its shores), cooperative international action is obviously the most direct way to deal with the resulting problems.

Unfortunately (although there are some notable exceptions), the history of diplomacy attests to the formidable obstacles to effective multinational programs. Certainly the recent negotiations concerning the Baltic Sea are not encouraging. Three of the seven countries bordering the Baltic are Soviet states whose attitudes toward environmental policy are often quite different from those of the other four countries. According to Swedish officials, it has so far been impossible for the seven Baltic nations to decide on any common policies.[14]

International cooperation on ocean oil pollution has been somewhat more encouraging. In particular, recent episodes of dramatic oil spills have generated sufficient common concern to spark some international agreements. Only twenty-five years ago a report to the United Nations commented, "Interested and responsible authorities in the United States are in agreement that pollution of the territorial waters of the country by oil is not serious and shows no sign of increase. . . . In respect to pollution of the high seas the United States has insufficient evidence that this is of such seriousness as to require international action."[15] Since then a number of significant oil spills (such as the sinking of the tanker *Torrey Canyon* off the British coast, the *Ocean Eagle* incident in the United States and Puerto Rico, and the leakages in Santa Barbara) have led to revision of such optimistic opinions.[16]

There are several international conventions for the prevention of oil spills, the most notable drawn up in 1954 and amended in 1962 by a conference of contracting governments. This convention establishes zones in which discharges of oil or oily water are forbidden; it requires that ships log their oil discharges

[14]Clyde H. Farnsworth, "Politics in Baltic Sea Hinders Coordinated Pollution Control," *New York Times,* October 4, 1970, p. 15.

[15]*Report of Studies by the United States on the Subject of Pollution of Sea Water by Oil,* Shipping Coordinating Committee, Economic and Social Council of the United Nations, March 31, 1952, as quoted by John W. Mann, *The Problem of Sea Water Pollution,* U.S. Department of State Bulletin, December 7, 1953, pp. 778, 779.

[16]The recent rash of serious oil spills has led to greater interest in international cooperation in this area. One of the most spectacular incidents occurred in December 1976 when an aging Liberian tanker, the *Argo Merchant,* ran aground twenty-three miles offshore from Nantucket Island; six days later the ship broke up, spilling over 5 million gallons of heavy oil into the Atlantic. Another huge spill occurred early in 1977 when an oil-drilling platform in the North Sea blew out and spewed over 7.5 million gallons of crude oil into the sea (*New York Times,* December 22, 1976, p. 1; *Newsweek,* May 9, 1977, pp. 47–50; *New York Times,* May 1, 1977, p. 1).

and losses at sea; it encourages the signatory governments to construct waste-oil receiving facilities in their ports; and it sets up procedures for the apprehension and prosecution of violators.[17] However, these conventions still suffer from a number of shortcomings.

First, the issue of liability of off-shore installations and drilling operations has not been settled, even though in the United States, for example, it has been estimated that these account for some 40 percent of the oil spills in domestic waters. Second, under U.S. law an oil spill is subject to penalties only if it can be shown to be "grossly negligent or willful." The discharger is, however, responsible for all the cleanup costs, unless the discharge is caused by "an Act of God."[18] Finally, and perhaps most significant, are the enforcement problems facing the international conventions. In the words of a former Assistant Secretary of the Interior, "There are no teeth in the prohibition against dumping in certain zones because the reporting of violations is on the honor system. Unfortunately, the pangs of a sea captain's conscience are not an adequate deterrent to oil pollution."[19]

While there has been *some* progress towards agreement on the use of the seas, it is slow and events are not always encouraging. Setbacks like that described in the following report are disturbingly frequent:

> Geneva, Aug. 29—National rivalries have again prevented a United Nations committee from agreeing on the basic principals for the internationalization of the seabed.
>
> The Committee on the Peaceful Uses of the Seabed adjourned last night after four weeks of meetings with no concrete results. The United Nations has enthusiastically endorsed the preservation of the seabed as "the common heritage of mankind. . . ."
>
> Leaders of the oil industry fear that in the meantime the worldwide race for offshore drilling concessions will induce coastal states to push their claims farther out to sea.[20]

In the case of river and air pollution, the prospects for truly effective international action seem at best highly uncertain. Though no truly international agreements regulate the use of rivers, there are many bilateral treaties dealing with the subject. There are now over sixty countries that have undertaken

[17]John O. Ludwigson, "Oil Pollution at Sea," in Stanley E. Degler, ed., *Oil Pollution: Problems and Policies* (Washington, D.C.: Bureau of National Affairs, Inc., 1969), p. 9.
[18]Max N. Edwards, "Oil Pollution and the Law," in Degler, *Oil Pollution*, p. 26.
[19]Ibid.
[20]Thomas J. Hamilton, "A Seabed Accord is Blocked Again," *New York Times*, August 30, 1970, p. 19. Three years later, matters seem not to have changed very much. See, for example, "Sea-Law Outlook Is Said To Be Dim," *New York Times*, August 26, 1973, Sect. 1, p. 11. Note also the continuing difficulties of the countries of the world to reach an agreement on the proposal to increase coastal nations' territorial waters to a boundary 200 miles from shore.

agreements to regulate the use of many international water courses and provide for compulsory adjudication or other third party determinations.[21] However, these agreements have generally established no really comprehensive rules. Some treaties, notably one between Denmark and Germany (1922) and one between Belgium and Germany (1929), prohibit pollution absolutely! Others prohibit pollution that damages a particular water use such as fishing or outlaws damage from "unreasonable use of the waters."[22]

The classic cases in international pollution control have occurred in the area of air pollution; here it is clear that countries are quite reluctant to give up any of their sovereignty. A typical case was the *Trail Smelter Arbitration* between the United States and Canada which arose out of a 1925 dispute and was not settled until 1941! The case involved a complaint by the United States about damage suffered by residents in the State of Washington from sulfur-dioxide pollution emitted by a Canadian smelter. A tribunal established by an arbitration convention in 1935 ruled "that under the principles of international law, as well as the law of the United States, no State has the right to use or permit the use of its territory in such a manner as to cause injury by fumes in or to the territory of another or to the properties or persons therein, when the case is of serious consequence and the injury is established by clear and convincing evidence."[23] Although the decision was hailed as a big step in international pollution control (since it involved an international tribunal which asserted the principle of state responsibility for extraterritorial injury), it must be recognized that the case was settled in this way only because the disputing parties were in agreement and not because they recognized general international obligations. Austin comments that "States are in fact most reluctant to refer such disputes to judicial settlement."[24]

This reluctance was later demonstrated in the dramatic case of the *Fukuru Maru*, a Japanese fishing vessel whose cargo and crew were injured by radioactive fallout from American H-bomb tests in 1954. The United States, whose attitude was "the same as any other State in similar circumstances where such important national interests as 'security' were involved" simply would not consider submitting to a decision by an international tribunal; the United States argued that its act incurred no liability under international laws.[25] The U.S. Government did pay $2 million to the victims, but did so "ex gratia" to avoid any concession of responsibility or precedent.

The history of international efforts to prevent the extinction of the whale

---

[21] Brice M. Clagett, "Survey of Agreements Providing for Third-Party Resolution of International Waters Disputes," *American Journal of International Law* 55 (July 1961): 645–69.
[22] A. P. Lester, "River Pollution in International Law," *American Journal of International Law* 57 (October 1963): 831.
[23] As quoted by R. H. F. Austin, "Air Pollution," *Report of Conference on Law and Science* (London: The Davies Memorial Institute of International Studies, 1964), p. 90.
[24] Ibid., p. 91.
[25] Ibid.

is also a mixed record of some successes and frustrating failures. The League of Nations recognized the need to slow the killing of whales as early as 1927. But there was no real hope for effective cooperation until 1946 at the International Convention for the Regulation of Whaling; that convention established the International Whaling Commission (IWC) which was to meet annually to set regulations on whaling activities. Through the years, the Commission has established numerous restrictions on the size and quantity of whales that could be killed. In June 1967, the Commission outlawed altogether the killing of the blue whale. However, compliance and policing has been another matter. Under the international provisions, a country can file a formal protest to any of the Commission's regulations and can then *legally* ignore the regulation! Japan and Russia, who together take over 80 percent of the world whale catch, have therefore simply filed objections to some of the IWC's restrictions on whaling and then violated them.[26] It has been impossible to do anything about it, one estimate indicates that the Japanese fleets alone have killed 550 blue whales off the coast of Chile since 1965.[27]

The 1970s have seen renewed attempts to achieve international cooperation to protect the environment. In particular, the participants in the United Nations Conference on the Human Environment held at Stockholm in 1972 tried to establish a global approach to environmental problems in terms of a comprehensive Action Plan. The Plan identifies six priority areas and three functional tasks for the United Nations Environment Program.[28] However, progress is slow and difficult; three years following the Stockholm conference, a petition signed by thousands from many different countries was presented to the United Nations asserting that "too little has been done" and pleading for intensified efforts to protect and improve the global environment.[29]

4. The Role of Unilateral Measures

If the countries involved find it impossible to resolve environmental problems jointly, there may be no choice for the aggrieved parties but to do what they can unilaterally. If the health of the inhabitants of one country is threatened by emissions from a bordering nation, the former may ultimately find it

---

[26]*Environmental Quality, The Fifth Annual Report of the Council on Environmental Quality* (Washington, D.C.: U.S. Government Printing Office, 1974), pp. 442-43.
[27]*National Parks and Conservation Magazine* 49 (October 1975): 28.
[28]The six priority areas are: (1) human settlements, human health, habitat, and well-being; (2) land, water, and desertification; (3) trade, economics, technology, and transfer of technology; (4) oceans; (5) conservation of nature, wildlife, and genetic resources; and (6) energy. The three functional tasks are: (1) environmental assessment: Earthwatch, (2) environmental management, and (3) supporting measures: information, education, training, and technical assistance. See, for example, *Environmental Quality, Fifth Annual Report*, Chap. 5.
[29]Gladwin Hill, "U.N. Environmental Effort: A Start, a Long Way to Go," *New York Times*, October 20, 1975, pp. 1, 14.

tempting to take matters into their own hands. Even if the two nations attempt
to negotiate the matter, it may not be easy to achieve an accord, and the victim-
ized country may have to resort to threats, which will very likely take the form
of economic retaliation.

Economists since Adam Smith have generally eschewed any sort of impediment to free trade between countries, since such impediments usually result
in an inefficient deployment of the world's resources. In consequence, new
trade restrictions will probably find little welcome, even if they are undertaken
in response to environmental problems. Nevertheless, in this case, it is possible
to argue on both practical and theoretical grounds that, where transnational
environmental damage is severe enough, appropriate trade restrictions may be
better than doing nothing at all. For example, there is something to be said for
the unilateral adoption by a country suffering from transnational pollution of
a duty on imports from the offending country, particularly a duty on goods
whose manufacture is a significant source of the pollution.[30] It is in fact the
nearest approximation available to the victim country (acting by itself) to the
emissions taxes which economists usually advocate. Such duties may directly
force the polluting business firms to curtail their emissions, and the threat of
duties or boycotts may smooth the path of bilateral negotiations and brighten
the prospects for an agreement that renders the trade restrictions unnecessary.

It therefore seems inappropriate to reject out of hand the concept of trade
restrictions to achieve environmental goals. It would be important, however, to
try to set out explicit rules for the operation of such a system of duties to prevent their misuse. Two such rules come to mind at once:

(a) A country that imposes trade restrictions on a polluting nation could
be required to specify the conditions under which the restrictions would be
dropped. That is, they could be expected to specify acceptable pollution levels
from the offending country. Once the standards had been met, the restrictions
would automatically be dropped (unless some substantial violation were subsequently detected). This means that the polluting country is effectively given
the power to end the restrictive duties; once it meets the specified pollution
standards, the importer would remove the discriminatory provisions.

(b) One might also require that no country impose pollution standards
that are more restrictive than those which it imposes on its own industries.[31]

---

[30] See Chapter 14 of W. Baumol and W. Oates, *The Theory of Environmental Policy* (Englewood Cliffs, N.J.: Prentice-Hall, Inc., 1975). Of course, such a program is unlikely to be
effective if it is attempted by a very small importer of the goods of the polluting country.
However, if a number of importing countries, each acting on its own initiative, decide
to impose such a duty, it is likely to work, even if some countries decide not to go along
with the program.

[31] This may not provide all the protection against discrimination that is desired. Suppose
country A can use nuclear power economically in producing its electricity, while B must
utilize coal. Then A may deliberately enact a levy that penalizes heavily only the pollutants
emitted by the burning of coal with its real objective being to impede imports from B. True,
the terms of the charge are nondiscriminatory, but their effects are not.

Obviously, other limitations on the use of such charges may be desirable. The preceding two suggestions are only illustrations. The adoption of such rules will itself require a painful process of international negotiation, but once the standards are agreed upon, the process of negotiation need not be replicated for each transnational environmental problem.

Any encouragement of restrictions upon free trade can be undertaken only with great hesitation; as economists, we cannot help having very mixed feelings about them. Yet where no other practical alternative is available, one may be forced to look for policies that the victim countries can employ on their own initiative, rather than passively waiting for international cooperation.

5. The Effects of Domestic Environmental Programs on a Country's Balance of Payments and Level of Employment

There is a second and equally important link between international issues and environmental policy. No government is anxious to impose an economic liability upon its industries in their competitive struggle for world markets. Yet that is precisely what every government fears will result from the unilateral adoption of a strong set of environmental measures. If environmental policies make a country's products more costly, it will certainly constitute a serious handicap for exporters. Looked at the other way, it becomes tempting for a country to hang back and let others protect their environments, while it takes advantage of the resulting reductions in its relative costs to improve its position in international trade.

The problem is a real one, but it is also true that business interests and politicians have exaggerated the potential damage from domestic environmental policies. Obviously, one cannot generalize about the price effects of environmental programs, since they can differ widely in range and magnitude. We can, however, get some feeling for the extent of these effects by examining some of the environmental measures that have actually received serious consideration. A few examples are the standards for water quality, automotive emissions, and other environmental targets that are contemplated by the U.S. government. The Council on Environmental Quality has made the following estimates of the added cost to customers for some of the products that will be most affected by the environmental standards: electric utilities, 7 percent; pulp and paper, 3.5 to 10 percent; aluminum smelting, 5 to 8 percent; iron, 1.7 to 5 percent; cement, 4 to 5 percent.[32] It has also been estimated that, using the current treatment processes, low-sulfur electricity production will raise the price of electricity by something between 6 and 10 percent.[33] Another system-

---

[32] "The Big Cleanup—How the U.S. Is Doing the Job," *Newsweek,* June 12, 1972, p. 48.
[33] Philip H. Abelson, "Progress in Abating Air Pollution," *Science* 167 (March 20, 1970): 1567.

atic analysis has estimated that, for a number of industrial countries, strong environmental programs will increase export prices from 3.5 to 9 percent.[34]

Such price rises are obviously not insignificant. But their effect on a country's competitive position in international markets is comparable to perhaps one or two years of regular inflationary price increases. Table 13-1, showing indices of consumer prices for some leading industrial countries for 1969-73, indicates that such price rises are hardly uncommon. It is true that inflation constitutes no competitive disadvantage if it is universal and proceeds at an equal pace in all countries. However, as the table shows, the rate of inflation has hardly been the same in all countries. Note that over the period 1969 to 1972, Japan, with its very strong trade position, had a price level whose *annual*

TABLE 13-1

CONSUMER PRICES (1963 = 100)

	1969	1970	1971	1972
United States	120	127	132	137
Japan	134	145	153	160
France	124	131	139	147
Germany	116	121	127	134
Italy	122	128	134	142
United Kingdom	127	135	148	159

Source: Organization for Economic Cooperation and Development, *Main Economic Indicators* (Paris: OECD, April 1973), p. 26.

---

[34] See Ralph C. d'Arge, "International Trade, Environmental Quality and International Controls: Some Empirical Estimates," Appendix F in Allen V. Kneese, Sidney E. Rolfe, and Joseph W. Harned, eds., *Managing the Environment: International Economic Cooperation for Pollution Control* (New York: Praeger Publishers, 1971), p. 298. These studies may, to some extent, overestimate the likely increases in prices inasmuch as environmental programs frequently rely on subsidies to polluters to offset, at least in part, the rise in abatement costs.

CONSUMER PRICES (1970 = 100)

	1973	1974	1975	1976
U.S.	114.4	127.0	138.6	146.6
Japan	124.5	153.4	171.4	187.5
France	119.9	136.3	152.2	166.8
Germany	118.8	127.1	134.7	140.8
Italy	122.4	146.2	171.3	199.6
United Kingdom	126.7	147.0	182.5	211.4

Source: Organization for Economic Cooperation and Development, *Main Economic Indicators* (Paris: OECD, March 1977).

rise was almost two percentage points greater than that of the United States, whose international financial position was much less strong during most of this period.[35]

In addition, rising export costs have often been incorrectly associated with a deteriorating balance of trade. Rising export costs can indeed reduce a country's net revenues from international trade, but they *need not* always have this effect. It is true that at higher prices we can confidently expect to sell smaller quantities of goods. But we will also get more money for each item we sell, and where one comes out on balance will vary from case to case. If the price of American machinery rises 20 percent and, as a result, their sales fall 15 percent, the total payments from abroad for these machines will rise (by about 5 percent). Only if the quantity sold falls by a larger percent than the rise in prices will one come out behind in terms of total money receipts. There is therefore no logical basis for the easy and widespread presumption that a rise in export prices must unavoidably affect the balance of payments adversely. One study, making what are admittedly very rough estimates, has in fact concluded that the unilateral adoption of strong environmental programs by any of the several industrial countries examined, can be expected to *improve* their balance of payments.[36]

It has also been assumed that rising export prices will necessarily increase unemployment. We have already considered this issue in the preceding chapter on the redistributive effects of environmental policies. However, we want to stress two points here. First, loss of foreign demand for goods and services need not result in unemployment. Modern governments have effective instruments to stimulate the level of national output and employment through their tax and expenditure programs and monetary policies. In addition, it requires labor and other resources to produce the instruments of environmental protection: the devices that control automotive emissions, municipal waste-treatment plants, and conservation projects. Even if environmental measures reduce imports, it is conceivable that they may, on balance, increase the demand for labor.[37]

What may be more troublesome is the unevenness of the resulting changes in demand among industries. It is true that increased costs in heavily polluting industries will typically require a flow of labor from jobs in these industries to employment elsewhere. This transition process can be made less painful by the adoption of "adjustment assistance" in the form of temporary income-

---

[35] When we look at the rates of inflation in more recent years (see table below) the increases and the differentials between countries become even more pronounced.

[36] See d'Arge, "International Trade," p. 307. The Council on Environmental Quality in its 1975 Annual Report cites several studies which found that U.S. environmental policies had no significant adverse impact on foreign trade; see *Environmental Quality, The Sixth Annual Report of the Council on Environmental Quality* (Washington, D.C.: U.S. Government Printing Office, 1975), p. 561, fn. 58.

[37] This is confirmed by several studies cited in *Environmental Quality, Sixth Annual Report*, p. 558, fn. 1.

maintenance payments, retraining facilities, and additional help in finding new jobs.

Finally, the evolution of the international monetary system may itself resolve any balance-of-payments problems threatened by environmental programs. Increasing reliance on flexible exchange rates has facilitated the adjustment of imbalances in international payments and is helping to mitigate many of the financial problems that are feared of environmental policy. Adjustments in currency exchange rates can automatically take care of any potential imbalances in international payments caused by the costs of pollution control. In particular, rises in a nation's costs of production occasioned by pollution-abatement programs can be offset, in terms of their effects on international financial flows and domestic employment, by a depreciation in the value of the country's currency.

6. The Special Problems of the Developing Countries

Transnational pollution and the trade effects of environmental programs create special problems for developing nations. For countries that are poor and very anxious for economic growth, it is tempting to opt for environmental damage if sufficient returns, such as a marked improvement in competitive position on international markets, can be gained. A newspaper story about the visit of three newsmen from mainland China illustrates the point:

> Above Wheeling, W. Va., the Ohio River flows past low forested bluffs and a series of decaying factory towns. . . . the smog from the steel factories and electric power plants hangs heavy over the river, obscuring the view of more smokestacks and more piles of coal farther upstream. . . . "What a beautiful sight," exclaimed Yeh Chih-hsiung, the third newsman, as we rounded a bend in the Ohio and saw two enormous chimneys belching white smoke. We stopped for a picture.
>
> For China, eager to achieve total industrialization, it was an impressive spectacle, Mr. Yeh explained.[38]

As recently as 1972 Brazil decided deliberately to expand its polluting activities:

> The Brazilian policy on pollution—seeking industries that cause it until it becomes a problem—is only one part of a nationwide drive for economic growth that has made Brazil a boom country. . . .
>
> Before the United Nations . . . Brazil has argued that her policy is the best for all of the world's developing nations and that poor, unpolluted countries should have the right to do some polluting of their own for the

---

[38]Fox Butterfield, "Reporter's Notebook: Chinese on Tour," *New York Times,* September 3, 1972, pp. 1, 2.

sake of the benefits that industry has already brought to rich, polluted countries.

"Brazil can become the importer of pollution," João Paulo Velloso, the nation's Planning Minister, said in a recent interview. . . . The idea is that a remote river estuary on the Brazilian central coast can take the polluted pulp wastes that Japan cannot.

"Why not?" Mr. Velloso asked. "We have a lot left to pollute. They don't." . . .

The state-owned iron mining enterprise, Vale Do Rio Doce Company, is now in negotiation for a $1.2-billion project to produce wood pulp for export to Japan, fully aware of its pollution potential. A company official estimated that the project would provide jobs for 12,000 people.

"And if we don't do it," he said, "some other country will."[39]

If a country is poor, that sort of decision may well be rational, at least up to a point. In our discussion of the distributive implications of environmental programs, we noted that environmental policies can sometimes be a better bargain for the rich than for the poor. Raising the standard of living may be well worth the price of malodorous fumes and desecrated natural landscapes, but a country that makes this trade-off should harbor no illusions about the nature of the price it agrees to pay. The willingness to accept more pollution may *appear* to permit a poor country to produce more cheaply than its competitors.[40] In the long run, however, the country absorbs part of the cost itself. It could just as easily produce "more cheaply" by giving away its copper, its lumber, or its labor. Sacrificing its clean air no more eliminates the real cost of this resource than the donation of some valuable mineral. Moreover, the underdeveloped country may make itself a dump for the waste products of the world. The virtues of the trade-off become even more questionable considering the health effects of many kinds of pollution.

Sometimes these implications become clear sooner than might have been anticipated. Barely a year after Brazil had rejected environmental programs as an obstacle to development, a dramatic change in policy seems to have occurred. A March 11, 1973, story in the *New York Times* was headlined, "Brazil Enacting Pollution Curbs. Development At Any Price No Longer the Rule."[41]

---

[39]Joseph Novitski, "Brazil Shunning Pollution Curbs," *New York Times*, February 13, 1972, p. 11.

[40]Moreover, as we stressed in the preceding section, under a system of flexible exchange rates, this "gain" in competitive positive will be largely illusory. Any such gain will result in a rise in the value of the country's currency and an offsetting loss in other exports and increases in imports.

[41]Sect. 1, p. 24, story by Marvine Howe. Some excerpts from the story are illuminating:

> Industrial development at any price has been the first priority of the military Government that took over this country nine years ago. Official policy held that problems of environmental pollution were a luxury that only highly developed countries could afford. . . .
> However, over the last two years there has been strong pressure from the municipalities and the press for a national antipollution policy.

From the point of view of the highly industrialized countries, there may be some merit in a pattern of specialization, with the poorer countries taking on the world's polluting activities. But even that is not without its problems, because pollution generated by the underdeveloped nations may refuse to remain within their borders. As we have seen earlier, all too often pollution seems to have a propensity to cross national boundaries.[42]

7. Conclusions

Our discussion of international environmental problems has raised more questions than it has answered. In part this is because the problems are predominantly political and not economic. If we can find ways to deal with political obstacles, the appropriate economic measures are already available. These measures are in essence the same as those that can be used in domestic environmental affairs, the policies which are the central focus of this book. If not, the crucial problem will be to find effective and appropriate unilateral measures which victim countries can undertake to protect themselves from the damage emanating from their neighbors.

Pollution entered the Brazilian vocabulary about two years ago. Since then not a day has passed without alarming reports about the country's diminishing resources: the contamination of the waterways, the poisoning of the beaches, the devastation of the Amazon forests, the dangers of air polluted by filth and noise.

The first major offensive against pollution was opened this week in the state of São Paulo, which contains the most highly industrialized area of Latin America–and some of the most urgent environmental problems.

The program will cost nearly $9-million and extend over three years. The United Nations development program and the World Health Organization will contribute about $2.3-million in technical assistance and equipment. . . .

The situation throughout the country is "terrible," according to O Estado do São Paulo. A survey it made recently concluded that air, soil and water pollution was increasing "at an alarming rate" in all the states. . . .

[For example] São Paulo's satellite towns of Santo André, São Bernardo do Campo and São Caetano have been described as "unlivable," but a total of 775,000 people live there. The air is said to contain tons of sulphur dioxide and is unbreathable, according to an official report. Fifty per cent of the children given medical treatment suffer from diseases of the respiratory tract. . . .

Even the handsome new capital of Brasília has pollution problems. The city's population has doubled to over half a million in the last two years and the authorities concede that they cannot cope with the garbage problems.

[42] Measures against major sources of international pollution raise other problems for less developed countries. Insecticides such as DDT have produced enormous benefits for their inhabitants. They have assisted in bringing malaria under control and in reducing other illnesses which sap the population's vitality. No other single discovery may have done so much for public health in the underdeveloped areas. In many respects DDT is ideally suited for use in places in which the population is scattered in remote areas, in which the level of education is low, and where public cooperation with the authorities is minimal. For, unlike medication that is administered to one person at a time, it does not require individuals to show up for injections or to take a sequence of pills. It can be administered without large numbers of expensive and scarce medical personnel. All one needs is an airplane with spray equipment that can distribute the insecticide over the countryside.

Part III

THE DESIGN OF ENVIRONMENTAL POLICY

14

Perfectionism and Priorities
in Environmental Policy

Before turning directly to the design of environmental policy, we want to establish three important matters of principle. The first concerns the unavoidable trade-offs among environmental policy objectives. The second is the irrationality of the view that all pollution can and should be eliminated completely. And the third is the priority of programs designed to protect life and health in relation to those that promise solely aesthetic and recreational benefits.

1. The Necessity of Difficult Choices

In the formulation of environmental policy, virtually any course of action may upset the ecological balance; well-intentioned, but misguided, attempts to interfere with that balance can produce results very different from those intended. For example, the complete protection of wildlife from hunters and fishermen can apparently cause overpopulation with severe costs to the health and welfare of animal life.[1] Similarly, many forestry experts now contend that

---

[1] It should be noted, however, that one reason hunters and fishermen are now needed to keep wildlife populations down is that so many of the *natural* predators have been killed off or driven away by man.

the campaign for fire prevention may have upset natural forest cycles. They believe that, if kept within reasonable limits, forest fires help to preserve the overall health of woodlands by keeping down the populations of certain types of vegetation that can crowd out and weaken the hardier species.

Even where ecological balance is not at issue, an environmental measure that offers benefits of one type can indirectly impose serious environmental costs of another sort. Thermal-pollution standards designed to protect fish life have resulted in the construction of huge, unsightly cooling towers which can cause heavy fogs as the water evaporates. The increased use of waste-treatment plants has given rise to a new disposal problem: the generation of enormous quantities of sludge. This sludge is usually dumped into the ocean where it can damage marine life and create health hazards along nearby beaches. As another example, some scientists believe that the emissions from certain catalytic converters on new automobiles may be more harmful than the exhaust they are designed to eliminate. Each of these cases involves trade-offs among differing environmental objectives.

In some cases, by effectively rejecting all the viable but unpleasant possibilities, public pressures have effectively produced an untenable state of inaction. A noteworthy illustration is the construction of new plants for the generation of electricity. In recent years many plans for new generating stations have been blocked by the protests of both environmentalists and the residents in areas for which the construction was proposed. Critics have opposed conventional plants as prime contributors to air pollution; they have also fought against nuclear plants on the grounds that they generate serious problems of disposal of radioactive wastes, that they create thermal and other types of pollution, and that they pose the threat of catastrophic accidents. This has led to mounting construction and legal costs, and to electricity shortages that can grow more acute from year to year. Realism and rationality require the community to face up to the fact that there exist only a few viable options:

a. Agreement on a suitable construction site and a suitable plant design (one which, incidentally, is not so costly as to render it totally impractical)
b. Agreement to prohibit new construction accompanied by a scheme for the rationing of electricity
c. Agreement to prohibit new construction and to free the price of electricity to rise to a point where demand is cut down to the available supply[2]

---

[2]There is one additional alternative which can ease somewhat the shortage of electrical power without mammoth construction of new generating capacity. Several European countries, notably France, have been using a *peak-load pricing* scheme under which power utilized when demand is low (e.g., nighttime or holidays) is substantially cheaper than during peak periods. This has apparently led to a considerable shifting of demand, particularly by industrial users, with declines as high as 15 percent in peak-hour usage not atypical. Since it is the level of *maximum* usage that determines required capacity, it seems clear that a peak-load pricing scheme can eliminate a considerable portion of construction demand.

Peak-load pricing may serve to reduce demand for congested facilities in other areas as

None of these possibilities is attractive, but the unwillingness to reach a decision is certain to produce results that are worse still: very likely a combination of rising prices, shortages, and the construction of a few badly located and uncoordinated plants, an outcome which is painful to consumers on every score.

2. Should We Eliminate Pollution Completely?

The pervasive notion that we can (and must) *totally* suppress all forms of environmental damage is a myth that can undermine rational and effective policy. Lest the reader think that we are constructing a straw man, we quote from the extensive amendments to the Water Pollution Control Act enacted by the U.S. Congress in 1972. The law aims "to restore and maintain the chemical, physical, and biological integrity of the Nation's water" with the goal that "the discharge of pollutants into the navigable waters be eliminated by 1985."[3] The Congress is thus on record that the objective of the U.S. government is the complete abolition of water pollution.

Not only is such a goal impractical, it is inherently undesirable. Since no production activity is 100 percent efficient in the engineering sense, every such activity must generate some minimal quantity of waste, and that waste must be disposed of somewhere, somehow—if not into our waters, then into the earth or atmosphere. Even human existence creates wastes which constitute a problem of public sanitation. The fact is that zero pollution implies not only zero economic growth, but zero production and zero population!

The design of an effective environmental policy is, by its very nature, a search for the best compromise. The more resources we use to clean up the air

---

well. Higher fares for transportation during rush hours is another measure long advocated by economists as a means to reduce the burdens of congestion upon consumers and reduce the demand for new highway construction.

Pricing measures can also be helpful in reducing the environmental costs of other policy alternatives. An example is the proposal for a fourth major jetport for the New York metropolitan area which a few years ago was widely considered unavoidable in light of trends in air traffic. No community was willing to accept a new airport with all its environmental side effects. Economists had long argued that, since small planes tie up a runway for about as long a period as a huge jetliner, they should have to pay similar landing fees. The small craft, with their few passengers, were in fact led to divert much of their traffic to smaller, less crowded airports that are not suitable for large jets. As a result, congestion was reduced to the point where one no longer hears of the proposed fourth jetport. The struggle for the new port has now been replaced by concern about the idle capacity at the new Newark facility. One must, however, be careful not to attribute all of the decrease in congestion to the diversion of small craft. "Jumbo jets," the unfavorable economic conditions which cut back on passenger traffic, reductions in the number of scheduled flights, and regulatory actions that eliminated a number of bargain-fare arrangements have also reduced the demand for air travel.

[3] *Environmental Quality, The Fourth Annual Report of the Council on Environmental Quality* (Washington, D.C.: U.S. Government Printing Office, 1973), p. 172; and Allen V. Kneese and Charles L. Schultze, *Pollution, Prices, and Public Policy* (Washington, D.C.: The Brookings Institution, 1975), p. 53.

and water, the fewer will be available to fight poverty and disease. This is the true social cost of overzealous environmental policy. We cannot be satisfied with the prospect of abundant material possessions, if they must be enjoyed in a world where smog has taken the place of air, lakes have been converted into cesspools, and trees, birds, and beautiful places are no longer to be found. But equally unacceptable is a world where nature is preserved virtually intact, but humanity has to reconcile itself to extreme poverty and discomfort and to deprivation of social and cultural amenities. The issue here is not whether we should avoid or accept some compromise, but which set of compromises makes most sense in terms of the general welfare.

3. By How Much Should We Reduce Pollution?

Rational strategy in the reduction of environmental damage requires that we begin by eliminating those sources of pollution that can be removed most cheaply and easily. Once we have done away with the bulk of the damage, still further reductions in pollution will usually prove more than proportionately costly and difficult. Just as a dieter finds it easy to lose a few pounds but more difficult to take off additional weight, the cost of additional reductions in waste emissions within a single industrial plant normally escalates rapidly as the level of discharges falls.

In Figures 14-1 and 14-2 we depict the marginal cost (i.e., the cost of cutting back emissions by one additional unit) of reducing pollutant discharges for a typical petroleum refinery and for a beet-sugar plant. The steep upward slope of both curves indicates the rapid rise in marginal cost. The petroleum refinery, for example, can eliminate 10 percent of its emissions at a cost of less than two cents per pound. But by the time 90 percent of the emissions have been eliminated, the cost of further reductions is more than twenty-two cents per pound. The beet-sugar plant displays similar cost patterns.[4]

The important point we make here is how steeply marginal cost rises with each successive increase in pollution-control objectives. Some estimates by federal agencies of the cost of reducing water pollution in the United States are quite revealing. The analysis indicates that the total cost over a ten-year period of eliminating 85 to 90 percent of the water pollution in the United States would be on the order of $61 billion. To raise this to a 95 to 99 percent reduction of water pollution would involve an *additional* cost of $58 billion, bringing the total to $119 billion. Moreover, to squeeze out the last percent or two to

---

[4]A second notable feature of these marginal-cost curves is how much cheaper in general it is for the beet-sugar plant to reduce emissions. This suggests that, if we are trying to clean up a river with both a beet-sugar plant and a petroleum refinery on its banks, we can do so much more inexpensively by concentrating on emissions reductions by the beet-sugar plant. This is a theme to which we will return later.

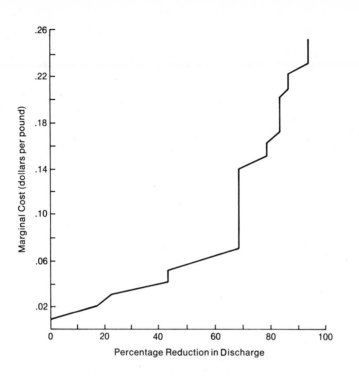

Figure 14-1 Marginal Cost of BOD-Discharge Reduction in Petroleum Refining.

Source: Allen V. Kneese and Charles L. Schultze, *Pollution, Prices, and Public Policy* (Washington, D.C.: The Brookings Institution, 1975), p. 21, who cite as their source Clifford S. Russell, *Residuals Management in Industry: A Case Study of Petroleum Refining* (Baltimore: The Johns Hopkins University Press, 1973).

reach total elimination of water pollution would require an additional $200 billion![5]

While costs of elimination of pollution rise with increasing rapidity as one approaches zero pollution levels, the gain in benefits will typically fall. That is, once concentrations of pollutants have declined sufficiently, further reductions will in many cases contribute little more to the general welfare. In fact, natural processes will often take care of low pollution levels. This is true of the emissions of small quantities of biodegradable wastes (wastes that are transformed into harmless substances by normal biochemical processes) into bodies of water. Similarly, air currents will quickly disperse minor amounts of air pollutants. Moreover, even where natural forces cannot automatically cope with environmental damage, in small amounts the effects may be minimal. Among thousands of acres of woodland, a small tract cleared by a farmer represents a minor loss to

---

[5] These figures are cited in Kneese and Schultze, *Pollution, Prices, and Public Policy*, p. 21.

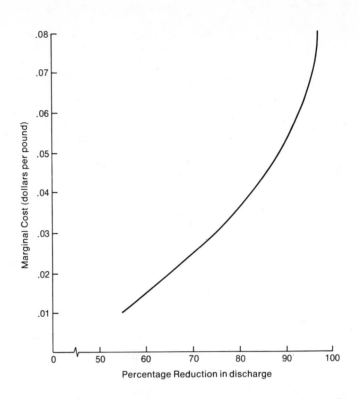

Figure 14-2 Marginal Cost of BOD-Discharge Reduction by a Beet-Sugar Refinery.

Source: Kneese and Schultze, *Pollution, Prices, and Public Policy*, p. 20, who cite as their source Clifford S. Russell, "Restraining Demand by Pricing Water Withdrawals and Wastewater Disposal," paper prepared for presentation at a seminar on the Management of Water Supplies, University of East Anglia, Norwich, England, March 1973; processed.

nature. And while an 85-horsepower motorboat creates an earsplitting noise, the sound of a fisherman's 10-horsepower outboard may be unobtrusive and inoffensive. Our point is that in many cases we gain very little by trying to eliminate the last vestiges of environmental damage.

All of this should surely make us think twice about our professed national objective of a total abolition of waste discharges into "navigable waters," or about the desirability of eliminating every trace of other types of pollution that do not cause much damage at low levels of concentration.[6] A rational policy requires that we compare the added benefits against the costs associated with proposed reductions in levels of pollution.

---

[6] A discerning reader points out to us that, when Congress sets "zero discharge" as an avowed goal, it may merely mean to indicate that it takes a reduction in pollution very seriously. It may simply reflect a congressional judgment that if the goal is stated as "reasonable discharge" then too large a discharge—an unreasonable amount—will be permitted by the workings of the regulatory process. While this may be the real intent of the Congress,

214

4. Health vs. Aesthetics in Environmental Policy

We turn now to the relative urgency of programs designed to protect human health, compared to those that offer aesthetic and recreational benefits. One of the curiosa of environmental policy has been the relatively low priority given to the various toxic substances that we discussed in Chapter 3. In the program for the cleanup of the Delaware River, for example, the prime criterion of environmental improvement has been the dissolved oxygen (DO) content of the water.[7] DO does have some significant consequences for water quality, and its widespread use *as one element* in the evaluation of water quality is certainly defensible. However, over a considerable range, improvement in DO may accomplish little but make the water more hospitable for fish. It will not suffice to make the water safe for swimming, and "If turbidity is reduced as a result of a BOD[8] clean-up campaign, the algae may be in a perfect position to multiply. Increasing DO may simply mean that the valley is trading a brown river for a green one. And one that will smell when the algae begin to die."[9] More important, the absence of "disease-carrying organisms and toxic chemicals . . . is not assured by high DO levels."[10] Thus, the program, which is expected to cost more than half a billion dollars, is likely to do virtually nothing to control the discharge of poisons into the river. It is difficult to disagree with the conclusion that "The most important problem in the Delaware River is not DO but the discharge of exotic chemicals and metallic compounds which may well be dangerous to human beings when they are present, even in small quantities, either in drinking water or in food. . . . Given the real life unquantifiable possibility of serious harm . . . a risk-avoidance strategy appears warranted in which a Poison Control Board should be given a strong statutory mandate to limit the discharge of any substances which there is reason to believe may significantly injure human health."[11]

The questionable ordering of priorities is by no means confined to the case of the Delaware. Early in the 1960s and 1970s Congress passed laws designed to promote air and water quality, and it has created national parks, seashore, and wilderness areas. But it was not until 1976, after years of delay, that a bill was passed to control the dispersion of toxic substances. Environmental legislation

---

our reading of experience with public policy suggests that the establishment of unattainable (and undesirable) goals does not facilitate the realization of the desired ends.

[7] The discussion of the Delaware River program is based on an excellent study carried out by an interdisciplinary group of investigators; see B. A. Ackerman, S. Rose Ackerman, J. W. Sawyer, Jr., D. W. Henderson, *The Uncertain Search for Environmental Quality* (New York: The Free Press, Macmillan Publishing Co., 1974).

[8] BOD, biochemical oxygen demand, is a measure of the oxygen depletion produced by an emission into a waterway.

[9] Ackerman et al., *Uncertain Search*, p. 27.

[10] Ibid.

[11] Ibid., p. 209.

has devoted itself primarily to the elimination of pollutants that can be seen or smelled and that are not always those that cause the most serious damage.

The important conclusion to be drawn from all this is that, in evaluating the evidence favoring a proposed environmental protection measure, it is important to balance off the imperfection of the evidence against the magnitude of the risk from which the measure is designed to protect the public. Where there is a real possibility that some pollutant constitutes a serious threat to human life, it is surely rational to take strong measures for its control based on less conclusive evidence than we would require for a form of pollution whose consequences are less threatening to life and health.[12] Only such a flexible standard can protect us from the dismal refrain repeated by so many industries seeking to protect themselves from the financial costs of some urgent environmental measure: the cry that the danger with which it is designed to deal is "unproven." A noteworthy case is the reluctance of the Environmental Protection Agency to take action against discharges of polychlorinated biphenyls (despite the evidence that these substances cause cancer, reproductive failure, and skin infections in laboratory animals), because it would be difficult to prove "in court that certain chemicals were creating specific illnesses during a given period."[13] Meanwhile, an EPA spokesman commented that "the agency believed there was an urgent need for more information [on cancer-causing chemicals in drinking water] and that it was pursuing that information as rapidly as possible through research."[14]

In practice, environmental programs seem to have developed rather haphazardly. They have tended to emphasize prevention of the most obvious and immediate sources of damage and have neglected other less visible, but possibly more insidious, sources. Current environmental policy does not consistently satisfy even the most basic requirements for a rational ordering of priorities.

We reemphasize in conclusion that there is a good deal more to the quality of life than the preservation of human life and health. We do, however, take the view that even a potential threat to life and health is always a matter of high priority, even where that threat is not embodied in something that can be readily seen and tasted. Here, surely policy makers have the responsibility of consulting experts in the relevant field and being one step ahead of public reaction, instead of waiting to be dragged kicking and screaming into awareness of the problem.

---

[12]For an excellent discussion of the issues raised by imperfect information in such cases, see Marcia R. Gelpe and A. Dan Tarlock, "The Uses of Scientific Information in Environmental Decision Making," *Southern California Law Review* 48 (November 1974): 371–427.
[13]*New York Times,* January 3, 1976, p. 25.
[14]*New York Times,* December 18, 1975, p. 36.

15

The Range of Policy Instruments

We arrive now at the section of this book that discusses how it can be done; here we shall examine the prime policy instruments for achieving our environmental objectives. This chapter catalogues the very wide range of broad legislative tools that are available, and also presents some techniques that are potentially useful for dealing only with particular and limited types of problems. The following chapters examine the most important of these methods in greater detail.

1. The Types of Available Policies

In Table 15-1, we classify the policy instruments that can be used for the preservation of environmental quality into four broad categories. The first three are techniques to influence polluters' behavior: moral suasion, direct controls (regulation), and methods that rely on market processes (price incentives). The fourth approach involves direct governmental expenditure, largely for the construction and operation of projects that improve the environment. For example,

TABLE 15-1

APPROACHES TO ENVIRONMENTAL POLICY

Part I: Policy Instruments

1. Moral Suasion (publicity, social pressure, etc.)

2. Direct Controls

   a. Regulations limiting the permissible levels of emissions
   b. Specification of mandatory processes or equipment

3. Market Processes[a]

   a. Taxation of environmental damage
      1) Tax rates based on evaluation of social damage
      2) Tax rates designed to achieve preset standards of environmental quality
   b. Subsidies
      1) Specified payments per unit of reduction of waste emissions
      2) Subsidies to defray costs of damage-control equipment
   c. Issue of limited quantities of pollution "licenses"
      1) Sale of licenses to the highest bidders
      2) Equal distribution of licenses with legalized resale
   d. Refundable deposits against environmental damage
   e. Allocation of property rights to give individuals a proprietary interest in improved environmental quality

4. Government Investment

   a. Damage prevention facilities (e.g., municipal treatment plants)
   b. Regenerative activities (e.g., reforestation, slum clearance)
   c. Dissemination of information (e.g., pollution-control techniques, opportunities for profitable recycling)
   d. Research
   e. Education
      1) Of the general public
      2) Of professional specialists (ecologists, urban planners, etc.)

Part II: Administrative Mechanisms

1. Administering Unit

   a. National agency
   b. Local Agency

2. Financing

   a. Payment by those who cause the damage
   b. Payment by those who benefit from improvements
   c. General revenues

218

3. Enforcement mechanism

    a. Regulatory organization or police

    b. Citizen suits (with or without sharing of fines)

Source: In the formulation of this table, we have relied heavily upon two exhaustive and illuminating discussions: René L. Frey, "Umweltschutz als Wirtschaftspolitische Aufgabe," *Schweizerische Zeitschrift für Volkswirtschaft und Statistik* 108, Jahrgang (September, 1972), Heft 3; and Bruno S. Frey, *Umweltökonomie* (Gottingen: Vandenhoeck and Ruprecht, 1972), especially Chap. 7 and 8.

[a]A reader points out that subsidies and taxes can also be distinguished by using a property-rights framework. Per unit subsidies implicitly confer ownership of the right to pollute on the polluter and these rights are then purchased by the government via the subsidy. Taxes essentially say that there is public ownership of usage rights which can be purchased from the public, through its agent, the government, by private parties upon payment of the tax (price).

in the control of water pollution these four approaches might involve:

1. Appeals to polluters to cut back, or eliminate altogether, their waste discharges for the sake of the public welfare;
2. Laws requiring polluters to cut back these emissions or to institute specified treatment procedures;
3. The levying of effluent charges or taxes on polluters, where the fee varies directly with the level of emissions;[1] or
4. The construction, at public expense, of waste-treatment facilities to purify the emissions from private industry and households.

These approaches are obviously not all mutually exclusive; in particular, it may be quite sensible to utilize the last instrument, publicly operated treatment facilities, together with one or more of the first three techniques to control the level of private waste discharges.

We shall focus most of our attention upon the second and third approaches, direct controls and market incentives. Direct controls are at present the most widespread form of policy instrument for environmental protection; they are the measures most popular among legislators and regulators, while many economists believe that market incentives constitute the only really viable alternative. This is not to say that moral suasion, which relies on voluntary compliance, is always foolhardy; in Chapter 19 we will, in fact, discuss situations in which this may represent the only feasible alternative. However, there are relatively few situations in which moral suasion offers significant promise as an effective means of dealing with environmental problems.

---

[1]There is some danger in the use of the tax analogy to describe the workings of a program of effluent charges. While economists have frequently compared emission charges to taxes, it turns out that from the legal point of view this terminology involves some difficulties. If the courts treat emission charges as taxes, past precedents indicate that they are more likely to

2. Two Types of Direct Controls and Regulations

In the United States and elsewhere environmental authorities have relied primarily on direct controls to regulate the polluting activities of private industry and individuals. Such controls may prohibit certain forms of pollution altogether or, alternatively, may place limits on levels of waste emissions or other damaging acts. In the fight against air pollution, many cities around the world have prohibited the burning of high-sulfur coal; similarly, many river authorities have imposed limits on the BOD discharges of water users.

In Table 15-1 we have distinguished between two types of direct controls: (1) the establishment of allowable levels of polluting activities, and (2) regulations requiring the use of specified procedures or processes that reduce emissions. By the first we mean the imposition of quotas or ceilings on the levels of polluting activities (e.g., waste discharges) of each firm or household. An example is a river authority that imposes BOD limits on the emissions of each polluter along the river. Under the second type of direct control, the environmental authority requires polluters to adopt certain techniques or equipment; the water authority, for example, may specify a type of treatment for all emissions, or the air-pollution agency may require that a particular smoke-cleansing device be installed in all chimneys.

The importance of this distinction will become clearer in subsequent chapters, but we note now that the first type of direct controls shares a problem with the market techniques discussed in the following section: it requires monitoring of pollutant emissions, which can be expensive and sometimes quite difficult. To enforce a quota on waste discharges, the environmental agency must measure the level of waste emissions of each polluter. If the regulatory authority chooses, instead, the second kind of direct control (e.g., requiring the installation of pollution-control devices), it may be able to avoid metering. The authority will, of course, have to insure the installation and proper operation of the device, but it may not have to measure the level of waste discharges.[2]

---

find them unconstitutional. Administrative agencies may not be permitted to set tax rates; moreover, indirect taxes collected by the federal government must be uniform throughout the United States, and a similar requirement holds in most states. Other problems also beset the tax interpretation. Emission charges may instead be treated as criminal penalties. But if this interpretation is used, the charge system is likely to be so burdened by procedural requirements that the efficiency and effectiveness usually claimed for a system of charges will be lost. A well-informed lawyer who has specialized in environmental law informs us that the most advantageous legal characterization of effluent charges would be as some sort of civil fine or, better yet, as a unique regulatory device. It would be helpful for this purpose for Congress to give specific statutory authority to agencies regulating environmental quality to use emission charges, although such authority may not be necessary in all cases. For a further discussion of these matters, see National Academy of Sciences, *Report of the Commission on Appraisal of Societal Consequences of Transportational Noise Abatement* (Washington, 1977), Chap. 2.

[2] A reviewer points out, however, that in some cases (automobiles, for example) operating effectiveness of the specified pollution equipment may deliberately or unwittingly de-

3. Price Incentives for the Control of Pollution

The idea of charging polluters a price for the damage they inflict on the environment seems, in principle, straightforward enough. However, as Table 15-1 indicates, this approach encompasses a considerable variety of different techniques. Instead of simply taxing effluents or subsidizing polluters who reduce their emissions, the environmental authorities can use the market in a somewhat different manner. They can auction off a limited number of pollution licenses, each of which permits a specified quantity of emissions. Rather than directly setting a *price* in the form of an effluent fee, the authority in this case determines the maximum *quantity* of pollution that will be tolerated, and then uses the market to ration this fixed quantity among polluters. This approach can be carried out either through a direct auction or the issuance of licenses on some equitable basis with provision for legalized resale.[3]

Taxes, subsidies, the sale of permits, and refundable deposits are the major techniques utilizing price incentives for the control of environmental quality. The next few chapters explore in depth their relative merits and disadvantages in principle and practice. Finally, we may sometimes be able to employ an alternative market process listed in Table 15-1: the redefinition of property rights. We shall examine this approach briefly in the next section of this chapter.

4. The Extension of Property Rights to Protect
National Resources

There is one method for the protection of environmental resources which is virtually paradoxical in its logic. It seeks to protect the resources of society by putting them into the hands of private individuals who consequently have a financial stake in their preservation. This approach is unlikely to recommend itself politically because of its implications for the distribution of wealth, but it is nevertheless instructive to examine its rationale. We saw in Chapter 7 that society's resources are often in far greater danger when they are held as common property so that anyone who decides to exploit them suffers only an insignificant share of the loss. One obvious cure for this problem is the elimination of common property or its reduction to a minimum, an idea that is not as far-

---

crease—and this can only be detected by periodic monitoring. The "required technique" approach may not always save much in monitoring efforts.

[3]The provisions of the licenses will have to be rather more complicated than Table 15-1 suggests. The licenses have to authorize some specified quantity of discharge of specified concentration. They may also have to indicate the location of emission and the time period for which the license applies: the time of day or season of the year, as well as the length of time for which the license remains valid.

fetched as it may seem at first.[4] J. H. Dales offers an interesting, if largely impressionistic, comparison of the condition of streams in Britain, where they are largely private property, and in Canada, where they are not:

> The island of Great Britain is moist and verdant, and blessed with innumerable cool streams that once were all haunts of trout and salmon. Most of them still are, even though they now flow through an industrialized countryside. The total poundage of fine game fish taken would put any accessible part of Canada to shame. We are so used to the idea that the waters of any industrial area are a write-off, so far as quality angling is concerned, that one cannot help but be curious as to how all that fishing is maintained.
>
> It is not because they do not have to watch out for pollution. There is an organization called the Anglers' Cooperative Association which has been in existence for nineteen years, which has taken over the watch dog functions formerly left to individuals. It is an interesting organization. It has a fluctuating and rather small list of members and subscribers, barely enough to keep an office open, but it is able to call on some powerful help, especially legal. It has investigated nearly 700 pollution cases since it started and very rarely does it fail to get abatement or damages, as the case requires. These anglers have behind them a simple fact. Every fishery in Britain, except for those in public reservoirs, belongs to some private owner. . . . Action is always entered on behalf of somebody who has suffered real damage. It has been that way from ancient times. Over here [Canada] the fishing belongs to everybody—and thus to nobody. The A.C.A. exists merely to take action where individuals may not act themselves. . . .
>
> What it amounts to is that you can have good fishing, which means good water, in a river in a populated British countryside if you make it your business to have it.[5]

In a few cases, this approach may constitute an easy, quick, and effective way of controlling environmental damage. For example, the city of Philadelphia has undertaken an ingenious application of this technique by selling, for almost nothing, abandoned dwellings to buyers (who promise to restore and reside in them), in the hope that individual private ownership will provide an incentive for the maintenance of these structures and the revitalization of decaying neighborhoods.

However, for a number of reasons, the applicability of the extension of

---

[4]For a fuller discussion, see J. H. Dales, *Pollution, Property and Prices* (Toronto: University of Toronto Press, 1968). U.S. water law in several western states uses appropriate property rights which result in a more restrictive definition of permissible uses. This type of property law has some "private" market contractual attributes and is quite different from riparian law.

[5]Ibid., pp. 68–69. (Dales attributes the passage to Douglas Clarke.)

private property appears quite limited. First, it can work only where damage to a natural resource comes from a few sources that are easily identified so that the proprietor of the resource can readily defend it against such ravages. But private guardianship is powerless in a case such as air pollution, where the sources of damage number in the thousands and where there is no effective way to exclude air pollutants from a particular area once they have been spewed into the atmosphere. Second, the approach is not useful in cases where private proprietors themselves are sources of environmental deterioration. Private land developers, in certain situations, cannot be depended upon to plan their land use to the benefit of public welfare. Finally, the private ownership of natural resources is unlikely to commend itself because of its implications for the distribution of wealth. The notion of the transformation of certain of society's resources into private property would be politically unthinkable, particularly if they were sold to the highest bidder.[6]

5. The Environmental Role of Government Investment Programs

Direct government investment plays a major role in both current and prospective environmental programs. The variety of purposes served by these outlays is enormous: waste-treatment plants, the disposal of solid wastes, slum clearance, reforestation, the designation and management of wildlife refuges, and so on. These merely begin to illustrate the range of governmental activities directly dedicated to the improvement of the environment. In addition, the public sector finances programs of research and education whose payoff is less immediate, but whose longer-run contribution may be enormous.

Table 15-2 provides a breakdown of federal environmental expenditures for 1975, 1976, and 1977. The first heading, protection and enhancement, encompasses activities ranging from recreation programs, preservation, and rehabilitation of historic sites to the protection of unique natural areas and endangered species. Under the second heading are programs for observing and predicting weather, oceanic conditions, and environmental disturbances (such as earthquakes); for locating and describing natural resources; and for ecological and other basic environmental research.

There are two fundamental reasons for the inclusion of government investment in an effective environmental policy. The first is the possibility that the most efficient scale of operation of pollution-control facilities may require more financial resources than private enterprise can (or is willing to) appropriate.

---

[6]There is, incidentally, nothing in principle that would require the auctioning of these resources; they could even be distributed on the basis of some sort of lottery. The essential matter is to establish private ownership with a subsequent right to sell the resources on the open market.

TABLE 15-2

BUDGET OUTLAYS—FEDERAL ENVIRONMENT PROGRAMS
(in millions of dollars)

Activities	1975 (actual)	1976 (estimate)	TQ (estimate)	1977 (estimate)
Protection and enhancement	1,128.5	1,242.6	328.5	1,327.0
Understanding, describing, and predicting	1,296.4	1,467.5	382.9	1,524.8
Pollution control and abatement	1,510.3	1,992.8	486.5	1,910.1
Construction grants[a]	2,060.5	2,474.4	633.7	3,913.0
Total	5,995.7	7,177.3	1,831.6	8.674.9

Source: *Environmental Quality, The Seventh Annual Report of The Council on Environmental Quality* (Washington, D.C.: U.S. Government Printing Office, 1976), p. 349.

[a]Includes but is not limited to grants under the Water Pollution Control Act Amendments of 1972 which provided $18 billion in contract authority to EPA. Obligations and outlays from this authority in 1976, transition quarter, and 1977 are funded from carryover balances.

Suppose, for example, that a large waste-treatment plant with many users can process liquid wastes at a cost per gallon far lower than if individual polluters were to do it themselves. The money needed for such a plant may exceed the amount private enterprise in the area can allocate without difficulty, and it may therefore be appropriate to use the tax and borrowing powers of the government to raise the funds.[7]

The second reason for government investment is one we examined in Chapter 4: the public-good character of many environmental services. Public goods typically cannot be marketed by private sellers, because no one can be excluded from consuming them. It makes no sense for a private citizen to go into the business of cleaning up the air of a city, because once the air is clean, that business can't charge for the use of it. People will not pay a charge for breathing the air when they can have it without payment.

---

[7]This argument itself is not really as persuasive as it may seem at first glance. If it is required that all polluters in an area treat their liquid wastes, they will presumably all be willing to pay a specialized firm to do the job if that firm can do it more cheaply. The treatment activity itself may then be a profitable investment opportunity for private enterprises, and if there are potential profits, there should be little trouble in raising the requisite funding on the capital market.

But the story does not end there. Where there are substantial scale economies, it is very likely to be inefficient for a multiplicity of firms to provide the service. Moreover, the largest firm may well be able to undercut and drive out any competitor. This threat of monopoly may well make the supply of these services by government enterprises the preferred arrangement, although the issue of the relative efficiency of regulated versus public enterprise is still far from settled.

The purification of air and water obviously has important public-good characteristics, and the same is true of more esoteric programs like the preservation of endangered forms of plant and animal life. The benefits conferred by the existence of the American eagle or the furbish lousewort are obviously available to everyone. Likewise, the research and information dissemination associated with environmental policy have public-good dimensions. Once a new discovery is made—a new engine that is less polluting or a cheaper recycling method—its use by a second firm does not require replication of its research or development costs. That is, once a new idea is discovered, its use by others is essentially costless to society. Moreover, such ideas are usually not easily kept secret, and once the pertinent specifications are reported in the scientific journals, exclusion becomes extremely difficult. So, in this area too there may be a natural role for the government.

6. Local, Regional, and National Policy

We have presented a menu of alternatives for governmental environmental policy, but up to this point we have treated the government as if it were a single, unified decision-making body. This is, of course, far from true, particularly in a relatively decentralized federal system like that of the United States. In addition to a large number of interested federal agencies, there are the fifty states plus thousands of counties, cities, municipalities, townships, special districts, and possessions, most of which have some responsibility for and authority over environmental issues. In fact, until quite recently the enactment and enforcement of environmental policy has been primarily a state and local matter.

One of the most difficult problems currently confronting the environmental movement in the United States is the determination of the appropriate scope of responsibility for different levels of government and the forging of an institutional structure to coordinate decisions effectively. The effort to develop a new "cooperative federalism" with environmental decision-making bodies composed of representatives from interested federal, state, and local agencies is one move in this direction, but the fruits of this effort are, at least so far, of doubtful value.[8] In this section, we simply want to set out some of the issues that arise in the formulation and enforcement of environmental policy in a federal system. In later chapters, we shall fill out the discussion by describing some actual experiences in environmental decision making.

The formulation of environmental policy in our federal system inevitably encounters one fundamental dilemma. On the one hand, *most* of our major en-

---

[8]For an enlightening description and analysis of federal, state, and local decision making in the selection of a program to clean up the Delaware Estuary, see Bruce A. Ackerman, Susan Rose Ackerman, James W. Sawyer, Jr., and Dale W. Henderson, *The Uncertain Search for Environmental Quality* (New York: The Free Press, Macmillan Publishing Co., 1974).

vironmental problems are regional or local in character: air pollution is typically a matter of the air-shed over a particular metropolitan area, while the control of water pollution is usually confined to a particular body of water or river basin. This suggests that localized policies are appropriate to deal with the problems in each pollution "district."

An extreme example will make the point. Consider two towns that have been emitting biodegradable wastes into two different rivers. The river next to the first town is deep and flows rapidly, so that the natural absorptive powers of the water assimilate the waste emissions without any significant degradation. In the second town, the river is shallow and slow moving; here, the effluents poison fish life and spoil the beauty of the river. Obviously, it makes no sense to require these two communities to reduce their effluent discharges by the same amount. In the second town the reduction would produce substantial benefits, but in the first town the reduction would have no important effects.[9]

This extreme example illustrates dramatically the deficiencies of a policy of uniform regulations. The same sorts of differences, although usually not as great, characterize virtually all cases of environmental damage. Where the diversities are small, little loss will result from uniformity of rules, but this is usually not the case. Table 15-3 shows for a sample of large U.S. cities the concentrations of several atmospheric pollutants. We see, for example, that average concentrations of sulfur dioxide vary all the way from 47 milligrams per cubic meter in Washington, D.C., to 236 milligrams per cubic meter in New York City, a ratio of more than five to one. Similarly, the number of one-hour periods exceeding the standard for total oxidants varies from 18 for Chicago to 602 for Los Angeles.

Moreover, the costs of emissions reduction also vary sharply from one case to another. In the preceding chapter, we saw how much more expensive it is for a petroleum refinery to curtail its BOD emissions than it is for a beet-sugar plant.[10]

---

[9]Another example of an efficiency problem posed by uniform regulation is the requirement that *all* new cars have identical pollution-control equipment regardless of where, when, or how they are used. This suggests that there is an important issue in balancing efficiency against ease of policy administration. See Donald N. Dewees, *Economics and Public Policy: The Automobile Pollution Case* (Cambridge, Mass.: M.I.T. Press, 1974). There are, however, many examples of pollution problems that are not local (ocean pollution, the acid rain problem in Europe, regional river pollution which traverses many states, Great Lakes pollution).
[10]Even if the federal government were willing (and able politically) to discriminate from area to area in the severity of its regulations, it would not find the task easy. The collection, evaluation, and coordination of the requisite data are likely to prove very difficult, and, as in the centrally planned economies, much of the task is likely to be shifted back to local authorities. These difficulties are compounded by the fact that the assimilative capacity of the environment in a given area is not stationary. It can vary sharply from season to season, and even from day to day. As will be discussed in greater detail in Chapter 20, recent heavy rainfall can sometimes increase the ability of a waterway to absorb pollutants, and an increase in wind velocity can decrease the damage produced by a given amount of emissions into the atmosphere.

TABLE 15-3

CONCENTRATIONS OF SEVERAL AIR POLLUTANTS IN A SAMPLE OF U.S. CITIES

City	Sulfur Dioxide (annual arithmetic mean— mg./cu.m.)	Total Suspended Particulates (annual geometric mean— mg./cu.m.)	Carbon Monoxide (annual arithmetic mean— mg./cu.m.)	Total Oxidants (number of 1-hour values exceeding the standard— 160 mg./cu.m.)
Los Angeles	54**	125	7	602**
Chicago	93**	195	7	18*
New York City	236**	123	4	NA
Washington, D.C.	47*	91	4	56*
St. Louis	58*	131	6	NA
Boston	NA	129	NA	NA

Source: *The National Air Monitoring Program: Air Quality and Emission Trends, Annual Report, Vol. 2, 1973* (Research Triangle Park, N.C.: U.S. Environmental Protection Agency, August 1973):

Sulfur dioxide: * Table G-3, West-Gaeke Colorimetric Method, pp. G-121–G-122;
                  ** Table G-4, Conductometric Method, pp. G-123;

Total Suspended
Particulates: Table G-1, pp. G-4–G-99;
Carbon Monoxide: Table G-6, pp. G-129–G-133;
Total Oxidants: * Table G-7, Alkaline Potassium Iodide KI Method, p. G-135;
                  ** Table G-8, Colorimetric Neutral Potassium Iodide KI Method, pp. G-136–G-138.

Note: NA = not available. Some measurements are for 1969, others for 1970. Where possible the same reporting stations were used for each city in the various categories of pollutants.

The other side of the issue is that policy planned and implemented at the local level runs the danger of being undermined by competition from other localities in which environmental policy is considerably less stringent. A factory in New Jersey that is required to meet strict and expensive emission standards may find itself at a severe disadvantage compared to a rival in Pennsylvania if the latter is permitted to dispose of its wastes in any way it chooses, with no financial penalty. With the best will in the world, the management of the plant in New Jersey may have no choice but to evade the legal restrictions by closing down, moving elsewhere, or seeking special exemptions. Faced with this sort of threat, local government may have to consent willy-nilly to the erosion of its standards and its regulations. This, then, is the dilemma: *the geographically specific character of most environmental problems invites a regional or local solution, but the constraints on local policy imposed by interjurisdictional competition may seriously inhibit the implementation of the appropriate measures.*

One proposed solution is the formation of larger regional units of govern-

227

ment which would be somewhat more insulated from the pressures of local competition and would also conform better to boundaries typically called for by environmental geography. The logical units of environmental authority may encompass entire air-sheds over metropolitan areas and whole river-basin systems for water-pollution control. However, it is difficult to be sanguine about the political feasibility of the imposition of yet another layer of government upon the American system.

A popular alternative these days is an exercise in "cooperative federalism": the formation of a regional agency with representation from the federal government and from the states and localities concerned. This sounds very attractive in principle; with all interests represented, we might expect a sensible compromise to emerge. Unfortunately, this doesn't seem to have been borne out by recent experience. One impressive example, the Delaware River Basin Commission, composed of the Secretary of the Interior and the Governors of New York, New Jersey, Pennsylvania, and Delaware, has hardly been a resounding success.[11] The biggest stumbling block seems to be the primary political commitment of each of the participants to a constituency other than the region itself. In the case of the Delaware, it is clear in retrospect that the primary concern of each of the Commission members has been his own political base. A distinctly regional orientation has never developed.[12]

The issue of the appropriate governmental structure for the design and implementation of environmental policy remains a very complex and difficult matter. But it is one we must keep in mind during the subsequent analysis of policy instruments.

7. Who Should Pay the Costs?

There remains one general issue to be dealt with in this broad survey of the options for environmental policy. If substantial outlays for environmental measures will be required of society, the apportionment of the burden must somehow be determined. In part, this is an issue of distributive justice involving the shares of the cost borne by the rich and the poor. We examined this crucial problem in Chapter 12, but it is one to which we shall have to return repeatedly.

Cost apportionment is not only a matter of distributive ethics; it also influences the *effectiveness* of environmental policy. Society must decide how to divide the costs among the beneficiaries of the environmental program, those

---

[11] See Ackerman et al., *Uncertain Search.* The book is primarily an evaluation of that performance.
[12] But see Edwin T. Haefele, "Environmental Quality as a Problem of Social Choice," in Allen V. Kneese and Blair T. Bower, eds., *Environmental Quality Analysis, Theory and Method in the Social Sciences* (Baltimore: The Johns Hopkins University Press, 1972), pp. 281–332, for general discussion and examples where regional commissions seem to have worked.

who do the damage, and the general public treasury. But this choice has important implications for the workability of the program. To illustrate the point, suppose that a plant pours wastes into a river, the banks of which were otherwise uninhabited when the factory was built. Later, however, a community came into being downstream, and the residents now suffer from the pollution generated by the plant. Who should pay for a treatment plant to clean up the river: the residents of the community who will benefit, or the owners of the plant that causes the pollution? Or should general tax funds be used?

As we shall see, the answer, strictly in terms of the economic effectiveness of the clean-up program, is straightforward: the polluters should pay an amount commensurate with the damage they do, for this will provide them with the appropriate incentive to reduce levels of pollution. Justice and equity do not enter into this calculation. Although the polluters can, in a sense, be innocent (as in our example), if they have to pay according to the damage they do, they will be given motivation to minimize that damage, and this is what matters for efficient pollution control. We will have more to say on this later.[13]

8. Concluding Comment

This completes our overview of the broad range of instruments and the options available for the design of environmental policy. In the next few chapters we examine in more depth several specific approaches: the taxation of polluters, the sale of pollution "rights," moral suasion, and direct controls. However, it should be clear already that there is no one approach or one technique that is best suited to deal with all problems in all circumstances. There is no panacea, no one simple approach, that is always best (or even always workable), and that is why the design of environmental policy requires such extensive analysis.

---

[13] It is sometimes argued that, in some cases, the potential beneficiary of a pollution-control program (i.e., the victim of the pollution) can do something about it. The laundry that suffers from the smoke emitted by a nearby factory can bribe the emitter to install smoke-control devices. But this can only work where the number of polluters and the number of victims are small so that they can get together and work out a suitable arrangement. In practice, most serious environmental problems involve enormous numbers of offenders (e.g., automobile drivers who pollute the air) and/or large numbers of victims (the residents of the city who breathe the polluted air), and in such a case the individual victim is quite powerless to do anything on his own to reduce pollution levels.

16

Direct Controls Versus the Pricing System

1. A Pluralistic Approach to Environmental Policy

While economists and other interested groups have agreed upon the desirability of environmental protection, they have taken quite contradictory positions on the best way to do the job. Economists have, with few exceptions, rejected both direct controls and calls for voluntary compliance, the methods preferred by many others concerned with the environment. Instead, economists advocate the use of pricing measures—monetary rewards and penalties—which they believe to be more efficient, more permanent, and more desirable for a number of other reasons. Other groups have often shown little interest in such pricing approaches and have instead turned to appeals to conscience or, more commonly, to the instruments of the law: the regulatory agencies, the police powers, and the courts.

Our own position is that the outlook of both groups is too narrow; neither view has taken adequate account of the merits of the other. In fact, we will argue that each of the available policy instruments has its particular virtues (and shortcomings), and that each is best adapted to deal with particular circumstances. Our purpose in the next few chapters is to indicate for each approach the cases for which that method is appropriate. In our view, effective policy requires a wide array of tools and a willingness to use each of them as it is needed.

We begin our study of policy instruments in this chapter with an examination of the role of price incentives; we shall explore the virtues of the fiscal approach in relation to those of direct controls. Let us stress that we do not do so because we believe price incentives are the only effective instruments for environmental protection. Rather, we want to show that the policy maker who is not prepared to consider their role in environmental programs embarks on a difficult task with one hand tied behind his or her back. This assumes a special importance in view of the demonstrated reluctance of environmentalists to make use of pricing incentives for protection of the environment.

2. The Economic Rationale of the Pricing Approach

The fundamental logic of pricing incentives is straightforward. Put very briefly and a bit superficially, the basic source of our environmental problems is the fact that the price system simply is not applied to many of society's resources. As we stressed in Part 1, the air and our other environmental resources can be used by anyone who chooses to do so, without payment for the privilege.

The proposal that the economist makes is, consequently, an obvious one: our scarce and valuable natural resources should be provided at an appropriate price. More specifically, the economist calls for a reorientation of the tax system—not necessarily increasing the overall level of taxes, but changing *relative* prices to provide incentives for the conservation of environmental resources. Once again, an example will help to clarify the issue.

Suppose we decide that the oil industry is currently paying the right total amount in taxes, but that it is also desirable to encourage the removal of lead from fuels. For this purpose one could *reduce* the tax on unleaded gasoline, and *increase* it on leaded gasolines. This would give the industry the opportunity to behave in a manner consistent with social goals with no loss to itself. Nor need this procedure constitute either a drain on the public budget or a subsidy to industry. Given the efficiency with which private enterprise pursues its profits, the speed of the resulting changeover to lead-free fuels would, no doubt, be impressive. Similarly, much could be done to reduce airplane noise by the imposition of substantial differentials in landing fees based on the noise level and pollution emissions of the airplane.[1] As another example, we can reduce the

---

[1] There have been a number of discussions of the use of fees in inducing reductions in aircraft noise. See, for example, J. P. Barde, "Aircraft Noise Charges," *Noise Control Engineering* 3 (No. 2, September-October 1974): 54–58, and David Pearce, "Charging for Noise," OECD (Paris, 1976). The Japanese have actually instituted "noise charges" for aircraft; in September 1975, they adopted a set of landing charges where the fee per aircraft landing is based on the noise category of the airplane.

flow of trash by imposing a significant tax on no-deposit, no-return containers, perhaps accompanied by a reduction in sales taxes on returnable containers (more is said on this in a later chapter). In each of these cases the basic notion is the same: by offering virtue its just (financial) reward, we change the rules of the game to induce industry (and individual consumers) to alter their behavior to promote an environmental objective.

3. Criteria for Evaluating Environmental Policies

Before examining in detail the advantages and disadvantages of the pricing approach to environmental protection, we want to consider the criteria on which to base the evaluation. The following list seems to us to encompass the most pertinent considerations for the appraisal of environmental policies:

a. *Dependability.* How reliable is the approach in achieving its objective? Are its workings fairly certain and automatic or does it depend on a number of unpredictable elements?

b. *Permanence.* Is the program likely to be effective only so long as it captures public interest, or can it be expected to endure even when other issues have seized the attention of the media and the public?

c. *Adaptability to Economic Growth.* Is the program flexible enough to adapt to normal expansion in economic activities and population growth, both of which tend to accentuate problems of environmental damage?

d. *Equity.* Does the program divide its financial burdens among individuals and enterprises fairly?

e. *Incentives for Maximum Effort.* Does the program offer inducements to individuals or enterprises to minimize environmental damage, or does it encourage no more than barely acceptable behavior?

f. *Economy.* Does the program achieve its results at relatively low cost to society, or does it waste resources?

g. *Political Attractiveness.* Is the method likely to recommend itself to legislators and to voters?

h. *Minimal Interference with Private Decisions.* Does the method tell the individual or the businessman exactly what to do, or does it offer the broadest scope of choices consistent with protection of the environment?

Let us now see how the pricing approach performs in terms of each of these criteria.

4. Dependability: Tax Measures vs. the Criminal Justice System

One of the fundamental differences between pricing techniques and the direct-controls approach to environmental protection is that the latter characteristically treats environmentally damaging activities as illegal acts, while the former considers them normal consequences of economic activity which should certainly be curtailed, but without the use of the police powers of the state. Economists maintain that, where a phenomenon such as waste emission is an inherent, regular, and continual part of human activity, it must be controlled by continuous methods that are correspondingly routine and regular. The fiscal approach typically uses the meter rather than the police inspector for enforcement. For example, the proposed tax on leaded gasoline requires no more than a record of how much of that type of gasoline has been sold. The emissions of pollutants by a factory can also, in principle, be metered, billed, and paid for like electricity, gas, and water. There are no crimes to be discovered, no legal battles over the level of fines. Enforcement is not sporadic: it is routine, continuous, predictable, and, consequently, effective.

In this respect, the use of pricing incentives, at least in principle, differs markedly from the reality of outright prohibition. The effectiveness of prohibition clearly depends on the vigor and clout of the enforcement mechanism. Violators of a regulation must first be caught in the act. They must then be prosecuted, found guilty, and given a substantial penalty. If any of these steps fails, the violators get away (virtually) free despite their disregard for the law. No such problem arises in a system of fees under which polluters simply receive their monthly bills as a matter of course.

A typical example of the workings of direct controls is the de facto erosion of the laws forbidding the use of garbage incinerators in apartment houses. Landlords, who are occasionally subjected to token fines on a rather random basis, find it far cheaper to pay the fines than to close down their incinerators. So the incinerators continue to pour forth noxious fumes, even though their use has been prohibited absolutely and categorically.[2] There are, in fact, many instances of fines so low as to render regulation ineffectual.[3] Enforcement by in-

---

[2] Another interesting case of the failure of a policy of outright prohibition is the ban on the sale of the skins of certain endangered animals in the United States. The result has been the creation of a lucrative black market, with an incentive for poachers to kill as many of these animals as they can. Alligators are one example.

[3] The following examples indicate the sorts of fines to which polluters have been subjected: "2 Companies Admit Polluting Harbor: Each is Fined $750" (*New York Times,* January 31, 1970, p. 25); "Consolidated Edison admitted that it was guilty of having discharged oil into the East River . . . [it is] liable to a maximum fine of $2,500 . . ." (*New York Times,* January 31, 1970, p. 22); "Ten Philadelphia firms were fined a total of $2900 Friday in the seventh week of the City's accelerated drive for violation of the air-pollution code" (*Philadelphia Inquirer,* October 30, 1970); "The Justice Department filed charges today against seven companies, including two steel concerns, accusing them of polluting waterways in the Chicago area. . . . The maximum penalty is a $2,500 fine for each offense" (*New York Times,* September 21, 1971, p. 74); "[New York City] has collected $800,000 in fines against air and noise polluters over the last three years . . ." (*New York Times,* June 25, 1974, p. 37). However, it should be noted that very recently financial penalties upon polluters have, in a number of cases, risen significantly. An example is the case of the discharge of the extremely toxic chemical, Kepone, into the Virginia-Maryland coastal region by an Allied Chemical plant. Allied was originally fined $13.2 million for damages to the

spectors, moreover, offers a temptation for evasion, and often for bribery and outright corruption. Tax collectors are probably no more law-abiding than inspectors, but the operation of the tax system is characteristically too business-like and the recordkeeping too systematic and routine to provide the widespread opportunities for evasion offered by periodic personal surveillance.

5. Permanence and Adaptability to Growth

A major problem that besets most regulatory efforts is that the effectiveness of the regulation is dependent on a high level of public concern. The effects of regulation are often transitory. In the first blush of public enthusiasm, an agency may uphold the severity of standards by relatively effective enforcement. However, some years later, when public attention has focused on other issues, the strength of the enforcement mechanism ebbs. The regulatory agency then takes on the characteristic bureaucratic lassitude that is compatible with self-preservation and the avoidance of trouble.

On the other hand, fiscal incentives, *once instituted*, need no reinforcement. "Nothing is certain," says the homily, "but death and taxes." It is this assurance of the arrival of the periodic tax bill that gives a fiscal program its reliability. A tax on smoke emissions that is billed monthly will continue to exert its influence on managerial decisions indefinitely. Unlike a program dependent on the vigor of a regulatory agency, the tax incentive does not require continued enthusiasm for the cause.[4]

There are, however, two possible sources of erosion of the effectiveness of a fiscal program: inflation and economic growth. A tax bill of a fixed number of dollars per unit, which might have been rather substantial twenty years ago, may have become relatively modest with a decline in the purchasing power of the currency. Moreover, if there is growth in population and industrial activity, pollutant emissions will rise unless the tax rate is increased steadily.

James River and surrounding area (the fine has recently been reduced to $5 million because of Allied's cooperation in mitigating the damages).

[4]It should be emphasized, however, that this conclusion holds only after an effective system of charges has gone into full operation. It would be naive to expect that those who seek to escape effective environmental measures will not find ways to combat a system of charges. One can be sure that, if such a program becomes a serious possibility, lobbyists will set themselves the task of inducing legislators to reduce the fees to a minimum—to a point where they become ineffective. One can also expect that such legislation, once passed, will be tied up in the courts for years by a variety of legal challenges. But there is still a difference here from the case of direct controls. In the latter, enforcement can require continual court battles—battles against the erosion of enforcement and penalty levels. In the case of a system of charges, once an adequate level of charges has been set by the legislature, and once the courts have confirmed its legality, its enforcement becomes largely automatic and requires little governmental vigilance except in billing for and collecting the fees. This has been demonstrated, for example, in the case of the Oregon Bottle Bill, which we shall examine in Chapter 18.

One way to get around the inflationary effect is to base tax payments on the price that polluters charge for their final output, which should increase with the general price level. Or, as we shall see in the next chapter, a fiscal alternative to effluent charges, the auctioning of pollution permits, can deal quite effectively with both the problems of inflation and growth. But tax measures themselves can be responsive to inflation. If they become an important source of revenue to state and local governments, rising budgetary pressures will generate inducements for increases in tax rates. In any event, it seems clear that, despite the problems of rising prices and economic growth, we can expect the effectiveness of fiscal programs to be far more durable than that of direct controls.

6. Equity

The regulatory approach is often thought to be superior to the use of pricing incentives in terms of fairness. Consider, for example, the case where an environmental authority determines that BOD emissions into a particular waterway should be cut in half. The most fair or equitable method of realizing this objective would appear to require all polluters to reduce their BOD discharges by 50 percent.[5] This would seem to allocate the necessary reduction in BOD emissions in a nondiscriminatory way.

Unfortunately, the appearance of fairness is largely illusory. We reemphasize the wide variations among industries and plants in the cost of pollution abatement. Some industries can easily recycle and make other adjustments in production processes, but for others, reductions in pollution are much more expensive. An order to reduce BOD emissions by 50 percent is likely to prove far more expensive for some firms than for others. If our objective were to distribute emission quotas fairly, perhaps we might do better to require reduction quotas such that the unit *cost* of the cutbacks were the same for all polluters. From this perspective, effluent fees may arguably be more equitable than a uniform percentage reduction in wastes.[6]

But even this is only half the story. If there remains any fairness in the uniform quotas among polluters, it will largely disappear in the chaotic process of issuing permits and administering the program. A recent study of the alloca-

---

[5] In fact, this is not how regulators have acted in practice. In part this is because they have responded to special problems of different polluters. The Clean Air Act, the Water Pollution Control Act, and the Noise Control Act all direct the regulator to take into account the individual polluter's cost of abatement and ability to reduce polluting activities.

[6] However, this is only part and, indeed, the less important part of the equity issue. Ultimately, a substantial part of the costs will be borne by buyers of the polluters' products, and the heart of the equity question is whether these customers will be predominantly rich or poor. This we have examined in Chapter 12. It must nevertheless be recognized that there is justice, in one sense, if costs are borne predominantly by consumers choosing to buy products whose manufacture generates a great deal of pollution.

tion of emission quotas among polluters along the Delaware Estuary provides some instructive insights into this issue.[7] The Delaware River Basin Commission (DRBC) selected a set of targets for levels of dissolved oxygen. Deciding against the use of fees, the Commission set a requirement for an essentially uniform percentage cutback (between 85 and 90 percent) in BOD discharges for all polluters.

This might seem simple enough, but the implementation proved far from easy. From what was the uniform percentage reduction to be made? Surely, a refinery that has already instituted extensive and costly treatment procedures should not be required to reduce its emissions by the same proportion as a neighboring factory that has been emitting untreated wastes into the river. To deal with this issue, the DRBC staff had to undertake the enormously complex task of determining the hypothetical "raw waste load" for *each* major polluter to serve as a benchmark for determining its pollution quota. The result was a case-by-case process specifying a quota, typically followed by a protest from the polluter, with some sort of compromise eventually emerging from a series of bargaining sessions. The anomalies in the final set of permits are quite striking: for example, the final pollution quotas for petroleum refineries on the estuary ranged from 692 pounds to 14,400 pounds of BOD per day! This experience suggests that neither in principle nor in practice are direct controls fairer than a system of fees that require the polluters to pay for the damage they do to the resources of the community.

7. Inducement for Maximum Effort

Since no manufacturing activity can be expected to reduce its wastes to zero, it becomes necessary, under direct controls, to assign some sort of quota or other behavioral rule to *each* polluter (i.e., to establish a clear definition of what constitutes violation of the law). If, for example, the environmental authority requires a polluting firm to reduce its emissions to 50 percent of the amount it discharged in the previous year, then a discharge equal to 49.7 percent of that base level is legal and presumably virtuous, while if the emissions equal 51 percent of that figure, they suddenly become illegal and reprehensible.

Aside from the inherent absurdity of such a thin separation between virtue and vice, this approach has an extremely questionable practical consequence. Consider a plant that can reduce its emissions to 50 percent of the base level by an investment of $1 million, while by an outlay of $1.1 million (i.e., for an additional outlay of $100,000) it can cut its discharges to a mere 20 percent of the base figure. The fine line between reward and punishment inherent in the

---

[7]Bruce A. Ackerman, Susan Rose Ackerman, James W. Sawyer, Jr., and Dale W. Henderson, *The Uncertain Search for Environmental Quality* (New York: The Free Press, 1974).

regulatory quota offers absolutely no incentive for this relatively inexpensive additional contribution to the welfare of society. Once it reaches the 50 percent reduction required by law, the firm has no inducement whatever to cut further its emissions one iota, no matter how low the cost.

The fiscal approach, however, need not be subject to such an anomaly; it can provide a continuum of rewards or penalties, defined according to a fixed schedule that is known by the polluting firm. The less it emits, the less its tax bill, and that is all there is to the matter. If by reducing its emissions from 50 to 20 percent, it can decrease its tax payments by $450,000 over the lifetime of its plant, it will obviously pay the firm to invest an additional $100,000 required for the purpose. There is no inducement to stop reducing emissions once the standard is reached.

Thus, one of the attractive features of the fiscal approach lies in its use of a more or less continuous schedule of financial inducements. The better the performance of the decision makers in reducing their pollutant emissions, the better off they will be financially.[8]

8. Economy

In choosing among instruments for environmental protection, economists place heavy emphasis on the efficiency with which they can be expected to do the job. We will argue that efficiency is one of the major advantages of fiscal methods.

It is all too tempting to decry the economist's preoccupation with "mere" dollars and cents, when the issues at stake for environmental policy are so important for the health and welfare of the community. Yet efficiency and economy in environmental protection measures are obviously important, if for no other reason than that, if the cost is unnecessarily high, it becomes that much more difficult to push environmental legislation through Congress.

But concern over social costs is not simply money grubbing. It represents a matter of profound importance for the interests of society. The community is constantly beset by many pressing claims upon its limited resources—health, education, sanitation, street maintenance, welfare programs—and there are never enough resources to do everything. No easy solutions have been proposed for the problems of poverty, decaying cities, crime and disease, but it is clear that each of them is going to require massive outlays of labor and other resources. Each

---

[8]There is, of course, the danger that in practice a legislature will produce a system of charges that is far from this ideal. If, for example, it is decided to assess charges only for "excessive" emissions, then even under a program of charges the polluter will lose any incentive to reduce emissions by any significant amount below the borderline between "acceptable" and "excessive" discharges. Obviously, a poorly designed system of fiscal incentives can perform just as poorly as any other instrument of control, and it is never safe to assume that in reality a system of charges will be well designed.

time we institute a wasteful measure for the protection of the environment where a more efficient alternative is available, we effectively undercut some other valuable service. The problems of society are surely too urgent to permit that sort of casual misuse of critical resources.

The possible savings in resources that the use of effluent fees can effect is readily illustrated. Suppose that we have a world of two polluters, each initially emitting the same quantity of effluent, but in which the first can reduce waste emissions at a cost of five cents per pound, and the second at fifteen cents per pound. In addition, assume that our environmental objective requires a 50 percent cutback in total effluents. If under a direct-controls approach, we require each of the polluters to halve its emissions, this would entail an *average* cost of waste reductions of ten cents per pound. However, we could obviously achieve our objective more inexpensively by placing the whole of the cutback on polluter number one (perhaps with some compensation paid to it by the other polluter); in this instance, the cost of the reduction would be only five cents per pound, and we would have cut the social cost of our environmental program in half.

The central point is that the second outcome is precisely the one that results from the pricing approach. Suppose that the environmental authority were to levy a tax on emissions of six cents per pound. All the reductions would then come from the first polluter which would find it profitable to avoid the tax altogether by stopping all its emissions; the second polluter would find it cheaper to pay the fee of six cents per pound and would maintain its level of waste discharges. The pricing method, in this instance, achieves the environmental goal at the least cost to society.

As a second and more realistic illustration, let us return to the case of the petroleum refinery and the beet-sugar plant that we examined in Chapter 14. In Figure 16-1, we display both of these cost curves for reducing BOD discharges on the same diagram. Suppose that, in an effort to cut down emissions, a regulation were passed which ignored this cost differential and required that each plant cut its discharges by 50 percent. Figure 16-1 indicates that the marginal cost of a one-pound reduction in BOD emissions would then be six cents in the petroleum refinery (see point *A*) but only about one cent in the beet-sugar plant (point *B*). This would be grossly inefficient, for society would effectively be paying six times the necessary cost for each additional pound of BOD reduction. By simply shifting a pound of the cutback from the petroleum refinery to the beet-sugar plant, we could reduce the cost of the marginal pound of emissions reduction from six cents to only a penny.

As in our preceding illustration, the use of effluent fees will lead automatically to the least-cost pattern of pollution reductions. In particular, if the environmental authority were to set an effluent charge of four cents per pound of BOD emissions, we can see from Figure 16-1 that the petroleum refinery

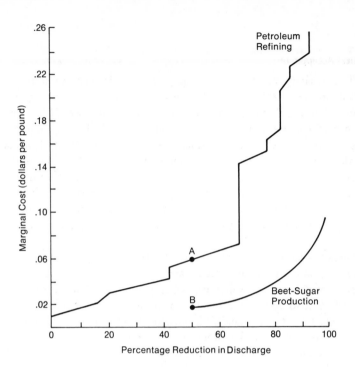

Figure 16-1   Comparison of Marginal Costs of BOD-Discharge Reduction in Petroleum Refining and Beet-Sugar Processing.

Source: See Figures 14-1 and 14-2.

would find it profitable to cut its discharges by about 25 percent, while the beet-sugar plant would reduce its emissions by roughly 75 percent. If the volume of initial emissions were the same in the two plants, this fee of four cents per pound would generate the targeted 50 percent reduction in aggregate emissions. Note that the cost of reducing emissions by an additional pound would never, in this instance, exceed four cents.

The pricing approach to pollution control thus promises significant cost savings in comparison with a set of quotas, because fees implicitly take full advantage of the difference in the costs of pollution abatement.[9] And, as we shall see in Chapter 18, in terms of some actual cost estimates the potential savings from the use of fees instead of direct controls is a sizeable sum, often of an order of 30 to 50 percent of the total costs of pollution abatement.

---

[9]It is possible to show that for a regulatory agency to select emissions quotas that are as effective in keeping down the total costs of the pollution program, it would have to have access to an enormous quantity of information of a sort which it could normally not obtain in practice.

9. Political Acceptability

Effluent charges certainly have met with very little success in the political arena. Both in the United States and in most other capitalist countries, they have so far proved uniformly unattractive to those in political power.[10] Yet the use of pollution taxes (or alternatively, the sale of effluent permits) does have one great political virtue. Unlike most other measures for pollution control, it need not add to the financial burdens of the public sector.[11] In view of the tremendous and growing fiscal pressures, particularly on state and local governments, the resistance of public officials to new programs making heavy demands on the public purse is understandable. For this reason alone, politicians should be far more receptive to a fiscal program that promises to bring in, rather than disburse, revenues.

The potential revenue contribution of these taxes is by no means negligible. Some recent, and admittedly rough, calculations for the state of New Jersey suggested that charges of twenty cents per pound on sulfur-dioxide emissions from fixed-point sources, ten cents per pound on BOD emissions into the water, and five dollars per ton for landfill disposal of solid wastes could together generate annual revenues on the order of $225 million. For New Jersey this is roughly equivalent to the revenues from an increase in the state's sales tax of 1½ percent.

When new tax programs are under consideration, there are good grounds for the inclusion of a program of charges upon environmental damage in the tax package. For such charges can achieve two goals for the price of one: an augmentation of the flow of revenues into the public treasury and the introduction of powerful incentives for improvements in the quality of life. Most taxes carry with them an incidental set of economic incentives leading to decisions *not* in the interests of the community; they may, for example, discourage saving or the rehabilitation of slum properties. Economists say such taxes impose an "excess burden" on the community (i.e., a burden of undesirable incentives above and beyond their direct dollar cost to the taxpayer). However, taxes on environmental damage, rather than imposing an excess burden, offer an offsetting benefit; they provide economic incentives for decisions that serve the public interest by, for example, inducing reductions in emissions of various pollutants.

10. Minimal Interference with Private Decisions

Before concluding our discussion of the virtues of pricing for environmental protection, we mention one noneconomic advantage of the fiscal approach: the fact that it keeps to a minimum governmental interference in the

---

[10] It is somewhat ironic that the Soviet economies seem far more willing to use the price mechanism and financial incentives to carry out their environmental programs! For a few examples, see Chapters 5 and 18.

[11] This obviously does not apply to the use of public subsidies.

individual decision. By relying on price incentives, the regulatory agency need not tell individuals or business managers what type of fuel they must use or what sorts of technology they must employ; the fiscal technique assigns no quotas, nor tells people how to run their life or their business. Instead, it merely modifies the structure of market prices by, for example, changing the relative prices of leaded and unleaded gasolines or of fuels with differing sulfur content, and leaves it to private decision makers to adjust to such price information as they see fit.

This, incidentally, can also result in an important additional benefit: it leaves greater scope for innovation. A regulation forbidding a certain process that creates a great deal of smoke, even if it contributes to a cleaner atmosphere, may not be the most efficient way of carrying out the task *for all polluters.* Suppose the addition of a system of filters to the old process is a cheaper way for some plants to achieve the same reduction in smoke. The business that is taxed for its emissions will seek the least expensive way of reducing them; in our example, it will compare the costs of an entirely new process to that of the system of filters and may select the latter. Even the best-intentioned bureaucrat cannot, in general, possess the detailed information needed to determine the least-cost method of compliance for each polluter. The fiscal approach, in an important sense, makes much less in the way of informational demands on the environmental authority.

If governmental interference is undesirable in itself, then the fiscal approach certainly comes out ahead on this score. It would seem that under these circumstances the business community would be unified in its support of fiscal methods as against direct controls. However, the reverse seems to be true. Our encounters with business managers have revealed a determined, and sometimes bitter, opposition to fiscal methods of environmental control. Two reasons for their opposition have been suggested. The first is that taxes on environmental damage, when once enacted, are not easily escaped or repealed; in short, they work. The enforcement of direct controls, on the other hand, typically allows a certain amount of leeway; the polluter may be able to negotiate with the regulatory agency or take its case to the courts, where for a variety of reasons, it may find an easy escape. Certainly, the low fines for violations of prohibitions that were cited earlier lend some support to this view. The assertion is that prohibition, for all its uncompromising aura, very often turns out to be a lamb in the guise of a lion.

James Buchanan and Gordon Tullock have recently proposed a second explanation.[12] They argue that, paradoxically, while emissions taxes will normally cause some reduction in the profits earned by a firm, direct controls can conceivably even increase profitability. If those controls effectively limit outputs and the entry of new firms into polluting industries, environmental measures

---

[12] "Polluters' Profits and Political Response: Direct Controls versus Taxes," *American Economic Review* 65 (March 1975): 139–47.

may succeed in restricting production. The result is, in effect, a legal cartel which, by enforcing scarcity, increases both prices and profits. The applicability of these hypotheses certainly requires further evidence. However, they do offer a somewhat plausible explanation of what otherwise seems a puzzling phenomenon: the business community's determined opposition to the policy approach which best preserves its freedom of decision making.

11. Some Limitations of Pollution Charges

We have built what seems to us a strong case for a widespread use of effluent charges to achieve our environmental objectives. However, it is also important to recognize several difficulties in their use. Though we are convinced of the great promise of pricing instruments in pollution control, we must not exaggerate the scope of their effective use.

One significant weakness of the tax method, which may account for much of its unpopularity among environmental protection agencies, is uncertainty about the magnitude of its effects. Suppose we enact a tax of five cents per pound on effluents. Just how large will the response of polluters be? Will it be enough to permit the community to achieve its environmental goals? If the response proves inadequate, one can try to return to the legislature to get approval for an increase in tax rates. But that certainly takes time, and the legislature may simply reject the proposal. We should not, however, exaggerate our inability to predict, at least roughly, the response of the level of waste discharges to fees. As we shall see in later chapters, considerable research has been devoted to the study of the costs of pollution abatement on an industry-by-industry basis. Consequently, we have a pretty good idea of how high a charge will make it profitable, for example, for a petroleum refinery to curtail its BOD emissions by 50 percent (recall Figure 16-1). We will see in Chapter 18 some actual calculations of the cost of BOD reductions in the Delaware Estuary, which are based on engineering cost data for the major polluters. This is not to say that such projections are highly reliable; there is surely a nonnegligible margin of error. But we do have a basis for reasonable estimates. Moreover, with more actual experience and research, we should become increasingly able to make reliable predictions of the response of pollution levels to varying schedules of tax rates.

A second, and perhaps more serious, difficulty besetting effluent charges is their relative inflexibility. For political and other reasons, it is typically a long and difficult process to change tax rates once a tax schedule has been established. The process often involves months of hearings, legislative wrangling, and other time-consuming steps. Moreover, it is expensive for business enterprises to have to adjust production to frequent changes in the level of fees; stable tax rates reduce uncertainty and lower costs of production.

A third problem of the tax approach is that the environmental authority may encounter troublesome political obstacles to levying different tax rates according to the *location* of polluters. In many cases such variations in tax rates are essential for the efficiency of a program. As we stressed in Chapter 15, a given level of emissions is frequently far more harmful in one location than in another; smoke spewn forth in a sparsely populated area will produce far less damage than in a residential neighborhood. Wind factors can also be important; the smoky factory will do significantly more damage to the community if it is located to the windward, rather than the leeward, side of the municipality. The problem is that identical tax rates in the two locations will provide equal incentives for the curtailment of emissions in areas in which it is highly beneficial and in those in which the advantages it confers are small.

Inflexibility of tax rates *over time* can also be highly disadvantageous. The reasons are essentially the same as for geographic uniformity: a given emission may cause more damage at some times than at others. A period of drought can reduce substantially the ability of a river to absorb and disperse pollutants; this obviously increases the potential damage from waste discharges. Similarly, in periods when low wind velocity and other atmospheric conditions combine to produce an atmospheric "inversion," emissions into the air can become much more dangerous than usual.

The dilemma here is that a tax rate sufficiently high to deal with such a pollution emergency will be far too restrictive and impose too high a level of pollution-control costs during normal periods. On the other hand, a tax rate low enough for ordinary purposes may be critically inadequate in times of adverse environmental conditions. Since we cannot predict such environmental crises very far in advance, we cannot expect to be able to adapt tax rates to them with sufficient speed. In addition, as already noted, the immediate effect of changes in tax rates on pollution is likely to be quite uncertain; this can obviously be of overwhelming importance in time of emergency.

We can reduce somewhat the inflexibility resulting from uniform charges by building variations into the schedule of fees itself. *Peak-load pricing* is widely used in a number of activities. Telephone rates, for example, are lower during periods of relatively unused capacity (the night hours and weekends) to induce a shift of calls away from the busy weekday hours. Likewise, a number of bus companies and railroads regularly charge reduced fares for off-peak travel. There is no reason in principle why an environmental authority cannot employ such pricing techniques. As one example, the authority may adopt two schedules of effluent charges for BOD emissions into a river, one for the winter months and a second with higher rates for the summer months, to encourage lower emissions when the river's absorptive capacity is at its lowest levels. As long as these schedules of charges are published well in advance, polluters will be able to plan their operations accordingly, thereby increasing the effectiveness of the measure as a protector of water quality.

As mentioned earlier, inflation and growth also constitute problems for the tax approach. A continuing rise in the price level will eat away at the real value of an effluent charge and will thereby reduce over time its effectiveness in the curtailment of effluents. Similarly, the growth of population and of industrial activity will generate increases in emission discharges at a given tax level. To hold the line on polluting activities, we shall probably find that periodic increases in fees are necessary; this is a distinct disadvantage, for it places the burden of maintaining environmental standards on the environmental authority, not on polluters.

Finally, we must mention one crucially important practical matter for the implementation of the pricing approach (as well as for at least some forms of direct controls): the monitoring and measurement of levels of polluting activities. In order to charge individual polluters for their waste emissions, the environmental agency must be able to measure the discharges. This may not be a simple matter. For example, in taxing discharges into waterways, the authority may want to base the charge on the BOD content of the effluent, the concentrations of various nondegradable chemical substances and suspended solids, and, perhaps, even the temperature. All this involves some fairly sophisticated problems in monitoring. The standard techniques for measuring the BOD content of effluents, for example, are still rather primitive, time-consuming, and not completely reliable (see Appendix A of Chapter 20 for details). They require that samples of the waste emissions be put to laboratory tests that reveal, some days later, a measure of BOD concentration.

The acceptability of metering procedures is often a matter of degree. In many cases, costlier metering techniques may provide more detailed and reliable data, but the additional information simply may not be worth the cost. An annual automobile inspection does not give as much information about car emissions as a weekly or even a monthly examination of the vehicle. However, the nuisance and administrative costs of the more frequent inspections are almost certainly not justified by the improved information they would provide.[13]

It must be admitted that taken overall the art of monitoring is in a relatively primitive state. There is often no way one can place a meter on the discharger's outflow pipe and expect the meter to keep a record of the quantities of the varying damaging emissions it spews forth. There may, however, exist some acceptable shortcuts; we will examine this in more detail in Chapter 20. Moreover, with increasing use and demand for metering, we can expect the development of less expensive and more effective methods of measuring polluting activities.

12. A "License to Pollute"?

One of the most persistent arguments against fiscal incentives is the assertion that pollution taxes (or the auctioning of pollution permits) are basically

---

[13] This point and the example were suggested to us by Professor William S. Vickrey.

immoral. Many environmentalists contend that a pollution tax is, in effect, "a license to pollute"—that whoever is willing to pay a price can abuse the environment. Economists have, of course, not been surprised at the united opposition to fiscal methods from those who have the most to lose—the polluters. More astonishing is this resistance by dedicated environmentalists. Two recent incidents will illustrate the fervor of the opposition. When a bill imposing effluent charges for the protection of our rivers was introduced into the Senate, an indignant editorial in a leading liberal newspaper asserted that this immoral piece of legislation *sold* the right to pollute our rivers. At about the same time, a group of public-spirited, liberal businessmen asked several economists to address them on environmental issues. The businessmen were shocked at the idea of a tax approach to environmental control; they asserted that business should cooperate *voluntarily* to protect the environment, simply because it is the just and virtuous thing to do. One of them asked, "Would you really tax General Motors for selling unsafe cars? Isn't that selling the right to destroy human life?" The economist thought for a moment and replied, "Surely, it is better than giving that right free of charge."

That is precisely the heart of the issue. Society has been giving away free too many of its precious resources far too long. It is *not* scandalous to decide that everything has its price; the real scandal lies in setting that price at zero or at some token level that invites us all to destroy these resources. By imposing essentially no cost on the individual for polluting activities, we have instead shifted the very heavy costs upon society. Unless we recognize the legitimate role of price incentives for the control of pollution, we may end up with our sense of morality intact but our environment the worse for continued abuse.

17

Pricing Techniques:

CHARGES, SUBSIDIES, SALE OF PERMITS, AND REFUNDABLE DEPOSITS

We noted in Chapter 15 that the pricing approach encompasses a number of different techniques, the most notable of which are taxes (fees), subsidies, and auctioning pollution permits. The purpose of this chapter is to examine the relative strengths and the weaknesses of these alternatives. We begin with a comparison of taxes and subsidies.

1. Effluent Taxes vs. Subsidies

In Table 15-1 we listed two basic types of subsidies: unit subsidies for the reduction of waste emissions and grants to defray the costs of pollution-control equipment. These are two very different sorts of programs. The first is a payment based upon a reduction in discharges, while the second is a grant of funds, typically to offset the investment costs of pollution-control equipment.

The use of unit subsidies to induce cutbacks in emissions is essentially an alternative to the use of effluent fees. In principle, it would appear that one is as good as the other; what we can accomplish with the stick, we ought to be able to

246

do with the carrot.[1] The basic argument runs as follows: with an effluent charge of ten cents per pound of BOD emissions, a polluting firm must pay ten cents for each pound of BOD it discharges into the environment; the cost to it of such effluents is obviously ten cents per pound. Alternatively, if the environmental authority offers to *pay* the polluter ten cents per pound of reduction in BOD emissions, then the net loss to the polluter per pound of BOD it emits is the same as it is under the tax program: for each pound of wastes, the polluter *foregoes* a ten-cent subsidy, so that the cost per pound is effectively ten cents.

It might appear that there is little to choose between the tax technique and an equivalent subsidy per unit of reduced emissions. However, the tax approach is distinctly superior to unit subsidies on two grounds. First, effluent taxes clearly reduce the net profits of a business, while subsidies increase them. It is possible for subsidies to keep alive a polluting enterprise that would otherwise have been unprofitable (even in the absence of an effluent charge). The subsidy program will induce a reduction in the emissions *per plant* (like the tax), but, by making the industry more profitable than before, it may also generate the entry of new polluting plants. Overall, total industry waste emissions may be unchanged, or may conceivably even increase.

The second objection to unit subsidies is a prickly administrative problem. In order to pay polluters according to their reductions in effluents, we must establish a benchmark from which reductions are measured; the question, in brief, is "reductions from what?" The environmental authority cannot simply take the initial wasteload for each polluter as the point of reference. It would hardly be fair, for example, to set a low emissions level for a firm that had already gone to the expense and trouble of adopting elaborate pollution-control techniques, while a competitor, who had continued to discharge raw wastes, receives a high benchmark with the potential for a correspondingly large subsidy payment. Moreover, such a procedure creates an immediate incentive for each firm to generate an initial waste discharge as large as possible in order to raise its benchmark. The environmental authority must determine some hypothetical "normal" level of emissions for *each* polluter to serve as the point of reference; this can obviously be a major undertaking and one that is likely to involve considerable haggling with individual polluters who feel that their assigned benchmarks are unfair.[2]

---

[1] For a formal analysis of the issue of taxes vs. subsidies, see W. Baumol and W. Oates, *The Theory of Environmental Policy* (Englewood Cliffs, N.J.: Prentice-Hall, Inc., 1975), Chap. 12. For an anticipation of many of the conclusions there, see Richard C. Porter, "The Long-Run Asymmetry of Subsidies and Taxes as Anti-Pollution Policies," *Water Resources Research* 10 (June 1974), pp. 415–17.

[2] Another problem raised by subsidies is a consequence of economic growth. As polluting economic activity expands, the budget of an effective subsidy program will also have to grow and this can impose a great strain upon the public sector.

Effluent charges avoid both problems: they discourage, rather than encourage, the flow of resources into polluting industries by making them less, rather than more, profitable; and, in addition, there is no need to determine a benchmark pollution level.[3] The authority can simply charge the polluter a specified fee per unit of waste emissions, whatever the previous or the "typical" level for the industry. Finally, as we noted in the previous chapter, taxes on pollution generate public revenues rather than depleting the public treasury. While such revenue generation for the government is obviously not the objective of a program of effluent charges, it may be considered an incidental benefit. In short, effluent fees are much to be preferred to unit subsidies as an incentive to reduce levels of waste discharges.

In practice, the use of subsidies has more often taken the form of government grants to assist in investments in pollution-control equipment. In the United States, for example, a major component of federal environmental expenditure has been assistance for the construction of municipal waste-treatment plants (running into many billions of dollars). The U.S. Congress has also offered attractive tax write-off provisions to private industry for expenditures on abatement equipment.

This type of subsidy program also suffers from a number of shortcomings. First, it reduces the firm's freedom of choice in the means it uses to decrease its damage to the environment. Investment in purification equipment is not always the most effective way to combat pollution. Yet this form of subsidy makes it relatively disadvantageous financially for the firm to use any other technique. Most notably, it provides no encouragement for the firm to decrease its output of goods that generate pollution.

Second, the structure of the subsidy may, in many cases, render it rather ineffective. Usually the subsidy will amount to only *part* of the cost of the installation of pollution equipment. A 50 percent subsidy reduces the cost of a $2,000 piece of equipment to $1,000, but if the use of the equipment brings in no revenue, that expenditure is pure loss to the firm. Only if the firm, under pressure from the public or the government, had already been considering the acquisition of such equipment, is this sort of subsidy likely to make the difference.[4]

The biggest problem besetting this sort of subsidy is that it rewards the wrong thing: not a demonstrated reduction in emissions, but something loosely connected with it, such as the purchase of control equipment. If the installation of pollution-control equipment is good for public relations, a subsidy makes

---

[3] In practice, such benchmarks have sometimes been used in the design of systems of fees. This is true, for example, in the effluent-charge programs in Germany, the Netherlands, and France. However, things need not be done in this way.

[4] One possible but noteworthy exception is the use of equipment used in recycling as a substitute for the dumping of wastes into the environment. Here the process does yield financially valuable products. If such a process is just on the borderline of profitability, a subsidy may indeed be able to bring it over the top.

that installation more attractive, but offers no inducement for effective use of the equipment. Thus subsidies turn out to be inferior to effluent charges on at least two of the criteria formulated in the preceding chapter: *effectiveness* and *economy.*[5]

These deficiencies are quite apparent in U.S. federal programs. The General Accounting Office (GAO) conducted a careful and thorough study of the federal subsidy program for the construction of municipal waste-treatment facilities; its report raises serious questions about the effectiveness of the subsidy approach.[6] It is not clear, for example, that the program even increased significantly the number of *effective* treatment plants.

> According to the Council on Environmental Quality, between 1957 and 1970, government subsidies of about $1.5 billion were provided for 10,000 waste treatment plants costing in total about $6.5 billion. Over this period the number of people served by some kind of waste treatment rose 51 million. But this gain was mostly canceled by sewered population growth of about 36 million. Moreover, as already noted, not only do some observers doubt that the federal subsidy program accelerated the construction of waste treatment plants; some believe that it actually slowed the process. Per capita expenditures in constant dollars have been just about level for the past fourteen years and dipped during the late sixties. Quite possibly there would be a greater degree of treatment of municipal wastes today had the federal subsidy program never been instituted.[7]

One of the important findings of the GAO was the extremely poor operation of many of the plants; in one-half of these plants, the service provided was "substandard," either because of improper procedures or a wasteload other than that for which the plant was designed. As Kneese and Schultze observe, "This is not really surprising, since the federal program emphasized construction exclusively; there were no incentives to spur effective and efficient operation."[8]

All this suggests that the effectiveness of subsidy programs for pollution-control is highly doubtful. We do, however, see one potentially useful role for subsidies: under certain circumstances, they can spread costs more equitably and thereby increase the political acceptability of environmental programs. Consider our earlier example of the plant constructed on the previously uninhabited

---

[5]It can also be argued that they are inferior in terms of *equity;* after all, fees require polluters to pay while subsidies reward them for reducing the damage they do to society. However we will see later that there can be significant exceptions to this argument.

[6]Report to the Congress by the Comptroller General of the United States, *Examination into the Effectiveness of the Construction Grant Program for Abating, Controlling, and Preventing Water Pollution* (Washington, D.C.: U.S. General Accounting Office, November 3, 1969, processed).

[7]Allen V. Kneese and Charles L. Schultze, *Pollution, Prices, and Public Policy* (Washington, D.C.: The Brookings Institution, 1975), pp. 42–43.

[8]Ibid., p. 43

banks of a river whose pollutants now have harmful effects on the new residents of the community downstream. Suppose that the construction of a waste-treatment facility beside the plant is the least expensive method to resolve the problem. It may be unfair to impose the full cost of the waste-treatment plant on the firm. After all, the owners took reasonable precautions against harm to others at the time they made their location decision and so have some sort of prior claim on the use of the water. Such conflicts have been exacerbated when the plant is an important source of local jobs, and the added pollution-control costs threaten to force its closure.[9]

The best feasible solution may, in such instances, be a public subsidy to underwrite the pollution-control investment. In Sheffield, England, for example, authorities chose subsidies to finance the changeover from coal to gas or oil furnaces; the argument was that people who had earlier installed coal-burning equipment had done so in good faith with no warning that such facilities would later be declared illegal. It was considered only fair, therefore, that the costs be shared by the entire community which would benefit from the cleaner air.

There is, however, another side to the matter. We noted earlier the importance of placing the tax on the polluters themselves to provide a direct incentive to reduce emissions and to leave them to find the least-cost method of compliance. To finance pollution-control abatement by subsidy obviously flies in the face of this dictum, and we would, therefore, warn that it is likely to be justifiable on balance only in rather special circumstances. In particular, such subsidies would seem to be justified, first, where the most effective method of pollution-control is readily evident, and, second, where the sharing of costs promises important benefits to the community in terms of a more equitable distribution of the tax burden and an enhancement of the program's political acceptability.

2. The Auctioning of Pollution Permits

A number of economists have suggested an alternative method of using pricing incentives for pollution control: the sale of pollution permits. Rather than levying charges on polluting activities, this technique involves the issue of a prescribed number of pollution permits each authorizing the purchaser to a specified quantity of discharges. The environmental authority determines the aggregate level of waste emissions that is consistent with the community's environmental objectives and then simply auctions off the rights to this limited quantity of emissions.

In principle, both effluent charges and the sale of pollution permits lead to the same outcome: with effluent charges, the regulatory agency raises the

---

[9]Some textile mills in New England have found themselves in just this sort of situation; some have actually closed under the threat of the added costs of newly required pollution-control measures.

fee until the target level of emissions is achieved, while under the pollution permit scheme, it offers for sale emission rights equal in total to the target amount. Moreover, the pollution permit approach has essentially all the same advantages we discussed earlier for effluent fees. It is *dependable,* because it is relatively automatic and routine (it involves a regular monitoring of effluents to be checked against the polluter's registered number of emissions rights). It is *permanent:* so long as it is not explicitly repealed, discharges will continue to be illegal without a permit. It is *equitable* in the sense that it requires polluters to pay for their waste emissions. It offers an incentive for maximal cleanup effort: every reduction in emissions reduces the number of permits the polluter has to buy. It is *potentially* (but is not now in fact) attractive politically because, like fees, it brings money into the treasury. It involves a minimum of interference with private decisions. Finally, and perhaps most important, this technique has the same cost-saving advantages as the tax approach: firms for which pollution abatement is relatively inexpensive will find it cheaper to install abatement equipment than to purchase pollution permits. In sum, if the public and government officials can ever be weaned from the idea that auctioning pollution permits is a wild, ivory tower scheme, they may find that the device has a good deal to recommend it.

In fact, the auctioning of pollution permits, besides possessing the virtues of the tax approach, also avoids several of its shortcomings. We noted earlier that, among the limitations of effluent charges, are:

a. Their vulnerability to erosion by inflation, which may transform a specified dollar fee per gallon of effluent from a heavy price on environmental damage into one which (in depreciated dollars) is little more than a token payment
b. Their inability to check expansion in waste discharges stemming from growth in population and economic activity, if the tax rate does not increase periodically
c. The political difficulty of varying the tax rate by geographic area despite the differences, from one location to another, in the social damage of a given quantity of emissions
d. The uncertainty of the response to a given tax rate (i.e., our limited ability to predict whether some proposed tax rate will be sufficient to achieve the intended reduction in the level of pollution)

In all four respects, the use of marketable pollution permits can do better than a tax:

a. Pollution permits are invulnerable to inflation. Since the quantity of pollution licenses is fixed, their price will rise automatically in an inflationary period. As the value of the dollar falls, polluters will bid more for each permit, so that no legislative action will be needed to produce a readjustment in the price of waste emissions.
b. As population and industrial activity increase, the *demand* for pollution permits will undoubtedly rise. If the number of permits offered for sale remains

the same, all that will happen is that their price will be bid up; potential polluters will either have to outbid current permit holders or curb their emissions. The point here is simply that emissions cannot increase without an expansion in the number of permits provided by the environmental authority.[10] Unlike the tax approach, this scheme puts the burden of initiative on the polluters, rather than on public officials.

c. If one area is more vulnerable to pollution than another, this can be dealt with simply by selling a smaller number of pollution permits (nontransferable from one area to another) for the first area than for the second.[11] Of course this might not happen in practice. Political pressures generally make for uniformity of treatment of different constituencies, and so it may not be realistic to expect the political process to yield significant differences in the abundance with which pollution rights are issued, even where there are good reasons for such differences. But, at least in principle, such variations are surely feasible.

d. The auctioning of a fixed number of pollution permits minimizes uncertainty about the resulting level of emissions (at least so long as there is no significant quantity of illegal pollution). We noted earlier that, in principle, the tax approach and pollution-permit schemes lead to the same outcome. In practice, however, the use of fees involves some uncertainty as to the outcome, because the public authority may not be able to predict with great accuracy the polluters' response to specific fees. Pollution permits eliminate this source of uncertainty by setting the level of emissions directly.

While its advantages are impressive, the pollution-permit approach does have some problems. For one thing, it does not seem to have a high degree of political appeal. Noneconomists usually regard it as an impractical and cumbersome product of the convoluted minds of academia. But then, the tax approach has not commanded an enormous nonacademic following either.[12]

Moreover, the use of pollution permits introduces an important risk of its own. This is the danger that society may find itself expending an excessive and unanticipated quantity of its valuable resources on pollution abatement.[13]

---

[10] The system could come under considerable pressure if an intransigent environmental authority refuses to concede any scope for economic growth and permits absolutely no change in the number of pollution certificates put up for auction. One prominent economist has argued that this is the most serious danger of the approach: it will simply be flouted if it grows intolerably restrictive.

[11] The sale of pollution permits may also cope better than taxes with temporal variations in the damage costs of pollution. For example, if the emission of BOD into a local river is particularly dangerous in the hot summer months when the water is low, one can require the purchase of a special summer certificate for emissions in these months; the environmental authority would issue a smaller number of these summer permits.

[12] In one sense, the pollution-permit approach may prove a less radical departure from existing programs than a system of fees. The current direct-controls strategy embodied in present legislation regulates waste emissions largely through the issuance of permits to individual polluters. The pollution-permit technique could simply amount to making such permits transferable at a market-determined price.

[13] This observation is taken from an illuminating discussion by James E. Meade, *The Theory of Economic Externalities, The Control of Environmental Pollution and Similar Social Costs* (Geneva: A. W. Sijthoff-Leiden, 1973), pp. 65–66.

Suppose that a certain number of permits have been offered for sale, but that the issue of 1,000 additional permits would make possible a substantial saving in pollution expenditures (i.e., that it would free substantial quantities of resources that could instead be used to build schools and hospitals). The decision to issue that fixed number of permits may impose a heavy cost on society—a cost that may be unanticipated by those who decide on the number of permits to be auctioned. The use of fees largely does away with this possibility. If the fee is set, say, at ten cents per gallon, this amounts to a ceiling on abatement costs, for no one will then pay twenty cents per gallon for abatement. A producer will simply reject any measure to curtail pollution that costs more than ten cents per gallon, because it is clearly cheaper to pay the tax than to adopt so expensive a technique to reduce emissions.

The choice between the use of fees and the auctioning of pollution permits may then be a matter of which risk constitutes the greater danger. If unanticipated future emissions are the most imminent threat to the public welfare, this argues for the auctioning of pollution permits, which leaves little doubt about the probable volume of pollution. On the other hand, if the prime danger is excessive use of society's resources needed for other pressing purposes, the fees approach, with its firmer control of abatement outlays, may be the preferable procedure. Finally, we must emphasize that both the fee and the pollution permit approach are feasible only if it is possible to identify the sources of the pollution, and if their emission levels can be monitored effectively. Where this cannot be done (as is true in a number of important cases), we must find other means of control.

3. The Use of Refundable Deposits for Pollution Control

There are a number of circumstances in which direct observation and detection of environmental damage are impossible or extremely difficult. It is not easy, for example, to determine whether an oil tanker has dumped some of its wastes at sea.[14] Likewise, in large cities, landlords (whose identities are concealed behind a maze of legal "front" organizations) abandon buildings which quickly become fire hazards, havens for criminals, and a blight on the neighborhood. As yet another example, when scrap metal prices are low, car owners sometimes find it cheapest to get rid of old vehicles by abandoning them on the street.

Robert Solow[15] and Edwin Mills[16] have offered an intriguing solution to

---

[14] See William J. Baumol, "Environmental Protection, International Spillovers, and Trade," *Wicksell Lectures 1971* (Stockholm: Almqvist and Wiksell, 1971), p. 24.
[15] Robert M. Solow, "The Economist's Approach to Pollution and Its Control," *Science* 173 (August 6, 1971): 502.
[16] Edwin S. Mills, *Urban Economics* (Glenview, Ill.: Scott, Foresman, and Company, 1972), pp. 259-60.

this problem: they have proposed that potential offenders be required to leave an appropriate deposit with the environmental authorities. For example, the owners of oil tankers might be required to pay to an international authority a deposit sufficient to cover the cost of cleaning up oil spills and compensating for any damage. The international organization could pay a suitable rate of interest on all such deposits and would be free to use the funds as it employs its other borrowed monies. It would be the obligation of the ship owners to present proof regularly, perhaps annually, that they had disposed properly of the cargo and all wastes. When a ship was sold, the owners would obtain a refund of their deposit from the agency. Similarly, the registration of a new automobile might be accompanied by a deposit to be refunded upon evidence of proper disposal of the vehicle.

The basic approach here, as in other uses in price incentives, is to make socially undesirable behavior unprofitable to the individual. Solow, expanding on this approach, has suggested that all users of raw materials might be required to provide a bond to assure the recycling or appropriate disposal of the materials. Indeed, one of the most promising applications of this technique is the encouragement of recycling or reuse. In the form of deposits on bottles it is a very old idea, one that is now used in many countries throughout the world, including the Soviet Union. In the next chapter, we will explore one experiment with deposits that apparently has been extremely successful: the use of deposits on returnable beverage containers in Oregon.

The use of deposits performs well in terms of most of our criteria for environmental policy instruments. It has been somewhat more attractive politically than the other fiscal methods, though still not an overwhelming success in the political arena. It may not offer the prospects for cost efficiency promised by the other fiscal methods, but otherwise it scores reasonably well, particularly where monitoring is impractical.

18

Experience with Price Incentives for Environmental Protection

Critics have expressed skepticism or outright opposition to effluent fees on a variety of grounds, but one continuing response to advocates of the pricing approach has been "It sounds fine in theory, but will it really work?" In answer to this important question, economists usually fall back on a theoretical discussion of the workings of the pricing system (like that in Chapter 16). Because of our limited experience with the use of fiscal incentives for environmental policy, they cannot produce much in the way of direct evidence.

For this reason, we have regarded the systematic collection of evidence concerning *both* the effectiveness and limitations of fiscal incentives as a critical part of our study. We have come up with a substantial body of evidence (drawn from cases ranging from municipal waste-treatment programs that levied fees on industrial discharges to deposits on beverage containers in Oregon) that suggests that the use of pricing incentives can be a powerful inducement for reduction of environmental damage by business firms and individuals. At the same time, it is clear that pricing incentives are subject to some important limitations; these we shall explore in later chapters.

1. Water-Quality Management in Europe[1]

Programs in the United States to reduce water pollution have placed very little reliance on pricing incentives. In contrast, there has been somewhat more experience with such fiscal inducements in Europe, and we therefore begin our survey with an examination of water-quality management in Europe.

The oldest and most widely publicized system of charges is that in the Ruhr River basin in West Germany.[2] The Ruhr basin is one of the world's most heavily concentrated industrial centers; it encompasses roughly 40 percent of total West German industrial capacity and includes between 70 and 90 percent of West Germany's production of coal, coke, iron, and steel. The river system of the Ruhr district, made up of five relatively small rivers, not only provides the water supply for the 10 million people in the area, but also the waste-carrying capacity to support this enormous industrial activity. Kneese and Bower provide some sense of the capacity of the system by noting that, "Their combined *annual* average low flow is only about one-fourth of the *low flow of record* of the Delaware River near Trenton, New Jersey, or about one-half of the low flow of record of the Potomac River near Washington, D.C."[3] Yet this system must absorb an immense quantity of industrial waste emissions: in fact, the annual average low flow in the Ruhr is *less* than the volume of effluent discharged into it.

One might expect to find signs of severe environmental degradation such as the absence of fishlife and the usual visual and nasal offenses. Yet, in all but one of the rivers, the quality of the water is high enough not only to sustain fishlife, but also to permit fishing and other recreational uses. This has been accomplished by a comprehensive system of water-control management established before World War II. The Ruhr district has eight large *Genossenschaften* (associations or authorities) that control the construction and operation of all waste-treatment plants, dams, and pump stations. In addition, the Genossenschaften impose effluent charges, which are dependent *both* on the quality and quantity of emissions, and thus provide direct incentives to industry to reduce waste discharges.[4] The results have been quite dramatic. For example, almost 40 per-

---

[1] This section draws heavily on Ralph W. Johnson and Gardner M. Brown, Jr., *Cleaning Up Europe's Waters: Economics, Management, and Policies* (New York: Praeger Publishers, 1976).

[2] In addition to Johnson and Brown, for a detailed description and evaluation of the Ruhr experience, see Allen V. Kneese and Blair T. Bower, *Managing Water Quality: Economics, Technology, and Institutions* (Baltimore: Published for Resources for the Future by The Johns Hopkins University Press, 1968), Chap. 12.

[3] Ibid., p. 240.

[4] The system of effluent fees employed in the Ruhr is a rather technical and complicated one. In particular, it doesn't correspond perfectly to the economist's ideal of a charge equal to marginal cost; the fees are, instead, based on something closer to average cost. See Kneese and Bower, *Managing Water Quality,* pp. 244–52. In addition, the Ruhr authorities have granted substantial investment subsidies for waste-treatment equipment.

cent of industrial acids used in the Ruhr Valley in 1966 were recovered. Kneese and Bower report that

> One steel plant at Dortmund introduced water recirculation, internal treatment, and materials reuse processes and virtually eliminated effluent from the plant. The incentive in this case was a combination of intake water costs and effluent charges. Other iron and steel plants in the area are gradually adopting measures to reduce their water intake and wastes generation.[5]

The Ruhr experience, extending over a period of several decades, is impressive and encouraging; it suggests that, at least in terms of water quality, high levels of economic activity can be consistent with the protection of the environment.[6] Although there has been little reliance on effluent charges elsewhere in Germany, a few other European countries have instituted systems of fees. In fact, the Common Market countries have adopted in the Rome treaty the general policy that polluters should pay for the prevention and cleanup of the nuisance they create. Some countries (the Netherlands and France in particular) have implemented the "Polluters-Pay-Principle" (PPP) by placing charges on both industrial and municipal sources of water pollution. These systems of charges differ in certain important respects from the "ideal" we described in Chapter 16; they are not, for example, based on levels of damages—they rely more on a compensation, than an incentive, principle in that the level of charges is set so as to cover the cost of water-quality management programs.[7] We will explore this in greater depth in a later chapter on the design of environmental programs, but it is important to note that the institution of actual systems of fees does require certain compromises with the conceptual ideal.

Moreover, it is still too early to evaluate the results of these relatively recent programs in Europe (other than the Ruhr). However, there are some encouraging signs. In France, for example, there was distinct disappointment by the end of the 1960s with the existing systems of direct controls based on pollu-

---

[5]Ibid., p. 252.

[6]Yet there is another side to the matter. The Ruhr program has dealt primarily with only one element of the environment: the protection of the quality of several of its rivers. One river (the Emscher) which has deliberately been left unprotected has consequently become a sink for a disproportionate share of the region's wastes, and has been described as little more than an open sewer. Moreover, Johnson and Brown (*Cleaning up Europe's Waters*, p. 131) point out that the stress on water quality has led industry to adopt measures that foul the air instead. In particular, the burning of wastes has generated serious air pollution.

[7]Somewhat paradoxically, the best system of pricing incentives in terms of principles of design seems to be the fee structure in Hungary. Johnson and Brown note that "The basic charge is modified to reflect the volume of receiving waters, the amount and extent of pollutants beyond the specified 31 [pollutants], the efficiency of treatment facilities, and the good efforts of the polluter to mitigate wastes" (*Cleaning up Europe's Waters*, p. 139). Unfortunately the level of the charges has apparently been so low as to blunt somewhat their effectiveness.

tion permits. As one observer pointed out, "most establishments simply find themselves in perpetual violation. . . . Over the years, the permit system has thus become the basis for a national 'tolerance policy' toward polluters. . . ."[8] In the 1970s in contrast, river-basin agencies have begun to assess and collect charges on polluters and to disburse these funds for pollution control. The results appear impressive. One official indicated in 1974 that "There has been more abatement in water pollution in the last five years than in all previous years."[9] Likewise, the early returns from the Netherlands indicate real progress. Since the introduction of fees in 1971, the pulp and paper industry, a major source of water pollution, has reduced its waste discharges by about 40 percent.[10]

2. Effluent Fees for the Management of Water Quality in the United States

The use of fees in the United States has primarily taken the form of charges on industrial emissions into municipal waste-treatment facilities. Such charges have become relatively common since 1930, but until recently they bore only the faintest resemblance to true effluent fees. The basic role of most sewer charges has been to cover the costs of the waste-treatment operation. To simplify administration, municipalities have typically spread the costs of waste treatment among users according to some easily measurable unit such as water intake (relying, for example, on a firm's water bill). Such charges bear no relation to the *quality* of the waste discharge; it is an incentive to economize on intake of water but not to clean up waste emissions.

This has led, over time, to an overload on many municipal waste-treatment systems, and some local officials have turned to sewer *surcharges* based on the strength or quality of the effluent. Normal wastes, for which the firm pays a regular sewer charge, are usually defined in terms of a ceiling on the BOD (biochemical oxygen demand) load.[11] For more highly concentrated effluents, the firm must pay a surcharge based on the number of pounds of BOD in excess of normal. The surcharge has typically been on the order of one to two cents per pound of "excess" BOD.

Such surcharges provide a direct incentive to firms with highly concentrated effluents to reduce the quantity and improve the quality of their waste emissions. Studies of the actual responses to these surcharges have been able to estimate roughly their effectiveness. The most ambitious of these studies was undertaken by Ralph Elliott and James Seagraves at North Carolina State Uni-

---

[8]Ibid., p. 40.
[9]Ibid., p. 64.
[10]Ibid., p. 97.
[11]Some municipalities have employed supplementary measures of the quality of waste emissions such as the level of suspended solids.

versity (Raleigh).[12] Elliott and Seagraves collected data on a group of thirty-five U.S. cities that had utilized sewer surcharges; they had information over a number of years on the levels of the surcharge and on the water intake and BOD discharges for a sample of firms in each city. Their procedure was to evaluate statistically how firms' water usage and BOD emissions varied over time and from one city to another, with the level of the sewer surcharge. Although differences in the industrial structure of the sampled firms obscured the results to some extent, Elliott and Seagraves found that the effects of the level of the surcharge on both water consumption and BOD discharges were statistically significant. For example, their results indicate that, with a surcharge of 2.7 cents per pound of BOD, a 10 percent increase in the surcharge (to about three cents per pound of BOD) will induce, on average, an 8 percent reduction in BOD discharges. The level of the surcharge also affects water usage substantially; Elliott and Seagraves found that, on average, a 10 percent increase in the surcharge was associated with a 4 percent reduction in water intake.

The Elliott-Seagraves findings provide some systematic evidence of the effectiveness of effluent fees in reducing industrial waste discharges, although, unfortunately, the highly aggregative character of their data relating both to different cities and various industries reduces somewhat the reliability of their results. There are some studies, however, of individual industries and cities that provide somewhat more dependable estimates. Don Ethridge, for example, has made a formal statistical study of the response of poultry-processing firms to sewer surcharges.[13] This is an intensively water-using industry, which generates a substantial BOD effluent. A typical poultry-processing plant handles about 75,000 birds per day and uses about eleven gallons of water per bird—a total of close to a million gallons of water per day! Using data for five different plants covering several years, Ethridge obtained results quite similar to those of Elliott and Seagraves. For the poultry-processing industry, he estimates that a 10 percent increase in the surcharge on BOD produces a 5 percent decrease in the pounds of BOD discharged per 1,000 birds. Again, water consumption appears to be price sensitive; Ethridge found that a 10 percent rise in the cost of water induced, on the average, about a 6 percent reduction in water used per bird.

To supplement Ethridge's statistical research on poultry-processing, there are also some "synthetic" studies of industry responses to fees. The synthetic approach proceeds by determining the cost structure of the industry (for a "typical" plant) and then using this cost information to estimate the adjustments in waste discharges that *would* result from various levels of effluent fees. The implicit assumption is that management will adjust the process of production so as to minimize costs including the payment of fees. One such study is

---

[12] For a summary of this study, see James A. Seagraves, "Industrial Waste Discharges," *Journal of the Environmental Engineering Division* 99 (December 1973): 873–81.
[13] "User Charges as a Means for Pollution Control: The Case of Sewer Surcharges," *The Bell Journal of Economics and Management Science* 3 (Spring 1972): 346–54.

that by George Löf and Allen Kneese of the beet-sugar industry.[14] Although this is an industry that does not often make the headlines, its levels of water usage and BOD emissions are enormous. Average water intake for a typical beet-sugar factory on-season is over 6 million gallons per day (about 9 gallons of water per pound of sugar produced). At the other end of the water-using process, each factory averages about 20,000 pounds of BOD effluent per day.

What is most striking about the Löf-Kneese findings is the tremendous variation in water intake and effluent among different factories. They found that water intake per ton of beets varied all the way from 270 gallons to a high of 5,250 gallons. This variation indicates that there is a great range of choice available in methods of beet-sugar production. By the recirculation of water and more effective treatment of wastes (both of which can be accomplished at rather modest costs), levels of water usage and the BOD and suspended-solid content of factory effluents can be cut drastically.

Trends in this direction are already evident in the data covering the period up to 1962. Taking the cost information provided by Löf and Kneese, Ethridge has gone on to estimate that the imposition of a typical municipal sewer surcharge per pound of BOD would induce extremely large reductions in waste discharges from beet-sugar plants. Ethridge's results indicate that, at a modest surcharge level, a 10 percent increase in the surcharge would generate, on the average, about a 60 percent reduction in BOD effluent.[15]

Clifford Russell has made a similar kind of study of the petroleum-refining industry.[16] After assembling a working model of the industry, Russell analyzed the scope for reduction in waste discharges into waterways, in particular for emissions of BOD, phenols, sulfide, and ammonia. He found that "The total costs of reducing discharges of waterborne residuals, even to zero, are a very small fraction, generally less than one-tenth of 1 percent, of refinery costs."[17] Russell's findings indicate, moreover, that most of these reductions could be induced by a relatively modest fee (five cents per pound) on effluents.

A recent study of the pulp and paper industry also indicates that there is a great range of possibilities in pollution control.[18] From a survey of 130 pulp mills operated by the 24 largest pulp and paper companies in the United States, the study found that, although some plants have excellent pollution-control records, roughly two-thirds of water discharged by the industry failed to meet the federal standard. Like the beet-sugar and poultry-processing industries, paper

---

[14] *The Economics of Water Utilization in the Beet Sugar Industry* (Baltimore: The Johns Hopkins University Press, 1968).

[15] Ethridge, "User Charges," pp. 349–50.

[16] *Residuals Management in Industry: A Case Study of Petroleum Refining* (Baltimore, Md.: Published for Resources for the Future by The Johns Hopkins University Press, 1973). The cost curve we presented in Figure 14–1 in Chapter 14 comes from Russell's study.

[17] Ibid., p. 155.

[18] The Council on Economic Priorities, *Paper Profits: Pollution in the Pulp and Paper Industry* (Cambridge, Mass.: M.I.T. Press, 1972).

and pulp mills use huge quantities of water. The 130 mills surveyed produce about 90,000 tons of pulp daily requiring a water intake of 2.7 billion gallons. In Everett, Washington, the four pulp and paper mills along with 60,000 residents use more water than the city of Seattle with 600,000 residents. The study makes clear that methods for treatment of the industry's effluents are available at reasonable cost and have in fact been adopted in a number of mills. Several companies, however, have simply neglected treatment of wastes because they have incurred no significant penalty by doing so. Although this particular study doesn't provide the kind of cost information needed to estimate the response to various levels of fees, the survey suggests that effluent charges would provide the necessary incentives.

When we turn to the cases of individual cities or metropolitan areas, the reports, although somewhat more impressionistic, again indicate a substantial response to sewer surcharges. Kneese and Bower describe the experiences of a number of local treatment systems employing such surcharges.[19] The experience in Springfield, Missouri, suggests the kinds of responses that sewer fees can induce:

> Faced with rising waste loads in 1962, Springfield decided to apply a surcharge on industrial waste discharges above the normal strength of sewage. The rationale was that the surcharge would provide an incentive for industrial operations to reduce waste discharges and/or would provide funds for expansion of the city's treatment plant facilities. . . .
>
> Even before the first official billing, some plants began to take action. A packing plant that faced an assessment of about $1,400 per month modified its production processes and ended up with a sewer bill of only $225 per month. A commercial laundry, faced with a large monthly surcharge because its waste discharge was warm and had a relatively high concentration of suspended solids, made changes that resulted in a significant *net* savings in its production costs even with the sewer surcharge. The principal savings came from the installation of a concrete sump, which functioned as a settling basin to remove suspended solids and BOD in the waste discharge, and as a heat exchanger, thereby reducing the cost of heating incoming water. Two potato chip manufacturers were stimulated by the imposition of a sewer surcharge to analyze their production processes to discover why the plant effluents were so high in BOD and suspended solids. When they found the answer to be the large quantities of cooking oils and potato peelings that were lost during processing, new processing equipment was installed in both plants. The losses of oil and product were reduced, and with the decrease in the strength of the waste discharge came a substantial reduction in the sewer charge.
>
> The responses of industrial operations to the imposition of sewer charges can be generalized as follows: First, the imposition of a charge or

---

[19]*Managing Water Quality*, pp. 165–70.

surcharge tends to encourage plants to make changes that in many cases reduce not only the volume of effluents and the wastes in the effluents but also the water intake. Second, sewer charges tend to induce an examination of production processes that often uncovers relatively simple modifications which may result in net reductions in total production costs.[20]

In addition to their potential effectiveness in inducing reductions in waste emissions, we stressed in Chapter 16 the cost-savings aspects of the fee approach. The scope for these savings has been documented by a study of the costs of reducing water pollution in the Delaware River Estuary. During the 1960s, a group of researchers constructed a detailed mathematical model of the estuary which described the biochemical relationships of this body of water.[21] In particular, the model examined the effects of changes in waste discharges at a particular point on water quality in all the different areas of the estuary. By appending to this structure a mathematical model capable of determining the nature of a (theoretically) most-efficient program, the researchers were then able to estimate the costs of alternate methods of achieving desired levels of water quality. This is an extremely suggestive exercise, for it makes possible comparisons of the costs of regulatory and fiscal programs to protect the estuary.[22] The findings of the study are summarized in Table 18-1. In particular, the table indicates the cost of achieving each of two possible levels of dissolved oxygen (DO) content for the estuary under four alternative programs:

a. The least cost program (determined directly by the mathematical program)[23]
b. Uniform treatment requiring identical percentage reductions in emissions by all polluters (characteristic of the direct-control approach)
c. Single effluent charge (a uniform tax per unit of emissions)
d. Zoned effluent charge (a tax on emissions varying with location)

The last program allows for a division of the estuary into three zones so that the

---

[20] Ibid., pp. 169–70. See also their description of the effects of surcharges in Otsego, Michigan, and in the Greater Winnipeg Sanitary District.

[21] For a discussion of the Delaware Estuary study, see Appendix C in Allen V. Kneese, Sidney E. Rolfe, and Joseph W. Harned, eds., *Managing the Environment: International Economic Cooperation for Pollution Control* (New York: Praeger Publishers, 1971), pp. 255–74.

[22] These results must, however, be treated with some caution, since they depend on the validity of the assumption that the relevant costs are, indeed, linear (that is, that they increase at a perfectly steady rate with the degree of improvement of water quality). We know as a matter of fact that such costs are likely to rise at an increasing rate. Moreover, there is evidence that mathematical programming calculations are very sensitive to such linearity assumptions. See W. J. Baumol and R. C. Bushnell, "Error Produced by Linearization in Mathematical Programming," *Econometrica* 35 (July–October, 1967): 447–71.

[23] It is worth noting that, while this is useful as a benchmark, it would be extremely difficult to administer as it requires precise information on both the effects of wastes and the costs of treatment at each point on the waterway with individually specified quotas for each emitter.

TABLE 18-1

COST OF TREATMENT UNDER ALTERNATIVE PROGRAMS
(millions of dollars per year)

Dissolved Oxygen Objective (parts per million)	Program			
	Least Cost	Uniform Treatment	Single Effluent Charge	Zoned Effluent Charge
2	1.6	5.0	2.4	2.4
3–4	7.0	20.0	12.0	8.6

Source: "The Delaware Estuary Study: Effluent Charges, Least-Cost Treatment Systems, and Equity," Appendix C in Kneese, Rolf, and Harned, eds., *Managing the Environment: International Economic Cooperation for Pollution Control* (New York: Praeger Publishers, 1971) p. 272.

fee can be set somewhat higher in a zone where effluents have a disproportionately deleterious effect on the estuary.

What is most interesting about the findings is the potential savings available from using effluent fees relative to uniform treatment of all polluters. For both DO objectives, the cost of treatment under a system of fees is only about one-half the cost of a program of direct controls utilizing a uniform percentage reduction in all waste discharges. If the environmental objective were three to four parts per million of dissolved oxygen in the estuary, this study suggests that the use of fees could save from $8 to $11.4 million *annually* when compared to uniform treatment, by no means a trifling saving.

3. Fiscal Incentives and Air Pollution

In contrast to water-quality management, we have hardly any direct experience with effluent charges to control the quantity and quality of air pollution. Programs to reduce levels of air pollutants in the United States and elsewhere have invariably employed direct regulations that require adherence to specified emission standards, rather than a set of fees to which polluters then respond.[24] However, there are several recent "synthetic" studies of industrial air pollution activities that provide rough estimates of the likely responses to various levels of effluent fees.

We turn first to an intriguing study by James M. Griffin of sulfur emissions in the electric utility industry.[25] This industry is the source of enormous quan-

---

[24] The only existing instances of fees to reduce air pollution are in Norway, the Netherlands, and Japan, where recent laws tax the use of sulfurous fuels. More on this in a later chapter.
[25] "An Econometric Evaluation of Sulfur Taxes," *Journal of Political Economy* 82 (July-August 1974): 669–88.

tities of pollution. The Environmental Protection Agency (EPA) estimated that in 1968 about 17 million tons of sulfur were emitted into the atmosphere, producing damage valued at more than $8 billion; power plants generate over half of the nation's emissions of sulfur dioxide.

Griffin began by constructing a mathematical model of electricity production and usage. The model allows both for shifts between fuels in the production of electricity (e.g., a substitution of fuel oil for high-sulfur coal), and consumer response in the form of reduced usage of electricity. Using statistical data in his model, Griffin analyzed the effect of an effluent charge on sulfur emissions. More specifically, he assumed the enactment of the proposed Pure Air Tax Act of 1972, which called for a fee of fifteen cents per pound on sulfur emissions beginning in 1976. Using what he saw as the most reasonable assumptions concerning the costs of alternative means for obtaining low-sulfur coal, Griffin estimated that the fee would induce an 85 to 90 percent reduction in sulfur emissions. This, incidentally, would be accompanied by a rise in cost that translates into an increase in the average price of electricity in the range of 7 to 19 percent.

Griffin's findings thus suggest that sulfur emissions in the electric utility industry would be very responsive to effluent charges. But is it justified in view of the higher costs of electricity? Griffin provides a rough answer to this question by noting that the EPA damage estimates imply an average social cost of sulfur emissions of $580 per ton. He then calculates that the reduction in damage from lower sulfur emissions would be more than three times as great as the addition to the cost of electricity. The answer seems to be yes—the benefits appear to exceed the costs.

William D. Watson has recently conducted a careful evaluation of the costs of reducing particulate emissions (another major air pollutant from power plants) and the likely response to the imposition of effluent fees on these discharges.[26] Watson estimates that the imposition of an effluent charge of about $75 per ton (four cents per pound) on particulate emissions "would induce all but very small plants to meet new-source performance standards."[27] For typical size plants, this would imply the removal of over 99 percent of particulate matter emitted. Like Griffin, Watson employs EPA estimates of the damages from particulate matter emissions to perform a cost-benefit comparison. EPA estimates suggest that in 1970 the benefits from controlling these discharges in terms of reduced ill health effects, decreased deterioration of materials, and a lessening of soiling and aesthetic insults would have ranged from a low of about $2.5 billion to a high of $7.7 billion with a mid-range estimate of roughly $5 billion. This is based on an assumed 87 percent reduction in total particulate emissions. Moreover, this could have been accomplished at an annual cost of about $130 million, so

[26]"Costs and Benefits of Fly Ash Control," *Journal of Economics and Business* 26 (Spring 1974): 167–81.
[27]Ibid., p. 177.

that the benefits from the effluent fee and associated decline in particulate emissions would apparently have far outweighed the abatement costs.

In the preceding section on water pollution, we described Clifford Russell's study of petroleum refining and, in particular, the potential effects of effluent charges on levels of waterborne discharges of various wastes.[28] Russell's study also includes an assessment of sulfur and particulate emissions into the air from petroleum refining. Here his findings are somewhat mixed. The costs of reducing sulfur-dioxide emissions in the industry appear to be quite high, for there are at present no feasible "treatment" alternatives; such reductions would require fundamental process changes that could increase refinery costs by as much as 8 percent. Russell estimates that a relatively high effluent fee of up to twenty-five cents per pound could induce reductions in sulfur-dioxide emissions on the order of only 30 percent (through switches to lower-sulfur coke). This finding underlines once again the (often large) differences in the cost of reducing waste emissions in different activities; it suggests, for example, that it is far less costly to reduce sulfur emissions by concentrating on electric-power generation than on petroleum refining. In contrast, Russell's study suggests that emissions of particulate matter would be highly responsive to modest charges; an effluent fee, for example, of two cents per pound would induce an estimated 82.5 percent reduction in discharges of particulates.

Since most air pollution is the result of fuel combustion, it is important to examine what we know about the price responsiveness of fuel usage. There is a substantial amount of recent work (much motivated by recurring fuel shortages) that is highly suggestive. A higher price of any particular fuel has two important effects: first, it discourages the use of energy in general by making it more expensive, and, second, it encourages shifts to other sources of energy which have become comparatively cheaper. Recent studies suggest that both of these types of effects are significant, particularly over longer periods of time when more permanent types of adjustment can be made.

The scope for shifts among fuels is, in many instances, fairly straightforward and has been illustrated by some of our earlier discussion. In the electric-power industry as we have just seen, a modest effluent fee on sulfur emissions can induce power plants to shift (quite quickly, incidentally) to lower-sulfur coals or petroleum as a substitute for cheap, but high-sulfur, coal. Over the longer haul, such taxes provide incentives to seek out other sources of energy (nuclear, solar, and so on) that produce even less airborne waste.

To illustrate the many ways price incentives can generate energy and fuel savings, it may be helpful to consider a familiar case: household energy consumption. Most Americans use large amounts of electricity for lighting and heating and the operation of various appliances. It might seem that there would be little scope for adjustment in these "necessary" uses in response to price

---

[28] Russell, *Residuals Management in Industry.*

changes. If, for example, we were to ask a sample of people how they would respond to, say, a 25 percent increase in electricity rates, they would probably wince and say that there isn't much one can do but pay the higher bill; they might instruct their families to be more zealous about turning out unnecessary lights, but that would seem to be about it. This, however, appears to be far from true. Robert Halvorsen (among others) has found a substantial price responsiveness of residential electrical use.[29] His estimates indicate, for example, that a 10 percent increase in the price of electricity will lead to a reduction in household electricity consumption considerably greater than 10 percent.

We have operated (until recently) in an energy-plentiful environment; fuel and electricity have been comparatively cheap, and there was little incentive for conservation. However, the growing scarcity and increased price of energy sources can be expected to induce more energy-conscious behavior on the part of individuals.[30]

In the preceding section we saw for the case of the Delaware Estuary that the use of fees, rather than direct controls, would result in large cost savings. The same appears to be true for the abatement of air pollution. A research team supported by the EPA has recently completed a similar sort of study for emissions of sulfur into the atmosphere.[31] They began by assembling engineering estimates of the abatement costs for the major point-source emitters of sulfur in two metropolitan areas, St. Louis and Cleveland (including, incidentally, a wide range of industrial activities: power plants, petroleum refineries, commercial, industrial, and institutional boilers, etc.) Second, the study assumed that the objectives of the program are given by current emission standards in the two metropolitan areas. The authors were then able to make the desired cost comparisons. First, they estimated the annual abatement costs of the existing sulfur-emission programs; these are programs of direct controls which specify maximum emission levels for each polluter in order to reduce aggregate sulfur discharges by 55 and 78 percent, respectively, in St. Louis and Cleveland. These cost estimates appear in Table 18–2; they are $49.5 million in St. Louis and $45.5 million for Cleveland.

Next, the research team made estimates of the costs of achieving these same reductions in total sulfur emissions by a uniform fee per pound of sulfur discharges. They found that an effluent fee of about thirteen cents per pound

---

[29] See his "Residential Electricity: Demand and Supply" (Ph.D. dissertation, Harvard University, 1973).

[30] There also appears to be considerable scope for adjusting the price of energy over different times of the day, week, and year to provide an incentive to shift usage to off-peak hours. As we mentioned before, the use of "peak-load" pricing has proved highly effective in the telephone industry. Differential charges for the use of electricity by time of day (and, perhaps, even by season) might serve to even out somewhat the demand for power. There is evidence that in Europe peak-load pricing has produced substantial reductions in peak demand for electricity by industrial users.

[31] Tayler H. Bingham and Allen K. Miedema with Philip C. Cooley and John C. Mathews, *Final Report, Allocative and Distributive Effects of Alternative Air Quality Attainment Policies* (Research Triangle Park, N.C.: Research Triangle Institute, October 1974).

TABLE 18-2

ESTIMATED COSTS OF REDUCTIONS
IN SULFUR EMISSIONS
(millions of dollars per year)

	Direct Controls	Emission Charges
St. Louis	$49.5	$29.1
Cleveland	45.5	34.2

Source: Tayler H. Bingham and Allen K. Miedema with Philip C. Cooley and John C. Mathews, *Final Report, Allocative and Distributive Effects of Alternative Air Quality Attainment Policies* (Research Triangle Park, N.C.: Research Triangle Institute, October 1974), pp. 54, 93.

would induce the required curtailment of emissions in St. Louis, while in Cleveland the charge would have to be approximately nineteen cents per pound. The estimates indicate a substantial savings from the use of fees: in St. Louis the savings are on the order of $20 million annually and in Cleveland roughly $11 million. In St. Louis the cost of compliance with current emission standards is some 70 percent higher if achieved through direct controls than by effluent charges.[32]

4. Reusable Containers: Oregon's "Bottle Bill"

We discussed in earlier chapters the growing problems of solid-waste disposal and resource scarcity. These problems are obviously not unrelated: the resources consumed in the production of disposable bottles and cans, for example, become wastes which must be dumped into landfills or bodies of water.

One promising approach for dealing simultaneously with both these problems is illustrated by Oregon's "Bottle Bill."[33] In 1971, the governor of Oregon signed into law an act to encourage the adoption of reusable beverage containers; the new legislation aimed at reducing the litter in Oregon but also it was hoped

---

[32] The source of these cost savings is the large differences in abatement costs among various polluters. It is much more expensive, for example, for petroleum refineries to reduce sulfur emissions than it is for steam-electric power plants. Effluent fees take advantage of these differentials by inducing a larger response from those with relatively low costs of abatement.

[33] Our discussion of the Oregon experience draws heavily on E. Claussen, *Oregon's Bottle Bill, The First Six Months* (Washington, D.C.: U.S. Environmental Protection Agency, 1973); Charles M. Gudger and Jack C. Bailes, *The Economic Impact of Oregon's "Bottle Bill"* (Corvallis, Ore.: Oregon State University Press, March 1974); and Don Waggoner, *Oregon's Bottle Bill Two Years Later,* Oregon Environmental Council (Portland, Ore.: Columbia Group Press, 1975).

to decrease solid wastes. The bill, which became effective in October of 1972, included the following basic provisions:

1. All carbonated beverage containers (with the exception noted below) sold in the state must carry a minimum refundable deposit of five cents.
2. Refillable containers used by more than one beverage manufacturer *may* be certified by the Oregon Liquor Control Commission. A certified container can have a minimum deposit of two cents.
3. The deposit on any carbonated beverage container *must* be refunded by any retailer or wholesaler who sells that kind, brand, and size of beverage.
4. Metal containers having detachable parts may not be sold in Oregon.

In brief, the intent of the legislation was to induce the re-use of beer and soft-drink containers through a mandatory refundable deposit. A reduced deposit for standardized containers was meant to encourage their use by several different beverage manufacturers to reduce the costs of sorting and returning them.

The effect of these price incentives on the composition and the return of containers in the first two years of operation was striking. In Table 18–3 we find that, during the first year of the new legislation (the "transition period"), non-returnable bottles disappeared from circulation. Returnable bottles accounted for 96 percent of take-out beer sales and 88 percent of soft drink sales. During the second year over 90 percent of both beer and soft-drink containers were of the returnable type with cans declining to less than 10 percent. The lower deposit has also been effective in producing greater uniformity of containers: by early 1973, nearly all nondraft beer was sold in standard, reusable eleven-ounce "stub-bies." (Even Miller High Life Beer, long associated with a tall, clear glass bottle, appeared in the brown stubby.)[34]

What fraction of returnable bottles are actually being returned? The evidence is again striking. Gudger and Bailes have found the Bottle Bill to be associated with an 88 percent reduction in the number of beverage containers found in the state's solid waste (see Table 18–4). This has as its counterpart a pronounced decline in the amount of roadside litter. The Oregon State Highway Department has carefully monitored the response through monthly litter counts on twenty-five to thirty one-mile sections of Oregon highway since October 1971. Although there has been some controversy over the precise comparability of some of the "before" and "after" litter counts, it seems clear that Oregon's

---

[34] Curiously enough, this seems to have been accomplished with little change in price to con-sumers (not including the refundable deposit), or impact on the volume of sales. In their recent study of the economic effects of the Bottle Bill, Gudger and Bailes of Oregon State University could find no support for the hypotheses that the Act would result in reduced sales of beverages or significantly higher prices to consumers. In fact, their calculations sug-gest that savings in container costs have more than offset the added expense associated with the retailer's collection and sterilization of the returned containers. Sales have continued to grow about in line with historical experience, and prices are about the same as those in neighboring Washington State with no such legislation.

TABLE 18-3

OREGON BEVERAGE CONTAINERS

	Before	Transition	After
Beer			
Returnable Bottles	36%	96%	96%
Nonreturnable Bottles	31%	0	0
Cans	33%	4%	4%
Soft Drinks			
Returnable Bottles	53%	88%	91%
Nonreturnable Bottles	7%	0	0
Cans	40%	12%	9%

Source: Don Waggoner, *Oregon's Bottle Bill Two Years Later,* Oregon Environmental Council (Portland, Ore.: Columbia Group Press, 1975) pp. 21-22.

highways are substantially cleaner. One study estimates the reduction in litter to be 72 percent.[35]

This evidence is quite impressive. A relatively modest deposit on beverage containers in Oregon has induced an increase in the use of refillable containers from 45 percent in 1972 to over 90 percent in 1973 and 1974, and a decline in the beverage containers found in solid waste and litter of about 90 percent and 70 percent respectively.

One further aspect of the Oregon experience is very revealing. Effective environmental programs will typically impose costs, sometimes in a relatively concentrated pattern, on certain businesses and individuals. The Bottle Bill is no exception. In particular, the increased use of refillable containers means reduced demand for the products of container manufacturers and increased handling costs for producers and distributors of malt and carbonated beverages. The proposed bill predictably generated an active opposition from these interests. Since the enactment of the Bottle Bill, the battle has continued in the courts, with attempts to have the Act declared unconstitutional. However, in December 1973, the Oregon Court of Appeals upheld the constitutionality of the Act and, in the following February, the Oregon Supreme Court refused to review the decision.

---

[35] Waggoner, *Oregon's Bottle Bill,* p. 16. This decline may seem a little less impressive in light of a national study which indicated that, in an item-by-item count, beverage containers constitute only about 20 percent of roadside litter. See Tayler H. Bingham and Paul F. Mulligan, *The Beverage Container Problem: Analysis and Recommendations,* prepared for Office of Research and Monitoring, U.S. Environmental Protection Agency (Washington, D.C.: U.S. Government Printing Office, September 1972). However, it is noteworthy that such containers account for over 60 percent of the *volume* of litter; moreover, one study in the midwest found that consumer perception of roadside litter seemed to be based more on volume than on frequency. See Midwest Research Institute, *The National Impact of a Ban on Nonrefillable Beverage Containers: Summary Report* (Kansas City, Mo., 1971).

TABLE 18-4

NUMBER OF BEVERAGE CONTAINERS PER YEAR
IN SOLID WASTE (millions)

	Pre-Bottle Bill	Post-Bottle Bill	Reduction
Bottles	174	40	134
Cans	263	12	251
Total Beverage Containers	437	52	385

Source: Charles M. Gudger and Jack C. Bailes, *The Economic Impact of Oregon's "Bottle Bill"* (Corvallis, Ore.: Oregon State University Press, March 1974), p. 67.

This experience reemphasizes the fact that the cost of environmental programs is likely to fall most directly and heavily on particular groups, and they can be expected to oppose such measures energetically. This is a matter of great importance, for we have stressed that it bears both on the essential equity or fairness of various environmental measures *and* on their political feasibility.

The apparent success of the Oregon Bottle Bill has generated great interest in other states; Vermont, for example, has followed suit with its own bill requiring deposits on containers, and there was, predictably, a strong reaction from container manufacturers. Gladwin Hill of the *New York Times,* in a survey in 1974 to determine the response in other states to the Oregon experience, found that powerful lobbies had sprung up to resist the introduction of similar legislation elsewhere and had, in fact, been extremely successful.

> One afternoon last spring, two buses pulled up at the state Capitol at Lincoln, Neb., loaded up with state legislators and public officials, and took them 60 miles to Omaha for a festive evening, courtesy of the Falstaff Brewing Company.
>
> A few days later a bill to ban nonreturnable beverage containers, opposed by brewing and other interests, was killed in a legislative committee.
>
> Nebraska was one of 15 states—among them New York—where, a New York Times survey shows, the "beverage lobby" so far this year has fended off proposals to emulate Oregon's widely acclaimed "bottle law." [36]

Industry has often sought to undermine such effective measures by suggesting that they amount to a denial of freedom to the consumer (the freedom to pollute unpenalized!) and that some vaguely specified alternatives (perhaps voluntary recycling) are the more practical alternative. As an example, we re-

---

[36] "Debate Widening on 'Bottle Law'," *New York Times,* August 3, 1974, p. 52.

print a letter to the Editor in the *New York Times* (March 11, 1974) from the director of communications services for American Can Company:

To the Editor:

The "bottle bill" now in effect in Oregon and Vermont, where it mandates a refund on beer and soft-drink containers, has met with less than the overwhelming success indicated in your Feb. 19 editorial.

Predictably, one-way bottles and cans have virtually disappeared from stores in those states, which accounts for the "resounding success" in reducing beverage-container litter. However, these containers, according to piece-count surveys by the Oregon Highway Department and others, never accounted for more than 20 per cent of total roadside litter.

What *is* happening in Oregon is that consumers are paying $10 million more a year for beer and soft drinks than they did before the bottle bill became law. Retail price increases due to costs of handling, storing, washing, returning and refilling bottles have far exceeded those in neighboring states. Oregon (and Vermont) consumers are denied their free choice of container, and they are asked to return only two types of packages out of thousands of one-way items stocked in stores. And finally, a large part of the Oregon cleanup results stems from the fact that the state has more than doubled its normal highway litter pickup effort.

The economic impact in these two states, where there are virtually no jobs related to can-making and bottling and where much of the system was in returnables to begin with, has been minimal. But in New York and in other heavily populated areas the impact on the processing and distribution system would be disastrous.

The real answer to product disposal lies in resource recovery and solid-waste management, not in a token return to a returnable system that would choke food stores with unsanitary empties. Resource recovery systems that separate and process garbage for recycling and energy recovery are coming on stream—in St. Louis, Chicago, Nashville, Baltimore, San Diego and other cities.

Simplistic, hurried responses to environmental problems do not address themselves to real issues.

New York legislators should be encouraged to reject Oregon-type proposals—as did lawmakers in 39 states last year—and to move forward to positive solutions to the litter and solid-waste problems.

John F. McGoldrick
Darien, Conn., Feb. 20, 1974

The battle over bottle bills thus continues with both sides recording victories and losses. In the fall of 1976, for example, bottle bills appeared on the ballot in four states. The voters of Michigan, despite vigorous campaigns by the container and beverage industries, enacted by a wide margin a law requiring a five-cent deposit on all standardized containers (usable by more than one company) and ten cents on all other containers. The electorate in Maine passed a bill which imposes a standard five-cent deposit on beverage containers. Both bills prohibit flip tops. However, bottle referenda were defeated in Colorado and Massachusetts. In the latter state, industry spent nearly $2 million in campaigns to defeat the proposed law, yet the bottle initiative lost by less than one percent of the votes. As of December 1977, there are four states which require deposits on beverage containers: Maine, Michigan, Oregon, and Vermont.

The response to the deposits continues to be impressive. In a summer-long experiment in California's Yosemite National Park during 1976, the park concessionaire charged a five-cent deposit on each beverage container sold (bottles and cans).[37] Midway in the experiment, the return rate was close to 80 percent. A park official noted that people of all ages were out picking up cans.

5. The Problem of Pesticides

An area of great concern in the ongoing ecological debate is the potential environmental threat from the heavy use of pesticides for pest control and the applications of other chemicals to the soil to increase crop outputs. The most dramatic case has been that of DDT. Its contributions to the well-being of humanity in terms of both the control of malaria in the tropics and notable expansions in agricultural production are matters of record. However, scientists have noticed side effects of an increasingly disturbing character. Early on they recognized the decline of certain bird populations as a consequence of decreases in eggshell thickness; there are now fears of a major degrading effect on the larger ecosystem with possible health dangers to humans as well. The result has been a series of state and federal restrictions on the use of DDT, which now amount to a virtual ban except for very restricted uses.[38]

The pesticide problem would, at first glance at least, appear to be one best handled by regulation—by the prohibition of the use of dangerous chemicals. This certainly is the approach that has generally been employed; we know of no case in which fiscal incentives have so far been used in this area. But there are a number of studies of agricultural production functions that indicate a wide range of substitutes for dangerous pesticides, whose use would be encouraged substantially by fiscal incentives.

Agricultural economists have for many years estimated "production func-

---

[37]Jerry Uhrhammer, "The Point of No Returns," *Sports Illustrated*, August 2, 1976, pp. 42–46.
[38]For a useful discussion of the DDT problem, see Orie L. Loucks, "The Trial of DDT in Wisconsin," in John Harte and Robert H. Socolow, eds., *Patient Earth* (New York: Holt, Rinehart, and Winston, 1971), pp. 88–111.

tions" for the outputs of almost all cash crops.[39] A production function is simply a relationship that describes how much output is generated by differing combinations of inputs. This sort of information permits one to determine the trade-off between different inputs (e.g., how much additional land a farmer must put into cultivation to compensate for a reduced use of a fertilizer). By altering the prices of different inputs (e.g., taxing chemical fertilizers), environmental authorities can induce desired modifications in patterns of input usage. The great range for substitution is apparent from experiments in agricultural production. As an illustration, we reproduce in Figure 18-1 a diagrammatic description of an actual production relationship involving outputs of corn. For example, the curve labelled "40" shows the variety of pairings of phosphates and nitrogen (fertilizers) that can yield an output of forty bushels of corn per acre. Note the striking range of substitution possibilities: forty bushels of corn per acre can be obtained, for example, by employing either 300 pounds of phosphates (P_2O_5) and 125 pounds of nitrogen (point A), or alternatively, by the use of only 100 pounds of phosphates and 235 pounds of nitrogen (point B).

Another feature of this production function is of particular interest. While in the intermediate ranges of input combinations there is a wide scope for substitution, the potential for additional substitution diminishes as the use of one input is continually reduced.[40] In Figure 18-1, for example, when the use of nitrogen is cut to 120 pounds per acre, it becomes extremely expensive (in terms of the additional phosphates necessary) to reduce nitrogen input even further and still maintain an output of forty bushels per acre. This is important for many production processes, because it may be relatively inexpensive to induce major cutbacks in certain inputs, but extremely costly to prohibit their use altogether. Fiscal incentives can be particularly effective here: by taxing inputs whose heavy use may cause substantial environmental damage, an environmental authority can eliminate them in all but their essential, most valuable uses.

Such a policy can, in principle, be applied to pesticides. Recent studies suggest that there is a considerable range of substitution of cropland for insecticide use (that is, the use of more acreage to compensate for reduced pesticides). But the scope of the substitution appears to exhibit wide geographical differentials: It is much cheaper in the Southeast and South Plains of the United States to substitute cropland for insecticides than it is in Appalachia.[41] One study estimates that, if the 40.8 million acres of cropland that were diverted from production under government land-retirement programs in 1967 had been culti-

---

[39] See, for example, the collection of studies in Earl O. Heady and John L. Dillon, *Agricultural Production Functions* (Ames, Iowa: Iowa State University Press, 1961).

[40] In economic terms, this is a diminishing "marginal rate of substitution."

[41] See the table below from Max R. Langhorn, Joseph C. Headley, and W. Frank Edwards, "Agricultural Pesticides: Productivity and Externalities," in Allen V. Kneese and Blair T.

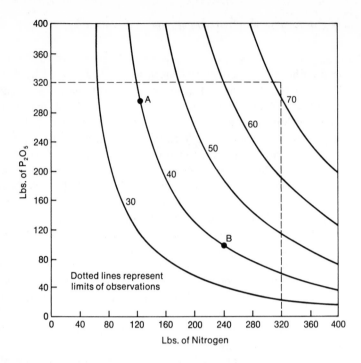

Figure 18-1   Corn Yield Using Different Combinations of Fertilizers.

Source: Reprinted by permission from *Agricultural Production Functions* by Earl O. Heady and John Dillon © 1961 by Iowa State University Press, Ames, Iowa 50010.

Bower, eds., *Environmental Quality Analysis* (Baltimore: Published for Resources for the Future by The Johns Hopkins University Press, 1972), p. 192.

MARGINAL RATES OF SUBSTITUTION AND ELASTICITY OF SUBSTITUTION
OF CROPLAND FOR INSECTICIDES, BY REGION, 1964

Region	Marginal Rate of Substitution[a]	Elasticity of Substitution[b]
Appalachian	-33.19	-2.70
Corn Belt	-10.03	-4.35
Delta	-256.47	-14.89
Lake	-0.80	-8.16
Pacific	-24.06	-6.49
Mountain	-0.97	-7.77
Southeast	-3,257.00	-326.67
South Plains	-547.17	-170.04
United States[c]	-13.24	-6.49

[a]Ounces of insecticide reduced per one acre increase in cropland.
[b]Percentage decrease in insecticides per one per cent increase in cropland.
[c]Excluding Alaska and Hawaii.

vated, farmers could have reduced insecticide use by 70 to 80 percent with no change in crop output.[42]

What is even more to the point is that there are a large number of different and substitutable pesticides, and the number is growing with the active research seeking more effective nonpersistent insecticides which promise fewer undesirable side effects. Moreover, farmers are finding a number of alternatives to the heavy use of pesticides. In particular, many are turning to a new strategy of "pest management" involving a variety of techniques to reduce damage to crops instead of a blind reliance on eradication of pests by use of hazardous pesticides.[43] The pest-management approach entails cultivation practices that discourage infestation and reproduction of the pest, the development and planting of varieties of crops that are pest resistant, the introduction of other insects or microbes that prey on the pest, and the use of pesticides only at the critical times of pest invasions when crops are vulnerable.

The use of price incentives to encourage the use of smaller quantities of insecticides and the substitution of those using more innocuous chemicals could be highly effective in reconciling our goals of increased agricultural output and improved environmental quality. Where there is evidence that a particular pesticide or chemical may constitute a serious threat to health, an outright ban on its use may, of course, be appropriate, but for less threatening products, fiscal inducements may permit more desirable adjustments in agricultural practices.

6. The Use of Fiscal Incentives to Reduce Congestion

Congestion and all its attendant discomforts—noise, air pollution, and time delays—have made life a good deal less pleasant in most of our cities and, more recently, in many suburban communities. The primary response to the congestion problem has taken the form of urban planning with reliance on architectural redesign and the encouragement of mass-transit systems. While these approaches are no doubt of basic importance, the relevant issue for our survey in this chapter is the potential role (if any) of price incentives, such as road tolls or parking fees, in the control of congestion.

A number of economists have contended that, in principle, the pricing of road facilities represents a most effective means to reduce traffic.[44] The argument is once again based on the concept of external costs: a driver entering a crowded road imposes costs on the other users of the road by slowing traffic.

---

[42] Ibid.

[43] Jane E. Brody, "Farmers Turn to Pest Control in Place of Eradication," *New York Times,* August 1, 1976, pp. 1, 22.

[44] See, for example, William S. Vickrey, "Economic Efficiency and Pricing," in Selma J. Mushkin, ed., *Public Prices for Public Products* (Washington, D.C.: The Urban Institute, 1972), pp. 53–72.

Empirical studies indicate that this effect is by no means minor; costs of congestion in terms of time delays rise rapidly with additional vehicles, once crowding sets in. A set of tolls is in many respects an appealing device for the relief of congestion, for it forces drivers to take into account the costs they impose on others. More specifically, by varying tolls by time of day with higher rates applying during peak-hour traffic, incentives can be provided not only to reduce the total amount of traffic in the course of the day, but also to shift vehicle trips to off-peak periods when there is less congestion. Similarly, parking taxes offer a means to reduce the number of automobile trips into a city.

Unfortunately, our experience with the use of price incentives to relieve congestion is rather limited; there are few careful studies of their effects and their findings are not wholly consistent. There are, however, two cases in which the effects of parking taxes have been shown clearly.[45] The first involved a dramatic increase in parking meter rates in 1966 in an area of about 1.7 square miles of Central London. In this area, the rates on about three-quarters of the meters were raised by 400 percent [from six pence (7¢) per hour to six pence per fifteen minutes], while the remainder were increased to six pence per half hour. London traffic authorities collected data on the time required to find a parking space, park, and walk to a specified destination before and after the rate increases; in addition, journey times through the affected areas were also measured. The findings, indicated in Table 18-5, are quite striking. Parking times fell dramatically in the zones with large rate increases. In areas with the greatest increases in rates, the time needed to find a vacant parking space declined from about six minutes to one minute. The London experiment thus suggests a substantial sensitivity to parking fees.

In contrast to London, a parking tax experiment in San Francisco appears to have had much more modest results. In October 1970, the San Francisco Board of Supervisors imposed a 25 percent parking tax on parking lots throughout the city; the tax continued in effect until July 1972, when it was reduced to 10 percent. While there are some serious problems of interpretation regarding the results, the evidence seems to suggest that there was only a relatively small reduction in parking in the city. Kulash estimates that a 10 percent increase in the price of parking would result in a 3 to 4 percent reduction in the volume of parking. While this is by no means negligible, the general effect on the overall traffic level in San Francisco was indiscernible. This emphasizes several major weaknesses of parking taxes as means to ease traffic congestion. First, they have no effect on "through trips," which constitute a significant fraction of the traffic in most cities. And second, they are likely to divert passenger traffic from private vehicles to taxis which obviously won't do much to relieve traffic con-

---

[45] For a survey of this evidence, see Damian Kulash, *Parking Taxes for Congestion Relief: A Survey of Related Experience* (Washington, D.C.: The Urban Institute, 1974); see also Kulash, *Parking Taxes as Roadway Prices: A Case Study of the San Francisco Experience* (Washington, D.C.: The Urban Institute, 1974).

TABLE 18-5

IMPACTS ON PARKING DIFFICULTY IN CENTRAL LONDON RESULTING FROM INCREASED PARKING METER CHARGES

Parking Rate Change	Average Number of Minutes Required to:											
	Find a Vacant Meter Bay			Enter & Vacate the Bay			Walk to & from Destination			Complete Entire Park-and-Visit Operation		
	Before	After	% Change	Before	After	% Change	Before	After	% Change	Before	After	% Change
None (6d/hr–6d/hr)	3.55	3.32	– 6	.47	.52	+11	5.75	5.53	– 4	9.77	9.37	– 4
100% (6d/hr–1s/hr)	3.45	1.40	–60	.50	.42	–16	4.19	3.24	–23	8.14	5.06	–38
400% (6d/hr–2s/hr)	6.10	1.04	–83	.56	.37	–34	6.04	2.94	–51	12.70	4.35	–66

Source: Damian Kulash, *Parking Taxes for Congestion Relief: A Survey of Related Experience* (Washington, D.C.: The Urban Institute, 1974), p. 28. Kulash cites as his source, J. Inwood, "Some Effects of Increased Parking Meter Charges in London, 1965," Road Research Laboratory Report No. 7, Harmondsworth, 1966.

gestion. What promises to be more effective (where feasible) are tolls on the roads, tunnels, and bridges which provide access to congested areas.

7. Summary and Conclusion

Our survey of the impact (both actual and potential) of fiscal incentives on polluting activity suggests that charges can be a powerful policy tool for protection of the environment. There is typically a considerable range of choice among methods of producing a particular output, and pollution charges can often tip the scale in favor of processes that do minimal environmental damage.

To help pull together the wide variety of material covered in this chapter, we present in Table 18-6 a systematic summary of the cases that we have examined. As the table indicates, the evidence supporting the effectiveness of fiscal measures comes from a wide variety of sources: *actual* responses to pricing incentives in terms of fees on BOD emissions, deposits on returnable beverage containers, higher prices for domestic use of electricity, and parking fees; studies of the *potential* response to fees on airborne emissions of sulfur and particulate matter; and studies of the wide scope of substitutability in processes of production. Moreover, studies of both air and water pollution suggest that the fee approach promises major costs savings in the achievement of our environmental objectives. We stress that, although our outline of case studies is undoubtedly not exhaustive, we do think that evidence is accumulating to make the most compelling case for the *effectiveness* of fees. The question posed at the beginning of this chapter, "But will fees work?" must be answered with an emphatic "Yes."

Before concluding our survey, we want to emphasize that the effects of fiscal incentives reported in this chapter are, in most cases, on the conservative side. We have examined, for example, a number of synthetic studies that predict the response to such things as effluent charges on the basis of *existing* techniques of production. Such studies, however, cannot take into account the development of new, less expensive, *and* less damaging productive methods. The imposition of fees on pollution emissions establishes incentives not only to reduce emissions but also to search for new ways to produce goods and services with fewer adverse side effects on the environment. In fact, in the longer run, this may be much the more important effect.

This does not mean, of course, that fees can always be employed or that they are necessarily the preferred policy instrument in every circumstance. There will surely be cases where other policy approaches are appropriate or where some mix of policies offers the best alternative. Our next task is to examine some of these other measures in the chapters that follow.

TABLE 18-6

EFFECTIVENESS OF PRICING INCENTIVES: OUTLINE OF EMPIRICAL STUDIES

Type of Study & Case	Description of Study	Findings	Comments
1. Studies of *actual* responses to systems of pricing incentives			
a. Ruhr River Basin (Kneese and Bower).	Historical description of water-quality management in Ruhr Basin.	High quality of water in presence of heavy industrial activity.	
b. Use of municipal sewer surcharges in U.S. on industrial waste discharges (Elliott & Seagraves).	Statistical study of comparative response in BOD emissions and water usage across 35 U.S. cities.	Significant reductions in both BOD emissions and water intake associated with higher level of surcharge.	Highly aggregative; findings not too reliable.
c. Effect of municipal surcharges on poultry processing plants (Ethridge).	Statistical study of response in BOD emissions and water usage in several plants.	Higher surcharges associated with significantly lower levels of both BOD emissions and water intake.	Less aggregative than Elliott-Seagrave study; findings more reliable.
d. Response of household usage of electricity to variations in its price (Halvorsen).	Statistical study of price responsiveness of residential electrical use.	Significant price effects of sizeable magnitude.	Longer-run response in terms of improved designs of dwellings and appliances promise yet greater savings in energy.
e. Recycling of beverage containers (Oregon's Bottle Bill).	Series of studies of effects of deposits on beverage containers, on extent of recycling, and reductions in litter.	Dramatic increase in use of returnable containers and measurable decreases in litter on highways.	
f. Effects of fees on traffic congestion (London and San Francisco).	Statistical studies of effects of parking taxes in London and San Francisco on amount of parking.	Large increases in parking fees associated with striking reductions in parking time in London; smaller fees with more modest effects in San Francisco.	

TABLE 18-6 (Continued)

Type of Study & Case	Description of Study	Findings	Comments
2. "Synthetic" studies of potential responses to fees.			
a. Sulfur emissions in electric-utility industry (Griffin).	Uses linear-programming model with cost data to estimate response of sulfur emissions to various levels of fees.	Modest fee should induce major reductions in emissions.	
b. Airborne emissions of particulate matter (Watson).	Uses cost and engineering data to estimate reductions in particulate matter from various fees.	Modest fee should induce striking reductions in emissions.	
c. Emissions of air and water pollutants by petroleum-refining industry (Russell).	Uses cost and engineering data to estimate effect of fees on several different pollutants.	Modest fees should induce major reductions in emissions of water-borne wastes; less effective in decreasing sulfur emissions.	
3. Studies of cost-effectiveness of alternative policy techniques.			
a. Costs of water-pollution abatement (Delaware Estuary study).	Study of comparative costs of uniform quotas versus effluent fees in attaining dissolved oxygen objectives.	Fees promise cost savings on the order of 50 percent (as much as $10 million per year).	
b. Costs of reducing airborne sulfur emissions (Cleveland and St. Louis).	Study of comparative costs of reducing sulfur emissions to target level by uniform quotas and fees.	Fees should result in savings of roughly 20 to 40 percent ($10 to 20 million in each city).	

TABLE 18-6 (Continued)

Type of Study & Case	Description of Study	Findings	Comments
4. Studies of substitutability in processes of production.			
a. Beet-sugar industry (Löf-Kneese).	Use cost and engineering data to determine cost of reducing BOD emissions.	Great flexibility present; large reductions in emissions achievable at small cost.	Implication: Modest effluent fee should induce quite large cutbacks in BOD emissions.
b. Pulp and paper industry (Council on Economic Priorities).	Study of water usage and emission of pollutants by different mills.	Indicates wide variety of processing with great potential for reducing emissions of pollutants.	Doesn't provide basic cost information.
c. Pesticides (Heady and Dillon).	Study of agricultural production functions including pesticides as inputs.	Find great substitutability among different pesticides and between pesticides and other inputs.	Implication: Taxes could have significant impact on types and quantities of pesticides used.

19

Moral Suasion:
USES AND ABUSES

There are a number of dedicated environmentalists who seem, in the last analysis, to pin their hopes on a moral resurgence: a resolve by the general public to stop damaging the environment. Campaigns of moral suasion have tried to persuade people to avoid wearing furs taken from endangered species, to stop littering, and to use products such as unleaded gasoline or phosphate-free cleansers. Voluntaristic response is the basis of many trash recycling programs, carpooling plans, and calls to industry to recognize its social responsibilities. The claim is that, ultimately, nature will be protected from man when and only when the public recognizes its moral responsibilities toward nature's gifts.

Economists have been highly skeptical of this approach; they generally have little faith in the dependability of good intentions and pledges of virtuous behavior. Instead, economic analysis focuses on the importance of policies that work to make individual self-interest coincide with the public interest. Even when they believe that something significant can be gained by trying to change public attitudes, economists usually doubt the availability of effective means to produce such a change. Judging from the record, government agencies are far more adept at levying fines, imposing prison sentences, and collecting taxes, than in changing public values.

Economists have also been wary of the use of voluntarism as a diversionary tactic. When an effective environmental program (that threatens some vested interest) is proposed, often those threatened find it expedient to urge the superiority of voluntary compliance, in order to block the enactment of the program. We will see that the fear of this sort of diversion under the cover of voluntarism has not been entirely groundless.

Since voluntarism has been closely associated with programs for the recycling of household wastes, we will begin with a study of voluntary recycling programs in a number of U.S. towns and cities.[1] The evidence indicates that prospects for an effective program of voluntary recycling of household trash and garbage are far less promising than is widely supposed.

Nevertheless, we will suggest in this chapter that voluntary compliance does have several significant and useful roles to play and that some of our colleagues have been a bit too ready to reject it out of hand. This does not mean that advocates of the approach have always sought to employ it where it is most appropriate, but appropriate uses it does have. One such case is the brief, but acute, emergency in which rapid implementation of alternative measures is difficult and costly. Happily, experience suggests that, in these instances, circumstances for effective voluntary cooperation are likely to be the most favorable.

A second category for which voluntarism may be appropriate encompasses instances in which the effectiveness of alternative instruments requires onerous and costly surveillance. This is apt to be true where (as in the case of litter in an isolated area) substantial environmental damage is the accumulated product of a large number of minor acts by many individuals, each act difficult to observe, insignificant by itself, and following no simple and regular pattern. In this case there may be no realistic and acceptable alternative to moral suasion, whatever doubts one may have about its effectiveness and practicality.[2] Ultimately, the issue of the effectiveness of voluntary compliance can only be settled by the facts and so we turn next to some evidence on this matter.

1. Experience with Voluntary Programs:
The Case of Recycling

Recycling is an instructive instance of the use of voluntarism for protection of the environment. In recent years, a number of local trash recycling centers have sprung up in various parts of the country. Their operations typically rely upon a considerable outlay of effort on the part of local residents; instruc-

---

[1] In addition to the issue of voluntarism, there are several technological problems inherent in the recycling of household garbage and trash that present formidable obstacles to recycling. For the interested reader, we describe the character of these problems in Appendix B.

[2] Obviously, voluntarism is not the only means available to reduce litter. We have already discussed the use of deposits on containers for the purpose; alternatively a few heavy fines on the individuals who are occasionally caught in the act can have a deterrent effect. But it seems unlikely that these methods can eliminate all but a negligible residue of litter.

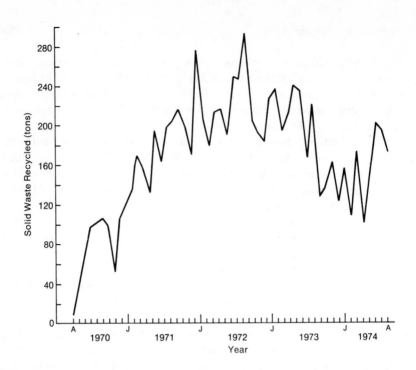

Figure 19-1   Total Solid Waste Recycled (tons), Berkeley Recycling Program, 1970-74.

Source: *Second Annual Report, 1973-74, Community Solid Waste Reduction and Recycling Program,* Berkeley, California, p. 28.

tions often require local participants to wash bottles and cans, separate bottles by color of glass, tie newspapers into bundles, and sometimes deliver them to a central collection place.

Before we accumulated any figures from voluntary recycling centers, we had some definite preconceptions about the likely findings. In particular, we expected to find that these programs would be launched in a burst of enthusiasm with rather respectable levels of initial participation, but would then gradually die off as interest flagged and the required labors came to seem increasingly burdensome. Our expectations were that, after the passage of some months, most recycling programs would simply have petered out.

This seems not to have been the case. Figures 19-1 through 19-5 summarize the available data for five different communities: Berkeley, California; the military installation at the U.S. Air Force Academy near Colorado Springs, Colorado; South Brunswick Township, New Jersey; the Park Slope district in Brooklyn, New York; and Princeton Borough, New Jersey.[3] The time series run

---

[3]These five recycling programs were selected because of the availability of systematically recorded data. The data themselves are reported in Appendix A to this chapter.

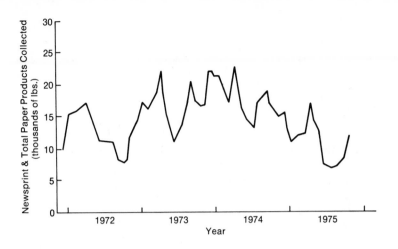

Figure 19-2 Total Newsprint and Paper Products Recycled, U.S. Air Force Academy Recycling Program, 1971–75 (thousands of pounds, three month running averages).

Source: 1971–April 1973: Col. G. Dana Brabson, Director, U.S. Air Force Academy Recycling Program; May 1973–November 1975: Capt. Harry E. Colestock, Assistant Professor, Department of Economics, Geography and Management, U.S. Air Force Academy, Colorado.

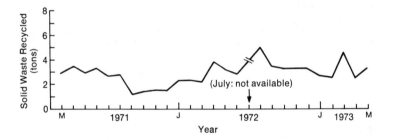

Figure 19-3 Total Solid Waste Recycled (tons), South Brunswick Township Recycling Program, Kendall Park, New Jersey, 1971–73.

Source: Mrs. Anne Kruger, South Brunswick Township Recycling Program, Kendall Park, New Jersey. For data from which figure was drawn, see Appendix A, Table 19-A1.

for about two to four years, and it is obviously dangerous to generalize from so brief an experience. Yet the figures do not indicate anything like the precipitous drop-off in participation that we had expected. In all the programs studied, the tonnage seems to have shown a mild increasing trend or to have remained about constant aside from more or less random fluctuations.

It would seem then that voluntary recycling programs, if they do tend to die out, certainly do not necessarily fade out in short order. However, these

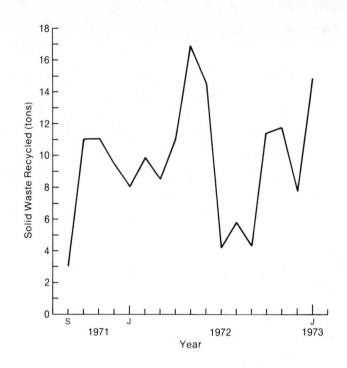

Figure 19-4   Total Solid Waste Recycled (tons), Park Slope Recycling Program, Brooklyn, N.Y., 1971–73.

Source: Mr. Bob Furman, Director, Park Slope Recycling Program, Brooklyn, New York. For data from which figure was drawn, see Appendix A, Table 19-A2.

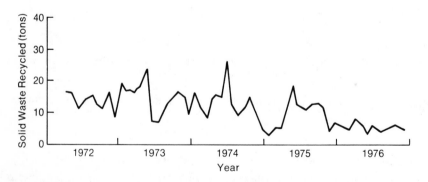

Figure 19-5   Total Solid Waste Recycled (tons), Princeton Borough Recycling Program, 1972–76.

Source: Sewer Operating Committee, Borough of Princeton, New Jersey. For data from which figure is drawn, see Appendix A, Table 19-A3.

TABLE 19-1

TOTAL AMOUNT OF SOLID WASTE GENERATED IN BERKELEY
COMPARED TO TOTAL AMOUNT RECYCLED, 1971-74 (tons)

Date	Solid Waste Generated & Not Recycled, (tons)	Recycling Program, Solid Waste Recycled, (tons)	Percentage Recycled
1971	39,582	2,036	5%
1972	40,898	1,940	5
1973	39,806	2,660	6.7
1974	38,814	1,783	4.6

Source: *Second Annual Report, 1973-74, Community Solid Waste Reduction Recycling Program,* Berkeley, California, p. 30.

observations do not mean that voluntary recycling programs have been a glowing success. Rather, they seem to have had a rather negligible (though constant) impact, when measured against the total amounts of waste generated in these communities. In Figure 19-6 and Table 19-1 total amounts of solid waste generated are contrasted with amounts recycled for Princeton Borough and Berkeley. In neither case did the voluntary recycling program handle more than 8 percent of the solid wastes of the community.[4]

This contrasts sharply with the experience in Hempstead, Long Island, where newspaper recycling was mandated by local ordinance. Householders there were required to put bundled newspapers out on their curbs on designated days. The reported compliance rate was extremely high: it was estimated that some 80 percent of the waste newspaper was handled by the program with much of the remainder apparently going to charitable organizations that had previously established newspaper-collection programs.[5] It has also been estimated that the town was saving approximately ten dollars per day in incineration

---

[4]Apparently elsewhere there have been programs that were somewhat more successful. In Briarcliff Manor, New York, it is reported that in 1971 a voluntary program managed to produce a 15 percent reduction in the amount of solid waste sent to local landfills (Linda Greenhouse, "Garbage Recycling Helps Out a Village," *New York Times,* March 15, 1972, p. 61). It is also reported that in Louisville a curbside pick-up was recycling approximately 16 percent of the newspapers in the city (David R. Stevens, "How Louisville, Kentucky Developed a Paper Recycling Program," *Rodale's Environment Action Bulletin* 3 [April 15, 1972]:2). We have been unable to get any details on these programs.
[5]We do not report the trends in collection figures, which show a sharp upward movement. However, that is misleading, since it reflects the gradual inclusion of more of the town's areas in the program's collection routes.

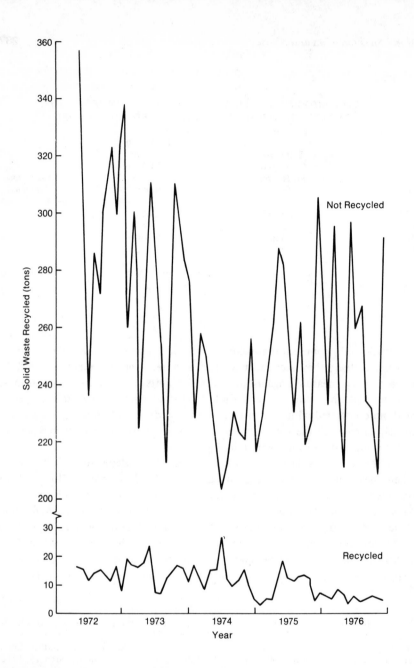

Figure 19-6   Total Solid Waste Recycled Compared with Total Solid Waste Not Recycled (tons), Princeton Borough, New Jersey, 1972–76.

Source: Sewer Operating Committee, Borough of Princeton, New Jersey. For data from which figure is drawn, see Appendix A, Table 19–A3.

costs.[6] (We should note that, despite the success of this program in terms of community participation, it was forced to discontinue in 1974, when the bottom dropped out of the newsprint market.)

2. Experience with Other Types of Voluntary Programs

Experience in a number of other voluntary programs suggests that they also have had little impact, *except where they provided tangible incentives for participation.*

A. Voluntary Use of Unleaded and Low-Lead Gasoline. Several years ago, in response to increasing public concern about air quality, a number of oil companies began to market unleaded and low-lead gasolines. It was hoped that consumers would switch voluntarily to the new fuels despite their slightly higher cost. In 1972 Shell Oil Company introduced "Shell of the Future," unleaded gasoline. It could be used only in late-model automobiles, and it was about two cents per gallon more than regular gasoline.[7] Shell of the Future captured only 5 percent of sales; the company was forced to take it off the market and replace it with "Super Regular," a leaded gas. Exxon's low-lead gasoline, introduced in August 1970, accounted for 21 percent of sales during the introductory phase (when heavily advertised), averaged 18 percent for awhile, but later declined to 15 percent of sales. Standard Oil of California introduced an unleaded gasoline in 1970; sales were less than 4 percent of its total volume.[8]

B. Sales of Auto Emission-Control Kits. Another interesting case of voluntary compliance was a recent attempt by General Motors to market relatively inexpensive auto emission-control kits in Phoenix, Arizona. The emission-control device, designed for use on most 1955-67 models, reduced emissions of hydrocarbons, carbon monoxide, and nitrogen oxides by roughly 30 to 50 percent. The cost of the kit (including installation) was about fifteen to twenty dollars. Despite an aggressive marketing campaign, only 528 kits were sold. From this experience, G.M. concluded "only a mandatory retrofit program for pre-1968 cars, based upon appropriate state or local regulation, can assure the wide

---

[6] Letters of November 28, 1972, and April 28, 1975, from William J. Landman, Sanitation Commissioner, Town of Hempstead, Long Island, New York.

[7] A better test of voluntarism would have occurred if there were no two-cent differential; as it was, the two-cent premium created an incentive against a voluntary appeal from the start.

[8] The sources for these figures are: Shell Oil Company–*Newsweek,* August 28, 1972, p. 71; Standard Oil Company–letter of November 17, 1972, from D. L. Bower, Director and Vice President, Standard Oil of California; Exxon Company–letter of January 19, 1973, from H. H. Meredith, Jr., Coordinator, Public Affairs Department, Environmental Conservation, Exxon Company.

participation of car owners that would be necessary to achieve a significant effect on the atmosphere."[9] The Chrysler Corporation had a similar experience. In 1970 Chrysler built 22,000 used-car emission-control kits. More than half remain in its current inventory; in fact after 1970 Chrysler's sales were negative, since about 900 more kits were returned than shipped.[10]

C. Car Pooling. Environmental awareness combined with recent gasoline shortages has led to renewed proposals for car pooling as a voluntary measure to save gasoline and reduce pollution. This is a rather old idea and several examples suggest how it is likely to work out in practice.

Operation Oxygen, a car-pooling program started in 1971 by the Burroughs Corporation in Pasadena, California was able to reduce the number of cars in the plant parking lot from 600 to 400. The key to the success of this program was human interaction and interest, lots of visibility for the program, and *many incentives* (e.g., free gas, preferential parking and raffles with prizes).[11]

Share-the-Ride-Day in October 1971 was an attempt by a Los Angeles citizen group, *Stamp Out Smog,* to reduce air pollution through car pooling. It was endorsed by many groups in the area and advertised on television and radio.[12] In addition, supporters of the program distributed 160,000 handbills and provided extra bus services. Unfortunately, the day was a dismal failure. There was apparently no difference in traffic density or air quality. Busses carried only a handful of passengers. The organizing group concluded that, while most people think car pooling is a good idea, when it comes right down to it they will not make the sacrifice.[13]

During the Second World War car pooling was promoted officially in many states because of fuel, rubber, and automobile shortages. The U.S. Office of Price Administration organized the car-pooling effort and took advantage of the gas-rationing rules to encourage participation. *In particular, they offered additional gas to people who were prepared to drive with a full car.* In order to qualify for the supplementary gasoline, a driver had to round up three additional passengers. From the outset, OPA made clear that this was a concrete way to help the war effort. Companies responded by coordinating car pooling for their employees. In 1943 the Office of Price Administration claimed that "the

---

[9] "Highlights of G-M Car Emission Control Kit," General Motors Corporation publication, July 13, 1972, p. 1.
[10] Letter of August 17, 1972, from D. A. Destino, of McCutchen, Black, Verleger & Shea, Counselors at Law, Los Angeles, California.
[11] T. B. Conerly III and F. F. Kroger, "Public Attitudes Towards Reducing Air Pollution Through Carpooling," Pacific Southwest Universities Air Pollution Association, Los Angeles, California, 1972, pp. 22–23.
[12] KFI, a Los Angeles radio station, in conjunction with Share-the-Ride-Day, offered its listeners matching services for car pools but less than 100 listeners responded. Many people in fact wrote to the station to express their disapproval of car pooling, and said they were afraid of strangers and did not like the inconvenience.
[13] Conerly and Kroger, "Public Attitudes," pp. 25–26.

nationwide average mileage has been reduced by over 50%."[14] Clearly, in addition to wartime patriotism, this program relied heavily on the very tangible inducement of supplementary gasoline; moreover, it is very likely that many of the participants had no other acceptable means of transportation available to them.

D. Voluntary Energy-Saving in Oregon. As a final illustration we consider Oregon's program for energy saving. According to the *New York Times*

> The experience of Mr. McCall [Governor Tom McCall of Oregon, a state noted for environmental awareness] and other residents of Oregon makes two points clear. Voluntary efforts can save small but significant amounts of energy. . . . In response to the emergency [the power shortage of 1973], Governor McCall last summer ordered [state agencies to undertake] a wide range of conservation measures . . . [and] asked the public to cooperate by similarly reducing uses of power. The state achieved savings of more than 20 per cent, but the public failed to respond. Consumption for the first month dropped only 2 per cent, considerably below the 7 percent target.[15]

The lesson to be drawn from the cases we have reviewed seems moderately clear. Voluntary programs can have an effect on environmental problems, but the magnitude of that effect is usually very small. There seems to be a highly reliable group of citizens (perhaps 5 percent of the population) whose consciences move them to participate voluntarily in environmental programs. However, where really substantial changes are considered essential, it appears that programs that require participation (or programs offering substantial and tangible inducements in the form of rewards or penalties) are usually necessary to carry out the job. The 80 percent participation rate in Hempstead's mandatory recycling program far overshadowed that of any voluntary program we studied. Similarly, both of the successful car-pooling programs in our sample offered tangible rewards to participants.

3. Voluntarism and Environmental Damage by Industry

Whatever the potential of voluntarism for individual behavior, there are overwhelming reasons to expect it to be ineffective in dealing with environmental damage whose source is private industry. It is important to recognize that we are not judging the morality and virtue of the individual business manager. What we are arguing is that management, whether it be composed of arch-

---

[14] Ibid., p. 2.
[15] Steven V. Roberts, "The Governor Has a Cold, or How Energy Saving Goes in Oregon," *New York Times,* November 12, 1973, p. 12.

angels or minions of Lucifer, simply does not have the option of voluntarily undertaking substantial and effective environmental programs.

The pressures of competition force the individual firm to struggle constantly to prevent its costs from exceeding those of its rivals. The same market forces that impose productive efficiency also effectively prevent management from making substantial expenditures, direct or indirect, to promote what it considers the social welfare. Even if a conscientious management were to consider the installation of expensive emissions-control equipment, it could not do so as long as a single competitor were prepared to continue business as usual (without emission controls) and pass the "savings" on to the consumer. A management willing to take that risk would soon find itself driven out of business with its conscience clear, but its gesture empty.

Predictably, in these circumstances, there has been a considerable gap between business' glowing accounts of its own accomplishments and the actual magnitude of its achievements. Newspapers report many cases in which public-relations releases have greatly exaggerated what companies have actually done. *Newsweek* reported the case of Potlatch Forests, Inc., a company with

> . . . the dubious distinction of being the only industrial mill in the U.S. to have been the subject of separate air- and water-pollution abatement hearings before Federal authorities. However, its advertising asserted, "It cost us a bundle but the Clearwater River still runs clear." . . . But what [the firm] neglected to mention in its national ad campaign was that the picture [in the advertisement, presumably taken near the plant] had been snapped some 50 miles upstream from the company's pulp and paper plant in Lewiston, Idaho [where it] dumps up to 40 tons of suspended organic wastes into the Clearwater and nearby Snake River every day.[16]

After citing several other such cases, the article goes on to report some more routine examples.

> Even without bending the facts, companies may inflate their ecological contributions with half-truths. FMC Corp. recently took out double-page spreads in national publications to boast of its participation in the $3.8 million Santee, Calif., water-reclamation project, which converts sewage into water fit for swimming and boating. Conveniently omitted was the fact that FMC did no more than sell the project some $76,000 worth of pumps and equipment. Nor was there any mention of the company's inorganic-chemical plant in West Virginia which daily dumps more than 500,000 pounds of wastes, mostly toxic, into a nearby river, according to the Federal Power Commission.
>
> Similarly, Union Carbide began an ad boosting its efforts to reduce auto pollution with the observation that "Driving through this beautiful

---

[16]*Newsweek*, December 28, 1970, p. 49.

land of ours, you can get all choked up." To the residents of the Kanawha Valley in West Virginia this is hardly news. So much smoke billows from the chimneys of Union Carbide's main ferroalloy plant there—28,000 tons of particulates a year—that a nearby Roman Catholic church had to encase an outdoor statue of St. Anthony in a fiber glass case to protect it from corrosion.[17]

We should reiterate that these illustrations are not meant to prove the dishonesty of businessmen, but rather to show that the rules of the game offer little leeway to firms. In the words of E. Lee Rogers, past general counsel of the Environmental Defense Fund, "If I were a company president right now, I wouldn't do any more than I had to on the pollution front, because that would hurt my company more than its competitors."[18]

Another aspect of the relationship between business and moral suasion is the use of voluntarism as a diversionary tactic. Those businessmen who have a vested interest in continued abuse of the environment can use this approach to lure public support from other programs that promise effective environmental protection. There is a wealth of examples of businesses providing active support for voluntary recycling as one strategy in their campaigns *against* fees or regulations on containers. The *New York Times,* for instance, cites a recent case in Minneapolis in which "the Theodore Hamm Browning Company and Coca-Cola Bottling Midwest, Inc., announced that they would sponsor 'the most comprehensive, full-time recycling center in the country'." This pledge, however, was apparently intended to forestall a proposed local ordinance to ban the use of nonreturnable beverage containers.[19]

EPA representatives recently resigned from the advisory board of Keep America Beautiful, Inc., the leading antilitter organization in the U.S. KAB is

[17]Ibid., pp. 49–50.

[18]Ibid., p. 51. To go a step further, the notion that firms should by themselves pursue what their managements consider to be the welfare of society is, at least to some economists, a rather unattractive (perhaps even frightening) proposition. Voluntarism suggests, or rather demands, that corporate managements use their enormous financial resources (which really belong to others) to influence the social and political course of events. But this amounts to asking business to select what it regards as *right* for society!

The danger is brought out most clearly by recent demands from various groups that business firms abstain from investment in certain countries whose governments pursue undesirable or "immoral" policies. The firm may be asked to eschew investment in countries that repress or persecute ethnic groups, whose governments trample civil liberties or are aggressive militarily, or whose leaders simply oppose with sufficient vigor United States foreign policy. But should one not question the wisdom of the notion that American business should attempt to arrogate to itself the determination of our foreign policy? An increase in corporate power is probably the last thing that those who call for greater "corporate responsibility" would want. Yet that, paradoxically, is precisely where some of their prescriptions lead.

[19]Robert A. Wright, "Waste Recycling Effort Found to Lag," *New York Times,* May 7, 1972, p. 57. For another example, see the letter from the Director of Communications Services for the American Can Company to the Editor of the *New York Times,* March 11, 1974, which is reproduced in Chapter 18.

owned and operated by the bottle and can industry and its Board of Directors includes the presidents of Pepsi-Cola, Coca-Cola, the U.S. Brewers Association, the Glass Blowers Association, National Can Company, and many others. What KAB's famous crying Indian television ad and its slogan, "People start pollution, people can stop it," never mention is the real cause of litter—the throwaway mentality encouraged by those same can and bottle manufacturers. KAB has never spoken in favor of returnables since that would be unprofitable for its backers.[20]

4. The Role for Voluntarism in Environmental Policy

Despite the reservations discussed earlier in this chapter, we believe that voluntary programs *do* have several useful roles. First, they can be of value where an imperfect budgetary process denies the public sector funds necessary to carry out the popular will. Second, they can be helpful in instances where policing is difficult and other policy approaches are ineffective. Third, and perhaps most important, they may be quite valuable in brief, unpredictable environmental crises.

A. Voluntarism and Imperfect Fiscal Arrangements. Our society has come increasingly to rely on volunteers to help out in hospitals, prisons, schools, and other institutions. In Great Britain, for example, there is a fine and effective system of volunteer lay magistrates, many without legal training, who handle the many minor cases which seem to have left the American court system hopelessly clogged. Though critics have raised questions about the competence and reliability of unpaid personnel and the equity of the system, more frequently supporters of the approach argue that without volunteers "society literally can't afford" the services they provide.[21] The workings of the budgetary process in a political environment may well result in a systematic underfinancing of certain public activities such as schools, hospitals, and the legal system. In such cases, the efforts of volunteers may be the only means to provide the service at adequate levels.[22] For environmental programs in particular, volunteers can (and do) assist with the upkeep of natural preserves, the improvement of slum areas,

---

[20]For more on this, see William H. Rodgers, *Corporate Country, A State Shaped to Suit Technology* (Emmaus, Pa.: Rodale Press, Inc., 1973).

[21] The approach has, incidentally, been attacked as an instrument of exploitation, particularly of women. See, "NOW Attacks Volunteerism—But Others Rally to Its Defense," *New York Times,* June 7, 1974, p. 41. NOW, National Organization for Women, is a feminist group.

[22]Voluntary contributions may sometimes also be of better quality than those available on a commercial basis; a notable case in point, to which we will return presently, is blood donations. Blood from paid donors is notoriously a more frequent source of hepatitis and other forms of infection than is that from volunteer donors.

the cleanup of accumulations of trash, and many other activities. In sum, the community may be forced to rely on voluntary personnel to carry out a number of its programs, simply because its fiscal processes have made it difficult to hire the necessary employees.

B. Voluntarism and Problems of Surveillance. The effectiveness of both direct controls and fiscal incentives depends on the ability to detect and monitor activities that damage the environment. If we do not know how much waste a plant discharges into a waterway, we cannot determine how much it should be taxed, or even whether there has been a violation of the legal standards underlying a program of direct controls. There are cases, however, where any sort of systematic surveillance, even a rough approximation, is extremely difficult. An example is littering by picnickers or campers in a wilderness area. The isolation and dispersion of these persons and the unpredictability of their movements mean that effective policing is all but impossible. Here only two approaches seem practical: (a) an appeal to conscience and (b) the imposition of disproportionately heavy penalties upon a few people who happen to be caught, "as an example to others." While the latter option might work, many people would surely consider it manifestly unfair.

That being the case, voluntarism may in such circumstances be our only acceptable alternative. And while its workings may be far from perfect, it is still better than nothing. Certainly, the protracted and extensive exhortations of "Keep America Beautiful" have not removed the beer cans from the banks of streams or picnic grounds, nor have they eliminated the litter from the city streets, yet one may conjecture that without such efforts matters might be significantly worse. An example of an apparently successful voluntary program of this sort is the "Smokey the Bear" campaign for the prevention of forest fires.[23] For over thirty years Smokey has been educating and urging Americans to prevent forest fires. In a study sponsored by the U.S. Forest Service, it was found that the program had been extremely effective in entering the consciousness of every age group: 98 percent of children interviewed, 95 percent of teenagers, and 89 percent of adults could identify the Smokey symbol correctly. Moreover, they associated the symbol with fire prevention (94 percent of children and 98 percent of adults understood the Bear's role), and were aware of Smokey's message that human carelessness is a major cause of forest fires.[24]

---

[23] In speaking of this program as "successful" we do not mean to enter into the dispute over the *desirability* of a substantial reduction in forest fires. Some biologists maintain that the program has interfered with the natural selection process and has thereby weakened in the long run the viability of the forests or, at least, of some of its species. We merely are suggesting that the program seems to have made striking progress toward its chosen objective by relying on publicity and voluntary cooperation of the public.

[24] "Public Image and Attitudes Toward Smokey the Bear and Forest Fires," A Study Conducted for Cooperative Forest Fire Prevention Program (U.S. Department of Agriculture, Forest Service, June 1968), pp. 7–52.

During the thirty years of the campaign, the number of forest fires caused by humans in the United States has been reduced from 201,511 in 1942 (when the program was initiated)[25] to about 105,000 in 1971.[26] Over this period, the burned area decreased from 31,000,000 acres to less than 3,000,000.[27] Moreover, "this reduction was achieved even though the land area for which statistics are kept has doubled."[28] One study calculates that this represents an "overall reduction by 75 percent in the number of fires which would otherwise be expected to occur."[29] Another notes that "Smokey Bear is credited with saving the United States more than $10 billion in timber that didn't burn, in recreation areas that were not destroyed, in watersheds that were not blackened."[30] These results are obviously subject to a number of important assumptions and qualifications. Nevertheless, the evidence is surely consistent with the conclusion that the program has been highly successful.

C. Voluntary Cooperation in Brief Emergencies. A third, and potentially very important, role for voluntary measures arises when society is threatened by perils that are brief and unpredictable but very significant. A sudden and unexpected atmospheric inversion over a city which leads to life-endangering pollution levels will require rapid changes in activity patterns and no time for the institution of elaborate enforcement machinery. Much may depend upon the willingness of landlords to cease operation of their incinerators, and upon the co-operation of myriad small enterprises each of which contributes only a small quantity of emissions. Authorities may be able to control the activities of the few largest polluters and certain very visible activities involving many individuals (such as the driving of private vehicles). However, they will find it far more difficult to supervise many other economic processes and may have to resort to moral and social pressures.

Fortunately, in such cases, where the need is urgent and the duration of the problem is likely to be brief, the record of voluntary cooperation seems to be relatively good. People do seem willing to rally round in emergencies, so long as the demands upon them do not drag on.[31] Two examples drawn from recent experience seem consistent with this evaluation:

---

[25] "Smokey Bear's Forest Fire Prevention Campaign," U.S. Department of Agriculture, Forest Service, Publication M-1920, p. 1.
[26] *America Burning, The Report of the National Commission on Fire Prevention and Control* (Washington, D.C.: U.S. Government Printing Office, 1973), p. 107.
[27] "Smokey Bear's Forest Fire Prevention Campaign," p. 1.
[28] Mal Hardy, "The Legend of Smokey Bear," *National Parks Magazine* 43 (January 1969): 18. (Reprinted by permission from *National Parks and Conservation Magazine*, January 1969. Copyright © 1968 by National Parks and Conservation Association.)
[29] *America Burning*, p. 107.
[30] "Smokey Bear's Forest Fire Prevention Campaign," p. 1.
[31] Another requisite for the success of voluntary programs in emergencies is that *universal* cooperation not be necessary. If 98 percent of the residents cooperate during an air inversion, the program may be completely effective. This contrasts with cases such as a wartime

a. A Blood Donation Case. Our first example is a case where blood supplies to hospitals were in short supply. Unlike the British voluntary blood program,[32] American hospitals rely mostly on paid donors for supplies of blood. The *New York Times* reported, "According to the American Association of Blood Banks, only a small fraction—about 3 percent—of those Americans qualified to donate blood actually do so. There is a definite shortage of blood donors."[33] This results in periodic blood crises. During one such crisis in September 1970, the blood reserves in New York City hospitals had fallen to less than a single day's supply. The response to a massive appeal for voluntary donations was described as "fantastic"; donors stood in line up to 90 minutes to give blood.[34] Two years later there was another major crisis. In December of 1972 blood reserves dropped to less than half a day's supply, and there was again an urgent appeal for donations. According to the *New York Times,* "The Greater New York Blood Program reported yesterday that the response to its appeal for blood donations to alleviate an acute shortage in the metropolitan area was slow, but improved as the day wore on."[35] By January 6, 1973, the *Times* reported that the response to appeals for blood donations was considerable. "The load of donors at [one] center soon jumped from the norm of 100 to 150 a day to a high of 500 on Thursday.[36]

b. A Water Shortage Case. A second illustration is provided by the appeals for voluntary conservation of water supplies in New York City in periods of shortage. During the mid-1960s New York (and the entire northeast United States) suffered severe droughts, which depleted the supply of water in the main reservoirs. During the worst of the shortages, New York City officials sent out appeals to the general public to conserve water. According to the *New York Times* of November 3, 1963, "Responding to water conservation pleas, New York residents used 343 million gallons less than they usually do. . . . Last week, daily water consumption in the city dropped 49 million gallons, or 4.4 per cent, from the usual 1.2-billion-gallon consumption."[37] Similar savings, amounting to some 4 to 6 percent of normal consumption, were also reported in succeeding weeks.[38]

---

blackout of a city where a single light may give the target away to enemy bombers. There, pure voluntarism is clearly impractical.

[32] For a fascinating study of the subject, see Richard Morris Titmuss, *The Gift Relationship: From Human Blood to Social Policy* (New York: Pantheon Books, 1971).

[33] Lawrence K. Altman, "Use of Commercial Blood Donors Increases With Shortage in U.S.," *New York Times,* September 5, 1970, p. 12.

[34] Marc Kalech, "The Blood Crisis: A Great Response," *New York Post,* September 4, 1970, p. 3.

[35] Will Lissner, "Response to Blood Appeal Here Is Termed Slow, but Improving," *New York Times,* December 31, 1972, p. 36.

[36] George Vecsey, "Business Booming at Blood Center," *New York Times,* January 6, 1973, p. 31.

[37] *New York Times,* November 3, 1963, p. 55.

[38] See, for example, *New York Times,* November 10, 1963, p. 56, and November 21, 1963, p. 47.

In the summer of 1965 a new water shortage threatened the City and the voluntary conservation program was resurrected and expanded. Again, the program relied primarily upon public cooperation, but in addition, the City adopted several compulsory measures including restrictions on car washing, filling of swimming pools, and the operation of public fountains and fire hydrants. However, these restrictions were quite modest; the result was summed up in the Annual Report of the Delaware River Master for 1965:

> During the year New York made great efforts to conserve water and to avert a critical water shortage in New York City. Prior to April 1965 the City had engaged in a water conservation campaign for a year and a half. In April 1965 the campaign was intensified to apprise even more

TABLE 19-2

WATER USE IN NEW YORK CITY, JANUARY 1–OCTOBER 2, 1965:
ACTUAL CONSUMPTION, ESTIMATED NORMAL CONSUMPTION AND
ESTIMATED SAVINGS (millions of gallons daily)

Period	N.Y.C. from Municipal Sources	Probable Consumption[a]	Savings due to Conservation
Jan. 1–May 1	1064		
May	1041	1133	92
June 6–12	1063	1189	126
June 13–19	952	1084	132
June 20–26	1043	1216	173
June 27–July 3	1024	1204	180
July 4–10	970	1198	228
July 11–17	979	1232	253
July 18–24	987	1173	186
July 25–31	991	1208	217
Aug. 1–7	983	1174	191
Aug. 8–14	1003	1220	217
Aug. 15–21	1006	1229	223
Aug. 22–28	979	1195	216
Aug. 29–Sept. 4	925	1162	237
Sept. 5–11	930	1235	305
Sept. 12–18	937	1195	258
Sept. 19–25	991	1259	268
Sept. 26–Oct. 2[b]	906	1162	256

Source: The City of New York, Environmental Protection Administration, Department of Water Resources.

[a]Probable Consumption: Based on temperature–water consumption relationships for the years 1963 and 1964. Separate relationships of temperature vs. water consumption were developed for Saturday, Sunday, and holidays, for Mondays, and for the other weekdays. From comparable temperatures the 1965 probable consumption was determined.
[b]From October 3 to the end of the year the average weekly savings ranged from 163 to 250 millions of gallons daily.

TABLE 19-3

AVERAGE CONSUMPTION FROM MUNICIPAL SOURCES,
JULY 1–JANUARY 1 (millions of gallons daily)

	1965	1964	Difference	Percent Change
New York City	938.2	1160.2	–222.0	–19
Outside Communities	72.8	88.0	– 15.2	–17
Total	1011.0	1248.2	–237.2	–19

Source: The City of New York, Environmental Protection Administration, Department of Water Resources.

people of the water supply situation and to enlist their full cooperation in eliminating waste of water in home, business, and industry. City agencies curtailed to a minimum the use of water in their equipment, services and facilities. The results of the conservation campaign were seen in a decrease of 20 percent in consumption of water by the City during the latter part of 1965.[39]

Tables 19-2 and 19-3 provide the actual and predicted data on water consumption that underlie these calculations.[40]

5. Concluding Comments

Our findings suggest that there is a place for moral suasion in environmental programs, one which the economics literature has neglected. In practice, however, public officials have frequently turned to voluntarism in cases ill-suited

---

[39] Delaware River Master's Annual Report of 1965, in *Water Shortage of 1965,* publication of The City of New York, Environmental Protection Administration, Department of Water Resources, p. 5. A somewhat more bizarre success story took place in the summer of 1977 in the midst of a severe drought in northern California. After adopting a rationing program aimed at a 25 percent reduction in water consumption in the San Francisco Bay Area, local authorities found that the active co-operation of Bay Area residents led to more than a 40 percent fall in water usage. Water officials, finding themselves facing a large drop in revenues, rewarded the populace with the threat of an increase in water rates if water consumption did not increase! See the *Los Angeles Times,* June 30, 1977, pp. 1, 26.

[40] Yet another illustration of the effectiveness of appeals to conscience in brief emergencies is the public's response to the shortage of pennies during 1974 and the Treasury Department's appeal for the return into circulation of hoarded coins. In a letter of November 12, 1975 to us, the Acting Assistant Director for Public Services of the U.S. Mint commented:

Although we did award 158,469 certificates to individuals or groups for depositing over 2 million cents, it is only a partial indicator. This figure recognizes only those

to this approach.[41] Appeals to conscience certainly seem unlikely to produce emission-free vehicles, the recycling of any substantial quantities of wastes, or the elimination of industrial wastes from our waterways. Yet in each of these areas voluntary individual action has been widely advocated and frequently attempted. Voluntarism has a role, one which is important, but used inappropriately it can undermine rational environmental programs and sap the enthusiasm of dedicated environmental groups.

APPENDIX A

TABLE 19-A1

SOUTH BRUNSWICK TOWNSHIP RECYCLING PROGRAM, KENDALL PARK, NEW JERSEY—RECYCLABLE MATERIAL (GLASS AND ALUMINUM) BROUGHT TO CENTER (tons)

Date	Amount	Date	Amount	Date	Amount
Mar. 1971	2.9	Dec.	1.5	Sept.	3.4
Apr.	3.45	Jan. 1972	2.3	Oct.	3.2
May	2.9	Feb.	2.3	Nov.	3.25
June	3.25	Mar.	2.25	Dec.	3.25
July	2.6	Apr.	3.8	Jan. 1973	2.52
Aug.	2.64	May	3.1	Feb.	2.5
Sept.	1.2	June	2.7	Mar.	4.7
Oct.	1.4	July	N.A.	Apr.	2.5
Nov.	1.5	Aug.	5.0	May 1973	3.3

Source: Mrs. Anne Kruger, South Brunswick Township Recycling Program, Kendall Park, New Jersey.

Note: Corresponds to Figure 19-3 in text.

N.A. means not available.

that formally registered for the award. It does not reflect the number of cents put back into circulation by responsive citizens.

The success of the program may . . . be partially measured at the Federal Reserve Bank level. As you know, they distribute coin to commercial banks and accept coin deposits from them. Reports of this activity show that cent deposits from commercial banks which were averaging about $2-$3 million before the crisis, dropped to $230,000 between January and June in 1974. About six months after the campaign began deposits had increased to nearly $500,000. Eight months later, deposits increased to $1,850,000.

[41] One may well argue that reductions in water use are an example of a goal ill-suited to voluntarism, particularly in the long run. Despite the success of the program reported in the preceding section, more might well have been accomplished by metering and charging for water usage.

TABLE 19-A2

PARK SLOPE RECYCLING CENTER, BROOKLYN, NEW YORK—
RECYCLABLE MATERIAL (ALUMINUM, GLASS, PAPER, TIN, PLATE-STEEL)
BROUGHT TO CENTER (tons)

Date	Amount	Date	Amount	Date	Amount
Sept. 1971	3.125	Mar.	8.5	Sept.	4.40
Oct.	11.0	Apr.	11.0	Oct.	11.40
Nov.	11.0	May	16.9	Nov.	11.75
Dec.	9.5	June	14.5	Dec.	7.75
Jan. 1972	8.0	July	4.25	Jan. 1973	14.90
Feb.	9.9	Aug.	5.75		

Source: Mr. Bob Furman, Director, Park Slope Recycling Program, Brooklyn, New York.

Note: Corresponds to Figure 19-4 in text. Updated figures were not available because the center has closed down.

TABLE 19-A3

PRINCETON BOROUGH RECYCLING PROGRAM,
PRINCETON BOROUGH, NEW JERSEY—
TOTAL AMOUNTS RECYCLED AND NOT RECYCLED, 1972-76 (tons)

Period	Not Recycled	Recycled[a]	Period	Not Recycled	Recycled[a]
May 1972	356.9	16.2	May 1974	232.4	14.8
June	336.2	15.3	June	217.5	15.3[b]
July	236.2	11.6	July	203.3	26.6[b]
Aug.	285.7	13.8	Aug.	213.6	11.8
Sept.	271.8	15.1	Sept.	230.3	9.9
Oct.	306.9	12.2	Oct.	224.2	11.8
Nov.	323.3	11.1	Nov.	221.3	15.1
Dec.	299.9	16.6	Dec.	256.1	9.4
Jan. 1973	337.2	8.0	Jan. 1975	217.0	4.7[b]
Feb.	263.5	18.7	Feb.	228.8	3.3[b]
Mar.	300.1	17.0	Mar.	245.4	4.9[b]
Apr.	225.4	16.4	Apr.	259.5	5.0[b]
May	302.4	17.7	May	287.5	11.1[b]
June	309.7	23.6	June	282.2	18.3
July	277.8	6.8[b]	July	251.9	12.2
Aug.	254.2	6.8[b]	Aug.	231.1	11.3
Sept.	213.4	11.6[b]	Sept.	261.9	13.0
Oct.	309.9	14.3	Oct.	219.3	13.3
Nov.	297.0	16.6	Nov.	227.7	12.0
Dec.	283.5	15.5	Dec.	305.2	4.6
Jan. 1974	276.2	10.5[b]	Jan. 1976	272.9	7.3
Feb.	228.4	16.7	Feb.	233.6	N.A.
Mar.	257.9	12.0	Mar.	295.0	5.3
Apr.	249.6	8.2[b]	Apr.	236.8	8.6

TABLE 19-A3 (Continued)

Period	Not Recycled	Recycled[a]	Period	Not Recycled	Recycled[a]
May 1976	211.8	6.6	Sept.	234.7	5.0
June	296.1	3.6	Oct.	232.2	6.1
July	260.0	5.8	Nov.	209.5	5.5
Aug.	267.2	4.6	Dec.	290.8	4.6

Source: Sewer Operating Committee, Borough of Princeton, New Jersey.

Note: Corresponds to Figures 19-5 and 19-6 in text.
[a] Clear glass, green glass, and newspaper.
[b] Some data not available.

N.A. means not available.

APPENDIX B: *THE RECYCLING OF SOLID WASTE FROM HOUSEHOLDS*

As we have seen, voluntary programs have been widely used for recycling household trash. Even aside from the participation problems inherent in voluntary programs, there appear to be serious technological obstacles to the success of household waste recycling. There *are* promising possibilities for expanded recycling of industrial solid wastes. In particular, industrial plants typically generate concentrations of refuse at specific locations, which keeps transportation costs down; moreover, these plants are usually able to keep solid wastes in homogeneous batches so that no heavy sorting costs need be incurred. Much can also be done to stimulate the *reuse* of household products *before they are disposed of as trash* (by the use of returnable, instead of disposable bottles, for example). However, the recycling of household garbage *after it has been generated* presents serious difficulties.

Stimulated by funding from EPA and other sources, a number of research and "demonstration" projects have brought significant progress in the technology of recycling of household garbage. New or improved techniques have been designed for the separation of different types of waste, for thermal decomposition using wastes as sources of heat and energy, and for the recovery of various valuable resources such as metals, chemicals, paper, glass, petroleum products, fertilizers, etc.[1]

Nevertheless, despite this technological progress, the rate at which household wastes are recycled has hardly been encouraging. Many of the new methods have not gotten far beyond the drawing boards or pilot projects of modest scale. EPA reports that the ratio of recycled materials to total materials used actually

---

[1] See, for example, Midwest Research Institute, *Resource Recovery: The State of Technology* (1973), report on a research project sponsored by the Council on Environmental Quality.

exhibits a declining trend. For example, "waste paper consumption as a percent of total fiber consumption dropped from 23.1 percent in 1960 to 17.8 percent in 1969."[2] Since 1965 some two-thirds of the nation's re-refineries, which recycle used oil, have closed down.[3]

The main reason for this is that recycling does not yet pay. For most purposes it is less expensive to use virgin materials. As we saw in Chapter 7, this is in part the result of some perverse incentives in the tax structure. Depletion allowances (which have even been provided for sand used in glass making!) and other substantial tax benefits provide powerful financial inducements for the use of virgin resources,[4] with no similar incentives offered for the use of recycled materials.[5] Railroad transportation rates (approved by the ICC) are also said to discriminate against scrap metal and in favor of virgin ore.[6]

A second reason is historical. In the past, industrial plants have usually located close to the sources of virgin materials: mineral deposits, energy sources, and forests. Recycled materials, however, are collected primarily from the heavily populated metropolitan areas. Consequently, it costs more to transport recycled materials to the manufacturing plants than to transport the corresponding new materials. (Of course, if recycling were to become sufficiently attractive economically, plant locations could adjust appropriately.[7])

To understand the third and most important reason for the high expense of recycling, we must digress briefly into the technology of recycling. We note first that, with current techniques, the direct recovery of materials can probably reduce solid waste by only some 10 to 20 percent of its total weight. The remainder must still be handled by incineration, landfill, or some other method.[8]

Popular discussions of recycling seem to proceed on the assumption that there is a great demand for recycled materials. Unfortunately, this is not always the case. The market for recycled materials often requires products of high quality, which current separation technology usually can't provide except at un-

---

[2]*Environmental Quality, The Fourth Annual Report of the Council on Environmental Quality* (Washington, D.C.: U.S. Government Printing Office, 1973), p. 204.
[3]Sonia P. Maltezou, "The Economic Determinants of Waste Oil Recycling" (Ph.D. dissertation, New York University, 1977).
[4]According to EPA, tax advantages to virgin materials, including the depletion allowance, the foreign tax credit, favorable capital gains treatment, etc., taken as a percentage of raw materials price, amount to 11 percent for aluminum, 10 percent for pulp wood, 7 percent for iron ore, and 3.5 percent for glass sand. See EPA Report SW-122, Resource Recovery and Source Reduction, Washington, D.C., 1974, p. 33.
[5]*Environmental Quality*, p. 204. As recently as 1965 virgin lubrication oil was largely exempted from an excise tax, while blends of recycled and virgin oil remained subject to a tax of three cents per gallon. See Maltezou, "Waste Oil Recycling."
[6]The issue has been the subject of some dispute, and the size of the discrepancy in the rates, if any, varies with the terms in which it is measured—whether by weight or bulk.
[7]However, a reviewer points out that, if material processing plants were to relocate closer to metropolitan areas, there might be a rise in external costs from *their* emissions (which now occur in relatively unpopulated areas).
[8]See National Center for Resource Recovery, Inc., *Resource Recovery from Municipal Solid Waste, A State-of-the-Art Study* (Lexington, Mass.: Lexington Books, 1974), p. 44.

acceptably high cost. Most garbage is a hodge-podge of substances, each of which interferes with the reuse of the others. Metals and plastics cannot be used as fuels; food products interfere with the recovery of glass and metals; and so on. Various methods have been designed to separate particular materials from the mountain of miscellaneous garbage, but only one of these is relatively cheap and efficient: magnetic extraction of ferrous materials. No such effective techniques seem to be available for the isolation of a number of other materials, including some that contribute heavily to the bulk of the garbage and are a prime source of its health hazards.

The trends do not promise any easing of the problem. Most of the cost of waste disposal, as much as 80 percent and more on some estimates, is the expense of transportation.[9] Although "compacting" (a process in which the bulk of the garbage is reduced by compression) can achieve major savings in transportation costs, it obviously makes separation more difficult and hence increases the cost and reduces the purity (quality) of the recycled materials. Work is underway on methods which make some inroads on the separation problem. For example, there is a separation technique in which trash is first chopped into small bits and then blown through a vertical zigzag duct in which the lighter materials fly to higher levels than heavier ones. However, even this method has serious deficiencies; it requires, for example, the inspection of all the trash before it is shredded in order to separate out very hard items (such as case-hardened gears) or those that are potentially explosive.[10]

The vulnerability of recycling activity to economic conditions is illustrated by the recent history of the market for reprocessed paper. During the recession of 1974 the market for used paper all but disappeared. According to the *New York Times*, "The market for waste materials—especially old newspapers—has dropped so severely that some [voluntary collection] centers have had to close. They are choked with paper that once provided the income to keep them going and that now they cannot even give away. . . . *Some environmental groups, just to keep the recycling idea alive, have considered continuing operations, telling people that the material is going to be reused, but then carting it off to the dump.*"[11]

Rising fuel prices have made a secondary form of recycling, the use of

---

[9] See, for example, D. Joseph Hagerty, Joseph L. Pavoni, and John E. Heer, Jr., *Solid Waste Management* (New York: Van Nostrand Reinhold Co., 1973), p. 77.
[10] National Center for Resource Recovery, *Resource Recovery*, p. 40.
[11] [Our italics.] *New York Times*, December 22, 1974, p. 1. With the rise in industrial activity toward the end of 1975, the demand for waste paper resumed (*New York Times*, October 26, 1975, Sect. 3, p. 13). Demands for several other types of recycled materials fell also in 1974 (lead, zinc, and copper among them). These declines were considerably smaller than the 35 percent drop in the recycling of paper in the first quarter of 1974 (*New York Times*, April 11, 1975, p. 45). Yet the decline in the price of scrap copper from $1 to 42 cents a pound was not negligible. Incidentally, the recession also affected the *production* of waste. It was reported that "For the first time in anyone's memory—and probably for the first time since the end of World War II—the amount of trash and garbage being generated

wastes for the generation of heat and power, increasingly attractive. The usual method simply combines standard incineration with some sort of steam generation plant.[12] Though the heat obtainable from trash obviously varies with its composition, it has been estimated to run to about 5,000 BTU per pound compared to coal which offers about 12,000 BTU per pound.[13] However, here too, there are some serious problems. Not all trash is combustible and the remains must still be disposed of. Also, while trash is sometimes low in sulfur content, it still gives rise to a variety of pollution problems of its own. The materials that are burned emit fly ash which is commonly collected in a (characteristically acidic) water mixture (slurry). When disposed of, the slurry can soak into the soil and cause damage to nearby areas. Even more important is the concomitant malodorous air pollution consisting of particulates and gaseous byproducts of the combustion process.[14]

Recent reports indicate that fuel generation from solid wastes is still quite unattractive economically, and that only some half-dozen incinerator plants in the United States are equipped to recover the heat they generate. The reasons include the cost of the equipment and the fact that users of the heat are not usually located next to the incinerator. But the main impediment is the fact that the heat potential of solid waste is highly variable, so that standby equipment must usually be held available in order to provide a steady flow of heat or power at times when the fuel content of wastes happens to be low.

Solid wastes can also be used as landfill, although this too has problems. Unless special precautions are taken, it can create serious sanitation dangers; it can easily become a breeding ground for vermin and disease. Rain and streams that make their way through the landfill can pollute the groundwater in nearby areas. In addition, such landfill typically produces carbon dioxide and methane which is both inflammable and explosive. Costly "sanitary landfill techniques" designed to minimize these problems usually involve interspersal of solid wastes with both vertical and horizontal layers of earth to block the trash off into individual cells. The entire mass is then covered with several feet of earth leaving venting arrangements to permit the escape of the methane gas before it can accumulate. Yet, even sanitary landfill sites have not overcome all pollution problems, and, in addition, are not suitable for building. The organic portion of the wastes will decompose over a period of two to twenty years with a resulting settling of the surface of the landfill of anywhere from 2 to 40 percent (with something over 20 percent considered normal). Decomposition may also generate the emission of hazardous gas. Certainly, the use of such land for deeprooted crops is undesirable since roots will reach the toxic decomposing solid

---

by New Yorkers is declining . . . apparently . . . the victim of the recession (*New York Times,* March 27, 1975, p. 33). All of these observations tend to confirm the power of economic forces to affect the prospects for recycling.

[12] Hagerty, Pavoni, and Heer, *Solid Waste Management,* p. 156.

[13] National Center for Resource Recovery, *Resource Recovery,* p. 45.

[14] Hagerty, Pavoni, and Heer, *Solid Waste Management,* pp. 158-60.

waste. For all these reasons, it is sometimes suggested that sanitary landfill be used for recreation areas rather than building construction or for agriculture.

At any rate, the disposal of solid waste presents us with a set of relatively undesirable alternatives. As expensive and difficult as the recycling of household garbage may be, the limitations of landfill space and the assimilative capacity of the seas may compel us to turn to recycling techniques. As one recent survey concludes: "In any case, the ecological cost both in terms of the raw materials removed from the earth and the waste material returned now outweighs, in the minds of many, the financial cost to the individual consumer when it comes to garbage disposal."[15] And, as our findings suggest, this is not a problem we are likely to solve through voluntary efforts to recycle household refuse.

---

[15] Terri Schultz, "Garbage is No Longer Treated Lightly," *New York Times,* Sunday, March 6, 1977, p. E6.

20

The Role for Direct Controls

The case for a heavy reliance on pricing incentives for environmental protection is, we believe, a very compelling one. Yet, though direct controls may have gotten much the worst of the comparisons with pricing measures in the preceding chapters, we shall contend now that there remain some very important circumstances in which direct controls seem distinctly superior to fees. In particular, we shall argue that there are three types of conditions that suggest the use of direct controls: cases where metering of emissions is impossible (or prohibitively costly); instances of rapidly changing environmental conditions that may threaten real catastrophe; and situations involving extremely hazardous pollutants.

1. On the Importance of Metering[1]

Implicit in our earlier discussion of the application of effluent fees is the assumption that it is practical to meter effluents. In order to charge polluters for the quantity and, perhaps, the quality of their waste emissions, we obviously

---

[1]We are grateful to Ralph Turvey for discussions in which he stressed the importance of the metering issue.

must be able to measure these discharges. Economists have often been somewhat cavalier in their single-minded advocacy of pricing techniques without much consideration of the metering issue. The point is simply that, where metering is impractical, the use of effluent fees has to be ruled out. We should also stress that this renders infeasible any direct-control programs that require the measurement of waste discharges. For example, a program under which the environmental authority assigns emission quotas to each polluter is obviously impossible to administer if the agency is unable to determine levels of actual discharges.

There is, however, another type of direct control policy for which the monitoring of effluents is unnecessary. Table 15-1 distinguished direct-control programs which effectively assign emission quotas from those which require the use of specified processes of production or treatment procedures. This latter class of policy typically does not require metering of emissions; environmental officials need only inspect periodically to see that the designated equipment or procedure is in use and is operated at some prescribed standard of performance. While the specification of treatment procedures may theoretically be distinctly second best to the use of fees, the former may be the only feasible alternative where metering is impractical.

We note here that it is difficult to generalize on the feasibility of monitoring effluents, for the method of measurement varies with different pollutants. While the quantity of BOD (biochemical oxygen demand) is not easily measured, in other instances (such as the disposal of beverage containers by a commercial establishment) a numerical count may be all that is required. Obviously, the cost *and* the accuracy of metering will vary widely from one case to the next.

The processes for measurement of emissions of BOD into waterways and for discharges of particulate matter into the atmosphere illustrate the complexity and the possibility of large margins of error in the monitoring of some of the more important types of emissions.[2] The tests for BOD and particulates each require samples of the emissions which must be subjected to extensive laboratory tests.[3] Moreover, these samples must be handled with great care to prevent contamination. In the case of BOD, for example, there is a standard five-day test, but it does not capture the full oxygen demand of the waste; more than 100 days, in which the sample must be kept at a constant temperature, are required for full stabilization. On the average, the five-day test seems to measure about two-thirds of the oxygen demand in the case of domestic wastes, but this fraction varies widely from one set of effluents to another. For the interested reader, we have included a more detailed report on the metering of BOD emissions as

---

[2] We are grateful to Linda Martin for her assistance in this study.
[3] A reviewer points out that, in the case of particulate emissions, a test based on opacity observations is relatively inexpensive. There is, however, some sacrifice in accuracy. At low levels of emissions, the accuracy problems become so severe that opacity observations are not used at all.

Appendix A to this chapter to provide some sense of the degree of complexity and accuracy of current measurement procedures.

This is not to say that the metering of BOD emissions is wholly impractical. On the contrary, we will contend in Chapter 22 that, in spite of its complexity, it may still make sense to monitor the BOD discharges of at least major polluters. A somewhat more surprising case in which metering (and hence a system of fees) seems out of the question, at least for the near future, is noise pollution in urban areas. This is surprising because we can monitor noise levels as well as their various attributes (e.g., pitch, duration, and regularity) with great precision. The problem lies in determining the individual sources of the noise: passing vehicles, individuals, or animals. Except in the case of aircraft (with carefully recorded flight times and paths) or stationary construction sites, it simply is not feasible currently to meter the noise discharges of individual emitters. It may seem that a reasonable substitute for a set of comprehensive fees can be provided by charges on motor vehicles assessed as part of a regular annual inspection, with charges varying with the noisiness of the vehicle. Even this, however, is not very promising since the noise produced by a vehicle depends on how, where, and when the driver operates a truck, car, or motorcycle. Instead of metering and fees, it would appear that the control of noise pollution will have to rely primarily on controls and regulations that specify the use of particular equipment or procedures (for example, prohibiting large trucks from using particularly noisy recapped tires, from driving through main streets in the center city, or from travelling through residential areas at night). There may still be some ways in which fiscal incentives can assist indirectly in the regulation of noise levels. Public subsidies for subways or railroads, for example, may serve to reduce levels of motor-vehicle traffic with consequent decrease in congestion and noise.

At any rate, the practical matter of metering emissions is one we must face up to. Where metering is infeasible, the only alternative may be to prescribe a set of procedures, perhaps involving the use of certain pollution-control devices, to which firms and individuals must adhere.

2. Direct Controls Under Adverse Environmental Conditions

A second role for direct controls has its source in the inherent uncertainty of future environmental conditions. The damage to the environment from the discharge of a certain amount of BOD into a river or sulfur into the atmosphere does not depend only on the quantity of the pollutant, but also on the absorptive capacity of the waters or the air. The ability of the environment to assimilate a given emission may vary widely from one period of time to another. Modest levels of auto emissions, for example, may pose a negligible threat to human health and well-being during normal weather conditions when air movements are sufficient to disperse the pollutants. These same emissions, however, may have grave consequences during an atmospheric "inversion" which prevents the escape of the pollutants. In the same way, a river at its average flow may easily assimilate a relatively small BOD discharge, but a drought may lower the flow so much that even this small quantity of pollutant will reduce the level of dissolved oxygen to a critical value.

The point is that emission levels that are acceptable and rather harmless under usual conditions can, under other circumstances, become intolerable. To make matters more difficult, these "other circumstances" are often not predictable much in advance. We typically have only a few days notice of impending meteorological conditions, and the forecasts themselves are far from perfectly reliable.[4]

The environment itself thus exerts an important influence on the purity of air and water, an influence which is largely beyond our control and which often does not provide much advance warning. For example, weather variables bear a strong relationship to concentrations of sulfur dioxide. Higher wind velocity, a higher mixing height, more precipitation, and a higher temperature are all associated with lower levels of sulfur pollution. An analysis conducted for us indicates that the weather accounts for a substantial fraction of the variation in sulfur-dioxide levels in New York City.[5]

This may seem to have little bearing on our analysis of the design of environmental policy. But, in fact, it poses a very troublesome dilemma. Suppose that we set as our standard for environmental quality some target level of sulfur dioxide in the atmosphere or dissolved oxygen in a river. We must now establish a set of effluent fees sufficiently high to reduce emissions to a level consistent with our environmental standards. The problem is that the levels of permissible emissions will vary with environmental conditions: during times of normal air movements or river flows, the environment will be able to assimilate greater discharges of effluents than during periods of adverse conditions (such as stagnant air currents or periods of drought).

How high should the environmental authority set effluent fees? High enough to meet pollution standards during normal circumstances or sufficiently

---

[4]For problems of air pollution, we should not, perhaps, exaggerate the importance of this. Lester B. Lave and Lester P. Silverman point out, "Lave and Seskin (1977) show that the emphasis on [air pollution] episodes is misplaced. The variables most closely associated with mortality rates are not the highest air pollution measures, but rather are measures of cumulative exposure. . . . Thus, it would seem that questions of timing ought to be put aside in favor of concern over lowering the average air quality level" (Lave and Silverman, "Setting Environmental Priorities: Amenity vs. Health?" [paper presented at the 89th Annual Meeting of the American Economic Association, Atlantic City, N.J., September, 1976]; the work they refer to is L. B. Lave and E. P. Seskin, *Air Pollution and Human Health* [Baltimore: The Johns Hopkins University Press for Resources for the Future, 1977]).

[5]To investigate this issue somewhat more systematically, we have explored both the variability and the extent of environmental influences on several measures of air quality in New York City. The findings are described in Appendix B to this chapter.

high to assure these standards even during times of the most adverse environmental conditions? If the environmental authority opts for the higher fees to deal with unfavorable (as well as normal) circumstances, it is likely to impose a considerable cost upon the community. Higher fees will induce lower levels of waste emissions, and this implies additional costs of pollution abatement. Moreover, the extra expense may not be trivial; we have seen that the incremental costs of reducing pollution tend to escalate rapidly once emissions have already been cut to a comparatively modest level. Not only will the costs of the additional reductions in discharges be high, but they will be largely unnecessary. Only during relatively infrequent periods of adverse conditions will they be justified; under more typical conditions, the environmental standards can be met without them. This suggests that the environmental authority will do better to ease restrictions on emissions during normal times and tighten them during adversity.

In principle, it would appear that this could be accomplished simply by varying the levels of fees. There would be a "standard" level of fees that applies during periods of normal conditions and a higher schedule of charges that the authority would invoke when unfavorable conditions prevail. Unfortunately, this may not be a practical solution. The main problem is the short time horizon associated with the onset of adverse environmental conditions. We rarely know more than a few days in advance of an impending atmospheric inversion which will prevent the escape of pollutants. Under such circumstances, we simply cannot rely on fees to induce the necessary cuts in emissions. Over a short period of time, the response to changes in fees is highly uncertain. A business may, for example, decide that it is less expensive to pay the higher fees for a few days rather than undertake the expense of temporary alterations in pollution-abatement procedures. However, it is precisely during times of adverse environmental conditions that such uncertainty cannot be tolerated. The environmental authority must be able to curtail these emissions quickly *and* reliably.

Direct controls have clear advantages over pricing incentives in such situations. The most expedient course may simply be to prohibit temporarily certain polluting activities when environmental conditions begin to deteriorate. Some cities have, in fact, done just this. When air quality falls to some specified level, environmental officials invoke temporary bans on incineration; this delays the burning of trash until atmospheric conditions are adequate to disperse the smoke.

Pricing incentives are better regarded as a longer-run measure to bring basic pollution-abatement procedures into line with normal environmental conditions.[6] In brief, what we envision is a system in which fees provide a first line of

---

[6]It might prove desirable to have some regular and planned seasonal variations in the schedule of fees to accommodate the *usual* fluctuations in the environment from one season to the next. As one example, officials could establish a higher set of effluent charges on BOD emissions during summer months when river flows are comparatively low. Such

defense for the environment, and where the authorities have in a standby status a number of direct-control measures to deal with periods of adversity.

3. The Regulation of Hazardous Pollutants

A third use for direct controls is the regulation of emissions of particularly hazardous pollutants. Where there is reason to believe that the discharge of even small quantities of a certain substance into the environment can have very serious consequences for human health, environmental officials should be able to prohibit them altogether, or at least to control them with great care. In such instances, the risk to human well-being may indicate that it is better not to rely on polluters' responses to a set of fees.

4. Direct Controls vs. Charges: Theory vs. Practice

Before leaving our discussion of the proper functions of direct controls, it is important to insert a word of caution. In discussions of such issues, it is all too easy to contrast an idealized version of the policy one is advocating with the messy, imperfect variant of the policy one is opposing. But in reality neither direct controls nor effluent charges is as neat or well-designed as its theoretical counterpart. This is so to some extent because of imperfections in political and administrative processes which always turn out imperfect compromises. Real effluent charges run into problems in the courts, jurisdictional barriers, and emasculative legislative provisions which can prevent them from being as automatic and effective as they are in theory.

But a more fundamental problem for the design of an effective system of fees arises from the intractable real-world complexities with which control techniques must deal. We have already seen how naive it is to think that the monitoring necessary for effluent charges can be accomplished simply by attaching a meter to a factory's waste pipes. Not only are there no such meters, but the sad fact is that many polluters do not even know how many such pipes are connected to their plants, or where the pipes are located. Nor is the setting of an effluent charge simply a matter of selecting a single fee. When, as is usual, plant emissions contain several pollutants—BOD, metallic wastes, chemical compounds, etc.—some care must be exercised in setting separate effluent fees on each of these, with relative fees designed to avoid encouraging the replacement of one pollutant with something considerably worse. The European experience with systems of fees to regulate levels of water pollution is particularly illuminating in this regard.[7] To keep the systems administratively manageable and

---

periodic alterations in fees would be published well in advance so that firms and individuals could plan the timing of their pollution-control measures.

[7]See Ralph W. Johnson and Gardner M. Brown, Jr., *Cleaning Up Europe's Waters: Economics, Management, and Policies* (New York: Praeger, 1976).

politically acceptable, fees in most instances apply only to a few critical pollutants and are often based on levels of output or employment in the plant to circumvent difficult metering problems.

We will have more to say on all this in Chapter 22, but we simply want to note here that anyone who (like ourselves) has been involved in the process of drafting effluent-fee legislation knows that it is inevitably a complex, untidy process which must produce results not fully satisfactory to anyone. In other words, there is little justification for the argument frequently made against direct controls that they are often so imperfect in practice. This is, of course, true, and it is obvious because we have seen direct controls in practice. But a real system of charges will undoubtedly also be plagued by imperfections, compromises, and outright irrationalities. The available choice is between imperfect direct controls and an imperfect system of charges, not between an imperfect version of the one and an ideal variant of the other.

5. Conclusion

In summary, we see three basic and important roles for direct controls in a comprehensive environmental policy:

1. The regulation of pollutants where metering is not economically feasible
2. The supplementary control of waste discharges subject to fees, to be invoked whenever adverse environmental conditions threaten to push pollution beyond tolerable levels
3. The prohibition or stringent limitation of emissions of substances that are particularly dangerous to human health

The last two of these roles relate directly to the avoidance of major environmental catastrophes; this must clearly be an integral part of a total environmental program.

With these "principles" as background, we turn in the next chapter to an examination of how direct controls have actually been used. It is here that we find the major failures in environmental policy, failures that are largely attributable to an inappropriate and indiscriminate use of direct controls and regulation.

APPENDIX A: *METERING OF BOD*

This appendix consists of a report by Linda G. Martin on the metering of BOD discharges. Although the report is fairly technical, it does provide some sense of the complexity of the prevailing technology of metering. In particular, it shows that, under the present state of the art, we cannot proceed by simply attaching a mechanical meter from which we can take direct readings. Instead, the process is a rather complex one involving sampling of effluents and laboratory tests.

BOD is the quantity of dissolved oxygen (DO) needed during stabilization by aerobic biochemical action of the decomposable matter in sewage, sewage effluents, polluted waters, or industrial wastes. Oxygen demand is exerted by three classes of materials: (1) carbonaceous organic material usable as a source of food by aerobic organisms; (2) oxidizable nitrogen derived from nitrite, ammonia, and organic nitrogen compounds which serve as food for specific bacteria; and (3) certain chemical reducing compounds, such as ferrous iron, sulfite, and sulfide, which react with molecularly dissolved oxygen. Most of the oxygen demand of domestic sewage is due to the first class of materials and may be measured by the BOD_5 test which involves incubation of the effluent for five days at $20°C$. For treated effluents most of the oxygen demand may be of the second class and may also be included in the BOD_5 test. However, the effects of the third class of materials cannot be evaluated by the regular BOD_5 test. Another imperfection of the test results from the complexity of most wastes other than raw or treated domestic sewage. In these cases the usual methods of seeding, as described below, and the incubation period of five days will not accurately measure the oxygen demands of these wastes. More than 100 days at $20°C$ is needed for complete stabilization. For domestic waste, BOD_5 measures about two-thirds of the oxygen demand required by an emission to time infinity. However, for other effluents the proportion varies widely.

In preparation for the BOD_5 test, several precautionary steps are required to insure accuracy. Since the dissolved oxygen in the effluent sample may not be sufficient for the complete test, oxygen must be added in dilution water or by aeration, with the amount to be added varying with the quality of the waste. The following dilutions are suggested: 0.1–1.0 percent for strong trade wastes; 1–5 percent for raw and settled sewage; 5–25 percent for oxidized effluents; and 25–100 percent for polluted river waters. The dilution water must be free from an appreciable oxygen demand of its own and must possess no germicidal properties stemming from residual chlorine, chloramines, caustic alkalinity, or copper. Most natural waters have a significant five-day demand at $20°C$, so synthetic dilution water is recommended. "Distilled water alone and chemically treated tap waters should not be used. Tap waters containing chlorine or chloramines should be passed through activated carbon filters before distillation to remove these volatile compounds."[1]

Another important step is the selection of the proper seed to be placed in the dilution water. The bacterial seed must be the same as that in the effluent, and the nutrients and minerals must also be representative. The choice of a seed depends on the type of effluent. For food-processing wastes, the supernatant

---

[1] Roy W. Hann, Jr., *Fundamental Aspects of Water Quality Management* (Westport, Conn.: Technomic, 1972), p. 123.

liquor from domestic sewage which has been stored at 20°C for twenty-four to thirty-six hours may be used successfully. "Many industrial wastes contain organic compounds which are not amenable to oxidation by domestic-sewage seed. In these cases, the analyst may use seed prepared from soil; acclimated seed developed in the laboratory; or the receiving water collected below the point of discharge of the particular waste (preferably 2–5 miles below)."[2]

Uninhibited growth of both bacteria and plankton cannot occur in the diluted sample if it contains caustic alkalinity or acidity, which must be neutralized to about pH 7.0 using H_2SO_4 or NaOH. If the sample contains residual chlorine compounds, standing for one to two hours may dissipate it. Higher chlorine residuals in neutralized samples should be destroyed by adding sodium sulfite (Na_2SO_3) in the amount determined by a test on the sample. In addition, samples containing other toxic substances, such as those frequently found in industrial wastes, require special treatment, as do those supersaturated with dissolved oxygen. The latter may be encountered during winter months or in localities where algae are actively growing.

The actual test is made up of the following steps:[3]

1. "Place the desired volume of distilled water in a suitable bottle and add 1 ml each of phosphate buffer, magnesium sulfate, calcium chloride, and ferric chloride solutions for each liter of water."[4] The water should be aerated, of the highest purity, and as near 20°C as possible.
2. Seed the diluted water. "Only past experience can determine the actual amount of seed to be added per liter. Seeded dilution water should be used the same day it is made."[5]
3. "Carefully siphon standard dilution water . . . into a graduated cylinder half full without entrainment of air. Add the quantity of carefully mixed sample to make the desired dilution and dilute to the appropriate level with dilution water. Mix well with a plunger-type mixing rod, avoiding entrainment of air."[6] Mixed dilution should be siphoned into two bottles each with 250–300 mil capacity and with ground-glass stoppers. One is for incubation and the other for determination of the initial dissolved oxygen (DO) in the mixture. The former should be stoppered tightly and incubated for five days in an air incubator or water bath, thermostatically controlled at 20°C ± 1°C. "As a precaution against drawing air into the dilution bottle during incubation [the bottle] should be water sealed by inversion in a tray of water in the incubator or by using a special water-seal bottle."[7] "All light should

[2]American Public Health Association, American Water Works Association, and Water Pollution Control Federation, *Standard Methods for the Examination of Water and Wastewater, Including Bottom Sediments and Sludges,* 11th ed. (New York: American Public Health Association, Inc., 1960), p. 319.
[3]Ibid., pp. 309–12, 318–24.
[4]Ibid., pp. 319–20.
[5]Ibid., p. 320.
[6]Ibid.
[7]Ibid., pp. 318, 320.

be excluded to prevent formation of [dissolved oxygen] by algae in the sample."[8]

4. "Fill two BOD bottles with unseeded dilution water. Stopper and water-seal one of these for incubation. The other bottle is for determining the DO before incubation. The DO results on these two bottles are used as a rough check on the quality of the unseeded dilution water."[9]

5. For seed correction set up a separate series of seed dilutions and select those resulting in 40–70 percent oxygen depletion in five days. "One of these depletions is then used to calculate the correction due to the small amount of seed in the dilution water. Do not use the seeded blank for seed correction because the five-day seeded dilution water blank is subject to erratic oxidation due to the very high dilution of seed, which is not characteristic of the seeded sample."[10]

6. Determine the DO in the unincubated samples and blanks and later in the incubated samples and blanks, using the Alsterberg azide modification of the Winkler method. To each bottle "add 2 ml $MnSO_4$ solution followed by 2 ml alkali-iodide-azide reagent, well below the surface of the liquid; stopper with care to exclude air bubbles and mix by inverting the bottle several times. When the precipitate settles, leaving a clear supernatant above the manganese hydroxide floc, shake again. . . . When settling has produced at least 100 ml clear supernatant, carefully remove the stopper and immediately add 2.0 ml conc. H_2SO_4 [sulfuric acid] by allowing the acid to run down the neck of the bottle, restopper, and mix by gentle inversion until dissolution is complete. The iodine should be uniformly distributed throughout the bottle before decanting the amount needed for titration [which should correspond to 200 ml of the original sample] . . . . Titrate with 0.025N thiosulfate to a pale straw color. Add 1–2 ml freshly prepared starch solution and continue the titration to the first disappearance of the blue color. . . . Since 1 ml 0.025N $Na_2S_2O_3$ is equivalent to 0.2 mg DO, each milliliter of sodium thiosulfate used is equivalent to 1 mg/1 DO if a volume equal to 200 ml of original sample is titrated."[11]

7. Calculate the biological oxygen demand using the following formula:

$$\text{mg/1 BOD} = \frac{(D_1 - D_2) - (B_1 - B_2)f}{P}$$

where

D_1 = DO of diluted sample 15 minutes after preparation,
D_2 = DO of diluted sample after incubation,
B_1 = DO of dilution of seed control before incubation,
B_2 = DO of dilution of seed control after incubation,
f = ratio of seed in sample to seed in control
$$= \frac{\%\ \text{seed in } D_1}{\%\ \text{seed in } B_1}, \text{and}$$
P = decimal fraction of sample used.

---

[8] Ibid., p. 318.
[9] Ibid., p. 321.
[10] Ibid.
[11] Ibid., p. 311.

"There is no standard against which the accuracy of the BOD test can be measured. . . . where interfering and toxic substances are absent, the standard deviation of the BOD test on sewages and effluents may range from 0.07 to 0.11 ml oxygen demand titrated. This should also hold true on wastes from food-processing industries or other organic nontoxic wastes. Industrial wastes containing toxic materials or substances which interfere with the DO determination have not been studied statistically."[12]

APPENDIX B: *EXTERNAL INFLUENCES ON ENVIRONMENTAL QUALITY* *

To explore in greater depth the role of external influences on the level of environmental quality, we investigated several measures of air quality in New York City. The findings indicate that levels of atmospheric pollutants vary widely among the different days and seasons of the year. Figure 20-B1 indicates the number of days that concentrations of five major pollutants achieved various levels; for sulfur dioxide, carbon monoxide, and particulates the time period studied was 1969-72, and for nitrogen dioxide and oxidants the period studied was 1971-72. For example, the shaded bar in Figure 20-B1 indicates that the concentration of sulfur dioxide in the air of New York City fell within the range 0.03-0.06 parts per million (p.p.m.) on about 430 days out of the total number of days in the sample. Note in particular that for most of the pollutants there are a substantial number of days for which levels of concentration exceed the range most frequently experienced (indicated by the highest bar) by several hundred percent. The most frequent range for suspended particulates, for example, is 90-120 p.p.m., but there are several days for which this concentration exceeds 200 p.p.m.; similarly, levels of nitrogen dioxide sometimes exceed four times their "normal" level.

Some of this variation is seasonal in character. Figure 20-B2, which shows concentrations of sulfur dioxide for each of the four seasons, indicates significantly higher concentrations during the winter heating season (most frequently observed range is 0.06-0.2 p.p.m.) than during the other three seasons of the year (in summer and fall the modal range is 0.03--0.06 p.p.m., and in spring it is still lower). It is interesting, however, that, even within each season, there still is considerable variation in the daily levels of SO_2.

The source of some portion of these fluctuations in levels of pollution is, of course, attributable to human polluting activities. Sulfur-dioxide levels are relatively high in the winter largely because of heating requirements. Our study was intended to determine the degree of the variability contributed by natural phenomena beyond human control or our ability to predict them accurately. To examine this in greater depth, we undertook a statistical analysis of the varia-

---

[12]Ibid., p. 323.
*We are grateful to Aristos Parris for his assistance in this study.

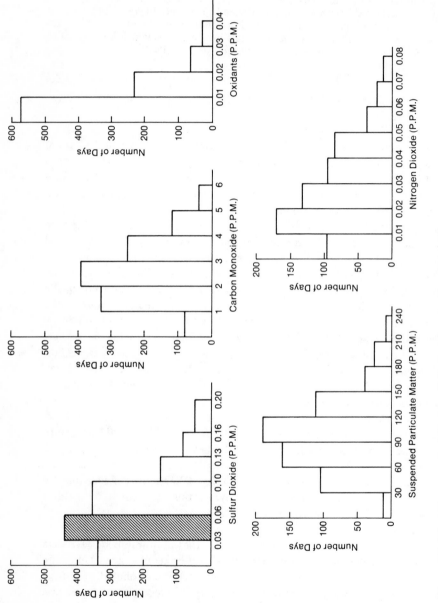

Figure 20-B1 Frequency of Various Pollutant Levels, New York City, 1969-72 (parts per million).

Source: Basic data supplied by the Department of Air Resources, New York City.

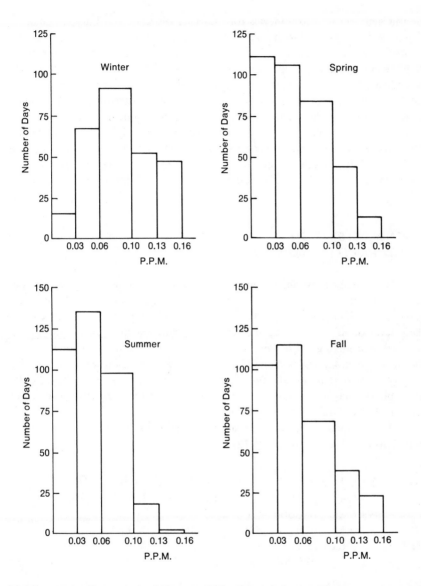

Figure 20-B2 Frequency of Various Sulfur-Dioxide Levels by Season New York City, 1969–72 (parts per million).

Source: See Figure 20-B1.

tion in daily sulfur-dioxide levels for the years 1968 and 1972. In particular, we explored the relationship between the daily concentration of SO_2 and "the weather," which we measured in terms of four dimensions of atmospheric conditions: wind velocity, precipitation, temperature, and mixing height.[1] The analysis indicated, not surprisingly, that our set of weather variables bears a strong (and statistically significant) relationship to the concentrations of SO_2. Higher wind velocity, a higher mixing height, more precipitation, and a higher temperature are all associated with lower levels of sulfur pollution. The weather, in fact, accounts for a substantial fraction of the variation in sulfur-dioxide levels in New York City. For the interested reader, we present the statistically estimated equations and some further discussion in Appendix C to this chapter.

APPENDIX C: *STATISTICAL ANALYSES OF NEW YORK CITY AIR QUALITY* *

We conclude by describing our calculations in somewhat greater detail. After collecting data on sulfur-dioxide concentrations and on four "weather" variables for each day during the two years 1968 and 1972, we regressed the daily level of SO_2 on the weather variables (wind velocity, temperature, precipitation, and mixing height) and on a dummy variable with a value of zero if the day was a weekday and a value of unity if the day fell on a weekend. This last variable represented an attempt to control for levels of emissions into the atmosphere; the presumption is that emissions tend to be greater on weekdays with the higher levels of activity in the city.

The estimated regression equations for each of the two years appear as equations (1) [1968] and (2) [1972]:

(1) $S = 0.4 - .008W_1 - .0003W_2 - .003W_3 - .00006W_4 - .01D$
           (24.1) (6.4)   (16.5)   (0.5)   (6.8)   (1.6)
                    $N = 366$ $R^2 = .46$

(2) $S = 0.1 - .002W_1 - .00007W_2 - .0004W_3 - .00001W_4 - .002D$
           (16.0) (5.4)   (10.5)   (0.2)   (4.5)   (0.9)
                    $N = 366$ $R^2 = .26$

---

[1] The "mixing height" is a kind of upper atmospheric boundary for the dispersion of pollutants. As warm air rises, it is gradually cooled; the point at which the cooling air meets its equal in temperature is the mixing height. At this point, there is little further upward movement to help disperse pollutants. The greater the mixing height, the more the capacity of the atmosphere to absorb and scatter gases and particles in the air.

*This appendix is rather technical and of interest primarily to readers with a background in statistics.

where

    S = Sulfur-dioxide content of the atmosphere in parts per million (p.p.m.);
    W_1 = Wind velocity in miles per hour;
    W_2 = Temperature in degrees Fahrenheit;
    W_3 = Rainfall in inches;
    W_4 = Mixing height in meters;
    D = Dummy variable: 1 if weekday; 0 if on weekend;
    N = Number of observations; and
    R^2 = Coefficient of multiple determination.

The numbers in parentheses below the estimated coefficients are the absolute values of their respective t-statistics.

    For both 1968 and 1972, the weather variables, as a group, explain a substantial fraction of the variation in levels of SO_2. Individually, each has the anticipated sign and is statistically significant (at a .01 level) with the exception of W_3 (precipitation). Some care, however, must be taken in ascribing all of the explained variation to weather influences (even aside from the small fraction explained by D, which, incidentally, did not prove to be significantly different from zero). There is an obvious problem of multicollinearity between some of the weather variables and the levels of sulfur emissions into the atmosphere. In particular, we would expect the temperature variable to be inversely correlated with sulfur discharges: during the cold days of the winter, more fuel will be burned than during the warmer days of the summer. Some of the explanatory power of W_2 must, therefore, represent differing levels of sulfur emissions.

    One interesting result is the differences in equations (1) and (2); not only does (1) explain a substantially larger fraction of the variation in S than (2), but it also possesses a much larger constant term. This suggests that, after allowing for the influences of weather, sulfur concentrations were a good deal higher in 1968 than in 1972. This, of course, comes as no surprise, for it was over this period that Consolidated Edison and others switched to low-sulfur fuels. To get a rough measure for this difference between 1968 and 1972, we pooled the observations for the two years and included a second dummy variable to reflect the year. The resulting regression equation was:

$$(3) \quad S = 0.3 - .004W_1 - .0002W_2 - .003W_3 - .00004W_4 - .01D - .12Y$$
$$\quad\quad\;\;\, (31.7) \;\; (6.8) \quad\;\; (17.8) \quad\;\;\; (1.0) \quad\;\;\; (8.3) \quad\quad\; (1.6) \;\; (35.3)$$
$$N = 732 \quad\quad R^2 = .68$$

where

    Y = Dummy variable: 0 for 1968; unity for 1972.

The dummy variable, Y, is highly significant with the expected negative sign; after allowing for the effects of the weather variables, a day in 1972 tended, on average, to have a lower sulfur level than in 1968. Moreover, this average difference is a quite substantial .12 p.p.m. (compared to a mean of .09 p.p.m. for the two years).

21

Current Environmental Policy:

A RELIANCE ON DIRECT CONTROLS

Direct controls and regulations, ranging from court injunctions that prohibit the emission of specific forms of pollutants to directives from environmental agencies requiring the adoption of particular treatment procedures, are the instruments that, by far, dominate environmental programs in the United States and other countries. In fact, with only a few exceptions public officials at the federal, state, and local levels in the United States have chosen to attack environmental problems almost exclusively by direct regulation of the behavior of individuals and business firms. This chapter, which outlines the main features of environmental policy in this country, will consequently concern itself largely with direct controls.[1]

Since no survey limited to a few pages can encompass all of the measures that have been undertaken to protect the environment in recent years, we shall attempt only to describe some of the highlights of the programs and shall confine our discussion to two of the primary concerns of environmental policy: air and water quality. Our objective will be to see what lessons we can learn from our nation's experience in the use of regulatory techniques.

---

[1] We stress that, in this chapter, we do not intend to provide a comprehensive and exhaustive documentation of U.S. environmental policy. Rather, our objective is to describe basic

1. The History of Federal Air Quality Programs

The history of federal policy relating to air quality is a story of increasing severity of regulation followed by a gradual retreat toward relaxation of the rules. Until comparatively recently, the federal government's role in the control of air pollution was largely passive. With the 1955 Air Pollution Control Act, Congress for the first time authorized a federal program of research, training, and demonstration for the improvement of air quality, but left the initiative for the adoption of pollution-control measures to state and local governments. The Clean Air Act of 1963 granted the federal government its first enforcement powers for the control of air quality. At the request of a state (or on its own initiative in the case of interstate pollution) the Department of Health, Education and Welfare was authorized to call a conference on the air pollution problems in a particular region or airshed. Such a conference was, in essence, no more than a public forum, empowered only to make recommendations for action to responsible state authorities. If these recommendations were not followed or if the pollution problem was not dealt with satisfactorily by some alternative means, HEW was empowered to appeal to the U.S. Attorney General to bring suit against the polluters in District Court.

In 1966, following an acute four-day pollution crisis in New York City (estimated to have caused eighty deaths), a National Air Pollution Conference was organized. This conference provided the initial stimulus for the eventual enactment of the 1967 Air Quality Act. The new legislation gave HEW the responsibility for formulating "criteria" relating concentrations of various atmospheric pollutants to "health and welfare." The states were then to establish standards of air quality and subsequently to design implementation plans for the attainment of these standards. Federal enforcement powers, however, were still limited largely to the calling of conferences.

During these same years Congress had followed a very different approach to the control of emissions from motor vehicles. Following the enactment of the Motor Vehicle Air Pollution Control Act of 1965, HEW adopted emissions standards for 1968 model automobiles which were roughly the same as those established in the State of California in 1966. Congress thus chose to set national standards for motor vehicles rather than rely on the initiative of the individual states, no doubt in part because in this area it was dealing directly with a single and tightly knit "oligopolistic" industry.

By the end of the 1960s there was widespread dissatisfaction and frustration with the modest rate of progress in air pollution control. The response of Congress to this apparent failure of the regulatory strategy was to enact further regulatory measures that were more stringent than their predecessors. The 1970 Clean Air Amendments greatly extended the powers of the federal government

---

policy strategy and to select some illustrative cases that indicate the strengths and weaknesses of direct-control programs.

to set and enforce air-quality standards and imposed much more restrictive limits on auto emissions. Under this law, which is still in effect, Congress adopted as a goal for the nation the attainment by 1975 of a set of national "primary ambient-air quality standards" with another set of "secondary" standards to be satisfied at a later time.[2] The primary standards were intended to set ceilings on concentrations of pollutants whose violation would pose a threat to human health, while secondary standards were designed to protect other aspects of human welfare including vegetation, property, and animals. The Act gave the Environmental Protection Agency (which oversees federal environmental programs) the power to translate these general goals into concrete figures intended to represent threshold concentrations of major pollutants, which *if exceeded,* would constitute an unacceptable degree of danger.[3] By April 1971, the EPA had formulated such national standards for maximum levels of particulates, sulfur oxides, carbon monoxide, hydrocarbons, nitrogen oxides, and photochemical oxidants.[4] These appear in Table 21-A1 of the Appendix to this chapter.

In addition to standards for ambient air quality, Congress empowered the EPA to set specific limits on emissions of "hazardous pollutants" which pose particularly serious dangers to health (including, for example, certain heavy metals). The Act also directed the EPA to establish "new source performance standards" for new industrial plants; EPA has responded by laying out detailed technical specifications for the operation of newly constructed plants. The reader can get some feeling for the form of these standards from Table 21-A2 of the Appendix.

The most dramatic part of the 1970 Clean Air Amendments was stringent new regulations on auto emissions that were intended to be met by 1975. These regulations specified maximum emission levels for hydrocarbons, carbon monoxide, and nitrogen oxides equal to only 10 percent of the maxima specified in previous legislation. Since substantial reductions had already been achieved, the new limitations required, approximately, a 97 percent decline in emissions from those that would occur in the absence of controls. This was coupled with a pro-

---

[2] The standards have been delayed for some states.

[3] The idea of "threshold concentrations" is a curious one implying that increasing concentrations of pollutants are relatively harmless until at some specifiable point, they suddenly begin to constitute a serious danger to health and life. As Kneese and Schultze point out, "The notion of threshold value can be regarded as a politically convenient fiction which permits the law to appear to require pollution damage to be reduced to zero—an absolutely ambiguous number" (Allen V. Kneese and Charles L. Schultze, *Pollution, Prices, and Public Policy* [Washington, D.C.: The Brookings Institution, 1975], p. 51). As we noted in an earlier chapter, such threshold figures provide no incentive for any further reduction in pollution.

[4] EPA sets ambient air quality standards for these pollutants. The states then get a chance to design a plan including emissions standards, which will achieve the ambient standard. If a state doesn't enact an adequate program within a given time, EPA imposes a plan upon the state.

hibitive $10,000 fine per vehicle for violations. In April of 1973, however, under pressure from auto manufacturers, the EPA granted a one-year extension in the deadline for compliance. Then, in the Energy Supply and Environmental Co-ordination Act of 1974, the statutory standards were revised once more in accord with the schedule outlined in Table 21-1. Early in 1975 the auto standards were again delayed for a year. Thus, one may well surmise that target figures are still subject to further revision. However, the general approach to automobile pollution control—the imposition of maximum emission levels for new vehicles—is clearly consistent with the overall approach of the federal government, and no deviation from this strategy seems imminent. We direct the reader to Table 21-A3 of the Appendix for a concise summary of federal legislation for air pollution.

Before we try to evaluate the effectiveness of the direct-control strategy for regulation of air quality, it will be helpful to examine some attempts by local

TABLE 21-1

AUTOMOBILE EMISSION STANDARDS
(grams per mile)

	HC	CO	NO_x
Uncontrolled cars (pre-1968)[a]	8.7	87.0	3.5
1970–71 federal standards[b]	4.1	34.0	
1972–74 federal standards[b]	3.0	28.0	3.1
1975[c] and 1976[d]			
Federal 49-state standards	1.5	15.0	3.1
California standards	0.9	9.0	2.0
1977[e] federal 50-state standards	1.5	15.0	2.0
1978 statutory standards	0.41	3.4	.4
Administration bill (January 1975)			
1977–81 50-state standards	0.9	9.0	3.1
Post-1981 50-state standards	(f)	(f)	(f)
EPA recommendation (March 1975)			
1977–79	1.5	15.0	2.0
1980–81	0.9	9.0	2.0
Post-1981	0.41	3.4	(f)
Revised administration proposal (June 1975)			
Through 1981	1.5	15.0	3.1
Post-1981	(f)	(f)	(f)

Source: *Environmental Quality, The Sixth Annual Report of the Council on Environmental Quality* (Washington, D.C.: U.S. Government Printing Office, 1975), p. 53.

[a]On the basis of 1975 test procedures.
[b]Imposed administratively by EPA.
[c]Imposed by EPA as interim standards after suspension of statutory standards, except for California's HC and NO_x standards, which were set by the state.
[d]Imposed by Congress in Public Law 93-319, except for California's NO_x standards, which were set by the state.[f]
[e]Imposed by EPA as interim standards after suspension of statutory standards, except for NO_x standards, which were imposed by the Congress (Public Law 93-319).
[f]Administrative discretion.

governments to control air pollution and to glance at federal policy for the regulation of water quality. We will then be in a better position to see some of the strengths and weaknesses of the regulatory approach.

2. Local Programs for Air Quality

Well before the federal government took an active interest in air quality, local governments had initiated air pollution programs of their own. Although most major cities adopted antismoke ordinances during the early part of this century, it was not until World War II that cities began to put together more sophisticated pollution-control programs. A look at the history of pollution control in Los Angeles and New York City, whose air pollution problems are among the worst in the country, will illustrate reasonably well the direct-control programs employed by local governments.

The mix of sources of pollution varies widely from region to region. Table 21-2 illustrates the contrast between New York City and Los Angeles: auto-mobile emissions are the dominant source of emissions in Los Angeles, while in New York pollution from power plants and space heating assumes a more im-portant role. In Los Angeles an aggressive and popular program for the control of stationary sources of pollution elicited general cooperation and compliance.[5] Although Los Angeles air quality had long been poor, by 1947 the acute attacks of smog in the Los Angeles valley, which were due in part to frequent tempera-

TABLE 21-2

COMPARISON OF POLLUTANT EMISSIONS IN LOS ANGELES AND NEW YORK CITY
(thousands of tons per year)

	Carbon Monoxide		Nitrogen Oxides		Sulfur Oxides		Particulates	
	L.A.	N.Y.C.	L.A.	N.Y.C.	L.A.	N.Y.C.	L.A.	N.Y.C.
Automobiles	2,850	2,084.5	275	243.4	NA	10.0	NA	13.3
Power Plants	neg.	1.1	24	192.0	27	263.2	2	52.1
Space Heating	neg.	4.4	2	27.9	neg.	697.8	neg.	18.2

Source: Reprinted by permission of the publisher, from Alfred J. Van Tassel, ed., *Our Environment, The Outlook for 1980* (Lexington, Mass.: Lexington Books, 1973), pp. 313, 314, 316, 368, 370.

Note: Neg. = negligible; NA = not available.

---

[5] Our discussion of the Los Angeles experience draws heavily on George H. Hagevik, *Decision-Making in Air Pollution Control, A Review of Theory and Practice, with Emphasis on Selected Los Angeles and New York City Management Experiences* (New York: Praeger Publishers, 1970).

ture inversions, prompted the California legislature to create the Los Angeles County Air Pollution Control District. The District was provided a wide array of direct controls with which it set out, rather single-mindedly and painstakingly, to halt virtually all emissions of air pollution from all *stationary* sources (i.e., sources other than motor vehicles). It made little or no use of air quality standards to gauge the emission reductions; the District simply decided that *all* stationary pollution sources were to be regulated, whether or not their emissions were demonstrably harmful.

The District laid down about 100 rules and regulations specifying permissible emission levels from stationary sources and then proceeded zealously to prosecute literally thousands of violators during the first eight years of its operation. In enforcing these regulations, written notices and cease-and-desist orders were issued for every violation reported and observed by the District staff. After office hearings and office notices, criminal actions and civil injunctions were applied.

By the mid-1950s the only significant and unregulated stationary sources of air pollution were the electric and steam power-generating plants which generated about one quarter of the sulfur-oxide pollution. Effective action against these sources had been delayed in part because of the relatively low visibility of the emissions from power plants and the lack of scientific evidence about the harmfulness of sulfur dioxide. Technological and resource constraints in the Los Angeles area left the burning of natural gas as the only feasible means to reduce sulfur-dioxide emissions. "Rule 62," enacted in 1959, which required the use of natural gas six months of the year and affected the power plants and 20,000 other fuel-burning firms, was passed and upheld despite much opposition from the power concerns.

In Los Angeles the control of stationary sources of pollution was aided by a very favorable political climate: polluters who considered refusing to comply with a District notice knew that public opinion would be against them, that a variance would be unlikely, and that a court battle would probably be lost. Under these circumstances even the influential power companies found it expedient throughout the hearings and court suits to attack only the elements of Rule 62 that they considered manifestly unfair.

Pollution control in New York City has taken a different course.[6] In 1952 the city's ineffectual Smoke Control Bureau was superseded by the Department of Air Pollution Control. The Department was given the power to license all new polluting equipment and to require necessary alterations in existing equipment. However, no large-scale enforcement campaign was launched until 1965, after a study initiated by the City Council had identified on-site incineration (largely that in apartment buildings), municipal incineration, and power plants as the

---

[6]For our discussion of New York, we again draw from Hagevik, *Decision-Making in Air Pollution Control.*

city's major sources of particulate pollution. New York's power plants were also shown to be the leading contributors of the city's other major pollutant, sulfur dioxide. The Council report led to passage of "Local Law 14" which required exclusive use of low-sulfur fuel by the 1969–70 heating season, prohibited the installation of any on-site incinerators in new apartment buildings, required the upgrading or sealing-off of all existing apartment incinerators, and banned all open burning.

Largely as a result of exemplary cooperation by the power companies, which were easily able to switch to one-percent sulfur fuels, total sulfur-dioxide emissions fell by 56 percent by the end of 1969. However, the city's proposed plan for incinerators encountered more difficult obstacles of a sort which illustrates the vicissitudes to which direct controls are subject. Local Law 14 laid down stringent requirements for the upgrading of old incinerators and prohibited the installation of on-site incinerators in new apartment buildings. This posed two sorts of problems. The first was the heavy cost of the necessary alterations. The second was the additional load that would have fallen on city sanitation and refuse-collection services if many owners had chosen simply to close down their incinerators. In an atmosphere of uncertainty of enforcement and continuing debate about amendment of the new law, the deadline for compliance arrived. Three hundred inspections on the first day of enforcement revealed two hundred violations. The authorities subsequently sent out about 1,400 notices of violation during the first month. It was rapidly becoming clear that the law was unworkable, and there followed a complex and prolonged process of negotiation and formulation of new proposals. At the end of March of 1969, three months after the deadline for the upgrading or closing of the first group of about 3,000 incinerators, only 375 units had been improved and a suit by landlords challenging the constitutionality of the regulation was in progress. To add the final touch, the New York Public Housing Authority announced in May 1969 that limited funds would prevent it from complying with Local Law 14 in its own apartment buildings.

Although the air pollution agencies in Los Angeles and New York followed somewhat similar regulatory approaches, their degree of success, as measured in terms of the compliance by polluters, varied widely. The difference illustrates the heavy dependence of a program of direct controls upon public enthusiasm and single-minded commitment of the regulatory agencies. In New York the program to upgrade incinerators was a source of intense conflict, not only between polluters and public officials, but among the city's agencies themselves. It may also be true, as Hagevik suggests, that the sense of crisis and the public support which it elicited was a good deal stronger in Los Angeles, because the physical discomfort and reduced visibility resulting from smog attacks made the population more aware of the benefits from the control of emissions.[7]

---

[7]Ibid., pp. 156–57.

The irony in all this is that it is New York rather than Los Angeles that seems to have achieved the greater improvement in its air quality. Because stationary sources have proved easier to control than motor vehicles, and because stationary sources were so much more significant a source of pollution in New York, the switch to low-sulfur fuels by New York's power producers sufficed to produce a significant improvement in the city's air quality despite the lack of cooperation by operators of incinerators.

3. Controlling Water Quality[8]

The current water quality programs in the United States have their origin in the Water Pollution Control Act Amendments of 1956. The 1956 Amendments adopted two basic instruments: federal subsidization of the construction of municipal waste treatment plants (which we examined in Chapter 17) and federal regulation of individual polluters. The regulatory framework, including the roles assigned to the federal and state governments, was similar to that embodied in the Clean Air Act. Before 1965, however, the federal government was limited to the conference technique as its means to enforce water pollution controls. The 1965 Water Quality Act provided for more direct federal control in the enforcement of the water quality standards set up by the states. The states' standards and their implementation plans required federal approval, and once approved they acquired the force of federal law. Under the 1965 Act the Federal Water Pollution Control Agency was given power to enforce standards without resort to the cumbersome conference procedure.

By 1971 virtually all of the states had chosen to use a permit system to control emissions into their waterways. Any plant or municipality wishing to discharge wastes into a body of water had first to obtain a permit from the appropriate state agency. The permit usually dictated, among other things, the quantity and/or concentration of certain pollutants allowable in the discharge. In this way, in principle, the discharges of polluters along a body of water could be adjusted until water quality standards were met.[9]

By the end of the 1960s, however, the slow rate of improvement in the quality of the nation's waters had produced widespread disenchantment. Con-

---

[8]For an excellent, concise description and evaluation of U.S. federal policy for both air and water pollution control, see Kneese and Schultze, *Pollution, Prices, and Public Policy.* We have drawn extensively on their Chapters 3-5.

[9]The FWPCA requires the adoption of specific abatement techniques for point-source dischargers. It also provides for the setting of water quality standards for various bodies of water. If the techniques-based standards for all dischargers on one body of water are expected to permit water quality to deteriorate beyond the water quality standard, then effluent limitations on those dischargers specified in individual permits must be more stringent than required by the technique-based standards alone. Thus, the more stringent of the two types of standard is the one that always applies.

gress responded very much as it did in the area of air pollution, with the 1972 Water Pollution Act Amendments, which authorized an ambitious and extensive set of federal regulatory measures whose avowed objective was that "the discharge of pollutants into the navigable waters be eliminated by 1985," and that "wherever attainable, an interim goal of water quality which provides for the protection and propagation of fish, shellfish, and wildlife and provides for recreation in and on the water be achieved by July 1, 1983."[10] To achieve these objectives, Congress granted the EPA broad new authority. The EPA was empowered to impose limits upon discharges directly on individual polluters and to issue permits based on these limits without establishing a link between water quality and the discharges of an individual polluter. In addition, the EPA was directed to require in new plants the adoption of the "best available technology" by 1981 as a prelude to the no-discharge objective for 1985. Congress also imposed more severe penalties upon violators: fines from $2,500 to $25,000 per day for a first offense and up to $50,000 per day for a subsequent conviction.

The 1972 Amendments included a number of other provisions such as the establishment of new federal standards for emissions of toxic substances. At the same time it expanded the commitment of the federal government to the subsidy of municipal treatment facilities. The new legislation increased the maximum federal contribution from 55 to 75 percent of total cost and authorized up to $5 billion in grants for fiscal year 1973, $6 billion for 1974, and $7 billion for 1975.[11]

4. The Results of the Direct-Control Approach

A. Air Quality. How effective has the regulatory approach to pollution control been? For air pollution, the record is a mixed one—some dramatic successes and other clear failures. The big success story is the reduction of sulfur dioxide. Referring back to Figure 2-10 in Chapter 2, we recall the marked reductions that have occurred in levels of sulfur dioxide in a number of major U.S. cities. In surveys of U.S. air quality in recent years, the EPA has found that, in ten of the nation's largest cities, the annual mean concentrations of SO_2 have been well below the level specified by the EPA primary standards (see Table 21-3). The explanation for this is quite straightforward: the state and local regulations that restricted the sulfur content of fuels have been very successful. Section 2 provided two examples of this: the cases of Los Angeles and New York City.

The record relating to other atmospheric pollutants is much less gratifying. For the ten cities in Table 21-3, the EPA found in 1972 that concentrations of "total suspended particulates" (TSP) in the air exceeded the EPA primary stan-

---

[10] Kneese and Schultze, *Pollution, Prices, and Public Policy*, p. 53.
[11] For a concise summary of the federal legislation on water pollution, see Table 21-A4 in the Appendix.

TABLE 21-3

SULFUR DIOXIDE: RATIO OF ANNUAL MEAN TO EPA PRIMARY STANDARD IN SELECTED CITIES

City	1967	1968	1969	1970	1971	1972	1973
Los Angeles	NA	NA	NA	0.14^a	0.26	0.30	0.23^a
Denver	NA	NA	0.22	0.17	0.10	0.09	0.18^a
Washington, D.C.	NA	NA	0.36	0.34^a	0.26^a	0.50	0.32^a
Chicago	NA	2.18	2.30	1.50	0.91	0.59	0.33^a
Boston	0.23^a	0.65	0.80	0.59^a	0.22^a	0.15	0.37^a
St. Louis	1.04	1.14	0.91	0.72^a	0.12	0.24	0.51^a
Cincinnati	NA	0.36	0.33	0.14	0.21	0.29	0.21^a
Philadelphia	NA	1.13	0.87	1.06	0.46	0.56	0.57^a
Pittsburgh	0.89	0.94	0.95	0.72	0.62	0.79	0.27^a
New York City	4.35	3.03^a	1.69^a	0.21^a	0.87^a	0.60	0.45^a

Source: *Environmental Quality, The Fifth Annual Report of the Council on Environmental Quality* (Washington, D.C.: U.S. Government Printing Office, 1974), p. 272.

Note: A ratio of 1.00 means that the annual average ambient concentration was exactly at the level of the primary standard (80 micrograms per cubic meter, annual average). An entry that is less than unity means that the corresponding concentration of SO_2 is less than the EPA standard. NA = not available.
[a]These readings do not meet EPA criteria for statistical validity, in most cases because an insufficient number of samples have been reported for the year.

TABLE 21-4

TOTAL SUSPENDED PARTICULATES: RATIO OF ANNUAL MEAN TO EPA PRIMARY STANDARD IN SELECTED CITIES

City	1967	1968	1969	1970	1971	1972	1973
Los Angeles	1.22	1.72	1.24	1.67	1.77	1.57	1.60^a
Denver	1.24	1.42	1.51	1.63	1.57	2.03	2.61^a
Washington, D.C.	1.13	1.14	0.98	1.01^a	0.97	1.11	1.08^a
Chicago	N.A.	1.49	1.80	1.49	1.53	1.30	1.16^a
Boston	N.A.	1.23	1.14	1.07^a	1.13^a	1.07	0.79^a
St. Louis	1.49	N.A.	2.48	2.04^a	1.17	1.24	1.28^a
Cincinnati	1.48	1.32	1.30	1.34	1.20	1.16	1.00^a
Philadelphia	2.00	1.49	1.69	1.80	1.33	1.03	1.16
Pittsburgh	1.78	2.15	1.92	1.69	1.48^a	1.80	N.A.
New York City	2.18	N.A.	1.41	1.64	1.41^a	1.27	1.53^a

Source: *Environmental Quality, Fifth Annual Report*, p. 265.

Note: A ratio of 1.00 means that the annual average ambient concentration was exactly at the level of the primary standard (75 micrograms per cubic meter, annual average).
[a]These readings do not meet EPA criteria for statistical validity, in most cases because an insufficient number of samples have been reported for the year.

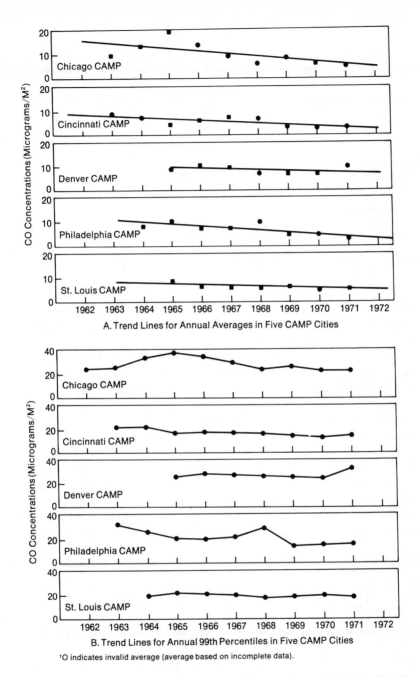

Figure 21-1 Trends in Carbon-Monoxide Concentrations, 1961–72, Continuous Air Monitoring Program (CAMP) Cities.

Source: *Environmental Quality, The Fifth Annual Report of the Council on Environmental Quality* (Washington, D.C.: U.S. Government Printing Office, 1974), p. 275.

TABLE 21-5

TOTAL NATIONWIDE EMISSIONS OF HYDROCARBONS AND NITROGEN OXIDES
(millions of tons per year)

	1940	1950	1960	1970
Hydrocarbons				
Controllable	10.1	15.6	18.8	22.5
Total	16.6	21.8	25.8	27.3
Nitrogen Oxides				
Controllable	5.5	8.2	10.9	22.0
Total	6.5	8.8	11.4	22.1

Source: *Environmental Quality, Fifth Annual Report*, p. 276.

dard in every case. Table 21-4 indicates that by 1973 only two of the cities appear to have met the standard, and, in some of these cities, TSP concentrations have actually risen in recent years.

The record for auto-based emissions is also mixed. While EPA air-monitoring programs report some recent reductions in carbon-monoxide concentrations in certain major cities (see Figure 21-1), nationwide emissions of other auto pollutants reveal dramatic increases. Table 21-5 indicates that since 1940, total national emissions of controllable hydrocarbons have more than doubled, while discharges of nitrogen oxides have quadrupled.[12]

B. Water Quality. Recent trends in water quality are also very uneven. In Chapter 2 we pointed out some impressive improvements in the dissolved-oxygen content of certain major rivers. The reappearance of fish in the Hudson River near New York City attests to a renewed vitality of the river (however, the enthusiasm that greeted the arrival of these fish was considerably dampened after warn-

---

[12]It is hardly surprising that the conference approach to enforcement of air quality standards has not proved terribly effective. Between 1963 and 1970 only eleven conferences on problems of air pollution were held and only one of these eventually led to the courts. This case, involving obnoxious odors from a chicken-rendering plant in Bishop, Maryland, illustrates the frustrating obstacles and delays inherent in a case-by-case approach relying on judicial enforcement. In 1965 a conference directed the firm to control its emissions by September of 1966. When Bishop Processing chose to ignore the deadline, hearings followed in 1967 with another order to control emissions. The owners of the firm again failed to comply and, instead, filed suit against the Clean Air Act. Finally, at the end of 1967 the U.S. Attorney General filed suit in District Court. By February of 1969 the Justice Department was able to ask the court to shut down the plant, but the court did not act until November, when the judge ordered the plant closed by February 1970. The closing thus came some five years after the initiation of the conference. On the Bishop case, see John C. Esposito, *Vanishing Air, The Ralph Nader Study Group on Air Pollution* (New York: Grossman Publishers, 1970), pp. 114-17.

ings from environmental authorities that the fish contained dangerous amounts of toxic pollutants, such as polychlorinated biphenyl (PCB), a chemical poison described in Chapter 3).[13] A more unmixed success story is the dramatic cleanup of the Willamette River in Oregon. After forty years of continuous and evolving efforts, environmental authorities and citizens were finally able, in the last decade, to deal satisfactorily with industrial and municipal effluents. Chinook salmon are now re-entering, in ever-increasing numbers, what was once one of the nation's most polluted rivers. However, as heartening as the story of the Willamette is, it must be recognized that this has been the result of an extraordinarily determined and persistent effort; moreover, without continuing vigilance, there is evidence that the river can easily return to its earlier polluted state.[14]

The Willamettes have been the exception rather than the rule. In a study of 600 water polluters in New York in 1971, officials found only 181 to be complying with current regulations. There is no reason to believe that this is atypical of other areas. Only a few states (e.g., Oregon, Washington, and Michigan) had by 1971 carried out adequate inspections of permit holders. Most states relied simply on self-reporting by the permit holders themselves! The state of Alabama, for instance, had "no routine monitoring program whatsoever" and depended entirely on a self-reporting system with which it was estimated that about twenty municipalities cooperated.[15]

It is difficult to provide an overall picture of nationwide trends in water quality because of the vast number and diversity of its waterways—which include everything from small ponds and estuaries to the Great Lakes and the coastal waters. Moreover, national averages reveal nothing about cases of dramatic local improvement or deterioration. Nevertheless, the EPA has attempted to provide an overview in the ambitious 1974 National Water Quality Inventory Report to the U.S. Congress. Analyzing the twenty-two major waterways in the U.S., the Report summarizes the trends over the period 1963–72 for a large number of measures of water quality. The picture it presents is very uneven. Table 21-6 indictates that, for some pollutants, the percentage of sampled "reaches" (sections of waterways) in which pollutant concentrations exceeded the EPA standard ("reference level") fell over the decade. In particular, counts of coliform bacteria and oxygen demand have shown general improvement over the past five years. The EPA found that the dissolved-oxygen content had increased in 61 percent of the reaches sampled, and that the oxygen-demand levels of pollutants

---

[13] Richard Severo, "State Says Some Striped Bass and Salmon Pose a Toxic Peril," *New York Times,* August 8, 1975, pp. 1, 56. For more on toxic substances like PCBs see Chapter 3, Table 3-2.

[14] For a discussion of the cleanup of the Willamette, see *Environmental Quality, The Fourth Annual Report of the Council on Environmental Quality* (Washington, D.C.: U. S. Government Printing Office, September 1973), Chap. 2.

[15] William N. Hines, *Public Regulation of Water Quality in the United States* (Arlington, Virginia: National Water Commission, December, 1971), p. 339.

TABLE 21-6

MAJOR WATERWAYS: REFERENCE LEVEL VIOLATIONS, 1963-72

Parameter	Reference level and source[a]	Percent of reaches exceeding reference levels		
		1963-72	1968-72	Change
Suspended solids	80 mg/l-aquatic life	26	14	-12
Turbidity	50 JTU-aquatic life	28	28	0
Temperature	90°F-aquatic life	0	0	0
Color	75 platinum-cobalt units-water supply	0	0	0
Ammonia	0.89 mg/l-aquatic life	16	6	-10
Nitrate (as N)	0.9 mg/l-nutrient	12	24	+12
Nitrite plus nitrate	0.9 mg/l-nutrient	18	26	+8
Total phosphorus	0.1 mg/l-nutrient	34	57	+23
Total phosphate	0.3 mg/l-nutrient	30	41	+11
Dissolved phosphate	0.3 mg/l-nutrient	11	22	+11
Dissolved solids (105°C)	500 mg/l-water supply	25	18	-7
Dissolved solids (180°C)	500 mg/l-water supply	28	12	-16
Chlorides	250 mg/l-water supply	12	9	-3
Sulfates	250 mg/l-water supply	12	12	0
pH	6.0-9.0-aquatic life	0	0	0
Dissolved oxygen	4.0 mg/1-aquatic life	0	0	0
Total coliforms (MFD)[b]	10,000/100 ml-recreation	24	13	-11
Total coliforms (MFI)[b]	10,000/100 ml-recreation	50	30	-20
Total coliforms (MPN)[b]	10,000/100 ml-recreation	23	20	-3
Fecal coliforms (MPN)[b]	2,000/100 ml-recreation	45	21	-24
Fecal coliforms (MPN)[b]	2,000/100 ml-recreation	17	43	+26
Phenols	0.001 mg/l-water supply	86	71	-15

Source: *Environmental Quality, Fifth Annual Report*, p. 286.

[a]With the exceptions that follow, reference level designations are from *Guidelines for Developing or Revising Water Quality Standards,* EPA Water Planning Division, April 1973; for ammonia, chlorides, sulfates, and phenols, *Criteria for Water Quality,* EPA, 1973 (Section 304(a)(1) guidelines); and for nitrate (as N), *Biological Associated Problems in Freshwater Environments,* FWPCA, 1966, pp. 132-33.
[b]Membrane filter delayed, membrane filter immediate, most probable number.

has been reduced in 74 percent. Similarly, bacterial counts were lower in 75 percent of the sampled reaches. This is, of course, of special interest because environmental authorities have used direct controls primarily to reduce the levels of these two pollutants.

Trends in other major pollutants are, however, not so satisfactory. For nutrients, the EPA discovered that "Up to 84 percent of the reaches exceeded phosphorous and phosphate reference levels associated with potential eutrophication, and up to 54 percent of the reaches showed increased phosphorus levels in 1968-72 over the previous years. Nitrate levels also increased in 74 percent of the reaches examined."[16] Another cause for concern was the frequency with which heavy metals and concentrations of pesticides exceeded their "reference levels."

5. Problems of Enforcement: The Reserve Mining Case

We have stressed at various points in Part 3 the serious problems and tortuous delays in enforcing regulations that environmental authorities have encountered under the direct-controls approach. Perhaps, we can best illustrate the nature of this problem with a particularly important and widely publicized example: the case of the Reserve Mining Company in Silver Bay, Minnesota. The company, which makes taconite pellets used in the production of steel products, discharges some 67,000 tons of waste into Lake Superior every day. The wastes contain microscopic asbestos fibers which have been found in the drinking water supplies of several lakeshore communities (Duluth among them) and are strongly suspected of causing cancer if ingested. (They are known to cause cancer when inhaled.) Since 1969 Reserve has evaded attempts by the federal government, environmental groups, and states adjoining Lake Superior to force it to halt these discharges.

In 1969 a water-quality enforcement conference failed to produce any results. In 1971 EPA gave Reserve a 180-day notice (which gives the violator the opportunity to comply voluntarily). By 1972, at EPA request, the Department of Justice filed suit in federal district court requesting a schedule from Reserve on its plans to abate the discharges. Finally, in March 1975 the court found that the discharges violated various state and federal laws, but ruled that the danger to residents of the north shore is a potential, rather than imminent, health hazard. The court told Reserve and the state to agree on a suitable onland disposal site for the discharges within a reasonable period, and granted Reserve time to convert to onland disposal (and said if no site were agreed upon within one year the plant must close). As of April 1977 the company and state officials had not yet come to complete agreement about a proposed disposal site, and Reserve continued to operate its plant. A federal judge, however, ordered a halt to the discharges into the Lake by July 7, 1977 (this was the sixteenth judicial decision in this controversy). Reserve, reacting predictably, requested an extension of this deadline until a proposed disposal site is ready, which is expected to take almost three years. At the time of last writing of this book, the federal government has just decided not to hold Reserve Mining to the July 7 ultimatum. The implication is that the company will continue to discharge its wastes into the lake for at least three more years until completion of the onshore disposal site.[17]

---

[16]*Environmental Quality, Fifth Annual Report*, pp. 284–85.
[17]*Environmental Quality, The Third Annual Report of the Council on Environmental Quality* (Washington, D.C.: U.S. Government Printing Office, 1972), p. 123; *Environmental*

6. Lessons From Experience in the Use of Direct Controls

As we have seen, our basic policy strategy for the control of environmental quality has been the adoption of a variety of direct-control programs to reduce air and water pollution. Both at the federal and state-local levels, environmental officials have sought to regulate the behavior of polluters by the issue of individual permits for waste discharges and the specification of detailed standards for the construction and operation of industrial plants and for household heating and waste-disposal systems. Similarly, to combat the environmental side-effects of the automobile, public policy has relied primarily upon the setting of emission standards for new models. To enforce these standards, environmental agencies have invoked penalties and have often turned to the courts for the validation of their decisions.

The U.S. government has thus been moving in the direction of a program under which a federal environmental agency, through a system of permits and other specified restrictions concerning treatment procedures, effectively regulates the activities of each polluter in the economy (with much of the implementation carried out by the states). The basic issue is whether such a strategy of comprehensive and individual central control is a sensible one.

In our judgment, it is not; we find it impossible to believe that such a system can function effectively and efficiently. It must be admitted that our reservations cannot be said to follow completely unambiguously from the actual record of performance of direct controls, for, as we have seen, that record is a very complex and mixed one. Yet, observation does give rise to strong doubts about the wisdom of complete reliance on direct controls to the total exclusion of any system of charges. We want to stress three primary grounds for this view.

First, there is the overwhelming administrative problem of prescribing procedures and issuing permits individually tailored to the different circumstances of literally thousands of polluters. In fact, recent reports indicate that there is an enormous backlog of unprocessed permit applications. Second is the tendency of direct controls to discourage innovation in pollution-control techniques. Third, and perhaps most important, is the potential waste and ineffectiveness of a policy that requires a centralized agency to determine levels of discharges and, in numerous instances, to specify actual treatment procedures for individual polluters.[18] The Clean Air Amendments of 1970 direct the EPA to set emission limits on newly constructed stationary sources of air pollution. These limits are

---

Quality, The Seventh Annual Report of the Council on Environmental Quality (Washington, D.C.: U.S. Government Printing Office, 1976, p. 48; "Obstacles Remain in Ore Waste Dispute," *New York Times,* April 18, 1977, p. 13; "U.S. Decides Not to Hold Reserve Mining to July Deadline on Dumping Ore Wastes Into Lake," *New York Times,* May 22, 1977, p. L-27.

[18] For an excellent discussion of enforcement problems under current environmental legislation, see Kneese and Schultze, *Pollution, Prices, and Public Policy,* Chap. 5.

not based on air quality standards, but rather on what the EPA determines to be the best "adequately demonstrated" technology for the reduction of waste emissions. Similarly, the Federal Water Pollution Control Act Amendments of 1972 direct the EPA to prescribe limitations on point-sources of water pollution, where the judgment again is to be based on feasible techniques subject to some test of "reasonable" cost.

The difficulty with all this is that it requires the EPA to determine specifications for new plants on a case-by-case basis. This involves, not only difficult engineering judgments about the effectiveness of alternative treatment techniques, but also highly controversial decisions about what is technologically feasible at reasonable cost. The initial efforts by the EPA to issue new-source performance standards for electric power plants and municipal incinerators has already led to objections with matters now in the courts. Kneese and Schultze conclude that:

> There seems to us no realistic way for the administrator to avoid negotiating and bargaining with virtually every individual source of waste discharge of any size. Even then he would probably face a huge bureaucratic and legal task, since some 33,000 plants have applied, and estimates of the total number of major sources run up to 55,000. The result will almost surely be long delays, a capricious distribution of control efforts, and, to the extent the program succeeds, an extremely costly way of achieving water quality goals.[19]

In Chapter 16, we noted that one of the deficiencies of most regulatory techniques involving specified limits or procedures is that they fail to provide much incentive for further improvement. This is particularly true of a technology still in its infancy, such as that for the control of air and water pollution. It is of great importance that our environmental policy include effective inducements for the development and introduction of superior pollution-abatement techniques. Where direct controls involve the requirement of particular equipment or techniques such as sound-absorbing materials in aircraft or scrubbers in chimneys, there is clearly little inducement for industry to seek a better way to do the job. In addition, a major shortcoming of our policy of direct regulation is that it may actually impede the development of new waste-control techniques; an industry that discovers a new method for curtailing discharges, rather than realizing cost savings, may simply find that its emission limitations are tightened even further under the requirement that industry use the best available technique.

An interesting example of this problem is provided by EPA's determination of performance standards for cement plants. In the process of setting standards for different industries, the EPA found that cement plants were

---

[19] *Pollution, Prices, and Public Policy,* pp. 62-63.

successfully removing more fine particulates from smoke emissions than were most electric power plants. The EPA's response was to impose a more restrictive particulate-emission limitation upon cement plants than upon plants producing electric power. This has given rise to vehement, and perhaps understandable, objections from the cement industry which claims that this type of discrimination penalizes the more innovative industry. The EPA won a court challenge to the Portland cement plant standards. The court accepted the argument that, if one industry can control emissions more effectively than another, it should be required to do so.[20]

We have also seen that, under current legislation, there have been numerous breakdowns in the enforcement mechanism. We have noted several instances where token fines have rendered regulations ineffective or where prolonged delays in the courts (as in the Reserve Mining Case) have frustrated the adoption of environmental directives. In the extremely important case of automobile emissions, efforts have bogged down in a series of hostile negotiations between environmental officials and the auto companies with the result that the enforcement of new emission standards has been pushed back time and again. Attempts to enforce the Water Pollution Control Amendments of 1972 have also encountered serious opposition and delays. The staff of the National Commission on Water Quality, in its 1976 report, notes that efforts to implement effluent limitations have elicited more than 250 lawsuits by industries challenging the promulgated guidelines.[21] The Commission goes on to point out that "at least 350 lawsuits have arisen under the Act, and more than 284 are still pending in the courts."[22]

Even where regulations are effective in curtailing waste discharges, we have stressed that they are unlikely to do so in the least expensive way. This is not, incidentally, a matter of peanuts. It is hard to get a reliable estimate of the anticipated costs of pollution-control programs, but it is clear that, over the next decade, this will run into hundreds of billions of dollars. The National Water Commission has estimated that, for the period 1972–83, the costs of adopting

---

[20] For an excellent study of the way in which enforcement procedures have discouraged the development of new techniques for cleansing of stack gases, see Richard E. Ayres, "Enforcement of Air Pollution Controls on Stationary Sources Under the Clean Air Amendments of 1970," *Ecology Law Quarterly* 4, no. 3 (1975), pp. 441–78. Ayres, who is Attorney for Natural Resources Defense Council in Washington, D.C., concludes that taxes on pollution are needed to provide a profit incentive for research and development of new pollution-abatement technology.

[21] *Staff Report to the National Commission on Water Quality* (Washington, D.C., April 1976), V-4.

[22] Ibid., V-6, 7. New systems of effluent fees will not, incidentally, be immune to challenges through the Courts. So we should not, perhaps, exaggerate the importance of Court delays under direct controls as compared to a system of charges. The uniformity of fees should, however, allow a more direct and speedy resolution of legal matters than the individually tailored permits and specifications of abatement procedures that have characterized programs of direct controls. The Oregon Bottle Bill, for example, was challenged in the Courts and rather quickly upheld.

the best-known technology (not of eliminating waterborne wastes) will be roughly $220 billion.[23] Similarly, the Council on Environmental Quality, in its 1973 Report, suggests an estimate for this same period of $135 to $140 billion as the cost of achieving the air quality standards set forth in the 1970 amendments. Kneese and Schultze provide what they see as a conservative estimate, a figure of roughly $400 billion, as the potential cost of pollution-control programs over the next decade. This suggests that even a modest percentage savings from the careful design of our environmental programs may avoid a huge waste of resources. If, for example, we could achieve a 25 percent saving by more efficient ways of cutting back on waste emissions (a rather low figure, to judge from the available estimates), we could release something like $100 billion in resources to meet other social and private needs. Such a saving would amount to about $500 for every man, woman, and child in the United States; it is more, for example, than the total annual expenditure for national defense or the total taxes collected yearly by all state governments put together. Resource costs of this magnitude should surely make us think twice about the relative expense of whatever environmental programs we are comparing.

In light of the discussion in the preceding chapters, all this may not come as much of a surprise. The basic deficiency in our approach to environmental policy is its excessive emphasis on programs of direct controls. As we stressed in Chapter 20, there is an important place for direct-control programs in our overall environmental policy. However, environmental policy in this country and abroad has attempted to accomplish virtually *all* its objectives via direct controls alone.

What is, perhaps, most discouraging is the reaction to the obviously mixed performance of our direct-controls strategy: the adoption of a series of regulations that are still more stringent and more complex in order to coerce polluters to reduce the damage they do to the environment. Instead of a rigid commitment to programs of direct control, what is needed is sufficient flexibility to make use of the full range of available policy instruments and design a strategy in which each policy tool makes its most effective contribution to protection of the environment.

---

[23] This and the immediately following estimates are cited in Kneese and Schultze, *Pollution, Prices, and Public Policy*, pp. 70–71.

APPENDIX

TABLE 21-A1

NATIONAL PRIMARY AND SECONDARY AMBIENT AIR QUALITY STANDARDS

Pollutant	Concentration Limit Micrograms per Cubic Meter	Concentration Limit Parts per Million	Averaging Time
Carbon monoxide	10,000	9	8 hours[a]
	40,000	35	1 hour[a]
Photochemical oxidants	160	0.08	1 hour[a]
Hydrocarbons (methane free)	160	0.24	3 hours[a]
Nitrogen oxides	100	0.05	1 year
Sulfur oxides	80	0.03	1 year
	365	0.14	24 hours[a]
	(60)	(0.02)	(1 year)
	(260)	(0.1)	(24 hours)[a]
	(1,300)	(0.5)	(3 hours)[a]
Particulate matter	75	–	1 year[b]
	260	–	24 hours[a]
	(60)	–	(1 year)[b]
	(150)	–	(24 hours)[a]

Source: *Federal Register,* Vol. 36, No. 84 (April 30, 1971), Pt. 2, p. 8187.

Note: Secondary standards are shown in parentheses; for some pollutants the secondary standards are the same as the primary standards.
[a]Not to be exceeded more than once a year.
[b]Geometric mean.

TABLE 21-A2

NEW SOURCE PERFORMANCE STANDARDS FOR CO, HC, NO_x

Source	Pollutant	Standards
Petroleum refineries	CO	Exhaust from fluid catalytic cracking unit catalyst regenerator may not contain more than 0.050 percent CO by volume.
Fossil-fuel-fired steam generators (heat input greater than 250 million B.T.U./hr)	NO_x	Exhaust gas may not contain more than: a. 0.20 lb. per million B.T.U. heat input, maximum 2-hr. average, expressed as NO_2, when gaseous fossil fuel is burned. b. 0.30 lb. per million B.T.U. heat input, maximum 2-hr. average, expressed as NO_2, when liquid fossil fuel is burned. c. 0.70 lb. per million B.T.U. heat input,

TABLE 21-A2 (Continued)

Source	Pollutant	Standards
		maximum 2-hr average, expressed as NO_2, when solid fossil fuel (except lignite) is burned.
		d. When different fossil fuels are burned simultaneously in any combination the applicable standard shall be obtained from the following proration: $$\frac{G(0.20) + L(0.30) + S(0.70)}{G + L + S}.$$
Nitric acid plants	NO_x	a. Exhaust may not exceed 3 lbs. per ton of acid produced, maximum 2-hr. average, expressed as NO_2.
		b. Exhaust may not exceed 10 percent opacity.
Storage vessels for petroleum liquids	HC	a. If the true vapor pressure of the petroleum liquid, as stored, is equal to or greater than 78 mm Hg (1.5 psia), but not greater than 570 mm Hg (11.1 psia), the storage vessel shall be equipped with a floating roof, a vapor recovery system, or their equivalents.
		b. If the true vapor pressure of the petroleum liquid as stored is greater than 570 mm Hg (11.1 psia), the storage vessel shall be equipped with a vapor recovery system or its equivalent.

Sources: For petroleum refineries and storage vessels: *Federal Register*, Vol. 36, No. 247 (December 23, 1971), Part 2, pp. 24878-81; for steam generators and nitric acid plants: *Federal Register*, Vol. 39, No. 47 (March 8, 1974), Part 2, pp. 9315-17.

TABLE 21-A3

OUTLINE OF MAJOR FEDERAL LEGISLATION ON AIR POLLUTION

Date of Enactment	Popular Title and Official Citation	Key Provisions
July 14, 1955	1955 Air Pollution Control Act (69 Stat. 322)	Authorized, for the first time, a federal program of research, training, and demonstrations relating to air pollution control. (Extended for four years by amendments of 1959.)

TABLE 21-A3 (Continued)

Date of Enactment	Popular Title and Official Citation	Key Provisions
December 17, 1963	Clean Air Act (77 Stat. 392)	Gave the federal government enforcement powers regarding air pollution, through enforcement conferences similar to 1956 approach for water pollution control.
October 20, 1965	Motor Vehicle Air Pollution Control Act (79 Stat. 992)	Added new authority to 1963 act, giving the Department of of Health, Education and Welfare power to prescribe emission standards for automobiles as soon as practicable.
November 21, 1967	Air Quality Act of 1967 (81 Stat. 485)	(1) Authorized HEW to oversee establishment of state standards for ambient air quality and of state implementation plans; (2) for the first time, set national standards for automobile emissions.
December 31, 1970	Clean Air Amendments of 1970 (84 Stat. 1676)	Sharply expanded the federal role in setting and enforcing standards for ambient air quality and established stringent new emission standards for automobiles.

Source: Allen V. Kneese and Charles L. Schultze, *Pollution, Prices, and Public Policy* (Washington, D.C.: The Brookings Institution, 1975), pp. 31–32.

TABLE 21-A4

OUTLINE OF MAJOR FEDERAL LEGISLATION ON WATER POLLUTION

Date of Enactment	Popular Title and Official Citation	Key Provisions
March 3, 1899	1899 Refuse Act (30 Stat. 1152)	Required permit from Chief of Engineers for discharge of refuse into navigable waters.
June 30, 1948	Water Pollution Control Act (62 Stat. 1155)	Gave the federal government authority for investigations, research, and surveys; left primary responsibility for pollution control with the states.
July 9, 1956	Water Pollution	Established federal policy for

TABLE 21–A4 (Continued)

Date of Enactment	Popular Title and Official Citation	Key Provisions
	Control Act Amendments of 1956 (70 Stat. 498)	1956–70 period. Provided (1) federal grants for construction of municipal water treatment plants; (2) complex procedure for federal enforcement actions against individual dischargers. (Some strengthening amendments enacted in 1961.)
October 2, 1965	Water Quality Act of 1965 (79 Stat. 903)	Sought to strengthen enforcement process; provided for federal approval of ambient standards on interstate waters. (Minor strengthening amendments enacted in 1966 and 1970.)
October 18, 1972	1972 Water Pollution Act Amendments (86 Stat. 816)	Set policy under which federal government now operates. Provided (1) federal establishment of effluent limits for individual sources of pollution; (2) issuance of discharge permits; (3) large increase in authorized grant funds for municipal waste treatment plants.

Source: Kneese and Schultze, *Pollution, Prices, and Public Policy*, p. 31.

22

Designing Effective Environmental Policy

In the preceding chapters, we have described each of the available policy techniques for the control of pollution, and, in each instance, have tried to analyze, both in principle and in practice, its strengths and its limitations in achieving particular environmental objectives. It is now time to attempt to draw together the various strands of the discussion into a more coherent, overall view of environmental policy. In brief, we shall try to outline the appropriate roles for our various policy tools to see how they can usefully complement one another.

We should caution the reader that it is *not* our objective to set out a definite legislative program for the control of pollution in the United States. As we have seen in the preceding chapters, the most effective technique for the regulation of polluting activities is likely to vary with circumstances. Nevertheless, the evidence does, we believe, point strongly to some important conclusions concerning the design of an effective environmental policy. As such, these conclusions can provide a set of principles for the integration of the various policy instruments into an overall program that will promote our environmental objectives without unnecessary waste of resources.

In brief, we shall conclude that, of the instruments of policy in our basic list,[1] there are valuable roles for direct controls specifying processes and equipment; for fees on emissions and/or auctioning of emission permits; for government investment in damage prevention and regenerative facilities and in research and education; and even, to some extent, for voluntary programs. On the other hand, we see only a limited use for subsidy programs in cases of extreme hardship or inequity or where political expediency permits no other option. Finally, we contend that it is inappropriate to use direct controls specifying permissible levels of emissions except where a particular pollutant is so dangerous that its emission should be prohibited outright.

Like most economists, we end up assigning a high priority to the fiscal instruments, that is, charges upon emissions and auctioned permits. Their cost efficiency, reliability, and durability argue that they should be a primary method for the control of emissions that are generated regularly and for which monitoring is practical and not excessively costly. In contrast, where the monitoring of emissions is not feasible, those direct controls which require the assignment and enforcement of emission quotas are also not practical. Other forms of direct controls will be necessary in such cases—perhaps directives that require the adoption of particular techniques (e.g., specified treatment equipment) or the prohibition of certain processes (e.g., the burning of high-sulfur fuels). Ideally, direct controls serve three primary roles: a substitute for fiscal measures when metering is impractical; a supplement to fiscal incentives in brief periods of emergency during which response to fees and permits is uncertain and slow; and finally, in cases where complete prohibition is appropriate.

We may also find voluntary measures (moral suasion) to be helpful in brief emergencies. In addition, such measures can be useful where not only monitoring, but even effective policing is not feasible (e.g., in the behavior of isolated campers in wilderness areas). Finally, where it is difficult to induce the private sector to undertake projects to promote environmental quality, direct government outlays will be necessary. For example, major projects involving the reoxygenation of bodies of water or augmentation of water flows will typically require governmental initiation and support.

In the remainder of this chapter, we shall explore in greater depth the rationale for this view of environmental policy. We do want to stress that our survey of current policy suggests that today's environmental programs are far from ideal; they have not, in general, made appropriate use of the wide range of available policy instruments. The result has been unnecessary cost, administrative complexity, and, most important, a set of programs significantly less effective in protecting the environment than they would otherwise have been.

---

[1] See Table 15–1.

1. The Use of Price Incentives Where Metering is Feasible

Our first conclusion is a strong presumption in favor of the use of fees to regulate individual waste emissions *in cases where the metering of waste discharges is technically and economically practical.* We believe that our survey of both the principles of pricing and regulatory techniques and our experience with such policies constitute a compelling case for the use of pricing incentives as a first-line defense against environmental destruction. Not only do devices such as effluent fees promise to be effective in reducing levels of emissions, but as we have seen, they can also yield very sizeable savings of our scarce resources. We are convinced that many of the shortcomings of our recent environmental programs are attributable to their undeviating reliance on direct controls; this has resulted in a series of programs that depend for their effectiveness on active enforcement by the police powers of the state and the courts, an enforcement which has proved erratic and often ineffective.

On the other hand, economists have gone too far in their single-minded advocacy of pricing techniques to the total exclusion of other policy methods. In taking this position, they have tended to neglect the operational problems inherent in a system of fees, in particular, the difficulties in measuring levels of emissions. Because of the central importance of metering in the choice of a control technique, we will have a few final comments on the subject in the next section. For now, we simply note the obvious fact that fees can work effectively only where the monitoring of levels of emissions is practicable.

We do not mean to imply that all types of fiscal incentives are equally desirable. On the contrary, their appropriateness varies considerably. For example, we strongly believe, for the reasons we examined in Chapter 17, that unit subsidies to reduce pollution are far inferior to fees. Any justification for the use of subsidies instead of fees must rest either on some extreme case of hardship or on political expediency. Where, for example, the burden of a program falls very heavily on the poor or where the polluter has a compelling claim for public assistance to help cover the costs of reducing effluents, we may wish to consider some form of payment to offset the financial burden implied by the program. In other cases, however, subsidies are difficult to defend either on grounds of efficiency or justice. They serve as a reward to polluters, or at least as a means to relieve them of the financial burden of cleaning up their own mess. Moreover, subsidies can serve as an inducement to enter the industry to which they apply, and in this way may well lead to an expansion of the activities that are most damaging to the environment—the very reverse of what the subsidies are intended to accomplish.[2]

---

[2] The real problem is largely a political one: subsidies have tremendous appeal in generating support for a program. We have noted the extensive use of subsidies in the United States. In their survey of pollution-abatement programs in Europe, Ralph W. Johnson and Gardner M. Brown, Jr., found that, in every country they studied, environmental legislation and control

In contrast, the auctioning of permits authorizing a limited quantity of emissions has nearly everything to be said for it but political appeal. The concept is unfamiliar and that in itself makes people suspicious of it. Add to that the fact that it *literally* entails the sale of licenses to pollute, and the difficulty of gaining acceptance for this approach becomes painfully clear. Yet such a program has many advantages to offer. It involves little risk of miscalculated environmental damage, since it sets a fixed and predetermined limit on the quantity of authorized emissions. Moreover, it may be somewhat more flexible than a program of fees in dealing with emergencies; for example, the environmental authority can simply declare such licenses invalid during pollution crises. Finally, unlike fees, the effectiveness of this technique is not subject to erosion by inflation or growing economic output.[3]

2. More on the Metering Problem

We have stressed the importance of the feasibility and expense of metering effluents in choosing the appropriate policy instrument to control waste emissions. This issue is not, however, so clear-cut as it may seem; under certain circumstances and with a little imagination in the design of a monitoring system, it may be possible to simplify measurement procedures. For example, there may exist some shortcuts that provide reasonably satisfactory estimates of emission levels. In the case of sulfur emissions, for instance, it may be unnecessary to measure what is actually emerging from the stacks; a determination of the sulfur content of the fuel prior to combustion may be an adequate, if somewhat imperfect, measure of the ultimate effluent. The environmental authority would, in this case, simply set a tax on the sale of fuels based on their sulfur content.[4]

---

relied heavily on subsidies. They found, in short, that polluters seek compensation for costly abatement procedures and are successful in obtaining it. See their *Cleaning Up Europe's Waters: Economics, Management, and Policies* (New York: Praeger Publishers, 1976), pp. 25–26.

[3] Some recent evidence suggests that the sale of pollution rights may encounter far less opposition than we have envisioned. In fact, it seems already to be taking place to a limited extent. In particular, the EPA has ruled that, where air quality standards have not been met, new polluting industries may enter an area only if existing emissions are reduced such that there is no net increase in air pollution. In California, for example, Standard of Ohio, wishing to construct a new unloading dock in Long Beach, has proposed "buying" the pollution of several dry cleaning plants and small factories. A spokesman for Sohio noted that "trade-offs have become almost a commodity." Similar exchanges of polluting emissions are taking place elsewhere in the United States. See "Expanding Plants Face Pollution Tradeoffs," *New York Times,* Aug. 1, 1977, pp. 29, 31. For a more detailed examination of the California experience, which has generated some proposed legislation, see Aileen Alfandary, "Air Trade-Offs: Attempting to Reconcile Industrial Growth and Clean Air in California," *Public Affairs Report* 18, no. 5, Bulletin of the Institute of Governmental Studies (University of California, Berkeley, October 1977): 1–6.

[4] The shortcoming of this method is that it does not provide any incentive for the cleansing of emissions during their passage through the chimney; a partial rebate of the tax could, perhaps, be made available to fuel users who employ such cleansing devices.

Moreover, even where the accurate measurement of emissions requires elaborate equipment and lengthy procedures at a substantial cost, it may still be worthwhile where the bulk of the pollution problem can be traced to a few major polluters. We have already identified a few cases of this sort. In the New York City area, for example, a sizeable fraction of sulfur emissions emanates from the operations of Consolidated Edison and the other major local sources of power; similarly in the Delaware Estuary, some forty-four polluters account for about two-thirds of BOD discharges. In such instances, a careful monitoring of the major polluters (based, for example, on expertly taken samples at frequent intervals) may be combined with admittedly less precise *and* less expensive measurement procedures for the larger number of minor polluters.[5] We saw in Chapter 18 that the estimated *annual* cost savings from effluent fees, as compared to uniform treatment, were on the order of $10 million for the control of BOD emissions into the Delaware Estuary and roughly $15 to $20 million for the reduction of airborne sulfur emissions in Cleveland and St. Louis. Such potential savings may well justify a considerable outlay, perhaps several thousand dollars per year per major polluter, on an effective system for metering effluents.

Finally, we should stress that the technology of metering is by no means static. Since widespread demand for metering systems is relatively recent, it is not very surprising that effective and inexpensive techniques do not yet exist for all pollutants.

3. Some Candidates for Effluent Fees

It may prove helpful at this point to consider the workability of pricing incentives for a few specific and significant pollutants. Our treatment will by no means be a comprehensive study of the full range of potential uses of fees, but rather an examination of some key pollutants for which price incentives seem promising.

A. BOD Emissions. It may seem paradoxical to begin the discussion with a pollutant for which we have documented the expense and difficulty of metering. Nevertheless, the evidence suggests to us that the potentially enormous cost

---

[5] This particular proposal may encounter some legal obstacles. Marcia Gelpe has pointed out to us that it may prove unlawful to measure the emissions of some polluters by a technique that is more precise than that used to measure the same type of emissions from other polluters.

In some fee programs in other countries, the environmental authorities have simply exempted small polluters. The French, for example, do not charge firms that emit only minor quantities of wastes into receiving waters. Likewise, the Japanese have restricted their sulfur tax to 7,400 facilities which account for over 90 percent of aggregate sulfur emissions into the atmosphere.

savings from the use of fees to regulate BOD emissions will, for the limited number of major polluters along most waterways, justify the adoption of what is
admittedly a rather costly and somewhat imprecise system of measurement.[6]
Even though the metering costs per polluter may be relatively high, the aggregate
cost of monitoring the effluents from major pollutant sources is likely to be
quite modest compared to the costs of other approaches. Moreover, BOD discharges are already being metered. We discussed in earlier chapters the enforcement of quotas on the Delaware River for the control of BOD emissions. The
evidence suggests that current monitoring procedures are rather erratic and
sloppy,[7] but this is in part attributable to the fact that they are not used for the
calculation of regular bills to polluters, but only to determine periodically if
polluters are complying with their quotas.

A number of bills proposing effluent charges on BOD emissions have been
introduced at the national and state levels. In 1971, Senator William Proxmire
of Wisconsin proposed "a schedule of national effluent charges" to apply to
"bio-chemical oxygen demand (BOD)" and certain other waste discharges.[8]
Proxmire's amendment was defeated, but the effort to increase understanding
and to generate support for these proposals continues.

B. Sulfur Emissions. Fees seem particularly promising as a means to control
sulfur discharges into the atmosphere. As we noted earlier, this is one case in
which actual metering at the point of discharge may be unnecessary. The sulfur
content of the fuel itself provides a measure of sulfur discharges, so that an
excise tax on the sale of fuels based on the amount of sulfur they contain may
be all that is necessary. There is, moreover, considerable scope for the processing
of high-sulfur fuels to reduce their sulfur content. A set of fees would provide a
powerful incentive for such processing.

The Japanese have recently introduced a sulfur tax of this variety. The tax
is based not on actual, but rather on estimated, emissions of sulfur oxides, where
the estimate depends both on the sulfur content of the fuel that the firm burns
and on the extent of stack-gas desulfurization that the firm employs. By including the latter, the environmental authorities encourage the use of "scrubbers"
and other devices to remove sulfur from the smoke as it passes through the
chimney prior to entering the atmosphere.

There has also been interest in this country in a sulfur tax. In 1972, responding to a number of studies urging the adoption of a sulfur tax, President
Nixon proposed the Pure Air Tax Act. This bill would have introduced, after

[6]In Europe, the French and the Ruhr authorities in Germany have chosen to include BOD
emissions in the formula for assessing charges for water pollution. In contrast, the Netherlands excludes BOD because of difficulties of measurement.
[7]See Bruce A. Ackerman, Susan Rose Ackerman, James W. Sawyer, Jr., and Dale W. Henderson, *The Uncertain Search for Environmental Quality* (New York: The Free Press, 1974),
pp. 69–73.
[8]*Congressional Record,* November 2, 1971, Vol. 117, Part 30, p. 38826.

1976, a tax on sulfur emissions, with the level of the tax depending on the region's air quality in the preceding year; the proposed tax was fifteen cents per pound where primary air quality standards had been violated, ten cents per pound where secondary air standards were violated, and zero where all standards were met. However, the Nixon bill encountered stiff opposition in the U.S. Congress for reasons that we will examine later in this chapter.

C. A Smog Tax on Automobiles.[9] The federal approach to the control of pollution from motor vehicles has relied primarily on the imposition of emissions standards for new automobiles. As we have seen, this has led to direct confrontation between the major auto producers and federal environmental agencies. The result has been protracted delays in deadline extensions, with the ultimate outcome still in some doubt. In particular, there are serious questions about the effectiveness of some of the new automobile pollution-control devices. Although these devices may initially meet federal standards, evidence suggests that they deteriorate quickly. Reporting on one set of tests following road use, the EPA noted in 1973 that, of the vehicles tested, over half had emissions in excess of the standards for their model year.[10] After only a few thousand miles of use, the effectiveness of many pollution-control devices appears to drop off to a dismaying extent. This suggests that our present strategy for the control of auto emissions faces formidable technological and enforcement problems.[11]

Some fifteen years ago, a group of economists at the Rand Corporation proposed an intriguing alternative to our present automobile pollution strategy: a smog tax. Under one form of this proposal, inspectors would test cars at regular intervals and assign a smog rating based on the concentrations of pollutants in the exhaust. This rating would then become the basis for a tax on purchases of gasoline; the gasoline station operator would charge the motorist a smog tax *on each gallon* of gasoline purchased depending on the car's smog rating.[12]

The appealing part of this proposal is that it offers motorists a number of ways to reduce their smog-tax bill. Testing has revealed, for example, that periodic emission "tune-ups" by a trained mechanic can yield sizeable reductions in exhaust pollutants. Alternatively, individuals can cut their tax bills by reduc-

---

[9]This section draws heavily on the excellent discussion of Allen V. Kneese and Charles L. Schultze, *Pollution, Prices, and Public Policy* (Washington, D.C.: The Brookings Institution, 1975), pp. 101–4.

[10]CALSPAN Corporation, *Automobile Exhaust Emission Surveillance: A Summary*, APTD–1544 (Research Triangle Park, N.C.: U.S. Environmental Protection Agency, Air Pollution Technical Information Center, 1973), pp. 4, 40.

[11]For a description and evaluation of alternative abatement strategies see Donald N. Dewees, *Economics and Public Policy: The Automobile Pollution Case* (Cambridge, Mass.: M.I.T. Press, 1974).

[12]The testing of the exhaust and assignment of a rating does not, incidentally, pose any insurmountable problem. The state of New Jersey, as one example, currently tests the exhaust of each automobile as part of the regular annual inspection; the test takes about thirty seconds and is carried out simultaneously with the remainder of the inspection.

ing the number of miles they drive, by living closer to their jobs or using mass transit more frequently, or, on older cars, they can install control devices. In Chapter 19 on voluntary compliance, we noted that General Motors and Chrysler had made available pollution-control kits at a cost of about $20 (including installation). However, sales of the kits were disappointingly (but not surprisingly) low. In contrast, a smog tax would give motorists a real incentive for the installation of such devices, for they could then save money.

Finally, and no doubt most important, the tax would constitute a powerful inducement to auto manufacturers to produce engines with better smog ratings. The potential purchaser of a new car would surely want to know its rating, as this would be an important determinant of the cost of operating the automobile. This is the kind of incentive to which we can expect auto manufacturers to respond most effectively. The smog tax thus promises some important and impressive advantages over our present strategy of emissions standards for new automobiles. It surely deserves more serious consideration than it has received.[13]

D. Deposits for Returnable Containers. Chapter 18 described the striking success of the Oregon "Bottle Bill" in the use of deposits for beverage containers. A small refundable deposit on standardized beer and soft-drink containers has induced the substitution of returnable bottles for throw-away containers; within two years of the enactment of the Bottle Bill, over 90 percent of beer and soft-drink containers were of the returnable variety. Moreover, this seems to have been accomplished at a relatively modest cost. This is one instance where "the metering problem" does not introduce any serious technological difficulties or impose costs that are excessively high. One might expect that this resounding success would have led the way to the universal adoption of such deposits. However, this has been far from true; at the time this was written, only three additional states, Vermont, Maine, and Michigan, had adopted similar legislation. As we noted earlier, powerful opposition (mostly from can and bottle manufacturers) has resisted the introduction of new bottle bills in other states. In spite of their demonstrated effectiveness, the fate of refundable deposits is yet to be determined.

4. Design of Effluent Fees in Practice

We turn next to two issues crucial to the design of an effective system of effluent charges: the selection of an appropriate base upon which to levy the charge and the determination of the actual magnitude of the fee. For both of

---

[13] Edwin Mills and Lawrence White have recently suggested a variation on the RAND smog-tax proposal. Their recommendation is that the EPA levy a tax on new automobiles at the time of sale, where the size of the tax varies directly with the level of emissions of each

these problems, economic theory provides simple answers, but the real world introduces serious complications.

The proper base for the assessment of charges is obviously the *actual* level of emitted pollutants. In principle, the firm should confront a schedule of fees with a separate charge per unit applicable to each of the pollutants it emits into the environment. That fee should differ from pollutant to pollutant depending on the relative damage it causes. For each pollutant, the fee provides an appropriate incentive for the individual emitting enterprise to cut the amounts of its discharges. In practice, however, this principle encounters two major obstacles. First, the number of different pollutants is very large. Hungary, for example, levies charges on its industries based on thirty-one different types of emissions into its waters. However, countries such as France and the Netherlands have selected two to four major pollutants upon which to base their charges. Some compromise on the number of pollutants to be included in a system of fees appears inevitable.

Second, and more serious, is the method by which the environmental authority determines the polluter's tax bill. Again, this is in principle quite straightforward. The bill should simply equal the number of units of waste emissions multiplied by the unit fee for each pollutant. However, in practice, this too has been a matter for compromise, in part because of the costs and difficulties in metering effluents. The form this compromise has taken in some of the European countries is particularly disturbing. In France and the Netherlands, for example, the environmental agencies have issued tables of "pollution coefficients."[14] These coefficients represent *typical* levels of waste emissions per unit of output (or employment) in each industry. Each firm in an industry is then taxed according to the pollution coefficient for its industry; its tax bill is essentially equal to the industry pollution coefficient times its level of production (or employment). Note that this avoids the metering of actual emissions of pollutants by each firm. At the same time, however, it emasculates the program, for a firm is not taxed on its waste emissions but rather on its level of output. The firm gains absolutely nothing by reducing its actual emissions so long as its output of products in unchanged. Such a system provides no direct incentive for the reduction of discharges; it only provides a very weak and indirect inducement which works by discouraging output through higher costs.[15] This is surely

model. In addition, they would levy an annual surcharge on the registration fee for each auto, with the charge again based on the level of emissions (as determined in an annual test). This would provide a set of direct incentives to *both* manufacturers and operators of autos to reduce the quantities of pollutants emitted by their vehicles. See Edwin S. Mills and Lawrence J. White, "Government Policies Toward Automotive Emissions Control," in Ann Friedlaender, ed., *Air Pollution and Administrative Control* (Cambridge, Mass.: M.I.T. Press, forthcoming in 1978). This paper, incidentally, provides an excellent description and critique of the U.S. experience with auto-emissions control.
[14] For a description of the determination of these pollution coefficients in each country, see Johnson and Brown, *Cleaning Up Europe's Waters.*
[15] This is a slight oversimplification. If a firm institutes pollution-abatement techniques in France, the Netherlands, or the Ruhr Valley in Germany, it can request the environmental

a compromise that is entirely unacceptable. In any rational system of effluent charges, the environmental authority must structure its fees in a way that offers direct cost savings to polluters who reduce waste discharges (regardless of what happens to levels of output or employment). This will require either actual metering of effluents or some sort of shortcut such as a tax on the sulfur content of fuels at the time of purchase. But, whatever its form, *it must reward directly the reduction in emissions of pollutants.*

A second major issue in the design of a program of effluent charges is the determination of the *levels* of the fees. How much should the polluter be charged per pound of sulfur emissions into the atmosphere or per pound of BOD released into an adjacent river? Economic theory once again suggests a direct answer: the fee should equal the level of damages that result from the pollutant. The idea is that, if we can put a dollar value on the damage to the community caused from a puff of smoke from a particular smokestack, then the environmental authority should charge the owner of the smokestack a fee per puff equal to the dollar value of its damage. If, for example, emission of an additional pound of BOD into a waterway causes damage valued at seven cents, the effluent charge for BOD should be seven cents per pound.

The reason for setting charges that way is straightforward enough: we wish to induce polluters to work hardest at curbing those emissions that are most harmful to the community. We can do this by imposing the highest tax rate on the most damaging emissions. Moreover, by making the charge *exactly equal* to the damage to society, the environmental authority makes it profitable to the polluter to invest in the reduction of emissions precisely to the point that is best for society. To see this, suppose that it pays society to reduce some particular emission (because the cost of reducing it is less than the damage it generates). Then with the fee to the polluter equal to the damage to society, the reduction in that emission must also become profitable to the polluter. For with cost of elimination less than damage cost, the cost of abatement must also be less than the charges on those emissions. In short, whenever the benefits to society of a reduction in an emission exceed the costs, the polluting firm will realize a net saving by cutting back on its effluents rather than paying the charge on them. The reverse is also true, for exactly the same reason: where a restriction in emissions is not worth its cost to society, it will be unprofitable to the polluter. In sum, with the fee equal to the damage from an additional unit of pollutant, the self-interest of the polluting firm is served when, and only when, it serves the interests of society.

This is all very well in principle. However, in practice the proposed rule is virtually impossible to use, because we do not know how to estimate with much precision the dollar value of most forms of pollution damage. How does one assign a dollar value to the effects on health and longevity of an increase in

---

authority to make actual measurements of its effluents and reduce its taxes accordingly. Such requests, however, appear to have been rather infrequent. See Johnson and Brown, *Cleaning Up Europe's Waters,* pp. 271-73.

emissions of sulfur dioxide? How does one evaluate the money equivalent of the aesthetic effects of an emission that contributes to smog? Since this damage cost will also vary from one geographic location to another (depending on how many persons are affected, how bad air quality is at the outset, and so on), and from one season to the next, it is hard to see how we can, in practice, determine what fee is equal to the appropriate damage cost as is called for by theory.[16]

Since the theoretical ideal is, in fact, unattainable, we have proposed a (more or less) second-best substitute. We have suggested that the environmental authorities begin their calculations, as they typically do, by formulating a set of standards for environmental quality. That is, they would specify target levels of particulates, sulfur dioxide, and other concentrations of pollutants in the atmosphere, target levels for dissolved oxygen in a waterway, etc. To some degree, the choice of such target levels must be arbitrary or the result of political compromise. But there can also be more rational bases for their selection. For example, suppose there is statistical evidence indicating that there is some threshold level of sulfur concentration below which the threat to health is minimal, but beyond which it becomes much more serious. Then one would have good reason to accept that concentration level (after adding to it an appropriate safety factor) as the target for sulfur concentrations. In fact, the accumulating evidence on the effects of various levels of different pollutants is reaching a point where it can provide substantial guidance in the determination of standards for environmental quality.

Once such target levels of concentrations have been selected, it becomes a matter of empirical analysis and experimentation to determine how high a fee is necessary to achieve each of them. We know that a very low fee will be ignored by polluters and a fee that is sufficiently high will eliminate the polluting activity altogether (Justice Marshall's principle that the power to tax is the power to destroy). Thus we can expect that there will exist a level of charges between the two extremes that will just be sufficient to achieve the selected standard.

To arrive at this fee may require some adjustments to the initial charge. If, for example, observed sulfur concentrations continue to be too high after the fee is first set, then the environmental authority will have to increase the rate. This does raise some administrative problems, for a series of adjustments in fees may not be very popular politically and may involve a delay in the attainment of

---

[16]Economists will recognize that the problem may be even more serious than these comments suggest. What is required in theory is that the fee be equal not to some average or total damage level but that it should be set equal to the *increase* in total damage resulting from a small increment in emissions (marginal damage cost). Moreover, it should be equal, not to the marginal damage cost at the current (nonoptimal) allocation of resources, but the marginal damage cost which would hold if an optimal adjustment had already been achieved. Since no one knows what that optimal reallocation of resources really is, the calculation of the corresponding marginal damage cost seems well beyond the realm of practicality. On all this, see W. Baumol and W. Oates, *The Theory of Environmental Policy* (Englewood Cliffs, N.J.: Prentice-Hall, Inc., 1975).

the target levels of concentrations. Still, such a procedure—the use of fees designed to achieve preselected targets in environmental quality—may well be the best that we can hope for in practice.

Moreover, it may be possible to reach a reasonably close approximation to the desired fee on the initial round. As we have seen in earlier chapters, there now exists a considerable series of engineering studies of the costs of pollution abatement (both air and water) for most of the major polluting industries. From such studies, it is possible to make forecasts of the response of waste emissions to different levels of fees. With such information, the environmental authority is in a position to set the fee initially at a level that equates the predicted response to the preselected target.[17]

Finally, we should emphasize that this approach offers virtually all of the advantages of the theoretically ideal effluent fee in terms of our criteria for the evaluation of instruments of environmental policy. Its only shortcoming is that, by not being based on an evaluation of the damage caused by the emissions in question, it will not achieve the theoretically ideal degree of environmental protection. It may be excessively severe or excessively lenient relative to that abstract ideal, for it can do no better than the targets that have been selected by the political process.

5. On the Use of Direct Controls and Moral Suasion

In preceding chapters, we explored the strengths and weaknesses of direct controls and moral suasion as tools of environmental policy and found two potentially important roles for them: the regulation of pollution where metering is impractical, and the temporary curtailment of certain forms of polluting activities in times of adversity, where the delays and uncertainty in response to a change in fees pose a serious danger. In addition, we noted a basic use for direct controls in cases where outright prohibition of certain types of pollution is appropriate.

A crucial issue is the determination of those cases in which a system of effluent fees is sufficiently cumbersome and expensive to make direct controls the preferred alternative. In some cases, the most effective regulatory technique will not involve exclusive use of either fees or controls. A mixed approach using charges and metering to regulate the emissions of the major polluters, and direct controls (or, perhaps, just moral suasion) for minor polluters may, in certain

---

[17]In Europe, the level of fees has typically been set neither on the basis of damages nor targets of environmental quality. Rather the authorities have employed schedules of fees that generate revenues sufficient to cover the costs of public pollution-abatement programs. This is surely a most unsatisfactory method for the determination of fee schedules, for it is not based on any goal for the changes in behavior that the fees are presumably designed to induce.

instances, be the best solution. Even if monitoring costs are high, a system of fees may still yield large benefits in the control of the major sources of pollution. At the same time they may not make economic sense for small or infrequent polluters. Where the expense of either fees or direct controls seems excessive relative to the likely effects on pollution levels, moral suasion may be of modest value.

We have also suggested that short-term emergencies may appropriately call for the use of all three of our policy approaches. A schedule of fees can serve to regulate levels of effluents during times of normal environmental conditions, but direct controls and even moral suasion can provide useful supplements during temporary periods of adversity.

A third and critical use for direct controls is the regulation of emissions of particularly hazardous pollutants. The 1976 Toxic Substances Control Act has just such an objective. However, even here, enforcement problems are formidable. One review of the first year under the new Act found that "enforcement gaps" were proving a serious obstacle to the control of dangerous pollutants.[18]

6. The Regulation of Pollution by the Public Sector

We turn next to a particularly difficult issue: the control of pollution emanating from the public sector of the economy. Government activities are themselves a major source of pollution: municipal waste-treatment plants release effluents into our waterways (and, in many cases, provide the bulk of these emissions), and public power plants pollute the atmosphere. The largest sulfur-dioxide polluter in the United States is a federal agency: the Tennessee Valley Authority (TVA), whose plants emit over two million tons of sulfur oxides each year—about 16% of all such emissions in the country.[19] An environmental policy that fails to come to terms with public sources of pollution cannot hope to succeed.

The central issue is whether or not we can expect effluent fees to induce public agencies to reduce waste emissions into the environment; if not, we presumably must resort to some form of direct controls. We have argued that fees are an effective measure for the regulation of *private* sources of environmental damage; fees make it less expensive for a firm or individual to reduce pollution than to pay the tax. The trouble is that this reasoning doesn't apply to government agencies. Most public authorities are either monopolies or "quasi-monopolies"; they are not subject to the competitive pressures for cost minimization that are found in the private sector. Moreover, since profits are not their primary objective, the probable response of such agencies to a regime of effluent charges is a very real question.

---

[18] See John Vinocur, "Major Enforcement Gaps Hobble Law to Control Toxic Substances," *New York Times,* Oct. 30, 1977, pp. 1, 60.
[19] See W. King, "T.V.A., a Major Polluter, Faces Suit to Cut Sulfur Dioxide Fumes," *New York Times,* July 4, 1977, pp. 1, 20.

If we could always expect public authorities to act in the social interest, there would, of course, be no problem. In this case, we would need no controls for this sector—fees or any other sort. The government agencies would, on their own initiative, cut pollution back to the socially desirable levels. But this view is patently naive. Not only are public enterprises major sources of pollution, but it is becoming increasingly clear that our system of political institutions does not always encourage public decisions that are consistent with the well-being of the people.

In our examination of pollution in planned economies in Chapter 5, we saw that public producers in the Soviet Union have frequently ignored the damage they impose on the environment, because their performance has been evaluated almost exclusively in terms of the level of their output. It simply was not in their interest to devote scarce labor and other inputs to pollution control instead of increased production. Government agencies in the United States are surely not subject to the same sorts of production quotas as those in the Soviet Union, but it may nevertheless be true that it is often not in a bureaucrat's interest to expend a significant part of his or her budget on pollution control. In fact, recent surveys have found that hundreds of government owned and operated facilities in the U.S. are in flagrant violation of antipollution regulations.[20]

The important question we must answer is: How can we expect such bureaucrats to respond to effluent fees? Suppose we adopt the hypothesis that heads of government agencies are interested in maximizing the size of their agency's budget.[21] Particularly in these times of fiscal stringency, such decision makers would view with considerable chagrin the allocation of a substantial portion of their budgets to pollution fees. These fees would represent a loss of resources that otherwise would have been at the agency's disposal. If so, it seems to us that it would typically be in the interest of bureaucrats to undertake pollution abatement as a means of increasing the *portion* of the budget under their control. Pollution control would increase the *effective* size of the bureau's budget.[22] It is thus our judgment that we should at least experiment with the use of effluent charges for government agencies, particularly since direct controls

---

[20] See Phillip Shabecoff, "Federal Violations of Water Act Cited," *New York Times,* Sept. 19, 1977, pp. 1, 25.

[21] There have recently been some intriguing attempts to provide a description of the kinds of incentives and behavior that characterize the public bureaucracy. For example, some of the studies emphasize the natural desire of the heads of government bureaus to increase the scope and size of their operations both in order to provide more services to their public and to enhance their own prestige (and, perhaps, their salaries). In fact, in one of the most penetrating of these studies, William A. Niskanen contends that the various objectives of bureaucrats imply that they will try to maximize the size of their agency budget. A larger budget will effectively enhance their power; it will enable them to have a larger staff and more of other resources which will extend the range of activities they can undertake. See his *Bureaucracy and Representative Government* (Chicago: Aldine-Atherton, 1971).

[22] For a formal analysis of bureaucratic response to effluent fees, see Wallace Oates and Diana Strassmann, "The Use of Effluent Fees to Regulate Public-Sector Sources of Pollu-

have apparently been so ineffective. Our tentative prediction is that such charges can provide a powerful incentive for pollution abatement in the public sector.[23]

7. Regional Variations in Standards and Fees

In Chapter 15 we discussed a formidable and complex problem in the design of a comprehensive environmental policy: the extent of regional and local differentials in programs for the control of pollution. The dilemma is perhaps best illustrated by the congressional controversy over the Administration's proposal for a sulfur tax. The proposed Pure Air Tax Act of 1972 would have taxed sulfur emissions at a rate dependent on regional air quality; the tax would have ranged from fifteen cents per pound in regions where primary standards had been violated to zero where no violations occurred. From an economic point of view, such differentials make good sense. They concentrate abatement efforts in those localities where environmental damage is relatively great; the proposed schedule of fees is probably sufficiently high to ensure that the EPA primary standards for sulfur concentrations in the atmosphere would be met on a nationwide scale. This was the obvious intent of the proposed legislation.

Such regional differences in fees do, however, raise some difficult issues. First, they put localities with poor air quality at a competitive disadvantage in attracting and retaining industry. A region in which firms are subject to a relatively high effluent fee is likely to find businesses moving elsewhere where costs of production will be lower. But perhaps this is as it should be; a dispersion of industry is one way of eliminating the concentration of effluents and congestion that seem to cause much of the damage to the environment.

Second, and more disturbing, is the recognition that this process of dispersion may involve the move of heavy polluters away from "dirty" localities to previously "clean" areas. While regional differentials in fee schedules may induce all regions to meet the primary standards, this may be accomplished to a substantial degree by shifting pollution from areas of industrial concentration to previously "unspoiled" locations. This prospect has caused great concern in Congress. To eliminate this incentive for the dispersion of pollution, Congressman Aspin and Senator Proxmire introduced alternative bills which would impose a uniform national tax of twenty cents per pound on sulfur emissions,

---

tion: An application of the Niskanen Model," *Journal of Environmental Economics and Management*, forthcoming.
[23]The alternative to price incentives, namely the use of direct controls, may present real problems in the public, as well as the private, sector. In a letter to one of the authors, Marcia Gelpe notes that, "I think enforcement of direct controls is also more difficult in the public than in the private sector. I am now working on air emissions from a state prison. It's a terrible problem. What do you do with a public authority that can't comply because the legislature won't appropriate funds for compliance?" (letter to W. Baumol, February 3, 1977).

regardless of the location of the polluter, to be fully effective in 1975.[24]

Although none of these bills was enacted into legislation, they do raise a most difficult problem for the formulation of an effective environmental policy. We must emphasize that this issue is not limited to a system of fees; it poses the same dilemma whether we adopt pricing incentives or direct controls. It is somewhat ironic that we seem to have adopted a system that implicitly *requires* differentials in the stringency of direct controls by the imposition of uniform national environmental standards for air and water quality. The enforcement of these standards requires restrictions on emissions to be tighter in areas suffering from relatively high levels of pollution.

The design of any comprehensive environmental policy will involve trade-offs among a number of competing objectives. It may well be that a single national fee, by virtue of its administrative simplicity and political acceptability, offers the greatest hope for an effective national policy. This is admittedly a complex matter and not one on which we wish to take a strong stand. Our biggest fear, however, is that proponents of these two positions will undermine one another's efforts and that as a result *no* program of pricing incentives will emerge.

8. Government Expenditures on Environmental Services

The programs we have discussed so far have all been designed to induce polluters—whether they be producers, consumers, or government agencies—to modify their behavior in ways that reduce the adverse effects of their activities on the environment. There is, however, another essential component of any comprehensive environmental program: the direct provision by the government sector of certain fundamental environmental services. Rather than seeking to persuade polluters to cut back on activities injurious to the environment, many governmental projects contribute directly to improve in environmental quality.

We can make this point best through illustration. Consider a comprehensive program to manage water quality in a system of rivers and estuaries. One critical element in such a program will obviously be a set of inducements for reduction of emissions into the waters. For this purpose, a set of effluent fees may provide the necessary incentives to induce the required cutbacks in waste discharges. But this is only part of the story. Another valuable component of such a program is the provision of certain "collective facilities" to enhance water quality. There may be a need for reservoirs to provide augmentation of water flows during low-flow periods; for systems to transport and treat wastes prior to discharge into the water; for artificial or induced oxygenation of watercourses;

---

[24] In *Sierra Club vs. Ruckelshaus* the courts ruled (in interpreting the stated purpose of the Clean Air Act "to protect and enhance the quality of the nation's air resources") that EPA must promulgate air pollution guidelines for the states that prevent significant deterioration in air quality. For more on this, see *Ecology Law Quarterly* 4, No. 3 (1975).

and perhaps for the construction of shallow oxidation reservoirs in the streams themselves.[25]

There is thus a substantial range of environment-enhancing services that the public sector must provide directly. In addition to dams and reservoirs for water-quality management, the government has taken an active role in the conservation and development of many outdoor recreational resources: national parks, seashores, and forests. The federal government in the United States owns and directs the use of some 760 million acres of land.[26] Finally, the public sector has a basic responsibility for another type of public service: research and education to help in the invention and adoption of new techniques for the improvement of environmental quality. This sort of program ranges from basic scientific research to extend our understanding of the ecological system to the development of better and cheaper metering devices.

9. Summary and Conclusions

The design of a comprehensive environmental policy is obviously a very complicated and difficult job. Rather than providing a detailed blueprint of such a policy, we have tried to sketch out a set of guidelines that can help in this task. The preceding chapters have presented a great deal of material relating to the actual and potential effectiveness and limitations of each of the available policy tools. To try to draw together and summarize the discussion, we present here two summary tables. Table 22-1 simply lists what we consider, on the basis of our analysis, to be the appropriate uses of each policy instrument. In Table 22-2 we attempt to evaluate these policy tools in terms of the various criteria

---

[25] On collective facilities for water quality, see Allen Kneese and Blair Bower, *Managing Water Quality: Economics, Technology, Institutions* (Baltimore: The Johns Hopkins University Press, 1969), Chap. 10. There are, incidentally, some extremely difficult conceptual and practical problems in determining the proper magnitude of such public projects. How, for instance, do we decide whether or not to build a dam at a particular site and, if so, of what size? Economists and others have labored in recent years to develop a systematic approach to such decisions and have produced an analytic framework known as "cost-benefit analysis." With this technique, the researcher attempts to evaluate in terms of dollars both the benefits and the costs of a proposed project. The cost-benefit study thus provides the decision-maker with estimates of how much the project is likely to cost in comparison to the value of the expected benefits. There are some troublesome ambiguities in principle and, even more, some knotty problems in practice in deriving dollar estimates of such things as recreational benefits or lives saved (!), but to explore all this in detail would take us too far afield from our central concerns. For an excellent introduction to cost-benefit analysis, see E. J. Mishan, *Cost-Benefit Analysis: An Informal Introduction,* rev. ed. (London: G. Allen and Unwin, 1975). For some applications to water pollution control policy, see Henry Peskin and Eugene Seskin, eds., *Cost-Benefit Analysis and Water Pollution Policy* (Washington, D,C.: The Urban Institute, 1975). A fascinating study of the actual use (and misuse) of this technique is provided by Ackerman, et al., *The Uncertain Search for Environmental Quality.*
[26] Joseph J. Seneca and Michael K. Taussig, *Environmental Economics* (Englewood Cliffs, N.J.: Prentice-Hall, Inc., 1974), p. 248.

TABLE 22-1

SUMMARY OF APPROPRIATE USES OF VARIOUS INSTRUMENTS OF ENVIRONMENTAL POLICY

Policy Instrument	Appropriate Use	Remarks
1. Direct controls	a. Where metering of individual polluters is not practical b. As a standby supplement to effluent charges and other fiscal methods to be used in periods of critical environmental conditions (e.g., serious atmospheric inversions) c. Outright prohibitions of emissions or activities that are extremely hazardous	Restricted to direct controls requiring use of particular types of hardware (e.g., smokestack scrubbers, catalytic converters) or specified procedures rather than emission quotas (which necessitate metering).
2. Moral suasion (voluntarism)	a. In brief emergencies, where effective direct controls are not available or practical b. In cases where effective monitoring or imposition of particular procedures is not feasible (e.g., careless causing of forest fires; littering in wilderness areas) c. Where volunteer personnel are available and can perform a useful role and the state of finances of the public sector restricts staffing by paid personnel	
3. Fiscal measures a. Subsidies	Usage generally limited to cases where no alternative fiscal approach is politically feasible or where fees have a very undesirable and inequitable pattern of incidence on different groups of individuals	
b. Fees on environmentally damaging activities (effluent charges)	A basic approach for the regulation of polluting behavior where metering of individual emitters is feasible	Widespread potential use which promises to be both effective and economical.

TABLE 22-1 (Continued)

Policy Instrument	Appropriate Use	Remarks
c. Auctioning of pollution permits	An alternative to fees for regulation of pollution where metering of individual emitters is feasible	Certain advantages over fees: eliminates uncertainty associated with polluters' response to fees and not subject to erosion by inflation or growth. Problems: risk of excessively costly environmental objectives and lack of political acceptability.
d. Deposits by potential polluters (refundable upon proof of acceptable behavior)	Attractive where direct observation and monitoring difficult, but burden of proof can be shifted to potential generator of damage	
4. Government projects to protect the environment (Public Works)	Where scale economies and public-goods characteristics of services make private supply of services undesirable	

TABLE 22-2

PERFORMANCE OF VARIOUS POLICY INSTRUMENTS BY SPECIFIED CRITERIA

Policy Instrument	Reliability[a]	Permanence	Adaptability to Growth	Resistance to Inflation	Incentive for Improved Effort	Economy[b]	Feasibility without Metering	Noninterference in Private Decisions	Political Attraction Actual	Political Attraction Potential
Moral suasion	Good[a]	Poor	Good*	Good*	Fair	Poor[b]	Excellent	Excellent	Excellent	—
Direct controls a. By quota	Fair	Poor	Fair	Excellent	Poor	Poor	Poor	Poor	Excellent	—
b. By specification of technique	Fair	Poor	Good*	Good*	Poor	Poor	Excellent	Poor	Excellent	—
Fees	Excellent	Excellent	Fair	Fair	Excellent	Excellent	Poor	Excellent	Poor	Good
Sale of permits	Excellent	Excellent	Excellent	Excellent	Excellent	Excellent[c]	Poor	Excellent	Poor	Good
Subsidies a. Per unit reduction	Fair[d]	Good	Fair	Fair	Excellent	Good	Poor	Excellent	Good	—
b. For equipment purchase	Fair	Good	Fair	Fair	Good	Poor	Excellent	Excellent	Good	—
Government investment	Good	?	?	?	—	?	Excellent	—	Good	—

*Authors' judgment based on little concrete evidence.

[a]For short periods of time when urgency of appeal is made very clear.

[b]Induces contributions from decision makers who are most cooperative, not necessarily from those able to do the job most effectively (most inexpensively).

[c]Tends to allocate reduction "quotas" among firms in cost-minimizing manner, but if the number of emissions permits is too small it will force the community to devote an excessive quantity of resources to environmental protection.

[d]Tends to allocate reduction quotas among firms in cost-minimizing manner, but introduces inefficiency into the environmental protection process by attracting more polluting firms into the subsidized industry, so that aggregate response is questionable.

formulated in Chapter 16. We emphasize that these "ratings" involve a good deal of personal judgment; in particular, we have, in some instances, collapsed a complex set of considerations into an admittedly simplistic evaluation of likely effectiveness. For this reason, the reader may have good reason to disagree with some of our evaluations. But it was not our objective to provide definitive judgments on environmental policy. Table 22-2 simply is intended to summarize our conclusions in a way that we hope is conducive to useful discussion.

23

Epilogue

A recurring theme in the environmental literature is the contention that capitalism and technology have run amuck and set off a cumulative process of environmental destruction that threatens eventual exhaustion of the world's resources and a series of man-made catastrophes. In this view the greedy pursuit of profits without regard for the wider interests of society and, particularly, of future generations is taxing the resources and the assimilative capacity of this planet's environment to an ever greater extent. It is held that at some point we inevitably will encounter limits to growth with truly frightening consequences. The only avenue of escape from this dire outcome is a radical restructuring of the economy and various social institutions to halt the expansion of the great industrial machine.

We have tried in this book to present a somewhat different perspective on the causes of environmental damage and the appropriate cures. We have seen, for example, that Western industrialized nations have no monopoly (either in time or space) on environmental destruction. Socialist countries and the less-developed nations have set a high priority on increased output, often with calamitous ecological side effects.

Whether an economy relies heavily on free markets or on directives from central planning agencies, we have argued that the basic problem lies in the set of incentives that confronts individual decision makers. Like labor and raw materials, clean air, pure waters, and the natural landscape are truly scarce resources. Yet we have treated them as common property; we have made them available for the taking at virtually zero cost to the individual. From this point of view, it is hardly surprising to find that the use of our environmental resources has been careless and unjustifiably damaging.

The economist's message is that, wherever possible, we should correct this malfunctioning of the economic system by making the use of environmental resources appropriately expensive. We should effectively place a price on clean air and water (and other amenities) in order to induce individuals to economize on their use. We cannot exaggerate the importance of this basic principle. The pricing system, driven by the pursuit of profits, contains within it an extraordinarily powerful set of incentives. What we must do is to enlist the profit motive in the cause of environmental protection. Not only must entrepreneurs be able to make their fortunes by inventing the better mousetrap, they must also be able to do so by providing the better pollution-abatement technique. The search for profits must promote, not discourage, efforts to improve environmental quality.

However, in their devotion to the use of financial incentives for environmental protection, economists have tended to neglect the role of other policy instruments. As we have seen, under certain circumstances systems of effluent fees or prices encounter difficult problems of implementation. There are clearly important roles for direct controls and even moral suasion in a comprehensive and effective program for the enhancement of the environment.

Determining an integrated program for protection of the environment using all of these approaches suitably is not a simple task. But neither is it an impossible one. We have at our disposal a wide range of policy instruments, and it is our firm conviction that an appropriate use of these policy tools can make continued economic growth consistent with an improved environment. We need not dismantle our industrial system; we must only provide the incentives necessary to give adequate weight to environmental protection.

None of what we have said is meant to imply that the environment faces no risks that are truly serious. Developments in nuclear energy production, for example, may pose a very real threat to humanity. In those areas where real catastrophe is even a remote possibility, we must proceed slowly and with the greatest of care. Some environmentalists may favor trying to turn back the clock and returning to a less-industrialized and, perhaps, simpler way of life. This does have a certain appeal. However, a world with no further economic growth could turn out to be a vicious place where the only way an individual or country could increase its standard of living would be at the expense of someone else. We do not consider "zero economic growth" as a viable alternative. The industrial machine has been set into motion and there really is no turning back. But society does have at its disposal the means to control this machine to harmonize its operations with the preservation of our environment.

In our view, the most serious and disturbing obstacle to this objective is a political one: the acceptance and adoption of an effective set of measures to enhance environmental quality. Economists stress that "There is no such thing as a free lunch." We have seen that an improved environment can be attained only at a substantial cost—and people must bear this cost in one form or another. One thing we can be sure of: those who are likely to bear these costs will seek ways to avoid them, and this will often take the form of active opposition to proposals for environmental protection. For example, we have noted the continued and powerful opposition of the can and bottle manufacturers and associated interest groups to the introduction of bottle bills in many states in the United States. Such opposition stands in the way of the adoption of truly effective policy measures. We have repeatedly stressed the distributive effects of environmental policies. This is not only a matter of social justice, but one of allocating the costs in a way that does not give unnecessary cause for political opposition. We know a great deal about the design of effective environmental policies. But we have yet to convince policy makers and their constituencies of the crucial importance and viability of these measures.

Index